# THE REBEL

is not only damn good, it's excellent!
—Guy B. Askew (Skidroad Slim, an IWW since 1917), 1964—

I like it! It's fresh, young, and daring, with lots of humor,
and true to the Wobbly revolutionary spirit.
—Jack Sheridan, old-time Wobbly & Dil Pickler, 1964—

Hmmm.
—Neal Cassady, 1964—

What impresses me most about *The Rebel Worker*
is that it deals with all sorts of questions which traditional
radicals consider "non-political," but which are actually
of the greatest concern to most ordinary people.
—Martin Glaberman, 1965—

You [*The Rebel Worker*] seem to be revolutionary in everything—hurray!
—Judy Kaplan, 1965—

Extremely interesting—could lead to very important things.
—Guy Debord, 1966—

The best magazine in the U.S. today is *The Rebel Worker.*
—Chris Pallis (founder of London Solidarity), 1966—

I've read and reread every word of every issue
of *The Rebel Worker*—it's a very important magazine.
—Murray Bookchin, 1967—

I liked *The Rebel Worker* immensely. No mere historical
curiosity, this hard-hitting, fearless little journal of the 1960s
remains startlingly relevant. A *Rebel Worker* anthology
would be a most welcome addition to our literature.
—Sam Dolgoff, 1983—

Specializing in topics other radical journals shied away from,
*The Rebel Worker* was one of the liveliest, most adventurous
periodicals of the mid-Sixties, [with] a revolutionary point of view
fundamentally different from all traditional concepts.
—Ron Sakolsky, *Surrealist Subversions* (2002)—

For comments on *Heatwave*, see page 325.

CHARLES H. KERR  SIXTIES SERIES

Featured on the inside front-cover of *Rebel Worker* 7 (1966),
this ten-word illustrated manifesto was also issued as a poster.
Words by Penelope Rosemont / art & calligraphy by Tor Faegre

# DANCIN'
# *IN THE STREETS!*

## Anarchists, IWWs, Surrealists, Situationists & Provos in the 1960s

*as recorded in the pages of*

THE REBEL WORKER

*&*

HEATWAVE

*Edited with Introductions by*

 **Franklin Rosemont**
**& Charles Radcliffe**

Chicago
**Charles H. Kerr Publishing Company**
*2005*

This book is dedicated to
**PAUL GARON,**
blues buddy & surrealist comrade,
opener of many doors,
and to
**MARTHA & THE VANDELLAS**
who suggested what we might do
once the doors were opened.

© Copyright 2005
Charles H. Kerr Publishing Company
Chicago

FIRST EDITION

ISBN 088286-301-0 paper
088286-302-9 cloth

## WANTED

For future publishing projects: Photos, publications, artwork, memorabilia,
and ephemera concerning the IWW, anarchism, the early Socialist Party;
Bughouse Square, Hobo College, the Dil Pickle Club, and other
free-speech forums; and early Charles H. Kerr publications.
Please write to the address below, or leave a message at 773-465-7774.

*Write for our free catalog.*
**CHARLES H. KERR PUBLISHING COMPANY**
*Established 1886*
1740 West Greenleaf Avenue, Chicago Illinois 60626
www.CharlesHKerr.org

# TABLE OF CONTENTS

# ACKNOWLEDGMENTS

Thanks above all to Charles Radcliffe—co-editor of *Rebel Worker* 6 and editor of *Heatwave*—whose invaluable collaboration, zealous fact-checking and enthusiastic good humor helped bring this long-delayed project to completion at last.

In the course of preparing this book, several others who once upon a time participated in *The Rebel Worker* and/or *Heatwave*—Joan Smith Cooper, Bill Corbin, Dorothy DeCoster, Lester Doré, Tor Faegre, Paul Garon, Robert Green, Bernard Marszalek and Deri Smith—communicated documents, memories and suggestions that did much to fill out the story.

Many other friends shared recollections of those days, including John Bracey, Paul Buhle, Leonora Carrington, Tom Condit, Polly Connelly, Carlos Cortez, Diane di Prima, Sam Dolgoff, Guy Ducornet, Rikki Ducornet, Schlechter Duvall, Richard Ellington, Archie Green, Philip Lamantia, Art Livingston, William J. O'Brien, Lorraine Perlman, Irene Plazewska, John Ross, Robert Rush, Ron Sakolsky, Ruth Sheridan, Gary Snyder, and Joffre Stewart.

Thanks to Gale Ahrens, Jen Besemer, Paul Buhle, Paul Garon, Don LaCoss, David Roediger, Ruth Oppenheim-Rothschild, and Tamara L. Smith for reading and commenting on the book as it took shape, and to Anne Condron and Justin O'Brien, who provided indispensable technical assistance.

And of course, in the spirit of Eiranaeus Philalethes and his "Great Wonder of Wonders," a very special *merci beaucoup* to Penelope.

By chance, as I was completing these Acknowledgments, I picked up a copy of Louisa May Alcott's 1872 novel, *Work*, that I had bought the day before. Opening it, I came across these words that could serve as a *Rebel Worker/Heatwave* motto: "I can't help feeling that there is a better sort of life than this dull one made up of everlasting work, with no object but money."

The struggle continues!

F.R.

Chicago, Bastille Day 2004

# A NOTE ON THE TEXTS

*A book can benefit only those who read it;*
*thus, everything which helps to make a book read*
*contributes to its usefulness.*

—Port Royal Logic (fifth ed., 1683)—

*The Rebel Worker*'s seven issues ran to 248 pages, our pamphlet series to 149 more. Numerous leaflets and a Chicago IWW Branch newsletter bring the total still higher.

Participants in the *Rebel Worker* group also contributed extensively to the *Industrial Worker* and, albeit less frequently, to other radical periodicals, including *Freedom* (London), *New Politics* (New York), and the Chicago *Seed.*

Similarly, although the two issues of our sister journal *Heatwave*, in London, came to only 76 pages, its editor, Charles Radcliffe, also wrote many articles for the biweekly *Freedom* and the monthly *Anarchy*, as well as *Blues Unlimited* and other publications.

A complete *Rebel Worker/Heatwave* compilation could therefore reach close to a thousand pages, without introductions or illustrations. The present volume offers instead a *selection*: several dozen articles, reviews, cartoons and letters.

We have not neglected what our many critics were wont to call our "eccentricity" (some used harsher words). A 10-year-old's science-fantasy-horror tale; a heroin addict's notes on addiction; sympathetic articles on comics, rock, and other aspects of popular culture; defenses of laziness; and critiques of everyday life: These were not, even in those stirring times, topics people expected to read about in "left" publications, but they were integral to *The Rebel Worker* and *Heatwave.*

In the selections published here, we have freely corrected typographical errors and culled some repetitions as well as superfluous adverbs. Readers should note that many reprints in *The Rebel Worker* were only excerpts, and that the versions included here are excerpted from those excerpts. For the most part, however, articles by participants in the *Rebel Worker/Heatwave* group are reprinted here "as is." For better or for worse, our 1960s penchant for overstatement and exaggeration remains intact in these pages.

In the *Heatwave* section, we have retained English spelling (labour, programme, etc.) but Americanized the punctuation. —F. R.

What causes sluggishness
in oppressed populations
is the duration of the evil,
which inclines the sufferers to believe
that their oppression will never end.
But as soon as they have hopes of overcoming their misery
—which never fails when the evil reaches a certain pitch—
they are so surprised, so happy, and so excited
that they rush all of a sudden to the other extreme,
and are so far from thinking revolutions *impossible*
that they now suppose them *easy*,
and such a disposition alone
is sometimes all it takes
to make a revolution.

**Jean François Paul de Gondi,
Cardinal de Retz**

Storming of the Bastille
(Paris, July 14, 1789)

# THE REBEL WORKER

&

# DANCIN'
## IN THE STREETS!

Calling out around the world.
Are you ready for a brand new beat?
Summer's here and the time is right
For dancin' in the street

They're dancin' in Chicago
There'll be music everywhere
There'll be laughing and singing,
Music swinging,
And dancin' in the streets.

Everywhere around the world
They'll be dancin',
Dancin' in the streets

**—Martha and the Vandellas—**

Franklin and Penelope Rosemont
Chicago, summer 1966

# TO BE REVOLUTIONARY
# IN EVERYTHING:
## THE *REBEL WORKER* STORY, 1964–68

Teenagers the world over are all walking firecrackers,
and everybody's scared of 'em.
Nobody knows why they're acting this way.

—Ed Lacy, *Harlem Underground* (1965)—

T HE *REBEL WORKER* WAS A MIMEOGRAPHED magazine published in Chicago in the mid-1960s by a group of recalcitrant
workingclass youths who regarded themselves as far to the left
of the far left. I was one of them. In fact, largely because I was a fast
two-fingered typist and nobody else wanted the job, I was the editor.

Our aims were simple: We wanted to abolish wage-slavery and to
smash the State—that is, to make a total revolution, and to have lots
of fun—really *live it up*—in a new and truly free society. Early in the
game one of our many detractors sneeringly called us "the left wing
of the Beat Generation." The tag caught on quickly in the local activist
community, and we ourselves never bothered to disown or dispute it,
for it clearly distinguished us from the squares who owned and operated the business-as-usual left. Ironically, by that time we no longer
really identified much with the increasingly irrelevant Beat scene. For
our part, we preferred to call ourselves anarchists, or surrealists—or
Wobblies, for we had all taken out red cards in the Industrial Workers
of the World (IWW).

Most of us were under twenty-one, but we had been active radicals for years, some since our early teens. Veterans all of the 1950s Beat
ferment, as well as of the civil rights and peace movements, a few of
us had also taken part in one or another socialist group. Our experiences in these movements and groups were very different, but all of
us had come to recognize the futility of reformism and knew that nothing less than social revolution could make life truly livable. For many
of us, the experience of *poetry*, more than anything else—poetry as
the exaltation of freedom and the marvelous—hastened this evolution.

By 1964 we were convinced of the inadequacy of the many sin-
gle-issue protest groups as well as the would-be "revolutionary" parties. The revolution *we* dreamed about went deeper than any and all
"politics." Already criticized as "ultraleft," we grew more and more
radical. We were sickened by the dull routine and lack of imagination
of what we called the "traditional left." One and all we yearned for

Something Else (the title of Ornette Coleman's first album). Tired of "senile dogmas . . . irrelevant concepts and old platitudes," we soon concluded that "the revolutionary movement, in theory and practice," had to be "rebuilt from scratch."

It was in that daredevil, all-or-nothing spirit that we started *The Rebel Worker*, and in the same spirit that we sustained our "wild-eyed journal of free revolutionary research and experiment"—along with an equally *outré* pamphlet series—for a frantic and fruitful four and a half years. As had happened before and surely will happen again, it was left to a bunch of naive and irresponsible adolescents, mad at the world but avid for life, to sound a new note—whole riffs of new notes—in American radicalism.

In this introduction I aim to tell the story of *The Rebel Worker*—the magazine, the group around it, our ideas, activities, and interaction with other groups, our successes and failures, our eventual dissolution as a group, and our overall impact. The opening sections—on *The Rebel Worker*'s 1950s and early '60s background—may seem a bit heavy on autobiography, but these preliminaries are intended only as one participant's account of where we came from and how we reached our collective point of departure. The experiences of others in the group no doubt differed from mine in many ways, but the similarities are probably just as great or greater. In any event, by the spring of 1964 we had all reached the same basic conclusions on what kind of world we wanted to live in, what needed to be done to make it a reality, and where to begin.

Readers who persist all the way to the end will even find some reflections on the whole adventure, and on its possible meaning(s) for today and tomorrow.

## HOW TEEN-AGE BEATNIKS BECAME REVOLUTIONARIES

*The Rebel Worker* was a homebrew—a special blend of catch-as-catch-can ingredients. It was about as far as you could get from those carefully planned and promptly forgotten journals issued by sects that pretend to have all the answers. The inspirations we drew on were many and diverse, and—like life itself—had their share of contradictions. Preceding them all was the so-called Beat Generation, an experience each of us had passed through as teenagers, and which gave us an initial frame of reference—a *revaluation of values*, no less—that helped us along as we each in turn grappled with the question: *Who am I?*

It is easy, today, to deride the ambiguity and incoherence of Beat "philosophy," but for many young people who were drowning in the humdrum horror of American life in the 1950s it was a life-saver that enabled us to make our way to new and unknown shores. It is impossible to grasp the liberating quality of the Beat message without understanding just how devastatingly empty life was for the generation that grew up in the wake of Hiroshima, Taft-Hartley, McCarthyism and Cold War.

Before the academics redefined it for their own confusionist purposes, everyone knew that the term Beat Generation signified a broad radical social/cultural movement involving thousands of young people all over the country and indeed, all over the world. Only much later were the professors able to reduce it to a mere literary current (and even a *respectable* literary current!) with an exclusive membership numbering—depending on which "expert" you consult—as few as three or four (Kerouac, Ginsberg, Burroughs, and sometimes Corso) or, according to Ann Charters, as many as sixty-six. Just as laughably, the academics also restricted the Beat Generation to two cities: New York and San Francisco.

Those seeking a truer picture of the breadth and scope of the Beat ferment would do well to go back to the articles and books written in the mid- and late 1950s and early 60s by observers who actually "made the scene." Lawrence Lipton, for example, whose 1959 study *The Holy Barbarians* was the first and remains among the best, focused on the thriving Beat community in Venice, California, and noted the existence of Beat activity in New Orleans, Chicago, Seattle and elsewhere.

In 1959, however, even the most astute onlookers were probably unaware that America's "beatnik problem" had reached such proportions that nearly every high school and juvenile home in the United States had beatniks of its own, labeled such by worried school authorities as well as the obedient majority of student slaves. Out of 5000 students at Proviso East High School in the Chicago workingclass suburb of Maywood, there were about a dozen of us.

I first encountered the Beat Generation in a dentist's office in late 1958. Looking through a copy of *Esquire* I chanced on a piece titled "Where Is the Beat Generation Going?" It was a tiresome litany of defamations by Norman Podhoretz, but what grabbed me, and changed my life forever, were the fragments of a message of revolt that broke out between the lines. As with many other rebel movements, the Beat Generation's enemies proved to be its most effective recruiters. Hostile sermons like the one in *Esquire* turned us on to the amazing and heartening fact that, somewhere out there in America, there were others like us, dreaming our dreams and living life as we wanted to live it, "to the hilt."

Right there and then, at the dentist's, I resolved to quit high school and take to the road. I didn't really know where the Beat Generation was going but I knew I wanted to go there with it. The next day I took the bus downtown to Chicago and picked up Jack Kerouac's *On the Road.* In a few weeks I read all of his books and got my friends to read them.

Some months earlier a small group of us at Proviso High had started a little magazine which, in the spirit of Diogenes—bitterly pessimistic about everything we were being taught—we named *The Lantern.* We mimeographed it on a hand-operated cast-iron antique machine—a "Rotary Neostyle"—that I bought for five dollars at Anderson's Typewriter Shop on Seventeenth Avenue in Maywood. In this paper we attacked every school rule and sparked as many controversies as we could.

With its second issue (April 1959) *The Lantern* became the voice of Proviso's growing interracial Beat community and started publishing Beat poetry. Page one of the fourth issue (June) featured, as a kind of two-line manifesto, Kerouac's warning: "Woe unto those who spit on the Beat Generation, the wind'll blow it back."

Most of what appeared in *The Lantern* was juvenile stuff, but it created a sensation among the students and faculty, and outright schoolwide scandal when the third issue (May) devoted a page to the horrors of atomic war and announced the formation of a school club to promote the abolition of nuclear bomb testing.

As the editor of this "nuisance," which is what the Dean of Students called it, I was frequently called into the Dean's and Principal's offices and threatened with expulsion. The *"Lantern* crowd" thus became the best-known kids in the school. More than one teacher singled me out for special ridicule as a "dangerous young man." A zealous right-wing gym teacher pulled me out of an outdoor gym class and shoved me to the front of his class. Pointing to me as I stood before this amazed assembly, he shrieked that anyone caught possessing the paper put out by "this Communist" (that was me, of course), or even seen talking to me, would be given a failing grade in "physical education," which meant not graduating at all, for in those gloomy times Illinois law bizarrely denied high-school diplomas to anyone lacking four years of such bullying.

All efforts to suppress *The Lantern* backfired. Some kids admitted that they were afraid to be seen with us at school, but wrote to me at home, and my school locker was always full of friendly notes. Every issue brought new contributors. Opinion polls of the "roving reporter" type, with brief responses to questions regarding school controversies ("Was the administration justified in sending home students wearing 'beatnik' clothes?") expanded student participation even more.

The attempts to redbait us also fell flat. I doubt whether they had any effect at all except to stimulate circulation of *The Lantern* and to interest a lot of students in subversive ideas. Before I was formally denounced as a Communist in gym class I had not read a single book on the subject and was probably even more ignorant of Marxism than my teachers were. One day a friend and I visited the office of the Chicago Committee for Soviet-American Friendship and brought back a stack of free literature which we distributed all over school just to antagonize the school authorities. The Russian propaganda was boring and repulsive, but we soon learned that there were *other* currents of socialism. In no time I was reading such books as Otto Ruhle's *Karl Marx: His Life and Work* and Paul Lafargue's *Evolution of Property*, which had been on our bookshelves at home for years (gifts to my father from fellow union printers).

In my third and last year of high school, the "*Lantern* crowd" expanded considerably as the paper became the recognized vehicle of the whole range of Proviso's "misfits," as some hostile administrators and faculty called us—a title we bore with honor, and used ourselves. ("Don't forget the misfits' meeting at 3:45.") We also grew steadily more radical.

Notwithstanding the fact that before my second year of high school my conception of Marxism was closer to the Cold War stereotype of *I Led Three Lives* than to the *Communist Manifesto*, my interest in revolutionary ideas could probably be traced back to fourth or fifth grade, when I learned about John Brown, one of the few figures in U.S. history who actually seemed interesting. By eighth grade I was following the progress of the Cuban 26th of July movement in the pages of the *Sun-Times* (my father was head proofreader there, and brought the paper home daily) and the Sunday *New York Times*, to which my parents subscribed. Toward the end of my first year of high school, several of Proviso's "26 de Julio" supporters, myself included, made vague plans to go to Cuba to join the revolutionary struggle. Alas, none of us knew Spanish, and we couldn't think of any way that teenage Anglos could find their way to the guerrillas. I can still recall our great rejoicing when news came of the Revolution on New Year's Day 1959. One of the longest pieces *The Lantern* ever published was an enthusiastic review of *Sun-Times* reporter Ray Brennan's 1959 book, *Castro, Cuba and Justice*.

All of us in *The Lantern* group were also excited by the Freedom

Rides and other actions of the 1960s civil rights movement. Since early childhood my parents had told me of the evils of race discrimination; both had been outspoken advocates of integration in the labor movement, my father as a member of Chicago Typographical Union No. 16, and my mother as a member of Musicians' Local 10. I had black friends—Negro was the word then—since the integration of Washington Irving School in Maywood during my sixth-grade year. Only with my discovery of the Beat poets, however, did I begin to appreciate the vitality and richness of African-American culture, and particularly jazz.

At Proviso, neither *The Lantern* group nor the anti-nuclear-weapons group were "recognized" student groups, and hence were not permitted to meet on school property. So we started our own "front group": The Proviso High School Jazz Club. In that heyday of rock'n'roll, *The Lantern* crowd—high-school hipsters—were in fact all militant jazz enthusiasts. I had grown up hearing jazz, thanks to my mother, but only in my second year of high school did I discover the new and wilder sounds. For me, at fifteen, listening to the marvelous music of Thelonious Monk for the first time was a breakthrough experience of unprecedented magnitude. Even today there's no music I listen to more than Monk's.

One morning, almost all the black kids at Proviso stayed outside when the bell rang. A couple hundred or more gathered in front of a student hangout across the street, on First Avenue. Most of them arrived in class about a half hour late; a few stayed outside even longer. The unmistakable *protest* character of this impressive "silent strike" was loud and clear, although I suspect that very few white kids, and probably none of the faculty or administration, had any idea of what was up. During this protest, non-black *Lantern* supporters throughout the school showed their solidarity by creating various classroom diversions.

Few of our "actions," however, were so charged with politics. Most were just pranks. One day a bunch of us brought alarm-clocks to school and set them to go off in our hall lockers. When the alarms sounded during the day, restrained titters grew into loud giggles as outraged teachers tried to figure out what was going on. Silly? Of course! We were *bored* silly. That's what high school is all about.

## POETRY: THE GREATEST FORCE ON EARTH

Poetry was a crucial part of our rebellion from the start, and grew more and more important as we began to regard ourselves as out-and-out revolutionaries. The first book I ever bought was *The Complete*

6

*Tales and Poems of Edgar Allan Poe*, and it meant a lot to me as a tormented eighth-grader. A few months later, on my first day of high school, I showed up in U.S. history class with a copy of Perry Miller's paperback anthology, *The American Transcendentalists*. To my astonishment, the girl seated next to me asked: "Are *you* a Transcendentalist? *I* am!"—and it turned out that she too had brought a copy of the same book—which was *not*, by the way, on our assigned or even "recommended" list. Funny as it may seem, the elder William Ellery Channing, Thoreau, Emerson, Margaret Fuller and Theodore Parker were major fomentors of the high-school rebellion that called itself *The Lantern*, and therefore ancestors of *The Rebel Worker* as well.

It was the Beats, however, who gave us—my high-school friends and me—our first glimmer of poetry as a living, breathing, here-and-now activity. Serious students of the work of Kerouac and his comrades—Gregory Corso, Bob Kaufman, Diane di Prima, Gary Snyder and others—we went on to read the work of authors they admired: Rimbaud, for example, and Baudelaire, and D. T. Suzuki's writings on Zen. Such reading was actively discouraged by our so-called teachers, but we couldn't have cared less. How excited I was when Okakura Kakuzo's *Book of Tea* (cited in *The Dharma Bums*) arrived in the mail! For months afterward several of us would get together at odd moments and sit around a circle in the full-lotus position in our own version of the tea ceremony. The spirit of the thing was surely closer to the Marx Brothers than to Buddhism, but that didn't bother us. Breaking out of the repressive machinery of suburbia wasn't easy, and we tried to make use of anything that came our way.

One afternoon in Miss Wolf's insufferable history class, I was doing my best to ignore her lecture by reading bits of *The Reader's Companion to World Literature* when I came to the page on Surrealism and was thunderstruck by the proverb "Elephants are contagious." A measureless new world of imaginative possibilities suddenly opened for me, and all manner of things I cherished—the poetry of Poe and Blake and Han-shan; the music of Thelonious Monk; Dixie Willson's stories that I loved as a child; my all-time favorite Bugs Bunny comic (*The Magic Sneeze*, 1952); the idea of Revolution—all seemed to fit into place in a way they never had before. My first experiences with automatic writing soon followed, and I began to read everything I could find having to do with surrealism, starting with André Breton's *Nadja* (his only book in English in those days), Gérard de Nerval's *Aurelia*, and Lautréamont's *Les Chants de Maldoror*.

As I explained to friends at the time, I dropped out of high school because it interfered with my education. Never had I studied so hard and read so much as I did during the last few months of my Junior year and the summer vacation that followed. But it was all "extracurricular" study, to say the least. I began going (eventually almost daily) to the library of the Art Institute and often spent most of the day there reading, rereading and copying things out of the books they had on surrealism in English. I spent whole days, too, looking through *La Révolution surréaliste, Le Surréalisme au service de la Révolution* and *Minotaure*.

I was surprised to learn how much of what had attracted me to the Beat writers had been anticipated by the surrealists and their precursors, where its expression tended to be much more powerful. Especially important for me were the poems of fifteen-year-old Philip Lamantia in the fourth issue of the journal *VVV*, which the European surrealists in exile published in New York during World War II. Lamantia's lightning-flash imagery, along with his extraordinary accompanying letter to André Breton, dated October 1943—the month and year of my birth—were decisive steps on my path to surrealism and revolution.

Many years passed before I came across Saint-Pol-Roux's maxim, "Poetry is the greatest force on Earth," but I had *known* it, and *lived* it—as if by instinct—since I was fifteen.

### North Beach 1960: Anarchy in Action

After discovering the Beat Generation, Thelonious Monk, Free Jazz, surrealism, and revolutionary politics at the age of fifteen, I realized there was no turning back. Naturally I dropped out of high school and went on the road. In the next few years I hitchhiked some 20,000 miles from coast to coast: to Los Angeles, San Francisco, Seattle, New York and Mexico.

On the first of these adventures, I lived for several weeks in San Francisco's North Beach. Those who had arrived there a year or two earlier assured me that the "scene" in 1960 was in an advanced state of disintegration. For me, however, and for others my age who had made their way there from points all over the map, North Beach was so much livelier than anything we had known before that we found it hard to imagine how it could have been better.

The neighborhood was hit hard by the massive publicity the Beat Generation was receiving—almost all of it hostile, some apoplectically so, like Alfred Zugsmith's ugly movie, *The Beat Generation*, which fostered the ludicrous misapprehension that the Beats were dangerous criminals. Ironically, this disinformation campaign brought square tourists by the thousands, especially on weekends, as well as "hippies," a term then used by Beats to designate the uncreative camp-followers who parasitically attached themselves to the Beat scene. Even worse, anti-Beat propaganda gave the police a pretext to escalate their war on all nonconformists. Police persecution, much of it aimed at interracial couples or groups, was an everyday fact of life in North Beach. I spent a large part of every day at two of the main Beat hangouts of those days: the Co-Existence Bagel Shop, a bar/deli at the corner of Grant Avenue and Green Street, and Lawrence Ferlinghetti's City Lights Bookstore a few blocks away, where I was able to relax in an armchair and read hundreds of poems as well as every book they had on surrealism and Zen.

My San Francisco sojourn retains a special luster in my memory as one of those rare experiences that are truly worthy of one's childhood dreams. My first sight of the Giant Redwoods, a couple of days climbing in the Sierras, hearing Ornette Coleman and John Coltrane live for the first time: How can one measure the impact of such privileged moments?

Intersecting with all the rest was a strong ancestral dimension, for my father's family were San Francisco pioneers, and I had grown up hearing stories not only about the city and its peculiar ways, but also about my grandparents, aunts, and uncles: true "characters" one and all. As I explored the city on foot, the very street-names echoed from my childhood. In 1960 my Aunt Helen still operated the old family printing office, Rosemont Press, at 21 Rosemont Place in the Mission District. In some ways San Francisco was more like home than home.

It was a season of lucky breaks; small incidents had a way of adding up to something grand. With two friends—bass-player John R. White and a black street-philosopher from New York, known only as Ike—I went to Monterrey for the Jazz Festival. By mid-afternoon half the population of North Beach was there. John, Ike and I took seats before the tickets went on sale, so we enjoyed the whole program for free. (None of us had the price of admission in any case.) The music that night had all the magic of dreams; I hear its golden echoes to this day. It was there that I first heard Ornette Coleman live. After listening to his rip-roaring oracular sounds we wandered off in the darkness dizzy with joy.

Brightest of all in my memory of that period is the unparalleled experience of community it provided. Life in North Beach was the closest thing to marvelous anarchy it has ever been my pleasure to enjoy. Despite battles with landlords, harassment by tourists, and mounting police terror, the Beats and their allies—old-time hoboes, jazz musicians, oyster pirates, prostitutes, drug-addicts, winos, homosexuals, bums and other outcasts—maintained a vital community based on mutual aid, and in which *being different* was an asset rather than a liability. In this community, made up of people of many races and nationalities, the practice of equality and solidarity was second nature. Almost everyone was poor, but no one went hungry, and newcomers had no trouble finding places to stay. In North Beach, 1960, what mattered most was poetry, freedom, creativity, and having a good time.

One of my Bagel Shop friends was a young woman who had taken part in the big anti-HUAC (House Un-American Activities Committee) protest earlier that year. Now she wanted to go to Cuba "to see what a Revolution looks like."

Police harassment finally shut down the Co-Existence Bagel Shop. The whole community turned out on its last day. Standing-room-only inside, hundreds more gathered out front on the walk and in the street. Many were grizzled old folks who had hung out there for years, but youngsters—my friends and I—were a sizeable and vocal contingent. Widely regarded as a symbolic event marking the end of an era, this was probably the biggest Beat protest demonstration of all time. A poet friend named Chris wrote an ode about it, mournful yet defiant. He hoped to publish it in a rumored forthcoming issue of the local mag, *Beatitude*, to which I too was urged to contribute some poems; as it happened, however, I soon left the Bay Area and never saw another issue.

I returned to Chicago flat broke, but highly charged, and eager to do things. But what to do, exactly? And with whom?

## CHICAGO BEATS & MAYWOOD RHAPSODISTS

Chicago did not have a Beat "scene" the way San Francisco or Los Angeles or New York did. Nonconformists were far from invisible in the Windy City, but they were scattered far and wide. Among them were numerous individuals who everyone called Beatniks, but there was no Beat "center": no neighborhood comparable to North Beach or Venice or the Village; few hangouts (what passed for "hip" bars in those days were mostly folk-music clubs), and—until *The Rebel Worker*—no periodical that free spirits could gather 'round. In 1959–60 a rather square Catholic college professor named Paul Carroll had edited and published five issues of *Big Table*, which featured "big name" Beat writers, but the journal never became a rallying-point for local poets and rebels: the only Chicago writer to appear in its pages was Carroll himself.

Meanwhile, out in Maywood, several veterans of the "*Lantern* crowd" and a few late arrivals started kicking up a little storm of our own. Militant poets and pranksters all, and not one over seventeen,

10

we boldly declared ourselves "The Rhapsodist Movement"—probably Maywood's only collective contribution to the last century's long succession of "avant-gardes." I mention it here not only because it prefigured some of the spirit of *The Rebel Worker,* but also and especially because Rhapsodism was a ferment we ourselves—kids of high-school age—dreamed up and put into action.

The expression of poetic exuberance deliberately carried to excess—in writing, speaking, drawing, and above all in living—particularly by means of deliriously extravagant imagery, was not only Rhapsodism's motivating principle but virtually the whole Rhapsodist program. We took the name from Emerson: "The poet must be a rhapsodist."

This is not the place to chronicle the turbulent, shadowy history of Rhapsodism. Few avant-garde movements enjoyed so brief yet so intense a life, and I doubt whether any literary or artistic current before or since produced less than we did in the way of "works." Rhapsodism was in fact less a poetic movement, in the usual sense of that term, than a way of applying poetry to daily life. Recognizing that certain rare moments in our lives radiate wonder, excitement, curiosity, and pleasure, we maintained that the central aim of poetry was to multiply those moments of perturbation and thus to create the conditions for a new (poetic) way of life for all. We saw ourselves, collectively, as the *spurs*—so to speak—of such moments, and just about all that we did together as Rhapodists was, in fact, strictly spur-of-the-moment.

Our public manifestations were rigorously unpublicized, enjoyed no official sanction, and tended to be clandestine and even against the law. At a Rhapsodist poetry reading at Prince Castle (a burger joint on Roosevelt Road), we asked no permission, and when the Manager angrily inquired of the astonished crowd, "What the hell is going on here?" we simply said, "We're just leaving," read a few more lines, and left.

Another Rhapsodist event took place around midnight on the steps of a large abandoned tomb in Waldheim Cemetery in Forest Park, less than half a block from the Haymarket martyrs' monument. Those attending had to climb over a high fence in violation of "No Trespassing" signs. Wine flowed freely as we bellowed poems to each other in the moonlit darkness. Despite the hour, bursts of loud laughter and other noise—not to mention the fact that in no time at all we were unquestionably drunk and disorderly—the police, oddly enough, stayed away.

Such fleeting and occult demonstrations did not enjoy a wide resonance. And yet Rhapsodism had ways of making its subversive presence felt. One week several of us, armed with crayons, pencils and ball-point pens, wrote "Elephants Are Contagious" on scores, probably hundreds of walls, fences, and other surfaces all over Maywood.

Half the village's 27,500 population must have seen this message at one point or another. Several years later, long after I had moved to the City, the words were still plainly visible in the Seventeenth Avenue station of the Chicago, Aurora and Elgin Railway. In ways impossible for us to know, difficult even to guess, this provocative proverb impinged itself on the consciousness of many a mystified passerby.

### BEATNIKS & BOOKSTORES

Despite problems of geographical separation and lack of common activity, most of Chicago's Beats and other "disaffiliates" knew each other, and we maintained a loose communications network, largely through the bookstores where, as it happened, many of us had part-time jobs. From time to time I enjoyed talking with playwright Dennis Jasudowicz, when he clerked at Kroch's and Brentano's big store on Wabash, in the basement paperback department. The first and for many years the only Chicagoan to have a book published by City Lights (*Flea Street: Five Plays*, 1965), Jasudowicz wrote short, frenzied, incredibly comical anti-Establishment plays. It was thanks to him that Kroch's carried the complete line of City Lights books and many other small Beat imprints. One day at Kroch's I ran into a San Francisco friend, Shig Murao of City Lights. A few years later *Rebel Worker* contributors Bernard Marszalek and Lester Doré also worked at Kroch's.

Brilliant, soft-spoken Robert Fitzgerald, a University of Chicago philosophy student and Beat "Dandy" in the Lord Buckley tradition, worked a few blocks south of Kroch's at the Summit Bookstore, which specialized in the literature of psychoanalysis and the "avant-garde." Maury's Bookstore, next door to Slim Brundage's College of Complexes on State Street, was more explicitly Beat, as were The Medici Bookstore on 57th Street in Hyde Park, and Bill Smith's Sedgwick store under the El.

My own erratic work-life almost entirely centered around bookstores: Solidarity Bookshop, Roosevelt University Bookstore, and finally, Barbara Siegel's store on Wells Street, which was modeled on City Lights and for several years in the late 1960s/early 70s had the largest selection of Beat, surrealist, and revolutionary literature in the city. *Heatwave* contributor Paul Garon worked there, too.

I've never heard it mentioned, but it's an interesting fact: In 1960s Chicago, the best bookstores fell into the hands of the Beat Generation.

Those Beats who, for whatever reason, were *not* involved in bookselling, nonetheless made the rounds of the bookstores and did much to keep us in touch. One messenger of the local underground was Eddie Balchowsky—Spanish Civil War veteran, one-armed pianist and abstract painter—who later lived for a time at the Gallery Bugs Bunny. Milton Monson, a veteran of *The Lantern*, peripheral Rhapsodist, practicing Buddhist and future Wob, was another indefatigable street-wanderer for whom bookstores were oases to relax in for a few hours on endless treks across the Chicago desert. And so was the poet/boxer Art Livingston.

The key agent of liaison, however, not only for the city's relatively small Beat and half-Beat population but for all of greater Chicagoland's rebels and radicals, was the one-man revolution known as Joffre Stewart. Constantly strolling from one end of the city to the other, Stewart always made the scene with two shopping bags full of anarchist, pacifist, IWW and other controversial newspapers and tracts, plus samples of his own literary and anti-political offerings. Alone and with no car, he distributed more subversive printed matter than any other five hundred people.

Stewart early on embodied the new rebel spirit that came to be known as Beat. In his teens he was close to the Workers' Party—or at least to C. L. R. James's faction—but he soon found his way to an unequivocally pacifist anarchism, and stuck with it. In his anti-segregationist activities, starting in the late 1940s on, he pioneered the tactics of nonviolent direct action later popularized by the Student Non-Violent Coordinating Committee (SNCC) and the Congress of Racial Equality (CORE).

Chicago's most notable participant in the Beat Generation in its late-'50s heyday, Stewart traveled to the West Coast mid-decade. In San Francisco he met Allen Ginsberg, who mentioned him, though not by name, in *Howl* (the long line beginning "who reappeared on the West Coast" and ending with "incomprehensible leaflets"), and in Venice, Lawrence Lipton included his replies to a Peacemakers' questionnaire in his *Holy Barbarians*. In Chicago, during the 1960 Presidential election campaign, he was the Beatnik Party's "anti-candidate" for anti-Vice-President, the running-mate of Bill Smith, a longtime associate of Slim Brundage at the College of Complexes. This anarchistic anti-campaign, typically ignored by the many historians of the Beat movement, was a scathing satire of Establishment politics and an assertion of the rising new radicalism's sweeping rejection of the entire military-industrial-political swindle. Widely covered in the media, the Beatnik Party served notice to a broad public that the social scene was changing fast.

Like the Transcendentalists and "Come-Outers" of the 1840s and '50s, we—dropouts of the next mid-century—were saying no to the whole despicable system: school, jobs, elections, government, organized religion, sexual repression, "official" culture, consumerism, and authority in all its forms.

## THE ANTI-POETRY CLUB: PROTESTING EVERYTHING

Unlike the upper- and middle-class New Left, which was just gaining a toehold on some of the more well-to-do U.S. campuses, the *Rebel Worker* group was made up entirely of young wage-earners. Notwithstanding the fact that revolutionary theory was one of our major passions, we started out and remained emphatically anti-academic. Curiously, however, we originally came together as students.

Chicago's Roosevelt University in those years was not typical of American academia. Housed in an elegant building designed by Louis Sullivan, it was and is a downtown commuter school with no campus (and only a few dormitories). Its students were overwhelmingly of proletarian background. Our generation (born in the 1940s/50s) was the first in which large numbers of workingclass parents could afford to send their kids to college.

Started in 1945 by dissident faculty from the local YMCA College who had unsuccessfully tried to overturn the latter's race-discrimination policies, Roosevelt in the 1960s still had a well-deserved reputation not only as the university of choice for young subterraneans from all over the Midwest, but also as a hotbed of social radicalism of all kinds. Detractors and admirers alike often called it "The Little Red Schoolhouse." An impressive number of its faculty and students were in fact outspoken leftists. The student population included what racists called a "disproportionate" number of racial and ethnic minorities, as well as of foreign students, mostly from "Third World" countries.

Because of its workingclass and minority student population, Roosevelt was a fertile recruiting ground for radicals of every description. Several top organizers of the Young Socialist Alliance—full-time students at such high-priced schools as Northwestern and the University of Chicago—enrolled in one class at Roosevelt just so they could "hang out" in the cafeteria and "win people over" to their version of Trotskyism.

The YSA (youth group of the Socialist Workers Party) always had an animated table of its own in the cafeteria, as did their chief competitors, the Young People's Socialist League (youth group of the Socialist Party). A small group largely concerned with Cuba, an even smaller group of Maoists, and other groups with highly specialized ideologies had tables, too. Each had its own "milieu" of listeners and hangers-on, but a lot of intermingling took place. Roosevelt's Communist Party-oriented students also had a table, but since they were mostly involved in promoting Democratic Party politicians, those who regarded themselves as revolutionaries usually preferred to go elsewhere.

The Black Nationalists (a.k.a. the Negro History Club) had the liveliest discussions of all, and many of us soon-to-be-Wobblies enjoyed listening in. Indeed, with the exception of the classes taught by anthropologist St. Clair Drake, my best "classes" at Roosevelt were between and after class, in the free-for-all discussions and debates with other radicals in the student cafeteria.

Every day we argued about the Russian, Chinese, Cuban, and African revolutions; problems of the "Third World;" U.S. trade union strategy; race, class and culture; the "Labor Party" slogan, and many infinitely more esoteric issues.

In these discussions, and in the mass actions of those days—for we all took part in civil-rights and peace demonstrations—those of us who evolved into the *Rebel Worker* group developed our own perspectives. Two years before the first *Rebel Worker* appeared we already recognized ourselves as "extremists" or—in the term employed in those days by some of our Very Serious critics—"left-wing adventurers." We disdained what we called the "traditional left" as little more than a "loyal opposition" of the old order. We saw ourselves as the radical *negation* of that order in its entirety, left-wing and all. We rejected, as if by instinct, the stifling ideological compartmentalizations which seemed to us to typify the overall bureaucratic sterility of so many leftist orthodoxies. Their indifference to "culture," for example—except as the direct expression of a "political line"—convinced us that their vision went no further than a "planned economy." What excited us, on the contrary, were the limitless possibilities of the free imagination in conditions of playful anarchy.

It did not take long for us revolutionary outsiders to establish a cafeteria table of our own. Characteristically, the first collective manifestations of what later became the *Rebel Worker* group took place under a banner that at first sight might appear to have nothing at all to do with politics. We called it the Anti-Poetry Club, and its sole aim was to ridicule the school's bourgeois Poetry Club. None of us was against poetry—several of us, indeed, were practicing poets—but the faculty-approved Poetry Club exemplified, in our view, everything that real poetry was not.

Because of a silly rule forbidding first-semester or below-B-average students from serving as club officers, our friend John Bracey of the Negro History Club graciously agreed to be the Anti-Poetry Club's Acting Officer. Active members of the Club included Lawrence DeCoster, Tor Faegre, Robert Green, and a quiet but supportive fellow named Scott Spencer, who went on to become a well-known novelist (*Endless Love, Men in Black*). I opened the first meeting by climbing onto the teacher's desk and, without introductory remarks, reading aloud—at the top of my lungs—an automatic text I had just written in the cafeteria. Others followed suit, and in no time several people were speaking or singing and/or laughing all at once. Joyful chaos prevailed. Aside from a few offended curiosity-seekers, including a spy or two from the Poetry Club, who quickly fled—perhaps in terror—a good time was had by all.

More like an indoor street gang than a student group, the Anti-Poetry Club had two main activities: goofing off and protesting everything. Several of the faculty and more than a few students called us "hooligans" and, truth to tell, unruliness was our only rule. When one of Chicago's dailies sarcastically noted the Anti-Poetry Club's existence—as a particularly hideous example of Roosevelt's Communist-Beatnikism—the great writer Nelson Algren telephoned Elaine Trojan, the Student Activities Director, and told her that the formation of the Club was the best news he had heard in Chicago in years. Algren also invited Robert Green, one of the Club's nominal "officers," out for an evening at Second City.

In some respects the Anti-Poetry Club could be considered the last bow of Maywood Rhapsodism, but it was also the nucleus from which the *Rebel Worker* group soon emerged. The Club was a souped-up Chicago-style mix of surrealism, Bugs Bunny, the Marx Brothers, Ernie Kovacs, Stan Freberg, and Bob Kaufman's Abomunism, but so heavily spiced with our own humor and revolt that it had a distinctive "flavor" all its own.

Friends and enemies alike had to acknowledge the Anti-Poetry Club's creative/destructive energy—its uncanny ability to draw attention away from allegedly More Serious matters. Dean Hoover, as quoted in the *Chicago Tribune*, went so far as to affirm that the Club was "more active than the Socialist organizations" for which Roosevelt was already infamous (Editorial, *Roosevelt Torch*, May 25, 1964).

After a few meetings, however, it was clear that the Club had nowhere to go—that every meeting would be the same, that the Anti-Poetry Club was getting to be as boring as the Poetry Club. Those of us who went on to start *The Rebel Worker* wanted not only to ridicule the existing order but also to *change* it. Several of us circulated a statement dissociating ourselves from those who had turned the Club into a repetitive farce devoid of even the slightest subversive quality.

By that time, most of the leading figures of the original Anti-Poetry Club now carried red cards in the Industrial Workers of the

World. Still in our teens, we were confident that we could organize One Big Union, overturn capitalism and still be young enough to enjoy a long and exciting life in our newfound freedom. We began calling each other Fellow Worker, the traditional IWW form of address.

And so it came to pass that a new group held its first meeting: the Roosevelt University Wobblies.

## BUILDING A NEW IWW IN THE SHELL OF THE OLD

Why did we join the IWW? Each of us no doubt had reasons of his or her own, but we all agreed that the IWW had very special qualities that other radical groups seemed to lack.

As one of us (was it Simone Collier?) pointed out a bit later: "The IWW is the only group that is *not* boring!" Wobbly history, for example—its incredible strikes and free-speech fights, its thousand-mile picketlines and direct action and sabotage, its wild humor, cartoons and songs—has no parallel. As a 100% *workers'* organization, moreover, the IWW always put freedom and solidarity first.

In glaring contrast, the left groups we ran into—the many varieties of social-democratic, Stalinist, Trotskyist, and Maoist organizations, as well as others that appeared to be floundering somewhere in-between one or more of these ideologies—were repulsively middle-class, authoritarian, dogmatic, narrow-minded, sectarian, humorless, and utterly incapable of even the smallest original idea. Most of them were hung up on electoral politics, and spent an inordinate amount of time denouncing sects even smaller than their own. Even those that went in for "violent" rhetoric (such as Progressive Labor), were hopelessly reformist.

We recognized the IWW as "Joe Hill's union" and the direct heir of 1880s "Chicago Idea" anarchism—a fundamentally anti-authoritarian group that left open lots of room for individual and small-group improvisation; the only group in which we could develop our wide-ranging inclinations: to rethink revolutionary theory, to explore the subversive possibilities of popular culture, and above all to pursue our passion for *poetic action*: that is, for *life as adventure*. We knew that IWW perspectives had a place for all these, and that no other group would even tolerate them.

I joined the IWW on September 19, 1962, at the union's international headquarters on the second floor at 2422 North Halsted Street. General Secretary-Treasurer Walter H. Westman (who had lined up in the IWW in 1916) handed me red card No. X322339 and welcomed me into the ranks. I was thrilled—all the more because it was not easy to join the union in those days. Fellow Worker Westman felt obliged to warn all applicants that the union was on the U.S.

17

Attorney General's list of "subversive organizations," and that IWW members were automatically disqualified for Federal government jobs of any kind. He would say: "Think it over, and if you still want to join, come back in a few months and we'll see what we can do." It took me several visits before I convinced him that I had thought the matter over carefully, agreed wholeheartedly with the IWW program, and really wanted to join.

I have often wondered how many prospective Wobs, less tenacious than I, never bothered to return.

On the 8th of April the following year, after the six-month waiting period required by the IWW Constitution, I was given organizers' credentials and immediately began signing up everybody I could think of.

At the first Chicago Branch meeting I attended, all seven of the old-timers present rolled their own cigarettes. They were a colorful and lovable lot, their basic unity enhanced by a charming diversity. Most of them had hoboed all over the country for years. Several, most notably Fred Thompson and Jack Sheridan, were fine storytellers— a result, no doubt, of decades of union soapboxing. Thompson, the IWW's own in-house historian, had served a few years at San Quentin in the 1920s for "criminal syndicalism" (*i.e.*, IWW organizing). Sheridan, a poet and great reciter of poetry, had longstanding hobohemian connections as a survivor of Chicago's old Dil Pickle Club. Walter Westman—IWW General Secretary-Treasurer for decades— had lost a leg leaping from a boxcar during a harvest drive way back when. Carl Keller edited the *Industrial Worker*. Softspoken Charlie Velsek had chaired the union's General Executive Board (GEB) in the 1930s. George Roby, a one-time carnival-worker, was a diehard Esperantist; at every meeting he made a motion that the IWW issue some literature in Esperanto. Carlos Cortez, linocut artist and poet, lived in Milwaukee but came down to Chicago for the monthly Branch meetings; the son of a Mexican Wobbly father and a German socialist/pacifist mother, at forty-something he was the youngest Chicago Wob besides me (I was nineteen).

At my first Wobbly "social," some months later, I met a few dozen more Fellow Workers: Czechs, Swedes, Finns, Hungarians, Russians, and others whose nationalities I never learned. Several had been "class-war prisoners." A couple were nudists. Some had been close to Ralph Chaplin and James P. Thompson in the old days. One elderly Swede cherished a 1920s letter in which his friend Big Bill Haywood told how discouraged he was living in the USSR. There was James "Bozo" Kodl, an actor/playwright who had appeared in several movies (including *Female Jungle*, with Jayne Mansfield) and on TV (often cast as a drunken cop). Among the many women Wobs were Aino Thompson, active in Women for Peace; Jenny Lahti Velsek, who had studied at Work People's College; the dynamic activist Ruth Sheridan; and Fannie Keller (Carl's wife), who told me that before we—the *Rebel Worker* group—showed up, the office mimeograph had hardly been used since she herself was our age, in the 1930s. "Just think," she said, "every page you print helps make the world a better place. Hearing that old machine is music to my ears!"

Some of the old Fellow Workers we met were no longer paid-up members, and a few had never even joined, but all were part of the broad Wobbly community. To give an idea of IWW non-sectarianism in those years, this milieu also included the anarchist Free Society Group, assorted oddballs from Slim Brundage's College of Complexes, and the old Proletarian Party, a jovial band of philosophy-minded worker-intellectuals who regarded themselves as America's only genuine Marxist-Leninists.

At this social, Fred Thompson introduced me to these oldsters as the "Fellow Worker who is responsible for the fact that there are some younger faces here for a change." Thompson called the 1960s IWW "a union of grandparents and grandchildren," for an entire generation had been skipped. Of the local old-timers, he was the most serious about reactivating the union, and more than any of the others he made it a point to keep in close touch with us younger Wobblies. After Branch meetings he often joined us for further discussion at the nearby Marquis Lunch on Fullerton, and several times invited us over to his and his wife Aino's apartment to plan leaflets or actions, or just to talk about IWW history and what kinds of things needed to be done now. Fellow Worker Thompson was a thoughtful and generous man and a walking encyclopedia of IWW history and lore; we all loved him and we all learned a lot from him.

We, of course—the soon-to-be *Rebel Worker* group—were bursting with ideas of all kinds. Thompson liked them all: a new Chicago Branch magazine, an IWW bookstore (the soon-to-be Solidarity Bookshop), a revival of farm-labor organizing. He also considered the Roosevelt University Wobblies an excellent starting point, particularly since Roosevelt was a workingclass school.

Indeed, the entire Old Guard turned out to be very supportive. They agreed that our proposals would benefit the IWW and help it grow, but they also pointed out how much work was involved, and made it plain that it was *we* who would have to do the work. The union would help, but basically it was up to us.

Our discovery of the works of the wonderful Wobbly writer

T-Bone Slim (Matt Valentine Huhta) provided clinching proof that the IWW was the group for us. Struck by the proto-surrealist quality of his text, "Electricity," in the October 1925 issue of the IWW magazine, *Industrial Pioneer*, I began reading his columns in the bound volumes of old IWW papers in the hall. In no time at all we were hooked. T-Bone's audacious imagination, flamboyant wordplay, and black humor, along with his marvelous maxims ("Wherever you find injustice, the proper form of politeness is attack"; "Half a loaf is better than no loafing at all") and his ability to regard old problems from the most improbable new angles (with results worthy of Alfred Jarry's Pataphysics), convinced us that the IWW project of workingclass self-emancipation went hand in hand with all that we meant by the word *poetry*.

## Free-Speech Fight at Roosevelt University

Forming the R.U.Wobblies broadened our field of action at Roosevelt. What had been a raucous gang around a cafeteria table had now become an organized presence and a real force. As a recognized student group, we were able to set up literature tables, and to bring in speakers, with the University paying the expenses. Several hundred students and faculty turned out to hear Marxist-Humanist Raya Dunayevskaya speak on the "Cultural Revolution" in China. *Industrial Worker* editor Carl Keller spoke on the contemporary relevance of the IWW. But when Roosevelt alumnus Joffre Stewart spoke on the antiwar movement, he incidentally precipitated the biggest scandal in the history of Roosevelt.

Stewart was an impressive speaker, with a flair for the controversial. In his Roosevelt talk (April 22, 1964) he exemplified anarchism's rejection of the State by burning several small flags, including a U.S. flag. The meeting was written up as a front-page feature in the *Roosevelt Torch* (April 27), and the following day President Robert J. Pitchell announced that the Wobblies group was suspended. We were charged with violating fire-safety regulations and an Illinois ordinance prohibiting flag-desecration. Pres. Pitchell added that the IWW—as a "subversive" organization, identified as such on the U.S. Attorney General's list—was also "in clear violation of the Smith Act" and therefore had no business on campus.

No group had ever been suspended at Roosevelt, and the news made all the Chicago dailies. "Fiery Substitute for Panty Raid" was the headline in one. Student papers at the University of Chicago, University of Illinois and other local and faraway campuses gave the suspension prominent coverage.

Pres. Pitchell and his henchman Dean Hoover found little support for their war on the Wobblies. Roosevelt founding president Edward Sparling defended us by telegram from his retirement in California. For weeks the affair dominated the pages of the *Roosevelt Torch*. The May 11, 1964 issue, for example, includes nine stories about it, plus an editorial, a letter to the editor, a cartoon, and even a mention in the gossip column.

The literature generated by the R.U. Wobblies' suspension was indeed enormous. Almost every campus political group issued at least one statement on the matter, as did the Student Senate and the Faculty. Several faculty members made individual statements. Except for a right-wing Republican club that demanded our "punishment," virtually everyone recognized it as a question of free speech, and demanded our immediate reinstatement. The most interesting response was a letter to the *Torch* from well-known social critic Paul Goodman, emphasizing how lucky Roosevelt was to have a group as relevant as ours (reprinted here on pages 282–283).

Throughout this crisis we Wobblies had a merry time. "Suspended" though we were, new people kept joining, and interest in the IWW and our ideas spread through the student body and beyond. Of course we continued to meet regularly, albeit "unofficially," in the school cafeteria. One day a group of six or seven Illinois Central Railroad conductors came to meet us. Dissatisfied with their own union, they wanted to learn more about the IWW. Nothing much came of it, but some of them did come back, and more than once, to buy IWW pamphlets and stickers.

In and out of school, we kept up a whirlwind of activity. The first issue of *The Rebel Worker* appeared a week after the free-speech fight started, and helped fan the flames of that struggle. We also held a big "Wobblies-in-Exile" meeting—with songs, music, and soapboxing— in Grant Park across the street from Roosevelt. We distributed thousands of IWW leaflets all over downtown Chicago. We set up an IWW literature table at the Maxwell Street open-air market on Sunday mornings. We soapboxed and sold IWW literature at Bughouse Square, and later on Wells Street in Old Town. Wobs were among those arrested at a big anti-HUAC demonstration. And we walked picketlines galore: at the Spanish Tourist Bureau, demanding freedom for political prisoners in Franco's Spain; at a police graduation ceremony near the old Haymarket cop statue; at Mayor Daley's house, for his stand on school segregation. We joined John Bracey and other Black students in shouting down a racist speech by the Mayor in Grant Park, and took part in the Congress of Racial Equality (CORE) Freedom Day marches. Most of us were also active in CORE, as well as in the Student Peace Union (SPU), and several members of these groups also took out red cards.

Meanwhile, Paul Goodman's letter (reprinted in *Liberation* and elsewhere) and a write-up by Sarah Murphy in a New York Students for a Democratic Society (SDS) bulletin brought our victorious free-speech fight—and more generally, the IWW revival—to the attention of students and young rebels all over the country.

No doubt about it: Thanks to the R.U. Wobblies and the *Rebel Worker* group, the IWW was noticed, talked about, and written about in the press more than it had been in many years. Several of the old-timers told us how pleased they were to see the union making headlines again.

## MAY DAY 1964: *REBEL WORKER* 1

The first issue of *The Rebel Worker* appeared on May Day 1964. As editor, I solicited the articles, wrote a lot of copy, typed the stencils and stayed up all night running it off—one page at a time—on the antique electric mimeograph machine at Wob headquarters. It was nearly sunrise when I collated and stapled the first few copies and bicycled twelve miles to my parents' home in the suburb of Forest Park.

We took the name *Rebel Worker* from an old Wobbly paper, *circa* 1919. For us it signified not only the worker as rebel, but also—and no less important—rebellion against work.

The original *Rebel Worker* group—those who planned and put out the first issue—consisted of Tor Faegre, Robert Green and me, soon joined by Bernard Marszalek, and then, in September, by Penelope Bartik.

Torvald Faegre had been active in the Committee for Non-Violent Action (CNVA), and had taken part in direct actions against the Polaris nuclear submarine on the East coast. His parents were "left of center," and a number of older radicals (Paul Mattick for one) were family friends and neighbors. Tor's own friends included many anarchist-pacifists, including Holley Cantine, Dachine Rainer, Virginia and Lowell Naeve, and Karl Meyer. Tor himself was definitely inclined toward anarchism, though also interested in the left currents of Marxism, and paid more attention than the rest of us to questions of wildlife preservation, ecology, nutrition, air-pollution, and what would later become known as "appropriate technology." A carpenter by trade, and an artist by inclination—always sketching—he was also deeply interested in traditional crafts, most notably calligraphy. His interests were impressively wide-ranging. When we met, he had just designed an italic font of the Cherokee syllabary, to be used in a revival of Cherokee printing. He did the covers as well as headlines and other lettering for all but two issues of *The Rebel Worker* as well as most *Rebel Worker* pamphlets and leaflets. It is also chiefly to him that we owe the beautiful series of Solidarity Bookshop Anarchist-Revolutionary Calendars.

Robert Green was born in rural Wisconsin and grew up on a small farm near Baraboo—a town best known as the summer quarters for circuses—where he became a skilled mechanic/machinist/carpenter, and eventually sculptor/cartoonist/inventor. A born agitator, he was also skilled in the art of getting into trouble, and spent more than his fair share of days behind bars. The day I met him in the Roosevelt cafeteria—he had just returned from a peace march in Indiana—he was wearing a foot-wide nuclear disarmament "button" he had made himself. That was his first semester at Roosevelt; before that he had gone to Wright Junior College, where he was active in civil-rights struggles.

Green was the first of us to move to Lincoln Park, in those days a semi-slum. His "pad"—to use the terminology of the time—was just a few blocks from the IWW hall. Not long afterward he was arrested in a ruckus at Bughouse Square, Chicago's famous free-speech park; the next day he took out a red card. His wife Judy joined shortly thereafter.

From early spring to the late fall of '64, Robert Green was a dynamo of IWW activity. When we revived Agricultural Workers' Industrial Union No. 110, he served as its secretary, and was instrumental in the Michigan organizing drive and The Great Blueberry Strike (the first IWW strike in many years). As Chicago Branch Secretary, he was also—with Faegre, Bernard Marszalek and me—a co-founder of Solidarity Bookshop. Even after he got involved in the short-lived Beatnik Coffee House (formerly The Erecthion Café) and transformed it into a co-op bicycle shop, he was still active in the IWW, although to a lesser degree.

I first met Bernard Marszalek at the Socialist Party office on Van Buren Street, downtown, and later noticed his name listed as the Chicago representative of Colin Ward's *Anarchy* magazine, published by Freedom Press in London. We met again at a demonstration at one of the big Chicago hotels, protesting the visit of the notorious Madame Nhu of Vietnam. Bernard promptly announced that he now considered himself a Bakuninist and favored direct action. His views seemed entirely compatible with ours, and we remained in close touch thereafter. Although he took no part in the first *Rebel Worker*, and was represented in the second only by a letter, from then on he was an integral and energetic figure in the group.

In our milieu, Bernard came closest to fitting the role of "left-wing intellectual," although he probably would have despised such a description. He was definitely a man of ideas, in any case, and the only one of us who regularly read such journals as *New Left Review* and *Studies on the Left*, or who paid much attention to what was published in the way of radical philosophy. Always volatile—the wild enthusiasm of one week might well be replaced by something entirely different the next—he often seemed to enjoy arguing for the sake of arguing. With his original turn of mind and sharp sense of humor, this made for a lot of truly amazing discussions.

Penelope Bartik, whose forebears were Czech freethinkers who had fled to the U.S. in the repressive aftermath of the 1848 revolutions, grew up around Fox Lake, sixty miles from Chicago. While still in her teens she was radicalized by reading Ruskin and Tolstoy, supported the 26th of July Movement, subscribed to *Liberation* magazine, and became an early and active member of the Student Peace Union. A chemistry major at Lake Forest College, she was also active in the radical Jacobin Club and part of the local "beatnik" scene. By that time Rimbaud's *Illuminations* was a major inspiration. In summer '64 she moved to Chicago and enrolled at Roosevelt, where—on her first day—she met the Wobblies and visited the still-under-construction Solidarity Bookshop. Fascinated by Vico, Hegel, Nietzsche, and later Spinoza, she expanded our collective consciousness in many directions and immediately became both a central figure in the *Rebel Worker* group and—as Penelope Rosemont—the lifelong companion of the author of these lines.

As we all got to know each other, we became aware of the IWW's presence in our own family backgrounds. Bernard's father had carried a red card in the 1920s. Penelope recalled her father singing IWW songs when she was a child, and my own father had IWW friends (Donald Crocker, for one) in the Typographical Union.

We were all very different, one from another—there never was a *Rebel Worker* "type"—but somehow our many differences strengthened and expanded our common project. When we were at our best, the mix seemed to add up to a kind of alchemy.

The *Rebel Worker* group also had a sizeable number of out-of-town friends, fellow workers, and contributing editors. Those most actively involved included Alan Graham and Barton Stone in Berkeley, Judy Kaplan in Philadelphia, Robert S. Calese in New York, Lawrence and Dotty DeCoster in various West Coast locales, and Louise Crowley in Seattle. IWW songsters "Utah" Phillips and Dave Van Ronk kept in touch via the Wob hall. Traveling in Europe, *Rebel Worker* cartoonist Lester Doré put us in contact with the Amsterdam Provos. Our early international correspondents included Jim Evrard in West Germany; Deri

Smith in Wales; Ian Bedford in Sydney, Australia; and in London, Charles Radcliffe, who quickly became our very closest co-dreamer.

## A VERY SMALL ONE BIG UNION

A tough old Wob who had known Joe Hill in Canada during the Fraser River Strike of 1912, Louis Moreau—still active and serving on the union's General Executive Board fifty years later—observed that of the 79 million wage-slaves in this country, probably 78,999,000 did not know that the IWW existed.

The One Big Union had fallen on hard times indeed.

None of us knew it then, but the IWW at the time I joined it had a membership of not more than 100, and probably less, of whom about twenty could be considered truly active. The rest, isolated in remote towns and villages across the continent, paid their dues by mail and occasionally sent in larger financial contributions to meet emergencies. Now and then an old-timer left his or her meager life's savings to the union. Together with income from sales of the perennially popular *Little Red Song Book*, these windfalls paid the headquarters rent, the modest salaries of the General Secretary-Treasurer and the *Industrial Worker* editor, and the printing bills.

At the time, the old guys at headquarters—General-Secretary-Treasurer Westman and *Industrial Worker* editor Keller—evaded our queries on the subject of membership, vaguely claiming "several hundred" members—many of whom, they conceded, were "way behind in their dues." The broad public was given even less candid information. To a *New York Times* reporter who phoned IWW headquarters and asked for membership figures, Westman simply explained that he was not allowed to provide such data; when the reporter asked whether the members numbered less than 10,000, Westman said yes. Next day, or so I was told, a *Times* filler informed the world that the once-great IWW now admitted that its membership was less than 10,000. All the News that's Fit to Print!

Not until decades later did we learn that we—the *Rebel Worker* group—had doubled and tripled the membership almost overnight. And only then, in the 1980s, did I realize what the generally taciturn Westman meant when he told me, *circa* 1963–64—and I still regard this as one of the most touching compliments I have ever received—that I was the best organizer the Union had had since its last resurgence among Kentucky miners and Detroit auto-workers in the early 1930s.

Our problem was not only organizing, however; it was keeping the organized active, and getting them to do some organizing, too. "Organize the organized!" was in fact one of our slogans for a time.

That the R.U. Wobblies was one useful model for growth was shown by the appearance of other campus Wob groups over the next few years. Momentum also played a role. The IWW resurgence in Chicago in turn inspired new bursts of activity elsewhere, most notably in the San Francisco Bay Area and New York. The fact that the IWW kept growing seems to indicate that we were doing something right.

## A WOBBY EXCURSION THROUGH NORTH AMERICA

Eager to meet as many as possible of the old-timers around the country, and to see for myself which locals showed greatest promise of expansion, I visited IWW Branches in San Francisco, Berkeley, Seattle, Duluth, Port Arthur (Ontario), and New York. These trips, mostly via hitchhiking, started in 1963 and continued in 1964–65.

On the first trip, Fellow Worker Lawrence DeCoster and I took a semester off at Roosevelt for what turned out to be a veritable Wobbly Grand Tour of North America. The first week or so had its share of frustrations, as we were unable to meet Houston IWW delegate Robert "Blackie" Vaughan, or Pedro Correa, the union's secretary in Mexico. In Mexico City, however, we did enjoy an afternoon of lively discussion with surrealist painter and writer Leonora Carrington, and later, in Acapulco, we met a representative of Lazaro Cardenas's short-lived Movimiento de Liberacion Nacional, which had been organizing huge direct-action land-expropriations.

After a glorious "sidecar-pullman" trip up the California coast (my first experience riding freight-trains), we hitched from Sacramento to San Francisco. The Bay Area IWW Branches—San Francisco and Berkeley—were, as we had expected, a direct outgrowth of the earlier Beat scene. Like the Chicago Branch, the Bay Area Wobs had their share of "characters." Several of the more prominent among them, including Dick Ellington and Tom Condit, were ardent science-fiction and fantasy fans, with huge collections; Condit had a complete run of *Weird Tales* and had met the great Clark Ashton Smith. Robert Rush, Secretary of the Berkeley Branch, had a degree in Egyptology from the University of Chicago, but made his living as a traveling brassiere salesman. One time he showed up elaborately costumed at a big ban-the-bomb demonstration and introduced himself to the crowd as a Martian who had come to thank the Earthlings for destroying this planet and thus facilitating Martian invasion. Such theatrical protests would become common later in the decade; in this as in many other matters Wobblies led the way for the New Left and the counterculture. It was not just an accident that some years later the whole Living Theater troupe joined the IWW.

The most surprising figure in the Frisco Branch turned out to be Philip Melman, the only Bay Area old-timer who regularly came to meetings. A one-time cellmate of Fred Thompson's in San Quentin, Melman was openly gay and a zealous devotee of marijuana. At the meeting we attended, he showed up a little late, placed a sheet of paper on the table, poured out a small bag of the stuff, announced that it was "Acapulco Gold," and invited one and all to partake thereof. What dismayed Larry and me about this incident was its irresponsibility: How did he know no informers were present? We could all have been arrested and kept in jail for weeks.

All in all, however, we found the Bay Area Wobs to be likeable, serious and well-intentioned. Their biggest problem seemed to be: What to do as an IWW Branch? They had almost no point-of-production presence, and—in a city that was then one of the most thoroughly unionized anywhere—saw no opportunity for effective organizing. Neither their one small strike at a small coffee shop, nor their forming of a short-lived Poets' Union, attracted much workers' interest. More significant by far was their appreciable role in the 1964 Berkeley Free Speech Movement (some months after the struggle at Roosevelt). Bay Area Wobs also did much to assist the struggles of the United Farm Workers' Union, and years later several became active in Earth First!

From Frisco we went by boxcar and thumb to Seattle, where the IWW had a large storefront hall on Yesler Way, in the original Skid Road, manned by a grand old Wob named O.N. Peterson. O.N., as everybody called him, gave us a rousing welcome, and for days regaled us with stirring tales of Wob splendor from the days of yore. Not only did he make it seem as if the 1919 Seattle General Strike was only yesterday; he made it clear that he expected even bigger battles in days to come.

One day a bent-over guy with long white hair and a long white beard came to pick up some copies of the *Industrial Worker*. After he left, O.N. told us that was Guy B. Askew ("Skidroad Slim"), a member since 1917, writer of countless letters to IWW headquarters and Solidarity Bookshop.

According to Carlos Cortez, who stopped in Seattle on a speaking tour some months later, O.N. and the handful of other old-timers who had wandered into the hall while we were there could hardly believe that there actually were people as young as us in the IWW again. Carlos quoted O.N. as saying: "We thought the Revolution was coming!"

O.N. was a magnificent fellow: fearless, unpretentious, full of the rebel spirit, and a first-rate *raconteur*. I wish I had gotten to know him better. Had there been ten more like him in Seattle, they could have given the boss class some bad days. In 1963, alas, the Seattle Branch did not have enough active members even to make a quorum.

A later trip, this time with Fellow Workers Tor Faegre and Robert Green, took me to Duluth and Port Arthur. In Duluth I had the pleasure of meeting Fellow Worker Abraham Wuori, an intrepid Finn whose tales of the "old days" were as good as O.N.'s. Wuori's depiction of the local situation was also unrelentingly bleak; the Duluth Branch had only three members, none at the point of production, and all too old to do anything.

At the Port Arthur Wob hall, Fellow Worker Alex Murto welcomed us heartily, and enjoyed talking with us at great length. But finally he had to confess—I think that was the very word he used—that he was the only active member of the Branch.

As we headed back toward Chicago, Tor said: "Well, I'm glad we didn't think rebuilding the IWW was going to be easy."

Sometime later I attended a meeting of the IWW Branch in New York. I already knew some of the old-timers there—my good friends Sam and Esther Dolgoff, Russ Blackwell, and Robert Calese, an important *Rebel Worker* contributor—and had met a few of the younger Fellow Workers, most notably Jonathan Leake and Walter Caughey, but this was my first encounter with the Branch as a whole. Like the Bay Area Wobs, their specifically IWW organizing efforts were few and far between; they were primarily active in local social struggles, including rent strikes, squatting, and defending the Harlem rioters. The Branch did issue leaflets, however, and members had seen to it that Wob stickers and graffiti were highly visible throughout the city. They hoped to open an IWW bookstore in the near future, as we had just done in Chicago.

## THE ONE & ONLY SOLIDARITY BOOKSHOP

Some people called it "the bookshop with the stop-light in the window." Others zeroed in on "the huge canoe on the ceiling." Still others remember "the motorcycle in the middle of the floor." Comic-collecting grade-school kids called it the "Solitary Bookshop." Jay Lynch, a pioneer of "underground comix," recalls it as "the hub of hippie activity in Chicago long before there were hippies." To the cops, according to the *Chicago Daily News* (December 23, 1967), it was always "The Anarchist Bookshop." What disturbed the FBI most about the place, as noted in a report on Bernard's draft status, were the "constant comings and goings of young people of all sexes and races at all hours of the day and night."

For one and all, Solidarity was a bookshop like no other.

Tor Faegre, Robert Green, Bernard Marszalek and I rented the original space at 713 Armitage Avenue in mid-summer of '64. We often acted as a foursome in those days. For Penelope, we were The Three Musketeers (in Dumas' novel, the "three" were also in fact four). Some of our detractors, who no doubt thought they were being abusive, called us The Fantastic Four. Word got around that when all of us showed up at picketlines, public events, or parties, "things started to get interesting."

After a few weeks of painting walls, building bookcases, gathering books and arranging them on shelves, Solidarity Bookshop opened informally in August, and we had an official Grand Opening party on the twelfth of December. Tor painted the calligraphed shingle that swung over the door: *Solidarity Bookshop. Industrial Workers of the World.*

The older Wobs loved the place. Carl Keller, Jack Sheridan, and Fred Thompson dropped by often, and usually bought a book or two, to help out. Fellow Worker Keller actually took the trouble to write me a letter to express how happy he was

> about the progress the Solidarity Bookshop is making. I already visualize it as the best thing we [the Chicago IWW Branch] have done in years. And I don't forget it is all the work of "young" members. (November 16, 1964)

A series of rummage sales helped us get acquainted with our workingclass neighbors, and even before the Grand Opening a group of black students from Waller High School (half a block away) asked if they could make Solidarity their noon-hour hangout. Of course we said yes! Mostly they came to listen to music and dance, but they also used our mimeograph machine to print leaflets for school protests. They also distributed IWW leaflets and anti-draft literature. Even grade-schoolers—second- and third-graders—used our facilities to make picket-signs and a leaflet for their very own lunchtime anti-Vietnam-war demonstration.

Solidarity was also the official headquarters of the Chicago Branch of the IWW (who paid half the rent), and that's where the monthly Branch meetings were held. But above all it was the headquarters and hangout for the *Rebel Worker* group.

From the start Solidarity was *the* place in Chicago to obtain new and out-of-print anti-authoritarian revolutionary books, pamphlets and periodicals. As our customers kept telling us, most of this material was "impossible to find" elsewhere. We carried all of Rosa

Luxemburg's in-print English-language works, for example, including many pamphlets imported from Ceylon. IWW, Anarchist, Syndicalist, Socialist, and Surrealist publications were the specialties of the house, but we always stocked a wide range of titles in other fields as well. The 55-page 1965 *Solidarity Bookshop Catalogue* included such categories as Anthropology, Calligraphy, Cinema, Labor History, Negro Freedom Struggle, Pacifism, Psychoanalysis, Psychedelics, and Spanish Revolution. We carried a lot of City Lights Books, all Freedom Press and Charles H. Kerr titles, and many mimeo'd poetry mags. At a time when H. P. Lovecraft and Clark Ashton Smith were no longer in print in paperback, we stocked all their cloth titles from August Derleth's Arkham House in Sauk City, Wisconsin. Wisconsin's best-known writer, Derleth told us Solidarity was the only store in Chicago to restock Arkham House books! (Kroch's had a standing order for new titles, but never reordered.) Derleth was no Wob, but he was always friendly to us. After one of our many battles with the authorities, he wrote: "Glad to hear that Solidarity has pulled through!"

Solidarity's Out-of-Print Department was awesome: a couple thousand old books from the IWW's Work People's College in Duluth; a comparable number from the Chicago IWW Branch library, long stored at the Halsted Street headquarters; and substantial quantities of material from several anarchist groups that were, so to speak, "going out of business": the Chicago Free Society Group, the New York Libertarian League, and the latter's Italian- and Spanish-language affiliates. At a fly-by-night resale shop we bought several large boxes of the old Haldeman-Julius Little Blue Books—some 5000 titles in all! Now and then, old-timers—known and unknown—dropped off a carton or two of old books as a "contribution to the Cause." And of course all of us young Wobs were constantly adding old books we found at Maxwell Street or at the many second-hand bookstores that flourished in Chicago in the Sixties.

We sold used comics, too. At least one Puerto Rican kid later paid his college tuition by selling comics he had bought at Solidarity.

To raise funds—and consciousness, too—we printed buttons. We didn't coin the slogan "Make Love, Not War" but we printed the first "Make Love, Not War" button, and sold thousands of them. Other Solidarity Bookshop buttons included "Burn, Baby, Burn!"—a disc-jockey's phrase that became the watchword of the 1965 Watts rebellion; "I am an Enemy of the State"; "Dodge the Draft"; "Abolish the Draft"; and a new IWW button—the first in many a year.

We also showed films, held parties, played records, drew pictures—and above all, we talked. Discussion and debate were often all-day affairs. As a meeting-place of the city's imaginative malcontents, Solidarity Bookshop in its early years had few equals.

There we were, a small, brave group at the service of the Revolution, determined and eager to abolish capitalist oppression and to transform the world. Though few in number, we were not dismayed. We were sure that our ideas and imagination, our passion for freedom, our unity and solidarity and—not least!—our *humor* made us (potentially, at least) a formidable force. In those glorious days, nothing seemed impossible.

All for One! One for All!

### REBEL WORKER WOMEN

By 1965, the *Rebel Worker* group included as many women as men, and they were active in every phase of our activity. Judy Green, Penelope Rosemont, Simone Collier, Joan Smith, and Anna-Marie Gibson were especially notable for their commitment and creativity. *Rebel Worker* women participated in formulating our collective plans as well as in realizing them. Side by side with the men, they took part in group discussions on "How can we become more effective?" and "What do we do next?" and countless other topics. They pitched in at our "collating parties," where we put together *The Rebel Worker* and our pamphlets. They joined the IWW/anarchist group on big demos, helped sell *The Rebel Worker* at street meetings, and kept hours at Solidarity Bookshop.

We were just the opposite of those New Left groups in which women's role was primarily to do the typing and/or make the coffee, for I did about 75% of the typing, Bernard Marszalek did most of the rest, and Tor Faegre usually made the coffee. This is not to say that the *Rebel Worker* group was innocent of sexism, but it certainly had much less of it than SDS or Progressive Labor.

As with the men, some women in the group were more active than others. Some focused on the Bookshop as their main sphere of activity, while others wanted to be in the thick of things. Judy Green, for example, was active in every aspect of our Michigan agricultural workers organizing drive: the early planning, organizing in the field, drafting leaflets, walking the picketline. Anna-Marie Gibson, too, was a real firebrand—a true-blue Wob, tireless in spreading the *Rebel Worker* word.

One thing most women in the group did *not* do was write articles, and that's why they are not better represented in this book. (Except for Penelope, the women contributors to *The Rebel Worker*—Leonora Carrington, Louise Crowley, Barbara Garson—lived far from Chicago.) Unlike the men, who tended to have irregular or part-time jobs—and even prolonged periods of unemployment—most *Rebel Worker* women worked full-time, and thus had less time for writing. Simone Collier, who worked at the main post office downtown, was a sharp critical thinker, full of ideas, and a fine writer. But when I asked her to write something she always said she was too busy working on a play—and in fact two of her plays were later staged in Boston. Charlotte Carter, another member of our post office nucleus, published a collection of her poetic prose tales in 1975, and went on to become a noted mystery writer, but we never saw any of her writing in *Rebel Worker* days.

Women were, however, active in the editorial discussions. Simone Collier, Dotty DeCoster, Penelope Rosemont, Joan Smith and others commented freely on incoming letters and other material for *The Rebel Worker*, and thus helped establish the content of each issue.

*Rebel Worker* correspondents Judy Kaplan in Philadelphia, and Louise Crowley in Seattle, made especially important contributions to the group's ideas. A seasoned veteran of labor struggles in the Northwest and a close friend of many old-time Wobs, Crowley later—around 1969—became a highly regarded theorist of the women's liberation movement.

In the opening rant of *Rebel Worker* 3 (January 1965) I announced a forthcoming "issue on women." This special issue was suggested by Dotty DeCoster, who hoped to edit it from her home in California. Alas, it never materialized. Among the proposed contents were Leonora Carrington's tale, "White Rabbits" (eventually published in *Rebel Worker* 7), and a compendium of short "profiles" of historic women we admired—French revolutionary Enragés Claire Lacombe and Pauline Léon; Mary Wollstonecraft; radical utopian Flora Tristan; poet Emily Brontë; feminist Transcendentalist Margaret Fuller; abolitionists Harriet Tubman and Sojourner Truth; libertarian Marxists Rosa Luxemburg and Mary Marcy; labor agitator Mother Jones; anarchists Louise Michel, Lucy Parsons, Voltairine de Cleyre, and Emma Goldman; and civil-rights activist Rosa Parks.

What, in the long run, did the *"Rebel Worker* experience" mean to the women who took part in it? No doubt its significance has varied as much among them as among their male friends and fellow workers. On a visit to Chicago in 2002, Joan Smith—a stalwart in the group who became a noted psychologist and now lives in Nevada—offered these reflections:

> I remember my first visit to Solidarity Bookshop. I thought there was a party going on, because there was music playing, and a lot of people were standing around talking, and everybody

was obviously having a good time. But later I realized that's just the way the place was—*always* music playing, *always* people talking, *always* a good time.

When I got to know the people involved, I knew I belonged to something special. The group around Solidarity Bookshop and *The Rebel Worker* weren't like most groups. They were more fun to be with—they had a real camaraderie, or rather, *solidarity*.

I knew some of the people at the Guild, too [a nearby bookstore with a strong Stalinist bias], but they were stuffy and rigid— yet every one of them seemed to have a completely different idea of what the Guild should be. They were always rather bureaucratic, too—when they showed their true colors.

At Solidarity, we Wobblies were more open-minded, much more close-knit, and we agreed on basics. Of course, we were also younger.

I have fond memories of those days: the "socials" at the IWW hall, with all the old-timers so happy to see us; and selling *The Rebel Worker* on Wells Street on weekend evenings; and all those IWW stickers pasted just *everywhere* at the Post Office!

I was young, I was in love. There was so much going on and I was glad to be a part of it.

## NOTES FROM AN UNUSUALLY HECTIC HISTORY (1964–65)

Imagine a sitdown strike of stand-up comedians in a cluttered, dimly lit bookshop and you will have an idea of what a typical *Rebel Worker* meeting was like, *circa* 1964–65. On these occasions, outrageous proposals seemed to be the order of the day—or rather *disorder*, for we often had a hard time getting down to whatever business it was that we were supposed to accomplish. Rarely if ever did we have an agenda, and by unanimous agreement we dispensed with *Robert's Rules of Order* (a book which was, however, in use at the monthly IWW Branch meetings, also held at Solidarity). We, the *Rebel Worker* "planning committee," preferred to hold *our* meetings in conditions of Perfect Anarchy.

Even when confronted with serious difficulties, these meetings tended to be enjoyable. Among the things that distinguished us from the New and Used Left was the fact that we laughed not only at the society of scissorbills and squares, but also at ourselves. We also realized that The Revolution itself was *funny*. I am absolutely serious: What on Earth could be funnier than overturning 500-odd years of capitalist slavery?

Of course each of us had his or her share of depressing moments, fits of melancholy, spells of despair. Together, however, more often than not, one good joke would lead to another and the three-ring Solidarity circus started up again.

I have been to many hundreds of other meetings since, and I can think of some that were far from boring, but few where there was more laughter or more all-around creative high-jinks than at the "planning sessions" of the good old *Rebel Worker*. The fact that we were all in our teens or early twenties probably helped.

Somehow, despite all the clowning (or was it because of it?) we did manage, at these meetings, to welcome newcomers, discuss pressing problems, make plans, reach decisions, and otherwise *get things done*— not only for *The Rebel Worker* and Solidarity Bookshop, but also for the IWW as a whole. A lot was happening in the union in 1964–65, and we were at the nerve-center of just about all of it. Looking back, it is hard to believe that so few people had so much going on all at once. Here are just a few of our activities for 1964:

*January-March:* Revival of Agricultural Workers Industrial Union No. 110, and plans for a summer organizing drive in Michigan. (The first contribution to the organizing fund was a $50 check from long-time labor agitator/writer Sidney Lens.)

*April-May:* Free-Speech Fight at Roosevelt; publication of *Rebel Worker* 1 (May Day);

*June:* Tor Faegre designs and prints a "silent agitator" for the Michigan drive—the first new Wob sticker in years; Jack Sheridan and Fred Thompson give us soapboxing lessons at Bughouse Square;

*July:* Blueberry-pickers' strike near Grand Junction, Michigan; front-page news for a week; two new leaflets issued;

*August-September:* Sunday morning soapboxing at Maxwell Street; publication of *Rebel Worker* 2;

*December:* Grand Opening of Solidarity Bookshop; also, a party there celebrating the publication of Joyce Kornbluh's *Rebel Voices: An IWW Anthology*.

All this was in addition to such routine chores as distributing IWW publications around town; leafleting Unemployment Compensation offices and various protest demos; joining workers' picketlines; running the mimeograph; and for most of us, holding down regular jobs. Once the Bookshop opened, we also had to keep hours there, put new books on the shelves, reply to correspondence, fill orders and take care of customers.

1965 was even more frantic, starting with *Rebel Worker* 3, the "young worker" issue, with an original red and black woodcut cover by Tor Faegre. The "young worker" emphasis continued with the famous "dropout leaflet"—"High School Students! Why Stay in School? Drop Out! Join the IWW!"—which appeared in February.

By far the most influential and talked about IWW leaflet of the decade, this one-page mimeo'd statement brought more attention to the union than any other single action had done in many years. Chicago's dailies reported it with indignation; the Board of Education was furious; William F. Buckley's right-wing *National Review* treated it as an example of revolutionary hysteria. More importantly, the news brought us phone calls from interested young people not only in Chicago but all across the country, and some joined up. Young Wobs and sympathizers in the Chicago suburbs of Glenview and Lake Forest reprinted the leaflet; it also appeared in the New York anarchist magazine *Resurgence* and later in *Heatwave*, edited by Charles Radcliffe in London. Local high-schoolers came to Solidarity again and again to get more copies.

As the Chicago *Seed* put it a couple of years later, the dropout leaflet earned *The Rebel Worker* and Solidarity Bookshop "a reputation [they have] been trying to live up to ever since."

That Spring we also revived the long-dormant local branch of the IWW's General Defense Committee, to defend and publicize the plight of class-war prisoners.

The first two *Rebel Worker* pamphlets—*Mods, Rockers & the Revolution*, and Robert Calese's *Blackout*, a first-hand account of the big New York power failure—were quickly followed by the 55-page *Solidarity Bookshop Catalogue*, with a calligraphed cover by Tor Faegre, and *Rebel Worker* 4, the "international issue," with a cover by Lester Doré, recently arrived from Tulsa, Oklahoma.

Chicago's black riots that August—the biggest workingclass uprising in the city's history—fully confirmed our sense that a radically new movement was in the air. Ten or so members of the *Rebel Worker* group piled into an old pick-up truck, eluded the police barricades, and drove through the riot zone for a couple of hours, hailing the surprised population with our raised fist salutes and loud cries of solidarity and Freedom Now! Symbolic of the mood of the time, someone had shot out the letter S in a huge illuminated SHELL gas station sign, so that it now read HELL—a classic of *détournement*!

In summer '65 the whole *Rebel Worker* group, plus many friends, turned out for the IWW's big sixtieth birthday party at headquarters. The farm-workers' drive that year focused on the apple harvest in Yakima, and several footloose Chicago Wobs hitched west to take part in it.

In November, to mark the fiftieth anniversary of the judicial murder of IWW songwriter Joe Hill, we organized two big memorial meetings (with 200-plus attendees at each) at Poor Richard's, featuring songs, poems and talks by Ginny Clemens, Tor Faegre, Jack Sheridan and others.

December marked Year One of Solidarity Bookshop, celebrated in rousing Wobbly style. Unfortunately, thanks to the Board of Education, that month also brought us an eviction notice. In the first four years of what the *Seed* called Solidarity's "unusually hectic history," we were forced to move four times.

Thanks to our activism, we were also able to learn—as the old-timers put it—"what the inside of a jail looks like." Almost everyone in the *Rebel Worker* group was arrested at least once, and several were carted off two or three times or more. None of us, as I recall, were convicted.

All year the Branch kept growing. Our Post Office group—consisting of Bernard Marszalek and three African American women: Simone Collier, Joan Smith, and Charlotte Carter—were especially active, not only on the job, but also as mainstays at Solidarity Bookshop. Other members were active in construction, factories, offices, restaurants, and the Chicago Transit Authority. Fellow Worker Charles Willoughby Smith, a conductor on the El, had the distinction of being one of Chicago's better Beat poets.

In a June 29, 1965 letter, Skidroad Slim (Guy B. Askew) wrote:

> If the IWW is growing today, it is because an active, young and vigorous generation is taking it over. For many long years the old-time members have done nothing but pay the landlord the rent and sit around the halls.

## The Best-Read Mimeo'd Mag in the World

In miserabilist society, most people don't recognize the real problems because they are too busy trying to justify their misery. The *Rebel Worker* group recognized the problems in all their boundless horror, and we did our best to let the whole world know.

The IWW's sudden and unexpected resurgence was covered in detail in all the Chicago dailies, as well as in magazines. The free-speech fight at Roosevelt, the announcement of the Agricultural Workers' Organizing Drive, and the blueberry-pickers' strike were major stories, and word of the dropout leaflet also got around. The "underground" *Seed*—which reached scores of like-minded papers all over the country—gave us a lot of coverage. Even the stodgy journal, *Studies on the Left*, published in Madison, begrudgingly acknowledged "a minor IWW revival."

Meanwhile, our literature tables at labor, radical, and countercultural events; our leaflets, stickers, graffitti, posters (including the first Lucy Parsons poster), and above all our well-attended street-meetings—frequently broken up by cops—and the many doings at Solidarity Bookshop made the Wobblies (and *The Rebel Worker*) a vital presence in the community.

The upshot was that the IWW and its upstart magazine were live topics of conversation and debate—denounced, belittled, scoffed at, and sometimes even admired and praised.

At an anarchist conference in New York, 1967, Murray Bookchin—who considered himself an anarchist at that time—announced loudly: "I've read and reread every word of every issue of *The Rebel Worker*—it's a very important magazine." Similar testimonials from a wide range of anarchists, socialists and independent radicals were far from rare. For a mimeographed magazine with a circulation that never exceeded two thousand, *The Rebel Worker* attracted an impressive amount of attention.

Notices of it, several of considerable length, appeared in some of the news and magazine stories noted above, as well as in such diverse publications as the New York Libertarian League's *Views & Comments; Direct Action*, monthly organ of the Syndicalist Workers' Federation in Britain; the Ohio Socialist Party's magazine, *Strike!*; the old Italian-language anarchist newspaper, *L'Adunata de refrattari*, from Boston; the Paris *ICO* bulletin; Jeff Nuttall's *My Own Mag* (at the time a major vehicle for the writings of William S. Burroughs); and in many other periodicals mentioned elsewhere in this Introduction.

In *The Rebel Worker*, we published very little of the fan-mail we received. The samples reprinted here, however, were typical of several hundred others. Comradely comments from old-time Wobs, young rock'n'rollers, and rank-and-file workingstiffs always boosted our morale. Now and then we received letters from students, prisoners, and unhappy guys in the army. Busybodies hoping to save us from the errors of our ways wrote often, urging us to read this or that pamphlet by Daniel DeLeon, James P. Cannon, William Z. Foster or the Jehovah's Witnesses. Letters and exchange publications came from dozens of countries.

Somehow, *The Rebel Worker* really made its way in the world. Fellow Workers "loaned" their copies to friends, who in turn—in the best hobo tradition—passed them on to others. Single copies sent as exchanges to radical groups were often read by twenty or more people. Many of our articles were reprinted or translated.

At Solidarity Bookshop, *circa* 1966, someone—I no longer recall who—said, "You know, *The Rebel Worker* might well be the best-read mimeographed magazine in the world!"

Who knows?

## What Made the *Rebel Worker* Different?

Few of us in the *Rebel Worker* group ever took a degree, much less became professors, but we never evinced the anti-intellectualism that so many observers discerned among New Leftists on the campuses in those days. It was not by chance that we had grouped ourselves around a bookshop and a journal largely devoted to ideas, imagination, and criticism.

What distinguished the *Rebel Worker* group from all the other groups that claimed to be against capitalism? What made us so different? The answers are obvious: *humor, poetry*, and *breadth of vision*—which are a large part of what make a revolution revolutionary. Our critique focused not only on Capital, work and the workplace, but also and above all on *everyday life*. Our aim, as our Philadelphia correspondent Judy Kaplan put it, was "to be revolutionary in everything."

In our view, the bleak humorlessness and thoroughly *prosaic* character of traditional left groups were definitive proof that their theory and practice were worthless, too. For most would-be radicals, "theory" is rarely anything more than a sack of abstractions that bumps along behind them, this way and that, in the wake of the books and "position papers" they read, with little or no relation to their own or others' real efforts to change the world. In contrast, the sometimes "wild" ideas advanced in *The Rebel Worker* developed directly out of our lives and struggles—more specifically, out of our many and varied experiences as so-called "undesirable elements": as "bad kids" in school, "trouble-makers" at work, dropouts, juvenile delinquents, hitchhikers, poets and revolutionaries.

Inevitably, the *Rebel Work* conception of revolution differed profoundly from prevailing left doctrine. For us, the abolition of wage-slavery and the destruction of the machinery of state were not postponable "stages" in a long-drawn-out revolutionary "transition," but rather the revolution's crucial starting-point, and indeed its *vital essence*. By abolishing all classes, the working class also abolishes *itself* as a class, along with the props of class rule: alienated labor, value, money, consumerism, bureaucracy, repression, boredom and all the rest. Sharply opposed to old dogma and new sectarian isms, we always emphasized workers' self-activity, creativity, solidarity and freedom.

Nonconformists by nature, we sought inspiration far from the beaten track. Unlike most young radicals, for example, the *Rebel Worker* group drew heavily on the IWW's hobo heritage—the nomadic tradition of the workingclass intellectual/poet/humorist who had been everywhere, done everything, and knew more about you-name-it than most college profs. No other group at that time had anything like the hobo education—from the horse's mouth—that we had. Old 'boes such as Fred Thompson, Carl Keller, Jack Sheridan, Charlie Velsek, Sam Dolgoff, O.N. Peterson, Guy B. Askew and Abe Wuori taught us a lot about history, philosophy, economics and poetry—to say nothing of point-of-production organizing, strike strategy and direct action—that somehow never came up in school.

Books were important for us, too—as they had been for the Wobbly hoboes of yesteryear—and at Solidarity we had quite a selection! For all of us, the *Rebel Worker* years remain memorable for their intellectual stimulation. Hardly a day went by without impassioned discussions of IWW history, new developments in capitalism and new forms of workers' struggle, the great revolutions of the past and the even greater revolution that needed to be made.

Naturally we identified ourselves with history's extreme radicals: the Diggers, Ranters, Shays' Rebellion, the Enragés of the French Revolution, slave rebellions, John Brown, the 1871 Paris Commune, the Haymarket ("Chicago Idea") anarchists, the IWW, Emiliano Zapata, James Connolly, John Maclean, the 1921 Workers' Opposition in Russia, the "Friends of Durruti" in Spain 1937, and the workers' councils in Hungary 1956. We also admired Black Hawk, Osceola, Geronimo and other great figures of Native American resistance.

Far more than most New Leftists, we were familiar with the Marxist classics, and with the less-well-known currents of later Marxism as well as anarchism. None of us—unlike many New Leftists—confused Stalinism, a crude and inherently anti-workingclass ideology, with Marxism.

Well-versed in Wob theory—the works of Vincent St John and Bill Haywood; the 1930 compilation, *Twenty-Five Years of Industrial Unionism*; and the more recent writings of Fred Thompson—we also read and discussed most of the theorists known to have influenced the New Left, including C. Wright Mills, Dave Dellinger, Staughton Lynd, Paul Goodman, and above all Herbert Marcuse.

We knew that the Leninist tradition was hopelessly infected with bureaucratic authoritarianism, but recognized that Lenin's views differed radically from Stalinism, and rather liked his *State and Revolution* as well as his notes on Hegel. Our "favorite" Marxists, however, were William Morris and Rosa Luxemburg, whose anti-authoritarian politics seemed to us perfectly compatible with our Wobbly approach (the old Wobs regarded them fondly as well). And we liked Paul Lafargue's *Right to Be Lazy* so much that we reissued it twice under the Solidarity Bookshop imprint. In our dream, revolution was a joyful jubilee.

We also admired the work of Anton Pannekoek and the "Dutch Left," and two of that tendency's outstanding U.S. co-thinkers, Mary E. Marcy and Austin Lewis, whose writings, published by Charles H. Kerr, we discovered at the Wobbly hall, and whose best work in fact articulated the experience of the IWW. In the same tradition was Paul Mattick, whose old pamphlets and journals we found at ridiculously low prices at Jerry Nedwick's used bookstore on Wabash Avenue, not far from Roosevelt University. Mattick had belonged to the IWW in the 1920s and '30s, and contributed to the *One Big Union Monthly*. Tor Faegre visited him in *Rebel Worker* days to discuss the past and present of the radical labor scene.

One day at the Wob hall Fred Thompson handed me a copy of Raya Dunayevskaya's *Marxism and Freedom* and said, "Here's a book that shows that old Hegel made some sense after all." YPSL acquaintances had never had anything good to say of Dunayevskaya or the "Johnson-Forrest Tendency" which she led with C. L. R. James, but this book—prefaced by Herbert Marcuse—piqued our curiosity.

By 1964 "Johnson-Forrest" had moved far from its Trotskyist origins, and had split into three distinct groups. We had friendly relations with them all, but were closest to Martin Glaberman's Facing Reality group, which concentrated on publishing the works of the eccentric Trinidadian Marxist C. L. R. James. Several of us read James's *Black Jacobins*, as well as his brilliant study of Melville, and I think the *Rebel Worker* group did as much as anyone to introduce his work to young radicals in those years.

The socialist group that influenced us most, however, was unquestionably the Solidarity group in London, England. I first learned of it around 1962 from friends in the "Libertarian Tendency" of YPSL. By the time we started *The Rebel Worker* we saw ourselves as *Solidarity's* U.S. equivalent.

London Solidarity was part of a larger current in post-World-War-II socialism whose principal vehicle was the French journal *Socialisme ou Barbarie* (Socialism or Barbarism), and whose best-known theorist was Cornelius Castoriadis. Under the name Pierre Chaulieu, Castoriadis had been a co-thinker of "Johnson-Forrest"; in *Rebel Worker* days he was known as Paul Cardan. In his book, *Modern Capitalism and Revolution*, published by London Solidarity, we found a critique of capitalism and a conception of socialism in many ways close to our own.

Unlike *Socialisme ou Barbarie*, which included a sizeable number of academics, the London group was made up almost entirely of wage-earners, and its mimeo'd paper reflected a devil-may-care shopfloor humor that we found very appealing. At the same time, it rejected traditional "workerist" limitations, and boldly took up topics that most radicals avoided. One article, for example, contrasted the uncreative and hierarchical structure of the traditional European orchestra with the playful, improvisatory emphasis of Ornette Coleman's "free jazz" ensemble. (The author was a young teacher at a workers' school in Munich, Jim Evrard, who soon became part of the international *Rebel Worker* community.)

Although *The Rebel Worker*—like the IWW—belonged to the revolutionary Marxist tradition, we rarely bothered to call ourselves Marxists. It seemed futile, and perhaps a bit silly, to quibble over labels. Besides, we were influenced not only by the "ultraleft" currents of Marxism, but also by anarchism. Fellow Worker Sam Dolgoff was a big booster of *The Rebel Worker* in its day, above all "because it presented the IWW from the anarchistic viewpoint," and of course we all appreciated his enthusiasm and support. In our view, however, Marx and Bakunin were no longer antithetical, and the IWW had always been a major locus of their reconciliation. In short, we were emphatically non-sectarian. Bernard Marszalek expressed a view we all shared when he wrote, in *Rebel Worker* 3, that anarcho-syndicalism remains "the most obviously relevant strain of anarchism," but we also admired much in the writings of William Godwin, Peter Kropotkin, Errico Malatesta, Emma Goldman, Voltairine de Cleyre and, more recently, the brilliant Marie-Louise Berneri. We would have loved Gustav Landauer, too, but we scarcely knew his work in those years.

Our indifference to the usual labels was inseparable from our rejection of the traditional left's ideological pigeonholing, and its pitifully narrow vision of life and the world. None of us regarded revolutionary theory as dogma to be memorized, or a "finished program" that needed only to be carried out. Theories at best were inspirations to play with, challenges to be taken up, suggestions to build on, or take apart, or push into unexpected directions. This open-ended outlook, largely inspired by the IWW hobo intellectual tradition, is also characteristic of surrealism.

When dogmatic Marxists or anarchists jeered at us as "utopians," we replied: "Long live Charles Fourier!"

In the opening article of *Rebel Worker* 1, Fred Thompson accused capitalism (quite rightly) of destroying the Earth. (Fellow Worker Thompson had years earlier given the IWW the slogan: "Let's make this planet a good place to live!") Ecological awareness and a specifically wilderness-inspired radicalism were central to the two principal sources of the *Rebel Worker* perspective: the IWW and surrealism. And yet, ecological concerns turn up in *The Rebel Worker* mostly "between the lines." This seeming oversight is all the more surprising in view of the fact that Robert Green, Tor, Penelope and I had all grown up in or around wilderness, and never made any secret of our love for wild nature.

These topics *did* figure in our discussions: I particularly recall an amazing fantasy of Tor's involving a band of superheroes who roamed the globe defending endangered species: elephants, rhinoceroses, giraffes, whooping cranes—a clear forecast of Greenpeace and Earth First! Tor also introduced us to Farley Mowat's fine book, *Never Cry Wolf*.

Living in a huge, sprawling city, we found the ecological crisis a staggering problem for which we did not pretend to have definitive solutions. All we had was our love for the wild, plus a good activist starting-point: *Abolish wage-slavery!*

It did not bother us in the least to be called dreamers; indeed, we took it as a compliment. The great bass-player Charles Mingus urged his listeners to "Think of the things you could be by now if Sigmund Freud's wife was your mother." That was the title of one of his compositions oft-played at Solidarity Bookshop, and it seemed to us to have methodological implications. Undisciplined and playful to a degree that surely seemed carnivalesque to our critics, we dreamed of the wonders of revolutionary thought and action free of the shackles of all hand-me-down ideologies.

Don't think we spent all our time reading explicitly revolutionary literature. Some of us were also impassioned readers of the poets. Like love and jazz, poetry provokes visceral anticipations of a happier world, and is therefore a liberating force that knows no bounds. Blake, Burns, Shelley, Emily Brontë, Lautréamont, Rimbaud, Jarry, Vaché, Breton, Péret, and Césaire were our inspirers and guides beyond all others. We liked the German Romantics, too, and the early Gothic novelists; Charles Robert Maturin's *Melmoth the Wanderer* was a favorite. We also read pulp-fiction—especially the works of H. P. Lovecraft, Clark Ashton Smith and their circle. And we all read comic books—*lots* of them, new and old. At Maxwell Street in those days, 1940s/50s comics were a nickel each, or three for a dime, and we often came back with a hundred or more. They were a vital part of our education as radicals. I like to think of *The Rebel Worker* as the first revolutionary journal influenced by Bugs Bunny, Scrooge McDuck, Plastic Man, The Incredible Hulk, and Harvey Kurtzman's *Mad*.

Passional attraction led us to the IWW and anarchism as well as to the dissident currents of Marxism. What is most original in *The Rebel Worker*, however, owes at least as much and probably a great deal more to other realms of thought—most especially to anthropology, Black radicalism, psychoanalysis, and, providing coherence to all the rest: surrealism. These inspirations, which we all shared, also did much to set us apart from the great bulk of what then passed for the "left press."

*Toward a Revolutionary Anthropology:* Several members of the *Rebel Worker* Group were anthropology students—specifically, students of St. Clair Drake at Roosevelt University. The "science of culture" interested us precisely because we were radicals. Aware of the racist/imperialist bias of the great majority of those who made anthropology their profession, we saw ourselves as learning what The Enemy knew so that we could develop it critically, in the spirit of revolt and freedom. We were all attracted by so-called "primitive" cultures, seeing in them much that "civilization" had lost and needed to recover. More generally, we sensed that the culture we ourselves lived in needed critical analysis that would go deeper than mainstream Marxism or anarchism had been willing to go. Consciously on the side of the "primitives" of the world, as well as of the oppressed in our own society, we wanted to develop an activist anthropology that would help the revolutionary cause.

Professor Drake's discussions—in class and after class, for he enjoyed talking freely with us Wobblies and other student radicals—were always inspiring as well as informative. His lectures on the roots of the U.S. Civil Rights struggle and the Revolution in Ghana were especially illuminating. One time he devoted a class to a line-by-line analysis of the revolutionary anthem, "The Internationale," relating it to the millenarian movements of olden times and contemporary Third World countries, as well as to May Day, our favorite holiday.

His lectures on American Indian cultures were also highly stimulating; we especially enjoyed his vivid discussion of Zuni and Hopi opposition to World War II. In contrast to other Roosevelt profs, Drake's recommended readings tended to be books that changed our lives: James Mooney's monograph, *The Ghost Dance Religion and the Sioux Outbreak of 1890*, for example, and Peter Worsley's *The Trumpet Shall Sound.*

Having read of Indian uprisings in the past, we were eager to know about Indian resistance today. Here again Drake pointed us in the right direction. In Edmund Wilson's *Apologies to the Iroquois* we learned about the contemporary Tuscarora agitator Wallace "Mad

43

Bear" Anderson, who had conferred with Malcolm X and Che Guevara. Later we began corresponding with the Survival of American Indians Association in Tacoma, whose "Plea to All" we published in *Rebel Worker 7*.

Drake's conception of an "urban anthropology," or the application of anthropological theory and methods to the study of modern city life, also intrigued us. Together with Archie Green's "laborlore" studies—which we read at the IWW hall—it influenced our exploration of popular culture and what some of us later began to call "vernacular surrealism." We in the *Rebel Worker* group were not only interested in workers at work, but also workers *at play*: jobsite bulletin board gags, graffiti, slowdowns, pranks, sabotage, Jacques Vaché's "desertion from within," and all the clandestine and semi-clandestine actions that have come to be called *infrapolitics*. Several of our articles focused on workers' leisure activities.

In more ways than I can describe here, Professor Drake shaped our knowledge of anthropological history and theory, and confirmed our hopes that a knowledge of "primitive" societies could deepen our radicalism. Tor Faegre's 1979 book, *Tents: Architecture of the Nomads*, and my 1989 essay "Karl Marx and the Iroquois" (in *Arsenal/Surrealist Subversion* 4) owe much to his early guidance.

When people asked me what I was "majoring in" at Roosevelt, I always replied: "St. Clair Drake."

*Black Radicalism:* Co-author with Horace Cayton of the classic study of Chicago's black community, *Black Metropolis*, Professor Drake was in close personal contact with black liberation struggles around the world. Naturally he influenced our appreciation of African, Afro-Caribbean and Afro-American radicalism, which in turn became a major part of our revolutionary project. Even before the first *Rebel Worker* stencil was typed, Nat Turner, Harriet Tubman, and Frederick Douglass were high on our list of heroes, and—like the Wobs of yesteryear—we regarded the struggle against wage-slavery as the logical and direct follow-up to the abolitionists' crusade against chattel slavery. The Cuban Revolution had opened our eyes to the reality of U.S. imperialism, and the saga of Patrice Lumumba in the Congo touched us profoundly. Drake discussed all this and much more in his classes, and got us to read Marcus Garvey, W. E. B. DuBois, George Padmore, Richard Wright, Oliver C. Cox, Kwame Nkrumah and other black radicals. Often he referred to his former student, James Forman, who became head of the Student Nonviolent Coordinating Committee.

The New Left, like the Old, approached the working class as "condescending saviors," and in turn viewed the Black struggle through lenses badly blurred by the myth of the "white man's burden." We were luckier; we knew St. Clair Drake. Thanks to his classes, his after-class discussions and fabulous reading lists, we knew far more about the black struggle, its history and global character, than most non-African-Americans enjoyed at that time.

The entire *Rebel Worker* group was active in the local civil-rights movement, and some of us had taken part in the August 28, 1963 March on Washington. We recognized—as Wobblies had for decades—that non-violence was a valid tactic in many situations, but we also affirmed the right of all oppressed peoples to self-defense. Drake's discussions of slave insurrections, the Marcus Garvey movement and the Mau-Mau Rebellion in Kenya sharpened our consciousness of the manysidedness of revolutionary struggle. He also talked about Malcolm X, whom we had seen and heard on TV talk-shows and read in *Muhammad Speaks*. We were all deeply impressed by Malcolm's views on the course of the black liberation movement, especially after his split with Elijah Muhammad.

With passionate interest and solidarity we followed the development of this movement. What attracted us most was the evident new *mood* in black America, especially among the young. Just as our labor perspective focused not on "leaders" but on "actions by the workers themselves, in or out of the unions"—as we put it in *Rebel Worker 2*— so too we identified ourselves strongly with the masses of black proletarian youth who outgrew the increasingly conservative older civil-rights groups and took up direct action in the streets. The Harlem Insurrection of 1964 was widely regarded at the time as an anomalous, isolated incident, but for us it marked the beginning of a new era.

The ensuing nationwide wave of "riots"—we preferred to call them "rebellions" or "insurrections"; the publication of Robert F. Williams's *Negroes with Guns*, the emergence of the Deacons for Defense and Justice, and the growth of SNCC into a fighting force for "Black Power" that dared to raise the question of armed struggle: These were critical moments in the rise of a new revolutionary generation. Our friend John Bracey, a fellow student of Drake's and a member of the black nationalist Revolutionary Action Movement (RAM), played a decisive role in the evolution of our thinking on these matters. Indeed, many of us at Roosevelt regarded Bracey as second only to Drake in advancing our education.

We knew all the Marxist and anarchist arguments against nationalism, but we also had the good sense to recognize that the emerging currents of revolutionary black nationalism in the U.S. were ra{...}different from—indeed, antithetical to—the reactionary tend{...}

commonly identified by the nationalist label. It was obvious, moreover, that with few exceptions the brightest, most daring and imaginative black radicals were those who called themselves nationalists.

*The Rebel Worker*'s support for the revolutionary currents of black radicalism also had a crucial cultural dimension. Having had the honor and joy of seeing and hearing Thelonious Monk, John Coltrane and Ornette Coleman several times, live, I say without hesitation that our most extravagant revolutionary dreams were summed up, renewed and expanded in the untrammeled loveliness of this music, in which human nature is no longer at odds with Nature writ large. As early as the 1950s some of us recognized the new jazz as the auditory equivalent of surrealism in painting. Our certainty that the coming revolution had to go further than any revolution had ever gone—and the particular tone of defiance we adopted to defend this view—would not have been the same without the inexhaustible wonders of "Great Black Music."

*Workingclass Psychoanalysis:* At Solidarity Bookshop we frequently discussed our dreams of the night before, as well as chance actions and "irrational" encounters that one or another of us had experienced, and these discussions drew appreciably on the literature of psychoanalysis. I doubt if there was any other revolutionary group in the U.S. in those years that had anything close to our enthusiastic interest in the work of Freud and his more radical followers. One of the things that repelled us most about the traditional left was its puritanical and positivistic character, exemplified by its anti-Freudianism, and the consequent shallowness of its social criticism—its inability to recognize the sexual and other unconscious factors in social development—which in turn led to its capitulation and defeat at every crisis. Interestingly, some of the old-time Wobs, especially those who had been Dil Picklers, shared our Freudian orientation.

Herbert Marcuse's *Eros and Civilization*, with its surrealist emphasis on the release of erotic energy as a defining element of revolution, was a particularly important book for us, and served as a guide through the maze of psychoanalytic literature. At a time when such liberal reformists as Erik Erikson and Erich Fromm were much in fashion, we vigorously upheld a radical, non-medical, non-therapeutic analysis—a kind of Wobbly anarcho-Freudianism, with crucial strategic implications. As Bernard Marszalek pointed out in the Chicago *Seed*:

> The kind of life we want to live cannot be served to us by
> reshuffling economic priorities. A new life can be found only
> by the release of Eros bringing about a transvaluation of all val-

46

ues and an existence that is fully cognizant of submerged realities. . . . Given our desires, we cannot make the mistake accompanying all reformism; we cannot confront the system on the system's terms. In short, we cannot make use of the *language of repression*.

Freud's *Interpretation of Dreams* and *The Psychopathology of Everyday Life* were key documents in the *Rebel Worker* library. Helpful too was the early work of Wilhelm Reich, most notably his critique of the USSR's sexual policies in the 1920s, and his fine study, *The Mass Psychology of Fascism*, which demonstrated the direct applicability of psychoanalytic theory and practice to the day-to-day revolutionary struggle.

*Surrealist Revolution:* Our interest in psychoanalysis was greatly deepened by surrealism. In our explorations of unconscious and irrational phenomena, we found what André Breton and his comrades had taught us to find: signal-lights illuminating the dialectics of internal and external reality. It would be no exaggeration to say that we used psychoanalysis just as we used Marxism, anarchism, anthropology and every other instrument of knowledge that came our way: that is, for explicitly surrealist purposes.

The *Encyclopedia of the American Left* is thus quite right to describe *The Rebel Worker* as "the first sustained U.S. surrealist-oriented publication." Our surrealism, more than anything else, differentiated *The Rebel Worker* not only from the left, right, and middle, but from *all* ideology. Recognizing no fixed boundaries between revolutionary activity and what we were already calling the "practice of poetry," we found in surrealism our basic world outlook and our conception of a future worth dreaming about—a *wildly desirable* future, vastly exceeding such reified categories as "politics" and "economics."

The fact that the IWW published a quasi-surrealist journal may be considered by some as one of the oddities of history, but Wobbly history is full of oddities, and there are those who look on the IWW itself as one of the oddest oddities of all. The perplexities of historians who have tried to tell the story of the One Big Union point to a simple truth that is rarely given proper emphasis: that U.S. history has never known a revolutionary mass movement more open-ended, imaginative, or creative than the Wobblies—or one more devoted to poetry, or more accomplished in the fine art of hardhitting humor.

Surrealists, in any event, seem to have a natural affinity for the IWW. My first close friend in the international surrealist movement— French poet Claude Tarnaud, who was living in New York in 1963—

was amazed to learn that "The Wobblies" were still around. Acquaintances had told him the union was long gone, but I had written him on the letterhead of the Berkeley IWW Branch. Claude was deeply interested in the subversive undercurrents in U.S. culture—from Charles Fort to post-bop jazz—and clearly enjoyed discussing the IWW's history and present prospects.

It is true that few old-time Wobs indicated even the slightest interest in surrealism, but none expressed hostility toward it, either—and surrealism was much in evidence not only in *The Rebel Worker* but also at Solidarity Bookshop (the Surrealism section of the Bookshop catalogue took up nine pages). Interestingly, the old-timers singled out for highest praise some of *The Rebel Worker*'s most surrealist contributions. In the first issue, for example, all the Old Guard liked René Daumal's story, "The Great Magician," which they read as a parable of the latent power of the working class.

Several old-timers also expressed admiration for the "crazy" cartoons we ran, by Roland Topor, Lester Doré, Tor Faegre and others. "They really attract attention," Jack Sheridan pointed out. "They make you sit up and take notice, and make you want to read the rest of the magazine." Our strong emphasis on cartoons and humor led Fred Thompson to liken *The Rebel Worker* to Art Young's early 1920s socialist jokes-and-cartoons magazine, *Good Morning* (which, by the way, none of us had ever seen). It's a long way from Art Young to surrealism, but we were rather charmed to have *The Rebel Worker* taken for a humor magazine.

In 1964, some of us had considered ourselves surrealists for several years—without, however, going so far as to constitute a formal organization. Not until two year later did the Chicago Surrealist Group come into being with our first tract, "The Forecast Is Hot!" In the meantime, *The Rebel Worker* served us well.

## THE *INDUSTRIAL WORKER* CRISIS

Basically we saw ourselves as the old-timers told us they saw us: as long-awaited reinforcements coming to the rescue of an embattled revolutionary outpost whose troops had "held the fort" valiantly for years. We regarded IWW theory—summed up in its beautiful Preamble—as fundamentally sound. What the union needed, we felt, was more members and more activity, and by organizing and agitating we were providing both. We also hoped to update and expand the Wobbly critique and methods, and to apply them to a wide range of current problems. Leaflets, strikes, picketlines, and participation in large multi-group demonstrations were all important, in our view, but we wanted to go further: to find new ways of disrupting routine, breaking habits, provoking inspiration, and in other ways helping workers realize that changing society was not only desirable and necessary but also *possible* and even *fun.*

One of the biggest problems for us was the *Industrial Worker*, the union's monthly newspaper. In the early and mid-1960s, it was an embarrassing anachronism, aimed at a readership of retirees. It did run some good material—Fred Thompson's articles, for example; Carlos Cortez's poems and linocuts; and an occasional angry outburst from Joe Hill's old friend, Louis Moreau. But too much of it read like a broken-down antique, and looked like it, too, with its oversized format, old-fashioned typography, and the same forty-year-old cartoons used over and over. Worse yet, a lot of the content was not only bad, but *awful.* Nick Steelink's column, for example (published under the name Enness Ellae), included a sickening amount of pro-Soviet propaganda. Shilly-shallying handouts from the AFL press service didn't help, either—to say nothing of the appalling ethnic jokes routinely used as filler.

It is no exaggeration to say that the *Industrial Worker* was an impediment to the growth of the union in those years—a real obstacle to our efforts to organize. Young people who liked *The Rebel Worker* found the newspaper repellent.

What to do? As we soon learned, the poor quality of the paper had been a topic of debate in the union long before most of us had joined. In his August 1, 1962 General Executive Board report, Fellow Worker Dick Ellington emphasized, in regard to the paper, that "we must make sharp and blatant changes in presentation, style, and content to attract new readers." No changes were made, however.

Many old-timers agreed with us that the *Industrial Worker* was inadequate as a vehicle for building the union; even editor Carl Keller admitted that he disliked a large part of what he printed, and he urged us younger Wobs to contribute more articles (which we did). It was Fellow Worker Keller who first suggested that I take over the editorship—but only after serving a year or so as his assistant. I agreed to help him one day a week: editing copy, selecting letters for publication, writing news stories, and trying to get others to write.

Meanwhile, from coast to coast in the IWW, things were heating up. Many members—old-timers as well as newcomers—did not want to wait a year to make changes. GEB discussions and minutes of Branch meetings focused more and more on the "*Industrial Worker* Question," and tensions mounted. Among the many foolish motions and counter-motions of those days was one from the Bay Area proposing to shut down the *Industrial Worker*—at least temporarily—and make *The Rebel Worker* the union's official organ. Making matters worse, several Bay Area Wobs adopted an increasingly belligerent tone in their letters to IWW headquarters. When Fred Thompson remarked that a few of the Bay Area members seemed to be either hopelessly immature or completely nuts, I had to agree.

In the midst of the ever-more-rancorous debate I received a phone call at Solidarity Bookshop—Penelope and I had no phone of our own in those years—from Bay Area Wobbly Patricia Ellington, the first woman to chair the GEB, and a serious, hard-working Fellow Worker, neither immature nor nuts. She called to urge me to formally apply for the editor's job by writing to the GEB, outlining the changes I wanted to make in the paper. She knew I had the confidence of the old-timers, and was sure that I would also be supported by both Bay Area branches, the New York Branch and many footloose individuals. In her view, resolving the *Industrial Worker* crisis in this way could stave off a major split in the union.

My proposal was simply to liven up the paper in every possible way: Switch to tabloid size and have it offset-printed in order to facilitate the use of new cartoons, photos, and color. Improve the typography and the proofreading. Include more point-of-production news; more on wildcats, black, antiwar and youth struggles; more news on IWW organizing and other activity; more on workingclass culture and revolutionary theory.

The proposal, however, never reached the membership. The whole discussion was sidetracked by a few Bay Area hotheads who persisted in sending insulting tirades to the Old Guard—especially to Fellow Workers Westman and Keller. As a result, many old-timers began to have doubts about young members—not only about the Bay Area bunch but others, too. In the end, the struggle to improve the *Industrial Worker* got lost in a spurious "young *versus* old" squabble.

The climax came when the GEB passed an absurd motion that Fellow Worker Keller be invited to remain editor "as long as he wanted the job." This was a pathetic moment. Wobs back in the union's early years had their problems, too, but they never handed out lifetime jobs!

A split was avoided, but an important momentum was lost. It was sad to realize how conservative some of the old Wobs were, and even sadder to see bureaucratic maneuvering triumph over workers' democracy.

At Solidarity Bookshop, the *Rebel Worker* group were too engrossed in ongoing projects to fret too much over the defeat. But Bernard Marszalek raised a question that would have been unthinkable a year before: Might we do better as a group *outside* the IWW?

Although I never heard the term "left wing of the Beat Generation" applied to others, the *Rebel Worker* group were not the only people who could qualify as such. Early on we received letters and/or publications from John Sinclair, Tuli Kupferberg, d. a. levy, Ed Sanders, Jeff Nuttall, Diane Wakoski, Wallace Berman, Jack Hirschman, Alexander Trocchi, rusel jaque, Mike Everett, Doug Blazek, Dick McBride, Carl Weissner, the Living Theater, various members of Fluxus, and the editors of such early "underground"papers as the Detroit *Fifth Estate*, the Milwaukee *Kaleidoscope* and the *East Village Other*. Some hoped we would publish their poems. A few said they had heard of *The Rebel Worker* from so-and-so and would like to know more about us. Others just wanted to exchange publications. Very few thought of themselves as revolutionaries the way we did.

At least two papers, however, not only had real affinities with *The Rebel Worker*'s revolutionary spirit, but actually said so in print.

In September 1964, four months after the publication of *Rebel Worker* 1, New Yorkers Jonathan Leake and Walter Caughey—anarchists, Wobblies, poets and militant supporters of surrealism—published the first issue of *Resurgence*, mimeographed organ of the Resurgence Youth Movement (RYM). The cover reproduced an automatic drawing I made in New York earlier in the year. Page one stated its outlaw themes: "permanent insurrection, anti-politics, cultural sabotage, juvenile delinquency, cosmogony, prophesy, autonomy, surreality, studies in the language of the night. . . ." For over a dozen issues *Resurgence* sustained an apocalyptic tone unparalleled in the history of American radical literature. Despite our many differences, no U.S. magazine was closer to *The Rebel Worker* than this irrepressibly strident voice of the "world revolution of youth."

Much later, in November 1966—a few weeks before the last *Rebel Worker*—a third U.S. publication took up the call for "Total Revolution." *Black Mask* was a four-page bulletin, printed rather than mimeo'd, and edited by Ben Morea, Dan Georgakas and Ron Hahne in New York. Inspired by Italian Futurism and Russian Constructivism, it focused largely on esthetic issues—a preoccupation that seemed a bit retrograde to those of us who made the supersession of such categories a priority. We nonetheless welcomed *Black Mask* as a publication of comrades who had come to share some of our conclusions, following a very different path.

*Black Mask* 2 (December 1966) published excerpts from *Internationale Situationniste* (Paris), *Heatwave* (London), *Rebel Worker*

(Chicago), and *Resurgence* (New York), as reflections of "groups which seem to be moving in the same direction."

Clearly, an authentically revolutionary movement was gaining ground. But recuperators were lying in wait. In spring '68 we received an urgent letter from Frankfurt, urging us to send—immediately—*The Rebel Worker* and a selection of our other publications. The writer's frantic and comradely tone led us to assume it was from fellow revolutionists involved in struggle. As it turned out, it was from academics organizing an exhibition/conference on the Beat and post-Beat avant-garde! The 184-page catalog featured *The Rebel Worker* and several *Rebel Worker* pamphlets along with a full-page reproduction (one of only sixteen illustrations) of the cover of the Chicago edition of *Rebel Worker* 6. The entire volume was an abject mishmash, largely devoted to people we regarded as reactionary—Allan Kaprow, Claes Oldenburg, the Art & Technology bunch—and we were appalled to be listed in such confusionist company. For us, Establishment flattery was worse than persecution.

## NEAL CASSADY DROPS BY

As the left-wing of the Beat Generation rapidly evolved into a new revolutionary current, the right-wing and so-called "apolitical" Beats were slowly absorbed into mainstream U.S. culture. The distance between the two expanded throughout the Sixties. Just how great the gap had become for some of us at mid-decade was somewhat eerily symbolized by the appearance one afternoon, at Solidarity Bookshop, of none other than Neal Cassady.

Robert Green brought him in—Cassady was staying at his place above the Beatnik Coffee House on Sedgwick Avenue—and introduced us: "Franklin, Tor—Neal Cassady." And that, as they say, was that. This was not one of the world's great interviews. The hero of *On the Road*, notoriously the most talkative man alive at the time, hardly said a word as he looked over our fine selection of subversive literature. It occurred to me later that he had probably never seen, in one place, so many publications aimed at fomenting revolt and revolution. Now and then he picked up a book or pamphlet, flipped through it, put it back.

At some point Green called his attention to *The Rebel Worker*, and a strange scene passed before our wondering eyes. Here was the journal we ourselves had dreamed up, written, typed, coaxed through the mimeograph, collated, stapled and put on display to attract the attention of each and all who set foot in our sanctum of solidarity. And here was Dean Moriarty himself, leafing through its pages, stopping momentarily to read a title or a few lines, now frowning a little, now smiling, once or twice muttering something like "huh!" or "hmmm"—inscrutable throughout.

I'm sure there was music on: probably Monk, maybe Mingus ("Pithecanthropus Erectus"). Tor turned to me and whispered: "This is crazy. Here's a guy we've read books about, a guy who loves to talk, and none of us can think of anything to say." I remember thinking: Should I ask Cassady if he still admires that fascist jerk Céline? (He had been a Céline fan some years before). And deciding no, it would sound unfriendly. I wondered, too: How to ask him about the Revolution—what he thinks of what's happening *now*, and how he sees himself in relation to it all. But the words never came together. When the moment arrived, we had nothing to say to each other.

Cassady stayed at Green's for several weeks, trying to work out yet another elaborate get-rich-quick scheme involving the importation (from Mexico) and sales (in the U.S.) of great quantities of his favorite medicinal herb. But after that one brief meeting at Solidarity Bookshop in the Fall of '64, I never saw him again.

## DANCIN' IN THE STREETS:
### MODS, ROCKERS & *THE REBEL WORKER*

*The Rebel Worker* was one of the very few radical publications of its time to take popular culture seriously. Comics, pulp fiction and movies were a significant part of what today's professors might call "*Rebel Worker* discourse," and we published some of the first radical criticism of rock'n'roll—perhaps *the* first, in the U.S. Our anthropological and laborlore studies helped us view the new tremors in popular culture not simply in terms of music or entertainment, but rather as part of the larger and more complex phenomenon of workingclass self-expression. For most Marxists in those days—and for almost all academics—the popular arts were anathema. Stalinists of all stripes heard nothing but "fascism" in the pop sounds of the day, which we found especially funny because the Far Right was busy denouncing the Beatles and other rock bands as propagators of Communism!

Most of us around *The Rebel Worker* were blues and jazz enthusiasts; we listened mostly to bop and the post-bop currents exemplified by Thelonious Monk, Cecil Taylor, John Coltrane, and Eric Dolphy, whose tragic death in the summer of '64 depressed me greatly. By then, however, I had lost touch with the local jazz scene. The clubs I knew best were gone. Muhal Richard Abrams, Joseph Jarman and others were forming the Association for the Advancement of Creative Musicians (AACM) around then, but the news took a long time to reach Solidarity Bookshop. We did, however, have a direct and personal link to the New Music: Anthony Braxton—who worked at the Roosevelt library while I worked at the Roosevelt bookstore—lived near Solidarity, and was in fact a frequent visitor. Penelope and I often enjoyed hearing him practice as we passed his place, and I'm sure we were among the first to hear his first album.

Meanwhile, during the mid-Sixties, the media were full of news and commentary on the Liverpool Sound, Beatle riots, Mods and Rockers riots, and miscellaneous rock'n'roll riots all over England and Europe and increasingly in the U.S. Most of this consisted of scare stories, panicky whinings, and other reactionary claptrap. We decided it would be a good idea for *The Rebel Worker* to run a sympathetic feature on the rebellious tendencies in teen culture and pop music. We ourselves enjoyed that anthem of global jubilee, "Dancin' in the Streets" by Martha and the Vandellas, and The Who's "My Generation"—songs that reinforced our utopian hopes in what our friend Jonathan Leake called the "world revolution of youth."

Charles Radcliffe's insightful article "Pop Goes the Beatle," in the London anarchist paper *Freedom*, confirmed and amplified our feeling that youth rebellion was neither "unimportant" nor a flash in the pan.

*Mods, Rockers & the Revolution*—including my article of that title, from *Rebel Worker* 3, Radcliffe's "Pop Goes the Beatle," and Richard Mabey's "Twist and Shout" from *Peace News*—appeared shortly afterward as *Rebel Worker* Pamphlet No 1. Tor Faegre, Bernard Marszalek and I—all in black cloaks—sold nearly all of the first printing (several hundred copies) at a Rolling Stones concert at McCormick Place. It proved to be quite a sensation, especially among teens. During the next couple of years, for example, a group of six or eight high-school girls who called themselves the Chicago Rolling Stones Fan Club regularly joined the *Rebel Worker* contingents on big street demonstrations. Some brought boyfriends along. Indeed, from 1965 on, teen-age boys—rock'n'rollers—began lining up in the IWW in ever-greater numbers. Word was getting around that joining the Wobs automatically made one a "subversive," and therefore ineligible for the draft. As the Vietnam War escalated, so did IWW membership. (Nixon abolished the subversive list in 1974.)

Apparently no radical group had ever thought of selling literature at a rock concert before. At another McCormick Place concert a couple of months later, half a dozen Old Left groups showed up.

One evening at Solidarity Bookshop, a dour middle-aged gent in a dark suit asked me: "Are you from the group that considers rock-'n'roll to be a serious force for proletarian revolution?"

## WITH THE SURREALISTS IN PARIS

Revolutionary internationalism was a *Rebel Worker* first principle, and our contacts with such groups as London Solidarity, the Japanese Zengakuren, the Dutch Provos and Scots Against War were very important to us. Every issue included at least one text by a comrade from outside the U.S., and *Rebel Worker* 4 was an "International Issue," with fourteen texts by fellow workers and dreamers from six countries. With its sixth issue, which Penelope and I co-edited with Charles Radcliffe in London in 1966, the *Rebel Worker* group itself became truly international.

At least one good thing came of the lamentably unresolved *Industrial Worker* crisis: Penelope and I decided to stop postponing that trip to London and Paris we had been dreaming about for over a year. We left in December '65, stopping off in New York to visit surrealist friends Nicolas Calas and Eugenio F. Granell. The day before we headed overseas we ran into a bizarrely-costumed character on the street who turned out to be the old hipster musician/composer Moondog. In the bitterest cold I have ever known we all stood on the streetcorner rapping at length. Poets in Antarctica! This chance encounter sounded an auspicious prelude for our transatlantic adventures.

What happened next seemed a real downer at first, but it proved to be the best of luck. A bureaucrat at London airport got it into his head that I was a draft-dodger—in truth, I still had a 2-S (student) deferment, left over from Roosevelt days—and refused to let us enter England, where we had intended to stay a few months. Marched off to airport detention quarters, we spent the night under the watchful eye of Her Majesty's police. (In the lavatory we noticed that each piece of toilet paper was emblazoned with the Queen's official seal.) Next morning a limousine drove us right to the ramp of a plane ready for take-off. A little over an hour later we were joyfully wandering the streets of Paris.

Our main reason for going to Europe was to visit André Breton and others in the Surrealist Group, and, more generally, to learn firsthand about the newest developments in the surrealist movement. We could hardly have arrived at a better moment. Much to our surprise, a major International Surrealist Exhibition opened that very month at the Galerie l'Oeil, and Gallimard brought out a new edition of Breton's *Le Surréalisme et la peinture*, with nearly two dozen new texts on painters and sculptors who had joined the movement in the 1950s and '60s. Posters for the exhibition were on walls all over Paris, and we saw the book in scores of bookstore windows. Proof of surrealism's vital presence was everywhere.

The exhibition—titled *L'Ecart absolu* (Absolute Divergence), a term of Charles Fourier's—signified not only the surrealists' vehement rejection of "consumer society," but also their revolutionary aspiration to subvert, abolish and supersede it. Articles in the catalog by Robert Benayoun, Vincent Bounoure, Alain Joubert, Gérard Legrand, Georges Sebbag and others added substantially to the surrealist critique of capitalist-christian-miserabilist civilization and its out-of-control technology, militarism, and bureaucratic unfreedom, as well as its concomitant fear and hatred of nature, eros, poetry and play. The exhibition itself enabled us to see the work of younger surrealist painters such as Enrico Baj, Jean Benoît, Jorge Camacho, Konrad Klapheck, Mimi Parent and Jean-Claude Silbermann.

A couple of weeks later at the café La Promenade de Venus—the surrealists' meeting-place in the 1960s—we met André Breton. Obviously charmed by the button Penelope had fastened to her cloak—"I am an Enemy of the State"—he greeted us with remarkable warmth, and was eager to know our estimate of the exhibition, and our plans for a Surrealist Group in Chicago. This first meeting with the author of *Nadja* and *Arcane 17*, and the comradely spontaneity with which he welcomed us into the Surrealist Group, was nothing less than exhilarating. My memories of the event (for it was vastly more than an "incident" for us) remain precise, vivid, intense—like one's first experience of mountain-climbing.

Indeed, despite cold weather, lack of funds, our difficulties learning to speak French, a bad case of *la grippe* that lasted three weeks, and other assorted frustrations, our whole several-months' sojourn in Paris lives on in an irreducibly euphoric light. The group's daily reunions at the café, the "introuvable" *Editions surréalistes* we kept finding at bookstores and bookstalls, and above all the friendship of many other surrealists—mostly among the middle generation, but also "elders" such as Jacques Brunius, Toyen, Jehan Mayoux, Man Ray, Elisa Breton; and even a fellow Illinoisan: the African American jazz poet Ted Joans—kept us in a state of continous poetic and intellectual effervescence.

Rarely have I met people who came even close to equaling our Parisian surrealist friends' knowledge of poetry, philosophy, history, revolutionary thought, painting, "primitive" art, alchemy, jazz, and cinema—or who did more to put their far-reaching knowledge and high-powered humor at the service of human emancipation. They had their problems and differences, but this was no ordinary group of "left intellectuals"—it was a *community of revolutionary poetic geniuses* whose aims and actions centered on transforming the world and changing life.

During our several months in Paris, we saw *nothing* to suggest that surrealism was "dead," or "finished," or "repeating itself," as Establishment critics have noisily pretended ("almost weekly," as Breton once remarked) since 1924. Throughout the Sixties and beyond, surrealists in France (and elsewhere) never ceased to turn out extraordinary, original work—in poetry and the arts as in criticism, theory and polemic.

The *L'Ecart Absolu* exhibition was an important initiative, as was the group's lively new journal, *L'Archibras*, then in the planning stage, and to which Penelope and I were invited to contribute (our article, "Situation of Surrealism in the United States," appeared in the second issue).

Our experience in the Paris Surrealist Group has profoundly influenced everything Penelope and I have done since. One measure of its impact is the durability of the friendships we made there. Forty years later, poets and painters we met at La Promenade de Venus remain among our dearest comrades. The excitement and inspiration of our first trip to Paris has proved to be inexhaustible.

One of the more anarchist-inclined surrealist poet/painters, Jean-Claude Silbermann, told us that the Paris group, in their frequent discussions of surrealism's international dimension, had concluded that there were two countries in which the appearance of a surrealist group would inevitably have a strong impact in other lands as well: the U.S.A. and the USSR. The latter, he added, did not look very promising just then.

"So you see," he told us with a big smile, "we're counting on you."

## GUY DEBORD, THE SITUATIONIST INTERNATIONAL, & US

Of our many encounters in Paris, meeting André Breton and the Surrealist Group was far and away the most important and had the most lasting impact on us and on the whole *Rebel Worker* group. Alas, our attempts to meet with other fellow revolutionaries were often frustrating, and the language barrier was by no means the only problem.

Shortly after we arrived we learned that the *Socialisme ou barbarie* group, whose politics were so close to *The Rebel Worker*'s, had disbanded some months earlier. Back issues of the journal were available at some bookstores, but no one seemed to know how to get in touch with any of the group's former members. We tried several times to meet with the *Informations correspondence ouvriers* (ICO) group, who had just published a French translation of my "Mods, Rockers and the Revolution" article from *Rebel Worker* 3, but somehow we never connected. Especially disappointing was our brief visit w anarchists of *Le Monde libertaire* at their bookstore (3, rue Te

Although most of them were our own age, they were decidedly incommunicative and even paranoid; I think they believed I was a deserter from the U.S. military.

On one of our countless aimless strolls through Paris—even our surrealist friends were amazed at how many miles a day we walked—we came upon "La Vieille Taupe" (The Old Mole) bookstore at 1, rue des Fosses-Jacques, a small shop which in many ways resembled Solidarity in Chicago. Among the many items we bought there were multiple copies of the 1848 edition of Victor Considerant's *Exposition abrégée du Système phalanstérien de Fourier*. At six francs ($1.20) each, these were destined to grace the shelves of Solidarity Bookshop, where they fit in well amongst the U.S. revolutionary antiquities, the hot-off-the-mimeo *Rebel Worker* pamphlet series, and the latest *Editions surréalistes* from France. (Now and then browsers asked how we happened to have back-stock of mid-nineteenth-century French utopian literature.)

More pertinently, at "La Vieille Taupe" we also found publications issued by the Situationist International. As early as spring 1965 a lone copy of *Internationale Situationniste* (No. 8) had made its way to Solidarity, and we had all found it intriguing, albeit rather mystifying. The material at "La Vielle taupe" made the situationist project much clearer. Particularly impressive was the English translation of the group's tract, *The Decline and Fall of the Spectacular Commodity Economy*, a remarkably insightful commentary—unsurpassed to this day, in my view—on the 1965 rebellion in Watts, California.

That very evening Penelope and I sent a note to the situationists' mailing address, explaining who we were, and suggesting a rendezvous. The next day we received a comradely invitation to meet the following afternoon at a nearby café.

We arrived at the café a few minutes early to find Guy Debord already sitting at a table waiting for us, accompanied by a young Asian woman who served as our translator. Debord greeted us warmly and ordered coffee. As we shook hands and seated ourselves, he asked where we were staying in Paris. When I replied, the "Hotel du Grand Balcon"— a graceful old building (without elevators) on the rue Dauphine, just off the rue de Buci—he was surprised and delighted. "That's a lovely hotel," he said, and went on to praise our "excellent taste."

Then he gave us (at no charge) a stack of back issues of the *Internationale situationniste* and other documents, and began asking the "big" questions: How many people belonged to the *Rebel Worker* Group? What were our backgrounds? What kinds of activities did we engage in? How had we become interested in surrealism? What did we think of the current Surrealist Group in Paris? How much had we read of situationist literature? How much of it did we agree or disagree with? Throughout the discussion Debord had at least as many questions for us as we had for him—and Penelope and I asked a *lot* of questions. He was clearly sympathetic to our rejection of the traditional left, and fascinated by what we told him of The *Rebel Worker* group: a free association of working-class youngsters drawn toward surrealism and old-time Wobblies who had not only fought long and hard on the front lines of the class war, but even served time in prison for their revolutionary ideals. Such a union, he said, was "extremely interesting," and "could lead to very important things."

Our biggest area of disagreement with him had to do with surrealism. All of us in The *Rebel Worker* group had listened to nauseatingly ignorant "critiques" of surrealism by various would-be Marxists and anarchists. Debord's criticisms were different. Indeed, they differed even from his own (and other situationists') criticisms, as published in the situationist journal. Again and again, in our discussion, he emphasized his ardent admiration for André Breton. He said he had read every book, every article, and—here he may have been exaggerating just a little—*every word* Breton had written, and that he regarded Breton as one of the greatest revolutionary thinkers. "If I had been young in the 1920s or early 30s," he told us, "I would have belonged to the Surrealist Group." At this point I raised my cup high and said, rather loudly, *"Moi aussi!"*—and we all laughed.

But Debord went on to say that times had changed and that the Surrealist Movement, in the situationists' view, had not kept up. He pointed out that in the 1920s/30s, surrealist books and tracts appeared one after another, in great quantity. The current surrealists, however—according to him—produced little. When Penelope and I mentioned Guy Cabanel, Gérard Legrand, Robert Benayoun, Vincent Bounoure and Joyce Mansour—all of whom published significant books around that time—Debord airily dismissed them as "not important." For him, Breton's 1947 *Ode to Charles Fourier* was the "last important surrealist work . . . a great poem, a revolutionary poem." As for Joyce Mansour, she was "a beautiful woman, but not a great poet." He was similarly indifferent to the younger surrealist painters: "Not important."

Even more severe was his negative judgment of contemporary surrealist politics. Noting that the early surrealists' experiment with Communism had inevitably ended in failure, he concluded that surrealism had never recovered from that debacle. In 1966 he was under the impression that the current Surrealist Group hardly concerned itself with politics at all. When we challenged that utterly mistaken belief, he made a dismissive gesture with his hand and said he no longer bothered to read the surrealists' journal.

It was obvious that he knew very few of the current generation of surrealists in France, and that he knew none of them well. He admitted that he knew even less about surrealists in other countries, but was certain they were "not important." In the U.S., he conceded, surrealism could (possibly) develop differently.

Our meeting with Debord lasted all afternoon—at least three hours, probably four. From beginning to end he was more than cordial toward us—he was *comradely* in the best sense. Not once did we see any indication of the arrogance or authoritarianism that so many critics have attributed to him. As with many other specialists in "politics," his attitude toward surrealism was narrow and full of misconceptions, but there could be no doubt about his admiration for André Breton. His expression of sympathetic interest in the *Rebel Worker* project also seemed genuine and heartfelt. In any event, we parted friends, handshakes and all.

As we were leaving the café, I told him that we could easily distribute a thousand copies (or even more) of the *Decline and Fall* tract in the U.S. Beaming with pleasure, he remarked to our translator that no one had ever asked for such a large quantity of their publications. He told us they probably did not even have a thousand copies, but would gladly give us all they had.

On the way back to the Rue Dauphine, Penelope said: "He was really trying to recruit us, wasn't he?" And indeed, Debord had scarcely concealed his yearning for a section of the Situationist International in the U.S. Meanwhile, however dismayed he may have been by our surrealism, he was evidently willing for us to become transatlantic couriers of S.I. literature. At least for the time being, then, our disagreements were just that: disagreements—not insurmountable barriers to cooperation.

A later meeting with situationist Mustapha Khayati did not improve matters. Khayati obviously lacked Debord's knowledge of surrealism; he was unfamiliar, for example, with the work of Benjamin Péret. He was nonetheless far more hostile toward surrealism than Debord had been, and abruptly brought our brief discussion to a close by saying "I see no point in wasting time arguing about something as irrelevant as surrealism."

In the meantime, Penelope and I had raised the question of the S.I. at a Surrealist Group meeting at "La Promenade de Venus." Passing out copies of various S.I. documents, we asked our friends what they thought of this group. The response was mixed, to say the least. Most antagonistic was Radovan Ivsic, who simply announced, loudly, "They are *not* our friends!" and turned away from us in a huff, just as Khayati had done. This curt decree, without any explanation, was disappointing, but not too surprising, for Ivsic—one of the least political of the surrealists—had the well-earned reputation of being the most timid member of the group. In stark contrast was Jehan Mayoux, whose response to the S.I. documents was genuinely enthusiastic. He not only read aloud from several of these publications, but also repeatedly interjected his hearty approval. Most of those present considered the S.I. texts of interest, and some wondered why they had not come across them before. (In truth, S.I. publications were not widely available in bookstores until much later.) I think it was Gérard Legrand who noted that, years before, the surrealists had attempted a joint action with some of those who later formed the S.I., but it had not worked out well. Unfortunately, before Legrand could elaborate further, the meeting turned to other items on the agenda.

Penelope and I left Paris in April 1966 with some 300-plus copies of the *Decline and Fall* tract. We gave away a few in London and more in New York, but the great bulk were distributed in Chicago, or mailed from Chicago to *Rebel Worker* supporters all over the country. From May '66 through the end of '68, the *Rebel Worker* group did more to promote the Situationist International than any group in the U.S. For a long time Solidarity was the *only* bookstore in the country to carry S.I. publications. *Rebel Worker* 7 (which appeared in December 1966) included the first translation of a French situationist text published in the U.S.: "Elementary Structures of Reification" by Jean Garnault. A little later, as part of our pamphlet series, we brought out a new edition of *The Decline and Fall*, with an introduction and epilogue by Bernard Marszalek.

Our relationship to the S.I. did not, however, grow closer. Apart from a two-line note from Donald Nicholson-Smith of the S.I.'s never-quite-real "English Section," we heard nary a word from Guy Debord or his associates. And despite Debord's avowed interest in our publications and activities, the *Internationale Situationniste* published only two—and not very friendly—references to the *Rebel Worker* group and our "anarcho-surrealism" (a term we ourselves never used).

Ironically, the most laughable—or, depending on your point of view, most pitiable—caricatures of the S.I. eventually came to be spawned in the U.S. From New York to California, hate-filled grouplets of former hippies and New Leftists began to proclaim themselves situationists, in each case combining an overabundance of ignorance, total absence of imagination, and full-time non-involvement in real struggle. Most ridiculous of all were the four white males who managed to get accepted, albeit briefly, as the S. I.'s official "U.S. Section." Their one lamentable issue of a journal was notable for its explicit racism (they reserved their harshest defamations for African American radicals). Just how well-informed they were on the matter may be gleaned from their mention of a certain "C.L.R. Jones."

U.S. situationist wannabes disagreed among themselves about practically everything, but they all shared a dogmatic hatred of surrealism. Starting around 1969, quotations from situationist texts have been widely used by academics and assorted pseudo-radicals to attack surrealism—especially surrealism in the U.S. Late as it is, a brief examination of the ideological basis of those attacks seems in order here.

In the naive and belligerent belief that they had already superseded the arts in theory, and would soon (come the Revolution) supersede them in practice, situationists let it be known that they were not interested in contemporary painting, poetry, or music. Indeed, they fostered the notion that such activities are anti-revolutionary, *passé*, part of the capitalist spectacle. Inasmuch as surrealists have always regarded the liberation of the imagination—and of all creativity—as the most essential part of social revolution, a considerable amount of situationist propaganda was directed against them.

Situationist ideology, and especially that part of it which pretends to be a critique of surrealism, involves several interconnected elements: antipathy to (*i.e.*, fear of) poetry and all forms of psychic automatism; the reductionist misapprehension that the unconscious is by nature impoverished, and that surrealism is "irrationalist"; insensitivity to the visual arts, especially painting and drawing; cynical indifference to love; and rationalist hostility to alchemy and the magic arts. All of these situationist prejudices are traceable to old-line leftist puritanism or, more precisely, Stalinist puritanism.

As an "International," moreover—one of the tiniest on record—the S.I. specialized in the most absurd and extreme sectarianism, which it justified solely by its delusions of grandeur: delusions based in turn on Debord's own crowning ideological delusion—that he and his constantly shrinking band of co-conspirators and yes-men had somehow managed, without actually doing very much, to "supersede" art, poetry, politics, and surrealism itself.

Situationist attempts at a critique of surrealism were rarely on target. Superficial at best, more often than not their criticisms were just plain wrong. Here as elsewhere Debord stands apart from most of his Situationist cronies. Truth to tell, his epigrammatic and not very numerous contributions to a critique of surrealism (barely a half-page in his *Society of the Spectacle*) are weak and unconvincing. In spite of himself, however, but true to his baroque propensities, and to the broad spirit of revolutionary romanticism that animated his whole life, he went on to do something much better: In effect, and evidently without even realizing it, he made an interesting contribution to the *surrealist* critique, very much in line with such surrealist social criticism as Crevel's *Le Clavecin de Diderot*, Cahun's *Les Paris sont ouvert*, Tzara's *Grains et issues*, Breton's *Position politique*, and Calas's *Foyers d'incendie*. It is high time to recognize that *Society of the Spectacle* is not only a work in the Hegel/Marx tradition, but also and more particularly *in the surrealist anti-tradition*.

Guy Debord never made his peace with Capital and the State. When he died (a suicide) in 1994—twenty-two years after the S.I.'s ignominious collapse in the wake of the May '68 near-revolution in Paris—he was still wholly unreconciled to the Old Order. Despite his crankiness, megalomania, and literary pretensions ("I am not someone who revises his work"); his aristocratic posturing, alcoholism, and sexism; his weird suspicious temper and goofy fondness for intrigues, schisms and exclusions—he remained to the last a real revolutionary—almost a novelistic caricature of a revolutionary. As such he differed radically from surrealism's real enemies: the mercenaries of misery and their minions, the turncoats, sellouts, cops, and false poets, along with the bourgeois, Stalinist, journalistic and academic critics, hacks, and other hired liars.

Rarely acknowledged by his numerous critics and commentators, Debord's admiration for André Breton tells us a lot about his true character. However oedipal that relationship may have been, the fact remains that the central elements of the situationist project—rejection of the pseudo-world of the spectacle; support for workers' self-emancipation, the passion for freedom and true community, revolt against work and affirmation of play, *détournement*, revolution as festival, "consciousness of desire and desire for consciousness"—were all essentials of surrealism's project long before the S.I. existed.

Significantly, the journal *Internationale situationniste*—whose unrestrained use of insult and invective almost matched *The Rebel Worker*'s own—never, in its twelve issues, insulted the author of the *Surrealist Manifestoes*. Breton's name figures in the "index des noms cités ou insultés" in the Raspaud/Voyer situationist reference-guide, but none of the seven citations could be construed as an insult. Only in the pre-S.I. mid-1950s, under the influence of Stalinoid ex-surrealists, did Debord refer slightingly to Breton (though not by name). Unlike some of his colleagues, moreover, Debord's concern was never merely to belittle surrealism, but rather to build a new world revolutionary movement on foundations that were, in essence—though he himself rarely dared to admit it—*surrealist.*

Like all those who enjoy thinking of themselves as History's Great Figures, Debord was more skilled than he knew in the art of self-deception. That he could pretend to have ventured far beyond surrealism when in truth he was making only a modest contribution to it speaks volumes not only about his vanity, but also his deeper insecurity—not to mention the shakiness of his sense of dialectics.

In his curious positive/negative links to surrealism—his odd mix of attraction and aversion—Debord in some respects resembles Antonin Artaud and Georges Bataille, just as his manic rationalism and conspiratorial zeal are reminiscent of Pierre Naville: *dissidents*, yes, and defiantly so, but dissidents *within* the ever-expanding orbit of surrealist revolution.

And that is how I recall Guy Debord: In spite of himself—and above all in spite of the *myth* of himself—the most surrealist of anti-surrealists!

## Laughing-Fits in London: *Rebel Worker* 6 & *Heatwave*

The second *Rebel Worker* attempt to invade England (April '66) proved successful. Officials at Dover limited our stay to ten days, but we managed to remain four weeks with no trouble. We stayed the whole time with anarchists Charles Radcliffe and Diana Shelley, in their big apartment at 13 Redcliffe Road. Charles had been a *Rebel Worker* correspondent for over a year. His articles on blues and rock in British anarchist publications had impressed us all, and his more "political" articles and letters made it clear that he shared our overall frenetic revolutionary outlook.

Our first talk in London showed that we had even more in common than we thought. In less than an hour we were fast friends and well on our way to what turned out to be a whole month of invigorating discussions on everything under the sun. This free exchange of ideas and inspirations often verged on delirium (a codeine-based cough-syrup may have contributed to this elation—I arrived in England with a bad case of flu, and Charles caught it). "You're all completely mad," Diana kept telling us, but of that kind of "madness"—the very stuff of poetry and revolution itself—the world can never have too much.

As had already been our experience in Paris, Penelope and I found that most Londoners our age were far more knowledgeable than our peers in the U.S. Among the Londoners, Charles and Diana stood head and shoulders above the rest. Their broad political culture was vastly richer than our own, as was their practical experience of direct action and large-scale struggle in the anti-nuclear-weapons movement. In short, they were considerably more "sophisticated" than we were, especially in regard to contemporary anarchism. Both were very critical of the existing anarchist movement in England, which, however small, was positively *immense* in comparison to its tiny U.S. equivalents then and since.

Day after day, and well into the wee hours, Charles and Diana patiently filled us in on the history and current situation of English radicalism, with numerous asides on everything from Robin Hood (a childhood hero all four of us loved) to the current jazz and pop music scene. I still recall illuminating discussions of Oscar Wilde, William Morris, Malcolm X, Luis Buñuel, and Ornette Coleman.

For several days running, we talked mostly about *blues*—for it was Charles Radcliffe who gave us our first lessons in the history of African American music. In my teens I had enjoyed Little Walter and Magic Sam live on the Big Bill Hill radio show in Chicago, and Penelope and I got to know the great blues harmonica player John Wrencher at Maxwell Street, but we knew next to nothing about the social/historical background of the music, or about the men and women who played it. Ridiculous as it may seem, Penelope and I first listened to Howlin' Wolf, Muddy Waters, J. B. Lenoir and other great Chicago blues-singers not in Chicago, but thousands of miles away in London.

During Charles's commentaries on blues, he often told us about a previous American guest, Paul Garon, who, he insisted, knew even more about blues than he did. Garon had moved into the Redcliffe Road flat just as a young British guitarist named Eric Clapton was moving out, and he left just before Penelope and I arrived. "I hope you get a chance to meet Paul some day," Charles told us. "He shares our interests and I'm sure you'd like him."

On Redcliffe Road, we also listened to a lot of great jazz: Charlie Parker, Monk, Cecil Taylor and much more. To Charles I owe my introduction to the music of Archie Shepp—which just goes to show that there's some truth in the old adage that "travel is broadening."

Charles also took us to the Freedom Press Bookshop, and introduced us—"anarchists and surrealists from Chicago"—to Lillian Wolf, whose friends from long ago included Peter Kropotkin. She told us she had also known the surrealists in 1940s London, all of whom frequented the Freedom Bookshop. Later, on a London Solidarity Group housing demonstration, Charles introduced us to Andy Anderson, whose excellent book *Hungary '56* Penelope had reviewed in *Rebel Worker* 3.

One day Dr and Mrs Chris Pallis, of Solidarity, visited us at

Redcliffe Road. Dr Pallis shook our hands vigorously and at once declared that "the best magazine in the United States today is *The Rebel Worker*." Mrs Pallis, however, was evidently quite alarmed to see comic books lying around, and wanted to know who among us read such trash. The visit was brief; Dr Pallis had an appointment elsewhere, but he invited us to the Solidarity Group's next meeting.

The Solidarity meeting turned out to be informative, if low key, and it was good to meet Bob Potter and Ken Weller, who had contributed to *The Rebel Worker*. We were a little disturbed, however, that everyone present seemed to be twice our age or older. Even more disturbing was Pallis's obvious role as chairman, main speaker, and peerless leader. The few others who spoke at all addressed their words not to the group, but directly to Chairman Pallis. For libertarian socialists, they seemed rather inhibited and cultish to us.

It was good to get back to Redcliffe Road, where the ideas were as hot as the music, and where our hopes for changing the world were not part of a "program," but a pleasure. Amidst this euphoria, our discussions recurred again and again to the urgent question: How can we help develop a new revolutionary theory and action for *our* time?

The first fruit of our free-for-all talks was *Rebel Worker* 6: the wildest issue yet. The very fact that we put out an issue at all, on such short notice and several thousand miles away from its home-base, conveys something of the contagious enthusiasm of those weeks in London.

The whole production was a Daffy Duck version of *Mutual Aid*. Notwithstanding the flu that had two of us on the sick-list, our exuberance was high and kept rising. Long coughing-fits were interspersed with even longer laughing-fits. In less than two days we planned the issue, wrote all the articles, and typed the stencils on the smallest, lightest typewriter I have ever seen—an Olympia 66 portable—while seated on scaffolding that workmen had set up just outside the second-story windows. And thus, with the volume turned up on the finest in recorded blues and jazz, the one and only "Anglo-American issue of *The Rebel Worker*"—and the only issue to be typed outdoors—was readied for mimeographing (indoors) on a machine kindly loaned by friends in London Solidarity. From start to finish it took us less than a week. On May Day, exactly two years since the first issue, we took armloads of copies to Hyde Park and sold every one.

This sixth issue did more than reaffirm the characteristic elements of *Rebel Worker* politics; it also expanded them and gave them greater coherence. Our opening declaration, "Freedom: The Only Cause Worth Serving," set the tone, emphasizing that *The Rebel Worker* expressed "a revolutionary point of view fundamentally different from all traditional concepts." Charles's critique of the peace movement concretized and elaborated our revolutionary/playful approach to mass struggles, and his appreciation of The Who extended our exploration of subversive moments in popular culture. My "Souvenirs of the Future" focused on what appealed to us most in the works of Sade, Blake, Fourier, Lautréamont, the early Gothic novelists and other precursors. This essay, with Penelope's "Humor or Not or Less or Else!," also broadened *The Rebel Worker*'s surrealist perspectives.

The "London issue," as it was called in Chicago, marked the beginning of the last and most fruitful period in the life of the *Rebel Worker* group—a period of expansive collective dreaming, in which the most far-reaching imaginative criticism and a truly desperate humor cleared the way for new revolutionary strategies and tactics responsive to *poetic* imperatives alone. "Desire at the service of Consciousness!"— the title we gave to a text by Pierre Mabille that we published in *Rebel Worker* 6—was our watchword, but so was "Consciousness at the service of Desire!"

Between the first of May and the end of December, our mimeograph machines were going full blast on both sides of the Atlantic. Although the "Anglo-American edition," as Charles called it, was conceived as a one-shot, the response it provoked—positive and negative—convinced him that there was indeed "an audience in Britain for an experimental, perhaps slightly crazed libertarian socialist journal." Two months after the appearance of the hottest *Rebel Worker* so far, the first issue of *Heatwave* hit the stands.

*Heatwave* lived up to its name; here were our most adventurous thoughts and dreams at fever pitch. The first issue's editorial declared that

> We intend to cooperate, ideologically and practically, with our Chicago co-dreamers; we see our task as being the same as theirs— to run a wild, experimental . . . journal which will attempt to relate thought, dream and action whilst pointing to the significance of movements, ideas and creations which are ignored by the stagnant, *fin-de-siècle* revolutionaries. . . . *Heatwave* wants to generate heat in every field.

The contents featured some excellent material by individuals who had responded to *Rebel Worker* 6, along with an excerpt from Paul Garon's harrowing "Expanded Journal of Addiction," showing how far *Heatwave* was willing to go beyond standard "left" themes. Most of the issue, however, was written by Charles (in part under the pseudonym Ben Covington). His short history of youth revolt and his eyewitness account of the Provo Riots in Amsterdam are surely among the high points of our collective effort to highlight new subversive strategies and thus to expand the consciousness of the emerging revolutionary movement.

On June 6, 1966 Charles wrote to me that he had met a "really groovy potential *Heatwaver*—guy in touch with Debord (no pun intended!)." This was Christopher Gray. None of us in Chicago ever met him; to us he was simply a guy who helped Charles put out *Heatwave*. It so happened, however, that Gray was, at least for the time being, a strict follower of the Situationist line, and would do much (perhaps unwittingly) to hasten *Heatwave*'s liquidation. By the 26th of July Charles acknowledged that *Heatwave* was "becoming very Situationist-oriented," and he and Gray began publishing translations of situationist texts in pamphlet form. But Charles continued to affirm that the *Rebel Worker* group was *the* U.S. group with which *Heatwave* identified.

After the appearance of *Heatwave* 2 in October, the picture gets murky, and then murkier. At a radical printshop Charles had helped start, one of the commercial jobs—brought in by an American involved in the antiwar movement—consisted of printing a black-and-white image of a U.S. dollar bill, with a message: "Is this worth the horror and murder in Vietnam?" Within days Charles Radcliffe was a hunted man, wanted for violation of the Forgery Act! He went into hiding; the printshop folded; *Heatwave* 3 never appeared. A fugitive on the run, Radcliffe wrote few letters, and those few were brief.

He did let us know that he and Gray had constituted an "English Section" of the Situationist International. I wrote him a letter regretting this move, criticizing what we in Chicago regarded as the Situationists' captious authoritarianism. The "English Section" proved ephemeral in any case. It survived less than a year and seems to have produced only a single pamphlet (*Ten Days That Shook the University*) and a rubber-stamp bearing its post-office-box address.

Too free a spirit to dally long in any centralized, hierarchical group, Radcliffe resigned from the Situationist International in November 1967—one of the very few to resign from a group noted for its "exclusions." His letter on the subject, and subsequent letters, detailed the seamier side of the S.I., which indeed suffered more than most groups from the pathology known as "cult of personality." A May '68 letter stressed "the situationists' failure to supersede either Dada or surrealism, or much else," and signed off: "Long live the Marvelous!"

## WHY *ZTANGI!* NEVER APPEARED

All through 1966–67 *Rebel Worker* activities continued to expand in all directions. Our radicalizing interventions at antiwar marches, labor rallies, sit-ins, protest meetings and "left" conferences attracted wide attention and were often noted and pictured in the press, sometimes with the names and addresses of our arrested members. Our critics—liberal, Old Left and New—wondered at our success in rallying young newcomers, even as these same critics conceded that we had the most eye-catching banners, the most provocative slogans, and a seemingly endless supply of humor and audacity. Though still a small subversive group, we were increasingly recognized as a growing revolutionary force.

In October '66 we organized a tenth anniversary celebration of the Hungarian Revolution. Attended by a standing-room-only crowd at the Wobbly hall, it proved to be our largest indoor public meeting. That same month we brought out one of our biggest publications. The 40-page *Surrealism & Revolution* was the first collection in English on the politics of surrealism, and surely one of the very few mimeo'd pamphlets ever to be noticed in the *New York Times*.

And then *Rebel Worker* 7 appeared in December—the last and by far the largest issue (56 pages), with the biggest press-run: 2000 copies. The contents were far-ranging even by *Rebel Worker* standards. Bernard Marszalek's exposé of media mystification and Jim Evrard's discussion of workers' hobbies enhanced our ongoing critique of everyday life. Robert D. Casey's "Plea for All"—on behalf of the Survival of American Indians Association—spotlighted a too-rarely-heard voice of revolt. Also included were many surrealist texts: by André Breton, Leonora Carrington, Benjamin Péret, my notes on poetry and revolution, and—as a folded insert—the first Chicago Surrealist Group tract, "The Forecast Is Hot!"

Carl Keller wrote to tell me that Jack Ujanen, editor of the IWW's Finnish-language newspaper, *Industrialisti*, liked the issue. I never had the pleasure of meeting Ujanen, but he must have been an unusually broad-minded Wob. Keller added that he himself did not think much of it *as an IWW organ*—and he was right: the only Wob-related material it contained were Guy Askew's "Reminiscences of T-Bone Slim" and the two pages of T-Bone's jottings. Even the Preamble had been left out. By the end of 1966 many of the *Rebel Worker* group had quietly dropped out of the IWW.

The one-page manifesto that opened *Rebel Worker* 7 announced it as "the last but wildly prehensile" issue. "Our aims," it went on to say, "remain essentially the same but now our war-cry shall be *Ztangi!*" For the title of our new journal, Penelope had suggested "Ignatz"—the brick-tossing mouse in the old George Herriman *Krazy Kat* comic strip we all loved. *Ztangi!* was Ignatz spelled backwards, with an exclamation point added to provide the requisite touch of hysteria. That the name had an African ring to it made it even more appealing.

Originally *Ztangi!* was conceived as a continuation of *Rebel Worker* without the organizational link to the IWW—that is, as a journal of free-for-all revolutionary/poetic theory, criticism and humor with a wide-open agitational and experimental dimension. Its "special tone" would surely have echoed my friend Claude Tarnaud's call for "a new defiance: hatred of all that is flabby, tepid, and accommodating." Of course we started by spray-painting ZTANGI! in huge letters, all caps, in Chinese red and day-glow orange, on walls, fences, boarded-up storefronts and other surfaces all over town. First things first!

As the months rolled by, however, it became clear that our individual notions of what *Ztangi!* might be—as journal and as group—were not only different but incompatible. Beyond wanting it to be as wild as possible, and printed rather than mimeographed, we never reached anything close to consensus about it. I had begun to put aside a few published and unpublished articles by members and friends of the group, for possible publication in a possibly forthcoming *Ztangi!* But that's as far as it got. The texts published in the "Ztangi!" section of the present volume could just as well have appeared as a new issue of *The Rebel Worker*. I do not think it would be unfair to say that our hopes and expectations for *Ztangi!* were so high that the project proved unrealizable. From 1967 on (that is, after *Rebel Worker 7*) our group publications consisted entirely of leaflets, posters, stickers, reprints of our pamphlet series, and—in a class by itself—the elegant *Solidarity Bookshop Anarchist-Revolutionary Calendars*, designed and calligraphed by Tor Faegre.

Meanwhile, several of us were turning our attention more and more to specifically surrealist activity, and actually assembling material for yet another much-delayed publication: the first issue of *Arsenal: Surrealist Subversion*. Despite growing friction in the group, this was a time of heightened adventure and discovery for all of us. Long, meandering walks; experimenting with LSD; spontaneous expeditions to heretofore unexplored areas of the city; rock-climbing in Wisconsin; bicycle excursions to the Friedrich Schiller statue in Lincoln Park; and seeing Luis Buñuel's *L'Age d'or* for the first time were all part of the manic restlessness that we liked to call our "research." We were especially devoted to radical forms of play, and even invented new games such as "Latent News" (rearranging lines cut out from news stories into completely new and hilarious stories).

Bernard wrote me around this time (from Buffalo, New York) that he regarded *Arsenal* to be of immeasurably greater importance than *Ztangi!*, an opinion evidently shared at that particular moment in history by almost all of the *Rebel Worker* group. Looking back on this now, it would seem that most of our friends were reserving their "best" efforts for *Arsenal*, in effect postponing the publication of *Ztangi!* Bernard and I were both doing quite a bit of writing at the time, but since neither *Arsenal* nor *Ztangi!* were shaping up on schedule, most of what we wrote either remained unpublished or appeared in publications over which we had no editorial control, most notably the Chicago *Seed*.

Everywhere—in Chicago, the U.S., all over the planet—the political temperature was rising. In the second half of the Sixties a youthful radicalism blossomed into a mass movement of unprecedented variety and scope, all the while remaining in the control of those who were well under the age of thirty. Nothing like it had ever happened before in this country or anywhere else. In the U.S., influenced by the black liberation movement, the ghetto uprisings and the Vietnamese struggle, SDS evolved from timid liberalism to revolutionary anti-imperialism. With a burgeoning membership increasingly made up of workingclass students, its earlier focus on electoral politics gave way to an emphasis on direct action. Roosevelt, where Wobblies were still an active presence, became an SDS stronghold. Joan Smith, and our other friends who were still in school, in turn helped "spread the word" to the larger community.

Naturally we followed these developments with the keenest interest, all the more so in that our publications and actions played a considerable role in hastening this radicalization. Countless SDSers, SNCC-workers and other New-Leftists passing through Chicago made it a point to drop in at Solidarity Bookshop, and most of them left with copies of *Rebel Worker* and at least some of our pamphlets (*Mods, Rockers & the Revolution* and *Surrealism & Revolution* continued to be the best-sellers). In spring 1966 several SDS chapters—Buffalo, New York, was one—proclaimed themselves anarchist. Some SDS members went on to take out red cards. The SDS turn toward "student syndicalism" in 1967 is only one of the more visible manifestations of *Rebel Worker* influence in the broader radical movement of the time.

Some Ztangi!s, however, were slower than others to recognize that SDS was no longer the same group that we had cordially disdained three years earlier. As a group, we never did reach agreement on the class character, revolutionary potential or, for that matter, much else having to do with the mass upheaval subsumed under the "New Left" label. I recall an especially heated discussion at Solidarity Bookshop, in which Bernard expressed an almost vitriolic hostility

71

toward SDS, which, however—to our astonishment—he joined the following day. I think he was the first of us to do so; Penelope and I joined a day or two later.

Not long afterward (late 1967 or early '68) several of us formed our own SDS group: the Louis Lingg Memorial Chapter, named after the youngest and most recalcitrant of the Haymarket Martyrs. However, this last effort to regroup the rapidly diverging *Rebel Worker*/Surrealist Group/Anarchist Horde/*Ztangi!*/Solidarity Bookshop forces proved chimerical. We did continue to do things together—on antiwar demonstrations, for example, where our contingents invariably were the loudest, most youthful and most boisterous—but we did them as Ztangi!s or "The Anarchists" or "The Anarchist Horde" or the "Solidarity Bookshop group" rather than as an SDS affiliate.

In 1967–68 the expectation of Revolution "next week"—or in two or three months at the latest—became increasingly widespread in the New Left and the black movement. It was not unusual to hear SDS neophytes declare that "The Revolution" would occur during summer vacation. Many Black Panthers shared similar illusions. The *Rebel Worker* group took a longer, cooler view; *we* argued that revolution might not happen for three or four *years*—maybe even five or ten.

Precise calculation of the date of capitalism's demise was not, however, one of our major concerns. We had problems of our own.

In the summer of '67 we learned, much to our surprise, that our good friends of London Solidarity had suddenly and inexplicably declared themselves enemies. The Paris group ICO was planning an international meeting of workers' groups in July, and naturally desired and expected the *Rebel Worker* group to participate. London Solidarity, however (Dr Chris Pallis presiding), stated that they would not take part in any meeting to which *Rebel Worker*, *Heatwave*, the Provos or the Situationist International were invited. London Solidarity had never sent us a word of criticism, and to this day we do not know why they insisted on our exclusion.

Silent, too, was the Situationist International in Paris, although packets of new S.I. publications continued to arrive at Solidarity Bookshop. In what seems to have been the first publishing effort by U.S. Situationists—a poorly printed version of *On the Poverty of Student Life* (April 1967)—a short "further information" list included not only the S.I.'s world headquarters in Paris and the New Yorkers' box number, but also *Heatwave* in London and *The Rebel Worker* in Chicago. You'd never guess it from reading *Internationale Situationniste* or other S.I. propaganda, but *Heatwave* and *Rebel*

*Worker* truly remained in agreement on just about everything, and continued to defend such heretical creative currents as blues and jazz, which were utterly ignored and even disdained by the S. I.

On the domestic front, locally and nationally, the IWW was in the doldrums. The old-timers weren't the problem. It was the influx of newcomers, most of them hippies: non-revolutionary non-workers, eager addicts of the consumer culture, whose politics rarely went beyond "white liberalism." Their activity concentrated on community clean-up programs and other petit-bourgeois reformism. Ignorant of IWW history and scornful of such "heavy theoretical stuff" as *The Rebel Worker*, these recruits were closer to the trendy confusionism of the latest guru-of the-month than to the irreconcilably rebellious spirit of Joe Hill or T-Bone Slim. Many once-active members stopped coming around; some, for various reasons, left town. Others made their way to the "underground press." After a stint at the San Francisco *Oracle*, Lester Doré devoted his time and energy to the Chicago *Seed*, and later to the *Heartland Journal*. Few indeed were still on the job trying to build the "One Big Union." Even an organizer as sharp as Anna-Marie Gibson found the situation perplexing, and she too drifted away.

Bad news kept piling up. Our home on Larrabee Street was raided by the police and for six months we were in and out of court. In August '67 our friend Walter Caughey in New York was stabbed to death by "person or persons unknown." *Resurgence*, which he had co-edited, soon devolved into a mystical Maoism. *Black Mask* also went into a decline, advocating a mindless violence that prefigured something of the later ludicrous "Weatherman" faction of SDS—whom we, by the way, always regarded as "silly bourgeois twits." (Ben Morea later inherited a fortune and quietly abandoned the radical scene.) Locally, on a big anti-war demonstration downtown, the cops went berserk. Many of us were arrested. (Although I escaped arrest, I was badly billy-clubbed for the first time.)

A veritable symbol of the manifold woes that beset us all was the fact that once again we were forced to move as a result of harassment by police, the Board of Education, and the Department of Urban Renewal. The last-named agency (we called it Urban Removal) seized the building at 1947 Larrabee Street that housed the latest edition of Solidarity Bookshop, and padlocked the front door; two of us were arrested and charged with "trespassing on city property," *i.e.*, entering our own bookshop to get our mail.

Meanwhile, one of our best friends and most creative collaborators—Charles Radcliffe—was still in hiding across the sea, and our sister journal *Heatwave* appeared to be gone. On top of it all, *The Rebel*

*Worker* was gone, too, and its announced successor was getting nowhere.

Is it any wonder that some of our friends got a bit discouraged?

Of course there were bright moments, too—mostly involving the Chicago Surrealist Group, which grew significantly in 1967. At the big anti-war march in New York that April, Dotty DeCoster's red-and-black surrealist flag attracted Guy and Rikki Ducornet, who immediately became our good friends, and have remained uninterruptedly active in the surrealist movement ever since. The Indonesian surrealist painter/poet Schlechter Duvall (then living in Ottumwa, Iowa) introduced himself to us in a letter c/o Solidarity Bookshop, and he, too, became a mainstay of Chicago Surrealism. The painter Eric Matheson, former Lake Forest beatnik then living in New York, also threw in his lot with us.

Toward the end of the year, a fellow came to Solidarity announcing that he was a friend of Charles Radcliffe's and had collaborated on *Heatwave*. With Charles on the lam, we were rather suspicious, but fortunately Penelope had the good sense to ask him *what* he had contributed to *Heatwave*. When he replied, "a piece on heroin addiction in the first issue," we suddenly realized: It's Paul Garon! Minutes later, recalling that Charles had called Paul his "mentor" in blues matters, Penelope also asked him whether he had any records by Peetie Wheatstraw, the Devil's Son-In-Law. Paul said he had all but a few, and that we were all welcome to listen to them.

In no time Paul, Penelope and I were close friends—a friendship that has endured unbroken to this day. Through Paul we also got to know such blues giants as Big Joe Williams, Johnny Shines, and Honeyboy Edwards. It also turned out that he shared almost all of the core *Rebel Worker/Heatwave* passions and preoccupations. Deeply interested in surrealism long before we met, he quickly became a central figure in the Surrealist Group, distinguishing himself above all as the author of *Blues and the Poetic Spirit* and other major studies relating surrealism and blues.

As 1967 drew to a close, surrealist revolution was definitely in the wind in the Windy City, and the coming year brought forth a veritable whirlwind of activity, including three issues of the large wallposter *Surrealist Insurrection* and the first Chicago Surrealist Group exhibition at our own Gallery Bugs Bunny.

## SPLIT

By year's end, however, it was also painfully obvious that the former *Rebel Worker* Group was in complete disarray, and that *Ztangi!* was not going to appear. By Spring '68, the group scarcely functioned at all except to maintain Solidarity Bookshop—which, incidentally, was no easy task. Now and then right-wingers, champions of law'n'order, would patriotically break our windows. Threatening phone calls were not uncommon. The local "Red Squad" pestered our landlords and neighbors with questions about "the anarchist bookshop" and the dangerous folk who frequented it. The many moves we had to make were time-consuming and exhausting, and each one required a new promotional effort to let people know our latest location.

Meanwhile, some of us had to take time off from all this other fun to convince the SS (Selective Service) that they really didn't want us to help fight the bosses' war in Vietnam. (After much trouble and fuss, I was eventually declared "morally disqualified" from military service.)

And don't forget that all of us, at all times, were afflicted with the day-to-day indignity of having to "make a living."

Clearly, then, in addition to our mounting disagreements regarding revolutionary theory and practical strategical and tactical matters, we had plenty of other problems to make our lives difficult.

Solidarity Bookshop was run by volunteers; it paid no wages. It was a rare month when enough money came in to pay the rent and bills from publishers. The hours were erratic, but we tried to keep it open weekday evenings and all day on weekends. Most of us also had "regular" jobs. When book-sales were slow, we had to pitch in toward rent.

In April '68 I started working at Barbara's Bookstore at 1434 North Wells Street. Right away I was put in charge of ordering "political" books, a category largely neglected up to then in what had been a somewhat genteel store that specialized in Classical and Modern Literature. Paul Garon got a job there a few weeks later.

Barbara's soon had by far the largest selection of anarchist, Marxist and surrealist books in Chicago—the Surrealism section alone had some two-hundred titles, many in French and other languages—as well as sizeable sections devoted to the Vietnam War, Black History, Women's History, Radical History, Native Americans, Utopianism, Black Music, and other subjects that interested us. All these books sold very well, so Paul and I were encouraged to order anything we thought the store should have.

During the week of protests at the Democratic Convention in August I was asked to do a "radical" window-display. It attracted so much attention that I did most of the window-displays thereafter, including several devoted to surrealism. In June '69 Barbara's was surely the only business in the city to welcome delegates to the SDS Convention (here we were satirizing the "Welcome Shriners" banners prominently displayed in night-club and restaurant windows).

Barbara's, which often took in more money on a Saturday night than Solidarity made in a year, for half a decade held the U.S. heavy-weight championship as purveyor of revolutionary literature. André Schiffrin, a *Radical America* contributor who went on to become chief editor at Pantheon Books and currently directs The New Press, told Barbara that she had "by far the finest bookstore in the country." Although it was never really the radical meeting-place that Solidarity was—and had none of the latter's old-time hobo charm—it did attract a sizeable left clientele. On any given weekend at Barbara's one could expect to meet members of the League of Black Revolutionary Workers, SDSers, Black Panthers, IWWs, Women's Liberationists, and all manner of anarchists, Trotskyists, and New Leftists as well as Diggers, Yippies and other exemplars of the "counterculture."Such unaffiliated radicals as Nelson Algren, Studs Terkel, and Jimmy Sheridan (Jack's soapboxing twin) were also frequent visitors. Now and then the Second City Players wandered in, too—drinks in hand.

Working at Barbara's thirty hours a week reduced the time I was able to spend at Solidarity, but multiplied my acquaintance with other radicals. Penelope, meanwhile, was working even longer hours at Liberation Press, the printshop at the SDS National Office at 1608 West Madison. Both of us were increasingly active in SDS, and had formed friendships with SDS members in Chicago and Madison, where Paul Buhle and others published *Radical America,* the leading SDS journal. *Radical America* later took up many *Rebel Worker* themes. It devoted entire issues to surrealism and to Guy Debord's *Society of the Spectacle* (translated by Fredy Perlman),while pursuing an approach to popular culture along the lines we had developed.

Our friends in "The Movement" also included John Higginson, Eric Perkins, Ernest Allen and other members of the League of Black Revolutionary Workers (the subject of another special issue of *Radical America*). A few other Ztangi!s had ties with radicals outside the small anarchist/Wobbly milieu. Bill Corbin, for example—a blues fan and student of Zen from Peoria, and the most active *Rebel Worker* group recruit during Penelope's and my sojourn overseas—came back from a Fall '67 trip to California full of enthusiasm for the Black Panther Party. For months Solidarity Bookshop was the only Chicago outlet for the *Black Panther* paper. By May '68 it was one of the best-selling periodicals at Barbara's.

All of us at Solidarity were elated by the May '68 General Strike in France—a massive uprising of workers, students, immigrants and racial minorities which in so many ways realized the *Rebel Worker* dream of revolution-as-surrealist-Wobbly-anarchist-carnival. It was plain, however, that we were far from agreeing on the analysis of what took place there, or what the May events meant for revolutionists in the U.S. and elsewhere. Many saw May '68 as a complete vindication of traditional anarchism, and simply blamed Stalinism for its defeat. A few of us, without minimizing the nefarious role of the French Communist Party, found the anarchists' self-congratulatory pose less convincing, and here as elsewhere favored Marx's call for "merciless criticism of everything in existence."

There appeared to be no shortage of things for us to disagree about. Then as now, for example, many anarchists looked on the would-be "vanguard parties" as their bitterest enemies, a far greater menace to the workers' cause than the minions of Capital. To others of us, however, such fear and loathing of tiny groups of Maoists and Trotskyists, not to mention factions of SDS, seemed absurd. In our view, the working class had long since superseded the "vanguardist" framework. Historically, the many self-styled vanguards were obsolete and irrelevant—no longer a discernible force in the workers' movement, much less a "threat." We argued that the American workers' refusal to join any of these groups, or to form a "labor party," were not indications of backwardness but rather, on the contrary, proof that they had moved beyond such outmoded categories. In the era of wildcat strikes, black liberation and youth rebellion it seemed more than a little ridiculous to hope for a revival of turn-of-the-century modes of struggle specifically designed to overthrow the Russian Czar. To us it was obvious that the new social forces and energies emerging all around us, unprecedentedly advancing the revolutionary movement in every direction, implied and called for new organizational forms.

On the practical level this meant that we accepted the fact that many latter-day "vanguardists" were active in the same broad movements that we were active in. Of course we disagreed with them, and fundamentally, but by and large we viewed them as fellow workers in the class war. Inevitably, they were naive, confused, and theoretically backward, but they were also relatively few in number and certainly not dangerous. The best of them—or so we thought—would sooner or later, *in the course of struggle*, free themselves of their anachronistic beliefs as the rapidly expanding revolutionary movement gained experience and self-confidence.

Such were the pressures of daily life that these disagreements, alas, and many others, not only went unresolved, but actually worsened.

The crisis came to a head in August '68. Large-scale antiwar demonstrations had been planned to take place outside the Democratic Party Convention in Chicago that month, and—thanks to the intoxication of the time—more than a few otherwise reasonable people actually expected hundreds of thousands or even a million or more young radicals to come "trash" the city. Anticipating that at least a few thousand would come, we met at Solidarity Bookshop (now at 745 Armitage) to discuss how we should approach this sudden influx. We realized that our political disagreements precluded a joint statement at that point, but—divergences notwithstanding—we were still together in running Solidarity Bookshop.

Some of us hoped that the throngs of young street-fighters descending on Chicago would provide a real boost for the Bookshop, not merely in terms of selling books, but in the wider sense of "spreading the word"—and that this might in turn reactivate the group. Others were more reticent; a proposal was even made to *close* the bookshop that week. As it happened, most incoming demonstrators congregated closer to the Convention sites—all of which were downtown, miles from Solidarity. Even the hippies' "Festival of Life" in Lincoln Park was a mile away. In any case, the "deluge" of visitors to the bookshop did not materialize. The only out-of-towner I recall meeting there that week was Fredy Perlman, from Detroit.

Many things happened in Chicago during Convention week in August 1968, but the rejuvenation of Solidarity Bookshop was not one of them. I guess we were better streetfighters than booksellers.

The actual "split" in the *Rebel Worker* group came shortly afterward, and was in fact anti-climactic. I say "split," in quote-marks, because there really were no clearly defined factions; indeed, the break-up came about not as a result of discussion, debate, and choosing sides, but by unilateral administrative decree. Penelope and I arrived one evening for our regularly scheduled hours at the Bookshop to find that we had been excluded by a simple expedient: the lock on the door had been changed, and we were denied a new key. Will any reader be surprised to learn that this incident did not heal the breach? Small as it may seem, the "lockout" generated bad feelings that lasted for years. For Penelope and me, as for others who quit in protest, and friends "on the periphery," it confirmed our suspicion that anarchists could be as authoritarian as anyone else.

In retrospect it is clear that, in the various disputes that brought the *Rebel Worker* group to an end and crippled Solidarity Bookshop, none of us had a monopoly on being right or wrong. All of us were gifted in the arts of obstinacy and impatience (traditional favorites of young radicals everywhere), and we practiced them aplenty. In the heat of argument, with (as we thought) the future of the Revolution at stake, passions ran high and rational debate ran low. As so often happens in polemics, verbal excess accompanied by more than a little foolishness entered the game and took over. We were good at rallying crowds, livening up dull protests, disrupting politicians' speeches, and dodging cops, but much less successful at settling differences among ourselves. Looking back now on the last days of the *Rebel Worker* group, it appears that an unexpectedly harsh sense of seriousness overwhelmed—at least for the moment—our far-famed sense of humor.

Like the much larger splits that it presaged—in SDS and the rest of the New Left, as well as in the black movement—the split in the *Rebel Worker* group was an ill wind that blew nobody any good. As old O.N. Peterson, the Wob sage of Seattle, would have said: Mr Boss and the Comical Party must have had a good laugh at our expense.

To our credit—the credit of all of us, on all sides of all the quarrels—not one of us ever went around claiming that the split was a great historic victory for the world proletarian Cause. Indeed, in flagrant contrast to most splits, which result in endless mutual denunciation, the dispersed *Rebel Worker* group avoided such sectarian idiocy and went on to pursue—albeit in very different ways—the basic aims and principles that we had all developed together in happier times. It is heartening to note in this regard that, notwithstanding the passage of many years—during which the Old Order has let it be known time and again that it is still running the show—not one of the characters in The *Rebel Worker* Story has defected to the side of Capital and the State.

## Forty Years After

*The Beautiful is the Splendor of the True.*

—Plotinus—

Was *The Rebel Worker*'s revolutionary quest "fraught with contradictions," as the platitude has it? And if so, what of it? We were not, after all, simply "applying" an abstract system in which all parts had been adjusted in advance to all other parts. Rather, we were trying—desperately, and I mean *desperately*—to think and dream and live our way out of History's deadliest dead-ends. Anyone who believes this can be done without false starts and wrong turns has yet to start living.

*The Rebel Worker* had all the vices of rebellious youth in ages past, plus a lot of new ones we invented for purposes of our own. Yes, we were insolent, cocksure, and headstrong—with too many chips on our shoulders, and too many jokes in our diatribes. Modesty was never our strong point. We were excessive in everything. Rebels against work, fanatics for poetry and play, we were sure we had the

Open Sesame of Total Revolution. While others patiently published platforms, programs and policy statements, we rushed into print with our wildest dreams and desires. Instead of discipline, dogma, bureaucracy and boredom, we practiced loud refusal, mad love, utopian revery, direct action. We laughed a lot, too, and had plenty of fun.

To what extent our revolutionary virtues may have outweighed our many adolescent vices is for the reader to decide. Those inclined to be more charitable than we were will not ignore the fact that when the last issue of *The Rebel Worker* rolled off the mimeograph in December '66, the oldest among us was only twenty-four.

But what really matters, today and tomorrow, is this: However wrongheaded we may have been about this or that detail, *fundamentally we were right*! Capitalism *does* stink! The State *is* oppressive! Revolution *is* the only solution! Freedom *is* the only cause worth serving!

And that is why, forty years later, *The Rebel Worker* and its sister magazine *Heatwave* are still as fresh as the revolutionary dawn, while 99.9% of today's media is nothing but lies, lies, lies, and more lies.

In *Les Chants de Maldoror*, Lautréamont wrote:

> It is good to look back over the course already traveled, and then, the limbs rested, to rush on again with an impetuous bound. To accomplish a journey in one single breath is not easy, and the wings weary much during a high flight without hope and without remorse.

The struggle for the abolition of wage-slavery continues! The question now is: What are *you* going to do about it?

We can be sure of this much: Nothing *less* than the *Rebel Worker/ Heatwave* dream can do the trick.

Trying to work *within* the repressive system only helps make the repressive system work. Refusal, saying no, defying consumerism, and outright revolt are still the healthiest responses to the unlivable.

Long live the Marvelous! Freedom *Now!*

Franklin ROSEMONT

*Chicago, May Day, 2004*

80

# Preamble of the Industrial Workers of the World

The working class and the employing class have nothing in common. There can be no peace so long as hunger and want are found among millions of working people and the few, who make up the employing class, have all the good things of life.

Between these two classes a struggle must go on until the workers of the world organize as a class, take possession of the earth and the machinery of production, and abolish the wage system.

We find that the centering of the management of industries into fewer and fewer hands makes the trade unions unable to cope with the ever growing power of the employing class. The trade unions foster a state of affairs which allows one set of workers to be pitted against another set of workers in the same industry, thereby helping defeat one another in wage wars. Moreover, the trade unions aid the employing class to mislead the workers into the belief that the working class have interests in common with their employers.

These conditions can be changed and the interest of the working class upheld only by an organization formed in such a way that all its members in any one industry, or in all industries if necessary, cease work whenever a strike or lockout is on in any department thereof, thus making an injury to one an injury to all.

Instead of the conservative motto, "A fair day's wage for a fair day's work," we must inscribe on our banner the revolutionary watchword, "Abolition of the wage system."

It is the historic mission of the working class to do away with capitalism. The army of production must be organized, not only for the every-day struggle with capitalists, but also to carry on production when capitalism shall have been overthrown. By organizing industrially we are forming the structure of the new society within the shell of the old.

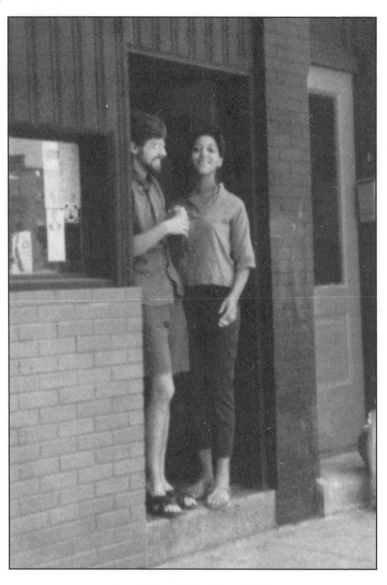

Bernard Marszalek and Joan Smith
at the original Solidarity Bookshop,
713 Armitage Avenue (1965)

# REBEL WORKER 1

The Rebel Worker

Published sporadically by the Chicago GRU Branch of the
· Industrial Workers of the World ·

number 1

"I'm organized, are you?"

May Day 1964 / Cover by Tor Faegre / 29 pages

*"From now on you won't be bored, I can promise you that," said d'Artagnan.*
—Alexandre Dumas, *The Three Musketeers*—

The first issue was in many respects a "traditional" IWW magazine, but the distinctive features that set *The Rebel Worker* apart from the rest of the "left" press were already evident, not only in the story by René Daumal (a French poet on the fringes of surrealism in the late 1920s) and the cartoons by Topor, but also in the editorial emphasis on our being "primarily a disruptive force against capitalism," and our interest in "problems related to but not traditionally part of the labor struggle." The T-Bone Slim selections (abridged here) were chosen explicitly for their surrealist quality. Writings by T-Bone, by the way, appeared in every *Rebel Worker* except 5 and 6.

Almost half of this issue consisted of reprints. Our policy was simple: "Anything appearing in *The Rebel Worker* may be freely reprinted, translated, or adapted, even without indicating its source, and we reserve the same freedom for ourselves regarding other publications." Although this notice did not appear until *Rebel Worker* 6, we practiced it from the start. In subsequent issues, however, original material greatly outnumbered reprints.

—F.R.

From the early 1930s into the 1970s the international headquarters of the IWW were located on the second floor of this old building at 2422 North Halsted Street, near the intersection of Lincoln and Fullerton. The Assyrian restaurant in the storefront below was a popular Wobbly eating-place.

# WHY REBEL?

WHY BOTHER REBELLING against capitalism if it is destroying itself anyway?

It is wrecking itself, damaging the earth that nurtured it, and threatening to drag humanity into oblivion with it.

But to conserve ourselves, to conserve the world so that later generations may blossom in it, to conserve whatever is worthy in our traditions, we must rebel.

We are an enslaved and manipulated class of hired hands. Our lot is that of trying to make a living by doing what we are told to do—and by people who cannot have our interests at heart. That is our destiny whether we have not learned to read and write or whether we are busy hawking our sheepskins to personnel managers. We cannot be aware of our situation and hold our heads erect if we do not rebel.

The intelligent rebel of today is concerned with somewhat different issues than was his counterpart of an earlier age. Then man rebelled against what was and what had been. The world we live in is phony and over-administered and self-destructive. We should rebel against it. But it is a world so obviously in the process of shifting and changing that today's rebel is primarily in revolt against what the world threatens to become.

Yes, capitalism is all too likely to disappear without our lifting a finger to end it. But in that case, what can we expect as a system to succeed capitalism?

Surely it will be succeeded by a society premised on those technical and traditional traits of our present order that survive it, organized and modified by the forces that have destroyed capitalism. The issue of what traits survive and how they are modified and organized depends on what forces do bring capitalism to an end.

If capitalism ends primarily because of the troubles it gets itself into or from the actions of the swollen bureaucracies it needs and engenders, or is given the final coup by the authoritarianism it seems likely to seek as a final refuge—what sort of world do we get from that?

Beware of the sort of "socialism" mankind can get without even trying. It is not only a hideous caricature of the dreams of the socialist pioneers, but it may so adroitly manipulate its antagonisms and administer its underlying population as to make itself rebellion-proof.

But—*If* capitalism is brought to an end by those who rebel against it, by those who despise its exploitation of labor, by those who condemn its devices for dividing humanity into warring collectivities, by those who cannot stomach its commercialism and who revolt at its commercials, who shudder at its glad-hand peddlers of mummified smiles and instant personality, who prefer the ancient verities to its tinkling baubles, who cringe at its ugliness, its stench and its moral degradation, but who refuse to cringe before its hireling watchdogs—then, and only then, is there a chance for a good world.

Rebel, while capitalism still makes it possible.

Fred THOMPSON

# THE WOBBLIES RETURN IN CHICAGO

THE RECENT RESURGENCE OF IWW ACTIVITY in Chicago—reported a few weeks ago in a long but somewhat confused article in the *Chicago Sun-Times* under the headline, "The Wobblies Return"—points to a general reanimation of the radical movement here, and the present situation seems to indicate a promise of continuous renewal of organization and education in several areas.

Plans for the agricultural workers organization drive this summer and fall have been discussed at length in recent issues of the *Industrial Worker* and elsewhere in this issue of *The Rebel Worker*. We've also been setting up a weekly literature table at the open-air street market on Maxwell Street.

The day-to-day struggle with the boss goes on, and workers are looking for answers. We in the IWW view ourselves primarily as a disruptive force within the capitalist system, seeking ways out of that system by demonstrating its uselessness and its miseries, and also by participating in all meaningful movements of protest and liberation.

We see much need at this time for rebellion by small groups of workers directed toward various problems related to, but not exactly traditionally part of, labor struggle. There is at present, for instance, no organized effort at opposing the draft, except by pacifists—yet increases in the draft are nothing more than efforts to artificially reduce unemployment, and therefore deserve our attention. It is problems like these that we are now working on.

Franklin ROSEMONT

*(excerpts)*

# A LONGSHOREMAN'S CALL

*8th October 1963*

**D**EAR BROTHER PORTWORKERS,
This is a plea for peace. A plea made by a dock labourer, the largest proportion of whose life must be spent amidst sweat, dirt, exhaustion and sometimes blood in the never-ending struggle for some sort of economic stability. A struggle which should and almost always does monopolize the whole of his consciousness and leaves no time for any original thought. This is the station in life into which I have been placed—one which, I am sure, you will easily recognize.

My position in society has been so carefully arranged by those responsible for such things that I am removed by only one week's wages from pauperism. Domestic tragedy, as you will well know, is always imminent. Sickness, accident, unemployment—the real ever-present enemies—always there to smash our pride and destroy any vestige of character and personality we might develop in spite of all the obstacles.

Is it of any wonder then that the vast majority of us concern ourselves less and less with the major international problems, and grab at the fruits of labour while they are going? We look at life through half-closed eyes and leave our destinies in the hands of people who have consistently betrayed us throughout the ages—and taught us to hate other working men just like ourselves.

We British portworkers have been taught in turn to hate Germans, Italians, Japanese, Russians, and Chinese—and we have complied with fervor. We have then been commanded to go out—shoot them or blow them to bits, and accepted as easily as if we were doing a normal day's work.

Such is the manner in which restricted minds react to abusive propaganda. I would willingly have machine-gunned an Italian portworker even though in the course of my whole life I have never met one. I could have quite easily condoned the slaughter of German workers' wives and children in Dresden or Hamburg, although my stomach would turn at the sight of a mutilated animal. I could have applauded the decision to atomise Hiroshima when the nearest I had come to a Japanese was at a performance of *Madame Butterfly*. And so it goes on. Tomorrow it might be the turn of the French. The day after that the man next door. Next year my own wife and children.

Authorities are rapidly failing to ensure the continued existence of mankind. We must begin to take control from them. We must reject the hate attitudes. Portworkers may be inarticulate, but they are also vociferous. They may be humble, but they can be equally as powerful. They are an essential part of any nation's economy and are in the position to terminate anyone's aggressive aspirations.

Only when we stand together as one race, mankind, can we begin to end forever man's greatest scourge.

Let us begin by starting to know each other, by meeting and talking and laughing with each other, and gradually find out that we are exactly the same, with the same kind of problems. Then we shall reject the swindle that we have been involved in for centuries and really think of each other, after the comradeship we would generate, as brothers.

Yours fraternally,

Jimmy JEWERS

From London *Solidarity*, 1963

# EDUCATION: WHAT IS IT?

I AM NOT READY TO ADMIT that the vast majority of workers are blockheads and consequently uneducable. I prefer to think that the majority of working men and women are victims of a false system of education. Educators are fond of quoting Solomon who was supposed to have said, "Train up a child in the way he should go, and when he is old he will not depart from it." Now, the thing that is fundamentally wrong with this formula is the fact that "the way to go" is determined by the traditional and personal prejudices of those who control the educational system, and once the minds of our youth are molded in accordance with these prejudices, intelligence ceases to function.

The character of true education seems to me quite clear and definite. It consists of, first, the ability to discriminate between relative values, and second, an attitude of sincere and honest doubt.

Any man or woman who possesses the two requisites mentioned in the above paragraph is an educated person, regardless of age or status in our social system, and anyone who does not possess these requisites is not an educated person. It is possible under the present educational system for anyone who possesses the financial resources to obtain a diploma and any number of degrees, even the much-coveted Ph.D., and not possess either of these requisites.

Any student who achieves superior marks in all his college courses is by necessity an extreme conformist who accepts everything on textbook and pedagogic authority, since he has not the ability to discriminate between the humbug taught by one professor or textbook and the science taught by another. If, by chance, a student readily learns that the professor he faces is a conceited clown despite all his pretensions and degrees, that student possesses all the requisites of an educated man, but he will absolutely be disqualified to receive superior scholastic marks and he will probably fail altogether.

We have been accustomed to the idea that education is a method of collecting data to be hurled at teachers and professors on an examination day, or to entertain our friends in idle parlor conversation, or marshal for purposes of propaganda. True education consists of knowing what to do with the tremendous volume of data that comes to us. The educated man has the power to analyze, interpret, appraise and classify data as to its relative value. He accepts none as facts unless they prove to be facts in the light of experience or by sense perception; and he knows that his senses are not always to be trusted.

The uneducated man accepts everything as fact that is in accord with his prejudices and will violently reject the evidence of facts that comes to him through his sense perceptions if it conflicts fundamentally with his prejudices.

It seems to me impossible to dissociate intelligence from education, or education from intelligence. Without intelligence there would be no education, and where intelligence is present there is always some type of education. Intelligence is the possession of innate powers or abilities, and education is the process of developing or intensifying these powers or abilities. Therefore, a child entering school for the first time has all the requisites of an educated person even though they are only present in a small degree.

All education outside pure science is a commodity to be sold to somebody, the selling of which is justified by any method that will bring the highest price. Consequently prestige, wealth and fame rather than truth and accurate knowledge become the goals for which those who survive a college education strive. This is why it is easier to "sell" or "teach" the false rather than the true notion about things. There is a great incentive on the part of the Board of Trustees of knowledge factories, euphemistically referred to as "institutions of higher learning," to silence a professor whose ideas are not in accord with traditional prejudices, since what he says attacks a racket from which multitudes of men derive profits.

Organized societies for various reasons have always been opposed to education. It was always considered dangerous by those in authority. From the days of the medicine man in savage tribes to the big businessman of modern democracies and functionaries in totalitarian states, authority has always been maintained by magic and hocus-pocus. The big business corporations of today and their chief mouthpieces, the political bosses, their editors and teachers, are just as much witch-doctors as the medicine men of ancient societies.

Nothing so quickly dispels witchcraft and magic as the free exercise of human intelligence. When workers stop attempting to reason about their place in the world in the light of the bunkum they have been taught, and begin to reason from what is obvious, that our industrial and social machine has broken down many times, that these breakdowns have caused unemployment and wars, and that the capitalist and communist alike, despite all their credentials and claims of competence, have miserably failed to maintain a social order worthy of the name—when the workers realize this and begin to apply the intelligence of a fourteen-year-old boy to the situation, they will have taken the first step toward their emancipation. And, who knows, they may decide that the kind of world that would offer a fuller and more meaningful life is the kind of a world built according to the plans drawn up by the Industrial Workers of the World.

Jack SHERIDAN

# THE GREAT MAGICIAN

THERE WAS ONCE A POWERFUL MAGICIAN who lived in a garret in the Rue Bouffetard. He lived there in the guise of a little old clerk, tidy and punctual, and worked in a branch of the Araganais Bank on the Avenue des Gibelins. With the wave of a magic toothpick he could have transmuted all the tiles of the roof into bars of gold. But that would have been immoral, for he believed that work ennobles man. And—to some extent—even woman, he would add.

When his Aunt Ursula, an old shrew who had just been ruined by the collapse of Serbian-Bulgarian stocks, came to live with him and demanded that he take care of her, he could have transformed her at will into a pretty young princess, or into a swan harnessed to his magic chariot, or into a soft-boiled egg, or into a ladybug, or into a bus. But that would have broken with good family tradition, the backbone of society and morality. So he slept on a straw mat and would get up at six o'clock to buy Aunt Ursula her rolls and prepare her coffee; after which, he listened patiently to the daily broadside of complaints: that the coffee tasted of soap, that there was a cockroach baked into one of the rolls, that he was an unworthy nephew and would be disinherited. "Disinherited of what?" you might well wonder. But he let her talk on, knowing that if he wanted to…. But Aunt Ursula must never suspect that he was a powerful magician. That might give birth to thoughts of lucre and close the gates of Paradise to her forever.

After that, the great magician would go down his six flights, sometimes almost breaking his neck on the murderously slippery stairs. However, he would pick himself up with a faint smile, thinking that if he wished be could change himself into a swallow and take wing through the skylight. But the neighbors might see, and so wondrous a feat would shake the very foundation of their naive but wholesome faith.

When he reached the street, he would brush the dust off his alpaca jacket at the same time taking care not to pronounce those words which would have instantly turned it into a brocade vestment. Such an act would have planted a sinister doubt in the hearts of the people passing and shaken their innocent belief in the immutability of the laws of nature.

He had his breakfast at the counter in a café, taking only some ersatz coffee and a bit of stale bread. Ah, if he wanted to… But in order to stop himself from making use of his supernatural powers, he would swallow five cognacs in rapid succession. The alcohol, dulling the edge of his magic powers, brought him round to a salutary humility and to the feeling that all men, including himself, were brothers. If the cashier repulsed him when he tried to kiss her, pretending it was because of his dirty beard, he would tell himself that she had no heart and understood nothing of the spirit of the gospels.

At a quarter of eight, he was in his office, his sleeveprotectors on, a pen behind his ear, and a newspaper spread before him. With only a slight effort of concentration he could have known straight off the present, past, and future of the entire world, but he restrained himself from using this gift. He made himself read the paper so as not to lose touch with the common language; it allowed him to communicate over an aperitif with his equals—in appearance—and guide them in the right direction. At eight o'clock, the paper scratching began, and if he made a mistake now and then, it was in order to justify the reprimands of his superiors, who otherwise would be guilty of the serious sin of having made a false accusation. And so, all day long the great magician, in the guise of an average employee, carried on his task as humanity's guide.

Poor Aunt Ursula! Whenever he returned at noon having forgotten to buy some parsley, that dear lady, instead of cracking the basin over his head, would certainly have behaved differently had she known who her nephew really was. But then she would never have had the opportunity of discovering to what extent anger is a momentary madness.

If he had wanted to!... Instead of dying in a hospital of an unknown disease in barely Christian fashion, leaving no more trace on earth than a moth-eaten coat in the wardrobe, an old toothbrush, and mocking memories in the ungrateful hearts of his colleagues, he could have been a pasha, an alchemist, a wizard, a nightingale, or a cedar of Lebanon. But that would have been contrary to the secret designs of Providence. No one made a speech over his grave. No one suspected who he was. And who knows—perhaps not even he himself. Still, he was a most powerful magician.

René DAUMAL

*Translated from the French by Charles Warner*

# WILL WE ALL GO TOGETHER WHEN WE GO?

I USED TO THINK NUCLEAR WAR HAD ONE ADVANTAGE over conventional war: the people who started it got killed just as surely as their working class cannon fodder. But, according to research conducted by the U.S. Office of Civil Defense, it seems that the

H-bomb is as class-biased as any bomb of World War II. It respects the lives of Top People.

I worked for four months in an American University Research Center studying "post-nuclear attack demography" for the government. For every possible pattern of nuclear attack, we would be given the number expected to be killed in each area. We would then check this against the U.S. Census figures on race, occupation, age, religion, political opinions, tolerance of communism, atheism, nonconformity, etc., for the area. We fed the data into an electronic computer, and up would come the probable social characteristics of the surviving population.

American cities are, of course, segregated by class and race. If you are Negro, workingclass, Roman Catholic or of recent immigrant stock, you tend to live near the center of the city. If you are white, Anglo-Saxon, Protestant and upper-class, you are likely to live in the "ex-urbs," semi-rural settlements as far as 50 miles from the center. The middle classes, true to form, live in between, in the suburbs.

Farmers, of course, are safest of all. But the American "family farm" was wiped out long ago. The few farmers remaining are prosperous businessmen who hire seasonal labor. Many of these farm laborers live in cities when they're not working.

I thought I saw a bright spot in the unusually low survival rates for Washington, D.C. A day-time attack would catch all the bureaucrats in their offices (day-time attacks are more egalitarian, because they get the upper classes in their offices rather than their homes). But there are two things to remember about Washington, D.C. First, its Negro population is about 55 percent (our rulers need a lot of servants). Second, it is the only place with deep *blast* (not fall-out) shelters, underneath buildings like the Pentagon. Foiled again! The day after a nuclear attack, then, the bureaucrats would be "safely" holed up either hundreds of feet below the Pentagon and White House, or, if it was a night-time attack, on their Virginia estates. With a year's supply of tinned food.

Safest of all of course would be the files and records. All important government records (and most trivial ones) are duplicated and stored in blast-proof shelters in the Virginia hills, far from Washington, D.C. Moreover, *all* bank records everywhere in the country are similarly duplicated and stored. So while you're floating 40,000 feet over the Atlantic as a radioactive dust cloud, they will know you owe $50 in taxes and $500 in hire-purchase, with $5 in the bank to take care of it.

More important than the study are the studiers. I never met the people in Washington who filed our results in duplicate (one copy for the wastebasket and one for the blast shelter in Virginia). But we six in the California Research Center all considered our job a patriotic duty: wasting government money helps stimulate the economy, you know. If someone came in fifteen minutes late, he was frowned upon as a slacker. Half an hour late was about right; being an hour late made you a hero of labor. In ways big and small we did our bit to avoid recession. Once we spent an entire day (48 man-hours) arranging to buy an unnecessary electric typewriter. And we took home paper clips whenever steel production dropped.

How did we feel about the exact nature of our work? Political consciousness in our office was high. Everyone was at the very least some sort of peacenik. Yet none of us felt guilt about our part in war preparations. Some rationalized that we were syphoning defense department money away from directly destructive weapon development into merely useless projects. Others felt that some of our startling findings might shock people into seeking peace. (Alas, the fact that an attack killing about 20% of the Protestants would also kill 35% of the Catholics and wipe out over 50% of the Jews would only encourage our generals!). But we all felt wasted: our brains and our hands were simply rented out. We worked all day (albeit sluggishly) without ever making anything that anyone wanted or needed.

We knew, of course, that *we* were not doing any harm. But we worried about the people in Washington. Did *they* take this stuff seriously? Or were they just helping avoid recession, like us? Perhaps there was a man in Washington whose sole job was to think up new projects. If they took it seriously, the implications were ominous. The questions they asked were aimed, crudely to be sure, at techniques of manipulating and dominating the surviving population. Only two of their factors—age and sex—were directly concerned with reconstruction work. All the rest were concerned with social background and political attitudes. They were in effect doing post-attack Gallup Polls.

Our rulers have learned to control the American population through a century-long process of trial and error. They know their public relations techniques will be disrupted by nuclear war. But they apparently think they will be able to adjust to the new situation. When the first politician crawls out of his blast shelter and grasps a microphone, will he "call on the peoples of the world to live in brotherhood now that the totalitarian threat has at last been overcome?" Or will he declare: "My fellow citizens, now that the niggers are out of the way, we can really get to work again to rebuild our great nation." Post-nuclear demography may help him decide.

Barbara GARSON

From *Solidarity* (London)

# INTRODUCTION TO T-BONE SLIM

MOST YOUNGER MEMBERS OF THE IWW probably know of T-Bone Slim only as the author of "The Mysteries of a Hobo's Life," "The Popular Wobbly" and "I'm Too Old to be a Scab," songs in the current edition of the Little Red Song Book. Older fellow workers who knew him describe him as a "fantastic character" who could hold his listeners spellbound with his rambling stories, raucous word-play, and violent humor.

Very little is known of his life. Of Finnish descent, he was born (I have not been able to find in what year) Matt Valentine Huhta in Ashtabula, Ohio, and drowned in 1942 while working as a barge captain in New York.

\* \* \*

If what is meant by "literature" is that tasteless soup of words shoved down our throats in high school, then clearly T-Bone Slim has nothing to do with it. His spontaneous notations riddled with explosive humor and his savage plays on words transcend all bounds of bourgeois propriety. He'll never make it in the college textbooks. Neither could he be included in an anthology of "socialist realism." Nor can T-Bone be simply and conveniently classified as a writer in the "folk tradition."

T-Bone obviously works out of a different bag. "True humor," he once wrote, "is the carefree manhandling of extremes." Hilarious rebellion against the rottenness of this system reverberates throughout his writings.

It is sufficient to know that T-Bone Slim was above all else a Wobbly, that his whole life (in his peculiar way) served the cause of freedom. "Freedom," as he once said, "is what makes life worth fighting for."

We look upon *The Rebel Worker*, in part at least, as a continuation of the revolutionary spirit which animated the life and work of T-Bone Slim. The following pages contain a few selections from old T-Bone himself.

Franklin ROSEMONT

*(excerpts)*

# SELECTIONS FROM THE WORKS OF T-BONE SLIM

BUGS HIDE UNDER ROCKS, germs under fingernails, and still other parasites under elm trees on country estates—garbage scow passing down the Thames stunk out the House of Commons.

\* \* \*

All leadership is based on the presumption of dictatorship, the very thing that the boss exercises. Dictatorship, no matter how well intended, makes for tyranny on the one hand and slavery—or rebellion—on the other. The rebellion is inevitable, though deferred.

These millions must be freed not by a leader but by an organization formed in such a way that all hands can get leverage on the problem and lend the weight of their considerations to balance the scales of justice.

\* \* \*

Workers should not under any circumstances accept the designation "lower class," because it is not so, and acceptance doesn't make it so. No debate here is necessary. Suffice it to say: *Nothing is lower than the parasite class.*

\* \* \*

*Tear Gas*: The most effective agent used by employers to persuade their employees that the interests of capital and labor are identical.

\* \* \*

I don't believe there is necessity for a news censor. Editors have been very careful not to let any news get into the papers.

\* \* \*

Reputation catches no herring. Past is buried, Future isn't born, Present is here. There are two words that cover it: *Now* and *Action*.

\* \* \*

The getting of results is simple indeed. For instance, the shorter workday requires no extended remarks. Just go out later and come in earlier.

# REBEL WORKER 2

The Rebel Worker

Official Journal of the Chicago GRU Branch of the Industrial Workers of the World

NEW MADISON HOTEL

THE SALVATION ARMY    HARBOR LIGHT CENTER

Aug.-Sept. 1964 / *Cover by Tor Faegre* / 31 pages

*Speak boldly when fear or doubt keep others silent.*
—Margaret Fuller—

Tor Faegre's first-hand account of the first IWW strike in many years made this issue an instant hit. Readers also enjoyed Daniel Thompson's hilarious send-off of the "Starvation Army," adapted from a paper written for an Urban Society class taught by St. Clair Drake at Roosevelt University. We found the sabotage lyric by "Shorty" (*circa* 1910s) in Archie Green's monograph, "John Neuhaus: Wobbly Folklorist." *Rebel Worker* 2 was the easiest issue to read because it was the only one *not* mimeographed; a friend employed by the U.S. government (!) offset-printed it during his lunch-hour.

—F.R.

IWW Picketers, Michigan Blueberry Strike,1964:
Judy Green, Robert Green, Tor Faegre, Franklin Rosemont

Tor Faegre designed this "silent agitator"
(the first new IWW sticker in years)
for the Michigan farm-workers drive

# Editorial:
# ON THE JOB

ONCE UPON A TIME there was a labor movement in this country. Hundreds of thousands of working men and women carried red cards—IWW cards—and pulled strikes that hurled the capitalist class into some of the most troubled waters it has ever seen.

Today the term "labor movement" is used to describe those massive bureaucratic structures, the actual function of which is to "keep the workers in line" by tossing them occasional bread-and-butter gains. The class interests of the bureaucrats who "lead" these organizations are identical with those of the exploiting class, rather than the working class. It is thus absurd to speak of such groups as composing a "labor movement," for it neither represents the interests of workers, nor is it a "movement" since it obviously isn't moving—at least not forward: its bureaucracy has bound it irrevocably to the ruling class mechanism. If the official trade unions "move" at all, it's downhill.

This is not to say, however,that there has not been a labor movement in this country for the last twenty-five years. We will leave such deprecations of "workers' apathy," "wrong historical period," etc., to the middle-class socialist intellectuals who invent the terms and find the means to theorize about them endlessly. That there *has* been a labor movement, in the real sense of the term, and that it is growing into proportions which may presently make it into a greater force than it has been for many years, we can see by looking to the actions of rank-and-file workers, rather than their "leaders." Every wildcat strike, every rank-and-file slowdown, every "unofficial" protest (*i.e.* without the imprimatur of the labor bureaucrats) or other direct action by the workers themselves, in or out of the unions, testifies to the intrinsically revolutionary spirit of the working class. These sporadic skirmishes, challenging the labor bureaucrats and the employing class, are the chief indications of the class struggle in our day, and are steadily growing in number and in significance.

We in the IWW suffer no illusions about our own role in this struggle. We do not pretend to be a large organization, but we *are* growing, and our influence is growing considerably beyond our own ranks. Press coverage alone is adequate evidence of this resurgence. The year 1964 marks the first IWW strike in many years. IWW organizers are becoming increasingly active in industries in which the voice of militancy has too long been drowned out by choruses of defeat and resignation. Our role is not only to foster solidarity among our fellow workers in industry, but also to help them apply their own leverage and their own solutions to the problems that confront them every day at the point of production.

As a writer in *Solidarity*, the journal of our English friends and fellow workers, wrote a while back: "Real power lies in our hands. If we use it, we will win. And as long as we keep it there, we can't be sold out."

In the factories, in the fields, in the shops and in the streets: the IWW is on the job.

*(excerpts)*

## ORGANIZING BLUEBERRIES

"BLUEBERRIES ARE WHAT TIDE YOU OVER between cherries and apples. You pick them because you got to, and you got no money." A fruit tramp, as he called himself, from Benton Harbor, Michigan told me this, but I was heading back to Chicago then and I couldn't have cared less....

Two weeks later, with three more Wobblies, I (we) returned to Michigan and discovered the great Blueberry Conspiracy was real. The blueberries don't just "tide you over"—they are a specially rigged economic trap. Workers come up from the south and pick strawberries, blackcaps (black raspberries) and cherries in early July. Then when the blackcaps are through and cherry pickers are allowed to pick only a few hours a day because of the glutted market, pickers turn to blueberries as a last resort. If they can last through blueberries, they can make good money again picking apples. In blackcaps I often made twelve dollars a day; in blueberries I couldn't make six. And this was a ten-hour day.

We entered the Michigan blueberry fields to fathom the extent of wage-worker discontent in agriculture, and to see how this discontent might be organized. We started with little enthusiasm, having been told all too frequently of the impossibility of organizing agricultural workers. "They move around too much...they don't understand unions." The A.F. of L., I was told, spent $100,000 in an agricultural organizing campaign and gave up. On the other hand, the old I.W.W.–A.W.I.U. #400 had organized the most unorganized workers in the grain belt. Well, we would see....

Discontent was rife. Except for a few workers who commented on "how nice this farmer is to work for," most were fed up with the whole deal. Just about every day we saw or heard of a "strike in detail," with a discouraged family leaving, usually not because of a better job elsewhere, but because they were living on savings from working for fifty cents an hour. Everyone was discouraged, but most had no choice but to stay.

The foreman told us that the berries would get better. We were encouraged. A veteran picker told us how they dropped the price down when they got better. "Wouldn't you know it," a picker commented, "you start to get ahead and they take it away from you."

Hodgman's Blueberry Farm, where we started to work, was a small farm—too small for our purposes, we decided, and prepared to get our pay and leave. Then on Friday night one of us, Bob Green, talked with a couple of class-conscious Arkansas boys who, before he knew it, declared that they would strike with us. From then on, around the cabins at night, and in the rows by day, we cautiously felt out the strike potential of each picker.

By Monday we were sure we had all but two families even though we didn't have a commitment from everyone. We were trying to figure out the best time to strike when a large family from Florida announced they wouldn't wait for a strike, but were leaving for home they next morning. That decided it; we would strike the next day.

Our questions to fellow workers were now bolder. "We're walking out. Will you come with us?" By night we counted five families who would strike or just leave, and three who were staying.

The next day we worked for an hour. Then each of us turned in his berries, had his card punched, and slipped it into his pocket. Our last striker joined us from his picking machine detail and we walked together towards camp.

"What seems to be the trouble?" we were asked by a frightened farmer.

"Can't make nothing picking these berries. We want higher wages—and showers."

"Well, you can go elsewhere then."

"Everybody tells us that, but they all pay the same. We're staying here on strike."

We argued further, but our "farmer-friend" was not willing to negotiate. He turned and started to walk away saying, "I'll pick them myself if I have to; now clear out of here."

Back at camp we packed and waited for the police. The fearsome police turned out to be a genial deputy sheriff who listened sympathetically to our tale of woe and then told us how he had been a union man since 1914, and was proud of it. Our deputy sheriff left, but the terrible state trooper arrived a minute later. He strolled on the scene with wrap-around sunglasses and cigarette holder, and after a detailed explanation of how and why he must carry out his obligations, he announced: "It's time for you to depart." So we left for Grand Junction to plan our next strategy.

Our fellow strikers, we found, were in bad financial shape, so they decided to work at a farm down the road for a couple of days and then return to picket with us. We left to make signs and work on a leaflet.

Just before dawn we returned and crept through each farm in the dark dropping a strike proclamation at the doorstep of each picker's cabin at every farm in the area. At seven we returned for our second attack with signs: FARM WORKERS ON STRIKE! JOIN THE IWW!

On Hodgman's farm the three remaining families went dutifully to work. But on an adjoining farm the workers were not returning to work but stood clustered about the camp watching us. The owner of this farm walked up to us. Her workers, she said, were afraid that if they returned to work we would "slash their tires and beat them up." She asked us to sign an agreement that her workers would not be injured and said that she would pay them ten cents a pint (they were getting nine cents) and promised to build a shower. We talked to the workers in her camp, explaining the situation at Hodgman's. We assured them that we intended no violence toward them or anyone, that we were trying to build a union of agricultural workers.

Unfortunately, our next-door neighbor did not keep her agreement, but lowered the price back to nine cents. We had no way to hold her to this, so we had to be content with her promise of a shower. It must also be noted that her price of nine cents was a penny more than we were paid at Hodgman's, her berries were thicker, and her camp was better (stoves and refrigerators in the cabins at no cost to the pickers).

The second day of the strike we paid a visit to our fellow strikers. We found them enthusiastic to hear how we fared. But in very short order we were surrounded by hostile faces and voices which declared that "You're not going to make us strike. We like it here. Why don't you stay at your own camp?" We left, posthaste, after receiving a few well-placed kicks. When we drove by the next day we saw that our friends' cars were gone. We weren't able to find them again.

It was amazing, the mystique our strike exercised in the minds of some workers. One camp was fearful that we would beat them up; another camp would beat *us* up if we "made them strike."

On Saturday, Fred Thompson and Jack Sheridan arrived from IWW headquarters in Chicago and agreed to assist us in union negotiations. They, together with Bob Green, talked with the Hodgmans. A very vindictive Mrs. Hodgman referred to the pickers as "filthy" and "slimy," and stated that if a shower were built the pickers would tear it down. A familiar tune, no? She then called over some of her loyal workers (we were in the habit of calling them scabs and scissorbills, however) and Sheridan had the chance to ask them a few questions:

"Do you want higher wages?"

"No."

"Showers?"

"No."

"Toilet paper?"

"No, we like it here."

At the end of the week we called a strategic withdrawal (never defeat!) and returned to Chicago to plan further assaults.

What did we achieve? At Hodgman's the only material progress we could see was garbage-can covers, put in after a visit (provoked by our picket lines) of a state employment commissioner. Next door we obtained a guarantee of showers. But more important, while picketing we talked with many sympathetic and interested workers—many more were friendly than antagonistic. A few actually took out red cards. Others put Wobbly Agricultural Workers stickers on the front windshields of their cars.

We had a strike in an area and an industry in which strikes are almost unheard of. The newspaper coverage, although hardly unbiased, was big, and the biggest headline—"PICKETS NOT UNION SENT"—was obviously designed to allay the fears of farmers.

Most importantly, we discovered that agricultural workers will respond to the call for an agricultural union and with many more IWW organizers in the field next summer, we should be prepared to strike to win.

Torvald FAEGRE

# KITTEN IN THE WHEAT

*A sab-cat and a Wobbly band,*
*A rebel song or two,*
*And then we'll show the parasites*
*Just what the cat can do.*

*From early spring till late in fall*
*We toil that men may eat*
*And "All for one and one for all"*
*Sing Wobblies in the wheat.*

*And have you fixt the where and when*
*That we must slave and die?*
*Here's fifty thousand honest men*
*Shall know the reason why.*

*The sab-cat purred and twitched its tail,*
*As happy as could be.*
*They'd better not throw Wobs in jail*
*And leave the kitten free.*

*The sab-cat purred and twitched its tail*
*And winked the other way.*
*Our boys will never rot in jail*
*Or else the plutes will pay.*

SHORTY

# THOUGHTS ON BUREAUCRACY

ONE OF THE GREATEST PROBLEMS facing the revolutionary movement today is that of bureaucracy. What is it? Is it a rootless "thing," floating between the working class and their rulers? Is it a "new class"? No other issue more clearly shows up the bankruptcy in ideas of the traditional "left" than its inability seriously to grapple with this problem.

The traditional "left" is incapable of looking at reality as it is, of analysing it here and now. Instead it gazes at society from the standpoint of political doctrines expounded a century ago, doctrines in many cases relating to very different social conditions and class alignments.

The contributions of Marx, Lenin, Trotsky and other "giants" of the past have been reduced to "sacred scriptures." They are quoted as "divine authority" on the assumption that "nothing has changed." The term "revisionist" has become a term of abuse. That the "giants" themselves constantly revised their ideas in the face of the constantly developing experience is conveniently forgotten.

This "religious" attitude to the past is a complete rejection of dialectical thinking. With such tram-lines firmly laid in their brains it is little wonder that so many self-styled revolutionaries fail to see that Russia today, for instance, is as much a class society as any Western country.

\* \* \*

The traditionalists, for instance, are all obsessed with the legal status of property, as if this were the fundamental thing. They fail to see that the bureaucracy in Russia has assumed the role of ruling class because it dominates production, manages it in its own interests and decides, through the exclusive control of the State, all about the distribution of the social product. State capitalism hadn't developed in Marx's day. His doctrines must be brought up to date in this respect.

Marx's dream of state ownership, centralised[1] and rapidly increasing productive forces, has been fulfilled *with a vengeance* in Russia today. But is this socialism? The Russian workers are never consulted in the important, everyday decisions that concern them most: hours or tempo of work, wages, consumption and leisure. They were never consulted about the resumption of nuclear tests (any more than ordinary people in the West were). Sometimes they are not even informed of such facts. And in the arts, what the Party says, goes.

Marx defines capitalism as a society based on commodity production and wage labour and in which "surplus value" is extracted from the workers. Part of this surplus value goes to capitalisation and part goes to the unproductive consumption of the rulers themselves. But many "marxists" fail to see that from this standpoint the Russian worker is exploited just as much, if not more, than his American counterpart.

The mere assertion that the State is "owned" by the workers has about as much relevance to the Russian worker as the fact that British Railways are "publicly owned" has for the rank-and-file member of the NUR. *The abolition of private ownership is clearly not enough.* Private ownership is only one "legal form" for the power of the ruling class. The ruling class has certainly perceived this. It is high time the revolutionaries did too.

The more far-sighted sections of the ruling class are beginning to realize that only by introducing State ownership can they effectively rationalize their economics, overcome the old type of economic difficulties, and thus maintain their rule.[2]

At the same time the rulers have learned that they *need* the Labour bureaucrats to discipline the workers, to tie them ever more closely to the job. They need the traditional unions as an outlet for grievances. In parallel with the increased State intervention in the economy, the Labour leaders and the unions have become increasingly integrated into the political structure of capitalism.

For the worker, these developments have meant increasing domination from above, both in work and in leisure. More and more the employer tries to fashion his employees along the lines so accurately depicted by Charlie Chaplin in *Modern Times.*

* * *

Many other "doctrines," unquestioningly accepted by the "left" today, are equally contradictory. For instance, some people pay lip service to the idea that "the liberation of the working class can be achieved only by the working class itself." But the same people act and speak as if the working class is an unintelligent herd, incapable of achieving socialism without an "elitist" party, "steeled in struggle," "disciplined," "centrally controlled," a party which would lead the class to revolutionize society by capturing political power.

Socialism to us means the maximum freedom for the worker in all his activities. It is the very opposite of the massive bureaucratic control which has developed on both sides of the Iron Curtain. The germ of socialism, *i.e.* maximum participation of the workers themselves, existed in the Paris Commune of 1871, in the Soviets or Workers' Councils of 1905 and 1917, in Spain in 1936 and 1937, and for a few weeks in Budapest in 1956. What has happened to that germ?

Millions of words have been written about the "degeneration" of the October Revolution and of the Bolshevik Party. The writers invariably miss the crucial point, namely that the seeds of the degeneration lay in the dual (and typically capitalist) conceptions of an elitist party and of the authoritarian management of industry. These ideas—or rather this mentality—was to govern all decisions on political and economic questions.

The elitist theory finds its highest expression in the works of Lenin. In *What Is To Be Done*, written in 1902, he argues that the the working class is incapable of independently developing "socialist consciousness," which has therefore to be injected from outside. "Socialist consciousness," he wrote, "arose quite independently of the spontaneous growth of the working class movement. It arose as a natural and inevitable development of ideas among the revolutionary socialist intelligentsia."[3]

From here it is a logical step to the overall conception of the ignorant herd of workers on the one hand, and the leading "cadre" of intellectuals on the other. The "cadre" do all the "thinking." The workers "test" the resultant "theories" in their everyday struggles with the boss. The division of labour between manual and intellectual, which capitalism developed, has now affected the ranks of the would-be "revolutionaries." Here is the ideological justification for bureaucratic politics.

Once these premises are accepted it matters little how opponents are fought, so long as workers "believe" the facts given them. In describing how one should deal with opposing factions (*i.e.* members of the same party) Lenin advocated "the spreading among the masses of hatred, aversion and contempt for the opponents." "The limits of the struggle based on a split are not Party limits, but general political limits, or rather general civil limits, the limits set by criminal law and nothing else." Modern "Leninists"[4] certainly seem to have learnt this part of the message!

In the field of production, this philosophy found expression in the doctrine of "one-man management," the militarization of labour and the determination to prevent the rank-and-file bodies from taking over the factories. It was presumed, in a typically bureaucratic way, that only those possessing technical knowledge were entitled to impose decisions concerning production. "In the interests of socialism, the revolution demands," Lenin wrote as early as 1918, "that the masses *unquestionably obey the single will* of the leaders of the labour process." Writing in *Terrorism and Communism*, Trotsky echoed: "The unions should discipline the workers and teach them to place the interests of production above their own needs and demands." Trotsky continued: "That free labour is more productive than compulsory labour is quite true when it refers to the period of transition from feudal to bourgeois society. But one needs to be a liberal to make that truth permanent and to transfer its application to the period of transition from the bourgeois to the socialist order."

These quotations show the contemptuous attitude held by the Bolshevik "vanguard" for the working class. It was to have disastrous results. It led for example to the bloody suppression of the Kronstadt mutiny in 1921, when workers demanded that the power stolen from the Soviets by the Bolshevik Party be returned to them. The mutineers were massacred by the Bolsheviks. Significantly, both Lenin and Trotsky publicly claimed that it was a counter-revolutionary rebellion, led by Tsarist officers. They both knew this to be a lie, but truth did not matter. Political expediency did.

The culmination of these doctrines was the introduction of completely capitalist methods into Russian production: speed-ups, piece-work, unpaid "voluntary" overtime, permanent labour control, time and motion study, and the open advocacy of a drive for "American efficiency." Engels could have been foreseeing modern Russia when he wrote: "The modern State, no matter what its form, is essentially a capitalist machine, the State of the capitalists, the ideal personification of the total national capital. The more it proceeds to the taking over of productive forces, the more does it actually become the national capitalist, the more citizens does it exploit. The workers remain wage workers, proletarians. The capitalist relation is not done away with. It is rather brought to a head."[5]

* * *

"Being determines consciousness" is an oft-quoted marxist truism. Related to a bureaucrat it means that any man possessing power over others cannot fail but to see society through the eyes of a master. So long as political power exists, class society will exist. So long as a specific social stratum manages production, the ruler and ruled relationship will persist. The political power held by Lenin and his elite over the rank and file of the pre-revolutionary Bolshevik Party was simply transformed, by the October Revolution, into State power. The Party appointed the industrial managers. It opposed workers' management of production. Its members took up key positions in the State apparatus. The Party built a society in its own image.

The trade union and Labour bureaucrat in this country plays the same role as his Russian counterpart. His prime concern is to maintain himself. This he has no difficulty to do as he is an essential cog in the whole edifice of bureaucratic capitalism. Socialism and workers' power would mean his extinction.

It is no accident that trade union and Labour bureaucrats, of every political colouring, instinctively and inevitably *must* oppose any form of rank and file activity. The bureaucracies are fully integrated into the structure of capitalism. Independent action by the working class is *the greatest* threat to their existence. To talk, therefore, of these leaders "selling out" the membership is absurd. There is no other way in which they could act. They differ with one another only in respect to the kind of class society they would choose: the Western, based to an ever-diminishing degree on private ownership, or the Russian brand, organized through total State ownership.

As capitalism develops, the State bureaucracy "takes over" managerial functions to an increasing degree until it becomes the ruling class. The economic basis for this new bureaucracy is the enormous concentration of capital and power and the increasing intervention of the State in all economic transactions, and finally in every aspect of social life. The old "property-owning bourgeoisie," which characterized the capitalism of the days of Marx, is dying together with the era of laissez-faire. It now has to share its power with the new bureaucracy. It will eventually be eliminated altogether, either gradually and piecemeal (as in the West) or suddenly, as the result of a violent struggle (as in Russia and China). In this respect the only difference between East and West is that the former has already achieved total centralization in the hands of the State, while in the West the process still continues. It is a quantitative difference...not one of quality.

In their attitude to rank and file ("unofficial") activity, the organizations of the "left" reveal most clearly their bureaucratic make-up. The great Frank Foulkes, then "Communist" President of the ETU, could say to the power workers (November 14, 1960) that "Unofficial bodies are not in the best interests of the industry." The Stalinist weekly *World News* devoted a major article, in May 1958, to attacking the "unofficial" attempts of sections of the London busmen to extend their strike. Even the ultra "r-r-revolutionary" S.L.L. declares its policy in all strikes is to make them official.[6] This is a permanent call for workers to leave control of the disputes in the hands of the bureaucrats. It goes hand in hand of course with calls for "better leadership" (*i.e.* themselves).

Experience has shown that movements relying on leaders can achieve nothing of fundamental benefit to the working class. Bureaucratic parties can only build bureaucratic societies. Socialism cannot be built with capitalist tools. The only saviour of the working class must be the working class itself—a statement that must be taken in its most literal sense.

Bob POTTER

NOTES

1. "...to wrest, by degrees, all capital from the bourgoisie, to centralise all instruments of production in the hands of the State, *i.e.* of proletariat organized as ruling class; and to increase the total productive forces as rapidly as possible." *Manifesto of the Communist Party*, Foreign Languages Publishing House edition, Moscow 1957, p. 85.

2. Bismarck and Churchill were advocates, in their time, of nationalisation. Even the Nazis put forward the following economic demand, in 1923: "We demand the abolition of unearned incomes and the abolition of the thraldom of interest. We demand the nationalisation of all industrial trusts." *History of Nazi Germany*, Pelican Books, p. 199.

3. *What Is To Be Done*, Foreign Languages Publishing House edition, p. 51.

4. Lenin, *Selected Works*, Vol. III, Lawrence & Wishart, pp. 493 and 494.

5. F. Engels, *Socialism: Utopian and Scientific*, Foreign Languages Publishing House edition, Moscow 1954, pp. 105–106.

6. Gerry Healy, letter to *The Guardian*, October 26, 1961.

From London *Solidarity,* 1963

# STARVATION ARMY 1964

AND WHO DOES JESUS SAVE? The old gray head, the lame, the blind, the young man on the bum, the wino, the Negro, the Puerto Rican, the poor white, the Indian, the Mexican, the Oriental, the one who speaks with an "old country" tongue, the homeless, the jobless, the hungry, the sick, poverty's children, that great American army of extraneous men, those who live mass lives of quiet desperation. *Jesus! Jesus! Jesus! Sweetest name I know!* Now clap your hands for God's Glory and *Make a joyful noise unto the Lord!* This is the Way, the Truth and the Light on the dark side of the American Dream. Are you poor and hungry? Is your life a failure? Then be a success, feasting on the riches of the grave of Jesus. Services every night at seven. The Harbor Light Center of the Salvation Army. Visitors Welcome.

Already well before seven p.m. over 200 men have assembled in the big chapel, while downstairs in the basement another 100 sit waiting

110

for the word of God to come from the loudspeaker hung in the corner. The service begins but the sea of voices drowns it out. I offer my seat, one of two together, to some late-comers. I want to get up front in order to hear better. There's an empty seat in the very front row. I sit down before a life-sized wooden cross, turned on its side and used as a hat rack by my neighbor on my left. On my right an old man sits reading his newspaper: "Daley Lauds LBJ War on Poverty."

A sign on the door: "Your life is but a little while. Do your job with a smile. Remember the Lord. He remembers you." Cripples on crutches are coming in late. They're singing hymns upstairs now.

The Brigadier is now going into his sermon. The Book of Daniel. The handwriting on the wall. The King shook in fear. We all act afraid in tight situations. Especially when we don't or won't listen to God. We must take His warnings and turn from our wickedness to Him before it's too late. The handwriting is on the wall etc., etc. He reaches eloquent heights of pleading. I'm reminded of Billy Graham, and like Billy, the Brigadier reminds us that this is our hour of decision, and that a collection will be taken up. He's asking us to come forward and make our decisions for Christ.

Someone gets up and I follow him into the big chapel. I sit down in the back row but an attendant tells me I have to keep moving. I find myself up front with about 12 others. We're standing before a large stage. Its curtain is drawn. Below there are a few rows of makeshift wooden benches. We kneel down, fold our hands in prayer and put them on the benches. Suddenly a group of men come down from the stage. They kneel down before us and put their hands on ours. I get Bob, a graying Negro of about 45. I know his name is Bob because it says so on his recently laundered bowling shirt. He asks me what my problems are. I tell him I just sort of got caught up in the current. No, I don't drink. He seems a little bewildered. Finally, he asks me to join him in prayer.

He then rattles off the routine I'm to follow. He gives me a slip of paper which he says entitles me to a meal. I ask a man next to me about the slip of paper. He says it's good for the six-o'clock meal. "You don't have to wait in line with the others—just come right in." "It's your press card," a man behind me jokes. I ask them about their decisions for Christ, whether it has any meaning in their lives. "We told you, you don't have to wait in line for breakfast."

I ask what they serve.

"You know, the same old shit: mush, sweet-rolls, milk."

"Yeah," another man joins in. "The same old shit."

We march downstairs. Half of the chapel is already there, in this large dining hall. There are about five rows of eight long tables. Each man is almost shoulder to shoulder and standing, since there are no seats. There's a bowl of vegetable soup, which I gobble up. I haven't eaten all day. I break the cheese in half and taste a small piece. I don't like it. The bread and pastry look and feel stale. I don't try them. I drink the milk. It's powdered.

I decide the best thing to do is wait in the bar across the street. I enter and sit next to an old Negro. I ask him if he had attended the service. No, he hadn't been there in over a month. I show him my slip of paper. Yes, he knows, he's been saved lots of times. We exchange information about our lives, our road experiences. He thinks Kansas City and Indianapolis are the best for missions. He's been hoboing since '28. He says he's been in a mission in every big city in the United States except Seattle. He never hitchhikes. He always rides the freights.

He tells me about the mission situation in Chicago. "It's too late to get put up now—you have to be there lined up already in the afternoon." I tell him I have a friend here I'm trying to get in touch with by phone. He tells me he's working now (washing cars) and he's going to eat now. "If you haven't reached your friend and you're still here when I get back, I'll give you forty cents for a hotel room. The same hotel I stay at."

I thank him and he leaves. I wait a while, then leave too. I pass another mission. It has a neon sign saying *Jesus Saves* and another saying "Please Stay Out of the Doorway."

When I cross the street and head toward the loop, a *Wall Street Journal* truck makes a sharp turn around the corner.

Daniel R THOMPSON

*(slightly abridged)*

# LETTERS

*The Rebel Worker* is Sure Damn Good. I bought 3 copies of it at IWW Hall here...

Guy B. ASKEW
(Skidroad Slim)
Seattle, Washington

I visited General Hdqrts. in February and talked to Carl Keller for some time about the Movement and the plight of migratory French-Canadian potato workers in Northern Maine.... I am an anarchist 1st, last and always; but I see the syndicalism of the IWW as one of the most practical ways of implementing anarchism. Direct action is the *only* action (I hate to sound doctrinaire, but...)

Bruce ELWELL<br>Westbrook, Maine

Received and enjoyed reading the first issue of your well-edited rebellious *Rebel Worker*. Hope we can have another issue soon. With my best wishes and thanks I enclose $1 to help meet the expenses that it took to give birth to this baby.

Abraham WUORI<br>Duluth, Minnesota

Here's a bit for your new IWW mag, *The Rebel Worker*. Needless to say, "I hope you make a great go if it."

George SLAVCHUK<br>(Syndicalist George)<br>Youngstown, Ohio

I was pleased to see your magazine *The Rebel Worker*, but I was more impressed by the organizational work you are doing....Would you send me information about the Agricultural Workers Organizing Committee of the IWW?

Hyatt BACHE<br>Kensington, Maryland

The four-hour day, four-day week proposal of the IWW...would open up countless opportunities for presently unemployed workers to directly control their destinies at the point of production. The four-hour-day, four-day week slogan is as applicable today as in the 30's; I think it should be revived and propagated and implemented by the workers today. Let's not wait for the tomorrows of the politicians.

Bernard MARSZALEK<br>Chicago, Illinois

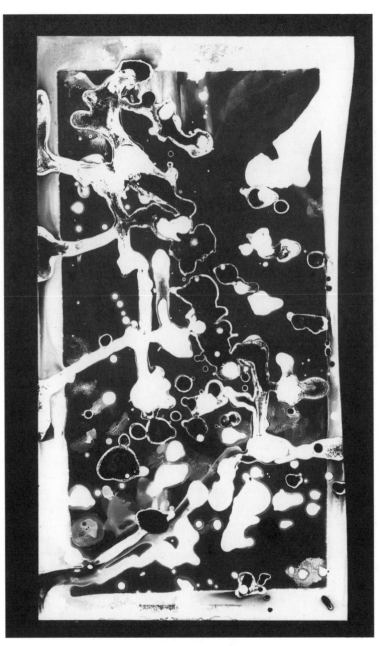

Penelope Rosemont:
*Zuni Tunes*
(Alchemigram, 1967)

# REBEL WORKER 3

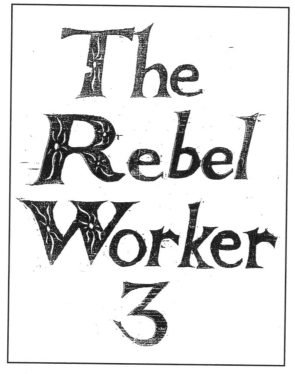

March 1965 / *Cover by Tor Faegre* / 37 pages

*The storms of youth precede brilliant days.*
—Lautréamont, *Poésies*—

With this "Young Workers" issue *The Rebel Worker* really hit its stride. The largest yet, it contained nine original articles, two reprints, and an original short story by the 10-year-old son of one of Tor's pacifist friends. The striking cover was an original woodblock, *printed* (not mimeo'd) in red and black. This issue also marks a deepening of our overall perspective: with its on-the-spot report of the 1964 Harlem rebellion and a survey of emerging "youth revolt," the *Rebel Worker* critique—not only of work but of "everyday life"—was moving ahead at full speed.

—F.R.

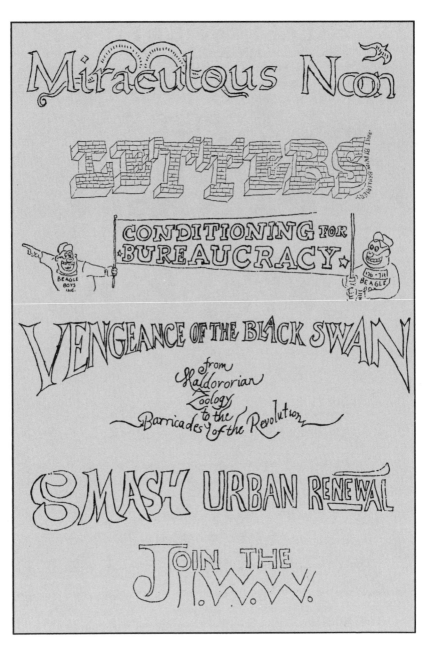

At a time when most "left" publications were visually boring,
Tor Faegre's inspired calligraphy did much to give
*The Rebel Worker* a distinctive sparkle

# THE UNFREE CHILD

IT MAY BE NO EXAGGERATION to say that all children in our civilization are born in a life-disapproving atmosphere. The timetable feeding advocates are basically anti-pleasure. They want the child to be disciplined in feeding because non-time-table feeding suggests orgastic pleasure at the breast. The nutriment argument is usually a rationalization; the deep motive is to mold the child into a disciplined creature who will put duty before pleasure.

One of the big tasks of today and tomorrow is the investigation of repressed sexual energy and its relation to human sickness. One day humanity may trace all its miseries, its hates and its diseases to its particular form of civilization that is essentially anti-life. If rigid character training makes rigid human bodies—cramped and confined instead of being alive and pulsating—it seems logical to conclude that the same rigid deadness will prohibit the pulsation in every human organ necessary to life.

Civilization is sick and unhappy, and I claim that the root of it all is the unfree family. Children are deadened by all the forces of reaction and hate, deadened from their cradle days. They are trained to say *no* to life because their young lives are one long no. Don't make a noise; don't masturbate; don't lie; don't steal.

They are taught to say *yes* to all that is negative in life. Respect the old; respect religion; respect the schoolmaster; respect the law of the fathers. Don't question anything—just obey.

The tragedy is that man, who holds his family in bondage, is and must be a slave himself—for in a prison the jailer also is confined. Man's slavery is his slavery to hate: he suppresses his family, and in doing so he suppresses his own life. He has to set up courts and prisons to punish the victims of his suppression. Enslaved woman must give her son to the wars that man calls defensive wars, patriotic wars, wars to save democracy, wars to end wars.

There is a great amount of good fellowship and love in humanity, and it is my firm belief that new generations that have not been warped in babyhood will live at peace with each other—that is, if the haters of today do not destroy the world before these new generations have time to take control.

The fight is an unequal one, for the haters control education, religion, the law, the armies, and the vile prisons. Only a handful of educators strive to allow the good in all children to grow in freedom. The vast majority of children are being molded by anti-life supporters with their hateful system of punishments.

It is a race between the believers in deadness and the believers in life. And no man dare remain neutral: that will mean death. The death side gives us the problem child; the life side will give us the healthy child.

A. S. NEILL

(From *Summerhill: A Radical Approach to Child-Rearing* (1960)

# THE VICTIMS OF THE BENEFACTORS
# OF THE POOR

HAVE YOU EVER BOUGHT A NEWSPAPER from a ten-year-old on a school day? Have you wondered why he is working? After all, there are laws prohibiting work for kids under 16 during school hours. The fact is that it is good economics for the newspaper to hire kids, and that fact determines child employment as much as any law or regulation.

Child-labor was an invention of the industrial revolution. As hand labor was replaced by machine production, children from six years and up provided a cheap and plentiful labor supply. As a result, the almshouses and jails were emptied of paupers and orphans. The employers advertised themselves as benefactors of the poor.

At the turn of the century the first laws began to be enacted to prohibit the more brutal labor practices, and at the same time, compulsory education became a nationwide law. Such laws continued to eliminate the worst ills—work at very early ages, sweatshop conditions, and work in hazardous occupations—but the effect was *not* a continuing decline in child labor.

The number of employed youth has always reflected the general labor market more than the law (economics precedes jurisprudence). The forced unemployment of the depression decreased the young labor force and increased school attendance. World War II greatly revived the employment of youth, which reached a peak in 1945 of 3

118

million kids from 14 to 17 working full- or part-time. After the war there was a steady decline which continues today.

The supposed problem of the young worker today is the lack of a job, not his exploitation by the boss. The excitement today is over the school dropout, not the young worker. This means that the on-the-job situation for youth is largely ignored. And because the bosses have the choice of many young workers, they can and do fix wages and conditions to their own liking.

The real problem with the young worker is that he has no recourse to action, while on the job he is often paid the lowest wages of any worker today. His only "choice" is to quit and take another job if there is one, or no job which is more often the case. He has no union to represent him. He is a victim of the benefactors of the poor.

Torvald FAEGRE

# EGYPTIAN TROUBLE:
## A Short Story

ONE DAY JOHN SKALACE GOT AN AIRPLANE TICKET to Egypt. He had been planning to go there for a long time. His brother, Tom, a scientist, wanted him to stay and help him in his work.

Finally the time came for him to go. The trip would take four days. When the plane left there was a hurricane blowing up. The trip was rough and they almost crashed twice.

They landed in a half-deserted area. All the people went to a city near there. Except for John. He stayed. He wanted it to be a surprise to Tom, who thought he was taking a vacation. He was on an expedition.

Finally he was alone. All alone. Except for one, who wasn't discovered yet. The thing that was not discovered was something that was terrorizing Egypt. Tom, his brother didn't know about the thing.

The thing was indescribable. It was ugly and terrible looking.

One day John was working, doing some research, when all of the sudden he heard this noise. It was getting closer and closer, and A—!

119

Yes, he was dead. Well at least we thought so.

When his brother Tom heard this, he immediately went to Egypt. Naturally he wasn't alone.

When they got there they found a note which he had written just before he was killed. Here's what it said:

> Dear Tom,
>
> *I have found the most ugly and devious "Thing" the world has ever known. Right now there is something coming. The earth is shaking like mad—The Thing*

When Tom and the police found this they knew he was dead. "But wait!" Tom said. The plane went down in the hurricane. Then out of nowhere, came John. Yes, it *was* John. John said he didn't have much time to live. He said if we don't stop testing bombs we would.... He was dead before he could finish, said Tom. Now we might end the world, he said.

Back home they found John's body at the bottom of the sea. They buried him before Tom got back.

One day Tom got permission to dig up his grave. When he did, he found him wrapped as a mummy.

Murray STEIB (age 10)

# HARLEM JOURNAL, OR
# HOMAGE TO PANDEMONIA

*Sunday July 19, 1964*

VISITING FRIENDS. Learned that "riots" had broken out in Harlem the previous night. Phoned CORE to see if they were doing anything about it. Informed, "There's a riot going on. That ought to be enough activity." Decided to go up and look around anyway. Live only 10 blocks away.

*11:00 p.m.*: Crossed 110th St. on 8th Ave. walking north into Harlem. Area strangely dark—resembled blackouts during war. Few pedestrians about, but lots of police cars and fire engines whipping around, sirens screaming. Progressed north. Area got ominously quiet …eerie. No police in evidence, streets dark and deserted, but bars going full swing on inside. Entered fish and chips place and ordered shrimp. Informed, "There's none left." Ordered fish. "Just sold the last order."

Went into bar, ordered beer. Received a few quizzical glances but most patrons didn't notice me at all. Bartender told me a gentleman wanted to buy me a drink. Turned out to be someone who thought he knew me. Couldn't place him but joined his party. Was asked: 1. What's your solution? 2. Are you a white liberal? Answered: 1. Didn't have any solution. 2. Didn't come up here to be insulted.

Left bar after a while and joined crowd of about 10 at corner of 125th St. Helped glare at police, visible for first time in large clusters. 125th St. blocked off by police barriers, though crosstown buses being allowed through along with police cars and ambulances. Whole block empty except for cops, mostly wearing aluminum helmets. (Usually they wear these only while turning off fire hydrants during the summer as kids throw beer cans at them for spoiling their fun.)

Ordered to move on by cop. Asked if could walk northward (barricades confusing). Was told yes. Went north a block or so, then started back meeting friends from bar. At 125th St. stepped inside barricades (had seen others do it) and phoned home from sidewalk phone booth.

Walked homeward on 8th Ave., emerging south of 110th St. with great relief. Immediately encountered fight, however; two Negroes— a cab driver and passenger. Two white cops interceding rather ineffectually. Nearby Negro onlooker commented, "Man, them cops can't even fight." Slipped in plug for non-violence; point out that the cops would have been better off interceding without nightsticks in their hands. Weapons are often an impediment—especially if accompanied by humane feelings or reluctance. Started discussing race problem, but condemned both Abraham Lincoln and recent Civil Rights Bill as equal farces, so middle-aged drunk took a swing at me. ("Son of a bitch, you don't want my people to ever have nothing.") Black Muslim warded him off and we continued discussion for an hour. Arrived home (100th St.) about 2:00 a.m.

*Monday July 20, 1964*

Left work in Bronx at 9:00 p.m., furious that police could just take over a whole section of city like Nazi Storm Troopers. They were in the wrong—the kid didn't shoot the cop. Where was CORE?? Why wasn't anybody protesting?

Left subway at 135th St. and Lenox Ave.—pretty much the same scene as previous night, except more people about. Decided to walk south on Lenox Ave. if allowed—police barricades were baffling. Asked fellow pedestrian. He didn't know either, though "swear to God" he'd tell me if he did. Started south tentatively—wasn't stopped— joined devout one. Was harangued with complications of his love life after cavalier disposal of racial crisis. ("Don't know nothing at all about that shit out there.") Selected a bar—companion wouldn't recommend one lest he be suspected of complicity "if everything wasn't just right." Atmosphere much colder than bar of previous evening, bartender barely civil—resented being kidded about policeman's nightstick he was armed with. Companion mentioned unlikelihood of a 15-year-old boy's being able to "whip the ass" of a grown man like Gilligan—evidently he did know something about "that shit out there" despite earlier disclaimer.

Bar patrons glaring out window at cops lining curbstone glaring in. Behemoth approached us, eyed first me then my 1 1/4" pin. ("Blood Brother" over a black and white handshake.) Told him handshake was a SNCC symbol. He'd never heard of SNCC, but ceded my right to wear it if I believed in it. He went away but returned a while later with a bar stool for me to sit on.

Left bar and continued south, feeling effect of beers on empty stomach. Companion explained that if he returned to bar now he'd probably get beaten up for having brought me in. Also, we might well "get our asses whipped right now" for walking down the street together. Pointed out that as a pacifist, wasn't taking my hands out of my pockets come what may. Little consolation to him.

Separated at 125th St. and ordered fish and chips at sidewalk counter. Teenager inside with head all bandaged. He'd arrived from Puerto Rico the day before and come to visit counterman, a former next-door neighbor. Waiting for a bus across the street he had encountered "law and order"—two cops came over and bludgeoned him on suspicion. Berserk cop had tried to club him, but missed, while he was in the act of loading another police victim into a stretcher.

Cops lined curbstone at ten-foot intervals, radiating hatred. Made it difficult to eat fish with *savoir faire*. Young, very conservatively dressed fellow walked by police line. Carried a larger poster with remarkable self-assurance: "Wanted For Murder/Gilligan, the Cop…". One-legged panhandler appeared—bought him some pizza. In front of building next door drunk with bandage—swathed head was heckling police.

Resumed course down Lenox Ave. acquiring Puerto Rican lady

with three infants. Walked them to 116th St. where she mooched a quarter in parting. Arrived home about 1:00 a.m.

Determined to continue going into Harlem, though not quite sure why. Walked up 8th Ave. about 11:00 p.m. Block after block deserted, still no street lights. Area seemed much more tense somehow.

Police barricades gone from 125th St. but whole block empty nevertheless, except for some teenage boys and girls in a doorway midway down. Police only at corners in clusters. Walked down 125th St. past teenagers, overhearing: "He wouldn't have come up here if the cops weren't here," (True.) and "He wouldn't dare walk down (unintelligible) street." Didn't stop. Wanted to locate CORE whose office used to be around corner in Hotel Teresa on 7th Ave. Got new address there, and turned back into 125th St. passing helmeted white news photographer, alone and unhappy in doorway.

Girl and three escorts, one wearing "Freedom Now—CORE" pin, walked right by without seeing me. Hailed them. Bizarre exchange: What are you doing here?...James Farmer announced on radio that all white civil rights workers should stay out of Harlem because white faces might inflame Negroes...Get out quick before there's one dead CORE sympathizer...Ask nearest cop (!!!) to put me safely on bus. *Exeunt* CORE.

Decided to talk to teenagers and possibly offer to walk down street they'd mentioned linking arms with them. Never got there. Police cars careened by, sirens wailing. Older group appeared from nowhere, one guy leaping out into street screaming "Mother Fuckers" after them. Accosted him—"want to shake your hand!"—which surprised him a bit, but we shook. Group evaporated, light-skinned guy popped up and asked, "What's happening?" Usual answer is, "Nothing much, man." Didn't seem appropriate. Strolled down to 8th Ave. chatting with cat—pretty far out panorama.

Ordered root beer at outdoor counter and dug scene. Groups moving up and down street giving out "Wanted for Murder" posters— police everywhere—squad cars looping back and forth. Same CORE group came up. Girl: "I thought I told you to get out of here." Noncommittal response elicited, "Farmer said..." etc. Answered: "Look, Honey, I don't take orders from Farmer." Immediately pictured half of Harlem clobbering me for putting down Negro chick siding with cops against them. Another CORE group appeared, including Bayard Rustin. Chick ran over and pointed me out. He merely shrugged.

Left on next bus, getting home around 12:30 a.m.

*Journal-American* ran front-page *exposée*, "What Sparks the Rioters" with picture of the poster. Naturally it wasn't the murder of a schoolboy, it was "known Communists" and "outside agitators" who were "fanning the flames of fury." Noted address of Progressive Labor Movement, the "Communist splinter group" which published the poster.

Phoned Committee for Nonviolent Action and War Resisters League to see if peace movement doing anything about Harlem. Told that civil rights "leaders" had asked them all to stay away.

After work went to hall of Progressive Labor Movement and got large batch of posters, plus leaflets announcing protest march that Saturday. No charge, but contributed $2.00. Was asked to give them out anywhere outside of Harlem. Refused. Walked home holding up posters, but giving them out only when specifically requested. Half gone on arrival.

By now had evolved plan of action: nod and smile with open countenance at every one met. Many nodded or smiled back; most didn't notice me at all.

Phoned a few friends. Only one wanted to join me but was tied up at other end of Manhattan. However assured me that mine was "correct" nonviolent approach. Others' reactions mixed.

At 11:00 p.m. pinned "Wanted for Murder" posters on front and back of my shirt with Nuclear Disarmament pins and set out uptown. Felt like William Moore. Everyone asked for posters and/or leaflets. One guy wanted an ND pin too. Around 114th St. two cops yelled "Hey, you!" Figured it was all over but they just wanted posters. Gave them leaflets also, then tried to shake hands. Was scornfully rebuffed. Woman at watermelon stand asked, "Is you from de CO'?" Refrained from giving opinion of "de Co.'"

Leaflets gone by 125th St., but plenty posters left. Intended to join anyone agitating, but street completely empty except for cops sheltering in doorways out of drizzling rain. Walked from 8th Ave. to 5th Ave. and back on 125th St. giving out posters to cops, usually with statement about everyone having to do what he believes in. One replied, "I didn't say anything." Cop wanted a poster "to show my kid"; another, one for a souvenir. Was scared half to death when a squad car pulled up—they asked for ten!

Towards 8th Ave. met some drunk with bandaged head who'd been heckling cops Monday night. Still drunk. Bought him root beer at corner stand. Learned that "cops" was right when clubbed him because he'd been bugging them. Hung around for a while, then took him to nearby bar. Still wearing the two posters. Spilled some beer on another fellow's coat but he wouldn't accept payment for cleaning. Bought him a drink instead. Explained how companion seemed to have something against police clubs—bangs his head on them. Walked home letting rain soak off the posters. Arrived about 1:30 a.m.

*Thursday July 23, 1964*

Learned a CORE demonstration at downtown Police Headquarters had been mobbed the previous night. Local neighborhood people—mostly Italians (my compatriots). The friend who had wanted to join me was there. Towards midnight went up to Harlem again. Kept posters folded, not wanting to agitate if everything was quiet. It was.

Hung around 125th St. for a stretch. Saw two white men walk by—first ones not there in obviously official capacity. Later discovered anther CORE protest had been mobbed at Police Headquarters.

*Friday July 24, 1964*

Went to Progressive Labor Movement's hall in afternoon for more posters. Few available—stock low, and being saved for protest march next day. Was asked why hadn't given posters out in Italian district instead of Harlem. Was told it wasn't "sound tactics" to have PLM literature given out in a Negro area by a white person. Also Harlem was already saturated (??) anyway.

About 11:30 p.m. walked uptown accompanied by musician friend. Area still quite dark and very quiet. Police outnumbered people. Stopped for soft drinks at 125th St., then started across towards Lenox Ave. Encountered Bayard Rustin—identified self with, "Met you in London." It was the truth! He was trying to get William Epton (of PLM) to call off the protest march; he had a forthcoming meeting with Mayor Wagner; and he was trying to get an injunction against the police's banning the protest.

Wandered by PLM, but hall was closed. Introduced friend to fish and chips at 125th and Lenox, then dropped by bar on 8th Ave. where bartender asked, "How are you tonight?"

Walked home discussing music business which is even worse off than Harlem.

Robert S. CALESE

# THE FLEAS OF THE FIELD

*Work with all your strength*
*Work on the land the streets the docks*
*and sow there what you will*
*paving-stones smoke or bottles*
*but work, work like a lunatic*
*and dung the stones*
*that they may sprout flags*
*even red ones*
*The rains and the winds will bless you*
*if you put the hands of a watch to your ears*
*and the harvest will be as good as your wife's stew*

*Work your own field and all the others*
*with your feet and with your nose*
*Break down the hedges like a bull*
*while singing*
*In the Revolution*
*there was a worker*
*who clinked with his spade*
*He had only one head and two arms*
*four feet and two eyes*
*one ear and three teeth*
*but he was a worker*
*who did not waste his time*

Benjamin PERET

*Translated by Ruthven Todd*

Cartoon by Roland Topor (*Rebel Worker* 3)

# MODS, ROCKERS AND THE REVOLUTION

WOBBLIES AND OTHER TRUE REVOLUTIONARIES are much less interested in the vague longings of college professors and Nobel prize-winners for a "better world" than in the day-to-day struggles of our fellow workers—not only the direct struggles against exploitation by the bosses, but the struggle to live some sort of decent life against all the obstacles presented by a society divided into classes. Thus it is essential that we concern ourselves not only with the job situation and economic questions but also with more "superstructural" anthropological factors: workingclass culture.

In this connection, the significance of rock'n'roll, and popular adolescent culture in general, has for too long been ignored. That rock'n'roll is one of the most important workingclass preoccupations (among the young, at least) is clearly evident. That it has been ignored by the "left" press is additional testimony to the isolation of the "socialist" intellectuals from the class in whose name they so often enjoy speaking.

Certain unfortunate souls, including many of traditional "left" orientation, have attempted to deny that rock'n'roll is really a workingclass phenomenon, even suggesting that it is imposed (!) on workingclass adolescents by Madison Avenue, etc., as a form of exploitation through cheap talent, record sales and juke-boxes. To them rock'n'roll is a sign only of the "decadence" of contemporary capitalist society. They can neither take it seriously as a form of music, nor see in it anything other than a possible "reliever of tensions" which they feel might better be expressed in more constructive activity. Thus Marshall Stearns, in *The Story of Jazz*, thoroughly puts down rock'n'roll as a form of music but claims that, by offering "release" to anxious kids, it actually contributes to the decrease of juvenile delinquency. This uneasy, patronizing anti-rock'n'roll "theory" is, amusingly enough, shared by Stalinists, liberals, Presbyterians, conservatives, and bourgeois sociologists.

We must have done, once and for all, with this kind of evasive excuse-mongering, and look at the situation as it really exists. Rock'n'roll must be recognized not only as a form of music (which, for its players and its listeners, is clearly as "serious" as any other), but also as an important expression of adolescent preoccupations.

As music, rock'n'roll is certainly "primitive," but this must not be assumed to mean that it is therefore inferior. No one is less able than musicologists and other prisoners of academic limitations to situate this problem in its proper context. For the importance of rock'n'roll lies not only in the music itself, but even more in the milieu which has grown up with it, characterized above all by delirious enthusiasm, a frenzy which is no stranger to tenderness, and which undoubtedly appears scandalous to the easily-outraged watchdogs of bourgeois morality.

Much could be said for the influence of rock'n'roll on the emergence of a new sensibility (intellectual as well as erotic and emotional). Much could be said, too, of its *unconscious* quality, which, with its roots in speed-up and automation (and thus in the class struggle) lends to its "subversive" aspect. For rock'n'roll is, more than anything else, a *latent cultural expression* of the age of automation. Indeed, a study of the psychoanalytical and anthropological implications of automation might well make rock'n'roll its point of departure. Witness the fact that almost all of the most popular rock'n'roll groups are from the most intensely industrialized and highly-automated cities: in the United States, Chicago and Detroit; in England, Liverpool, where one out of every fifteen "Liverpudlians" between the ages of 15 and 24 now belongs to a rock'n'roll group.

The best of the new groups—Martha and the Vandellas, Marvin Gaye, The Jewels, The Velvellettes, The Supremes, Mary Wells (all from Detroit), and The Kinks, The Zombies, Manfred Mann and, of course, The Beatles (all from England)—have brought to popular music a vitality, exuberance and rebelliousness which it has never seen before.

The Beatles are the most successful group in entertainment history. Their flippant replies to interviewers; their wild, raucous behavior; their riotous and insulting sense of humor remove them far beyond the pale of "respectable entertainers." Their first movie, *A Hard Day's Night*, will remain one of the greatest cinematic delights of 1964, a lone cry of uninhibited freedom and irrationality in a cold desert of "seriousness" and pretentiousness.

The legendary quality, which can almost be called *mythical necessity*, of The Beatles, has not failed to attract the critical attention of some perceptive commentators. Consider this judgment from the pen of Jean Shepherd, who interviewed The Beatles for *Playboy* magazine (February 1965):

> In two years they had become a phenomenon that had somehow transcended stardom or even showbiz. They were mythical beings, inspiring a fanaticism bordering on religious ecstasy among millions all over the world. I began to have the uncomfortable feeling that all this fervor had nothing whatever to do with entertainment, or with talent, or even with The Beatles themselves. I began to feel that they were the catalyst of a sudden world madness that

would have burst upon us whether they had come on the scene or not. If The Beatles had never existed, we would have had to invent them. They are not prodigious talents by any yardstick, but like hula-hoops and yo-yos, they are at the right place at the right time, and whatever it is that triggers the mass hysteria of fads has made them walking myths. Everywhere we went, people stared in open-mouthed astonishment that there were actually flesh-and-blood human beings who looked just like the Beatle dolls they had at home. It was as though Santa Claus had suddenly shown up at a Christmas Party.

Another British group, The Rolling Stones, has risen to popularity more recently, bringing with them a more disquieting, more sinister, more violent attitude into the rock'n'roll arena.

It is in England where the adolescent revolt (of which rock'n'roll is only one constituent element) seems to have assumed its largest proportions. In England the kids are categorized into two "tendencies": Mods, fashionably (often bizarrely) dressed, and who are associated with motor-scooters; and the Rockers, who prefer black leather jackets, blue jeans, and motorcycles. In both cases the boys wear their hair long, considerably longer than in America, and (according to a *New York Times* writer from Britain) "the word in London and Liverpool is that male hair is going to get longer and longer." The girls' hair is usually straight and worn down to the middle of the back.

The hair itself deserves comment, particularly since hair is growing longer in the United States as well as in England and elsewhere in Europe. The social implications of hair fashion have been inadequately studied, if studied at all. Some psychologists and sociologists have confined themselves to brief, unexplained remarks on "sexual confusion," "identity problems," and the like, which help very little. Others, it is true, have gotten a *little* closer to the heart of the matter. Thus the *New York Times* writer referred to above mentions that "sociologists, always a pessimistic lot, look on our jungled tresses and prophesy a future filled with indulgence and rebellion." For it is an undeniable fact that *short* male hair has always been a characteristic of submission to authority. The police, prisons, army, schools, and employers are all in agreement in insisting on short hair and regular haircuts. Also, crew-cuts are the symbol, almost, of Goldwater conservatism. Before making unfounded judgments on the "identity problems" of today's kids, one might consider the problems of a culture so obsessed with keeping male hair short.

The riots and brawls of the Mods and the Rockers have also called attention to another aspect of the youth revolt: that rock'n'roll represents the only *mass protest music* today—another reason why it deserves the sympathetic appreciation of revolutionaries. The most popular jazz has entered the colleges and become respectable. The most important developments in jazz during the last few years (Ornette Coleman, Eric Dolphy, Charles Mingus, Roland Kirk, *et al.*) are hardly known outside a small audience of connoisseurs. It is useless to point out that jazz is, *musically*, ten thousand times better than rock'n'roll; that's not the point. The audience for contemporary "classical" music is even more limited.

As for "folk" music and its derivatives (country-and-western, bluegrass, etc.) these have become the official expressions of today's college fraternities. (Real folk music is primarily of historical interest.) Those unhappy souls of the traditional "left" who try to pretend that the "folk revival" has some sort of revolutionary content reflect only their sentimentality and intellectual superficiality. I do not mean to imply that there's not much that is beautiful and important in the folk tradition, and certainly it deserves serious study. But it can no longer be assumed to have anything to do with the working class. At any rate, workingclass kids are bored by it. Like it or not, what today's workingclass kids are listening to is rock'n'roll.

The rise of the Mods and Rockers indicates to some degree a rise of young rebellion everywhere: the "new youth" of Tokyo, Berlin, Moscow, etc. Inevitably, this has provoked innumerable journalistic scare-stories about "new parent-teen crises" in Sunday supplements throughout the world. Such articles contribute nothing of importance to the understanding of the contemporary adolescent, though they do shed a little light on the problems and preoccupations of adults. Repressed adults, attempting to understand younger people, often merely project their own problems onto the kids.

Many parents, for instance, afraid of participating in uninhibited dancing, approach the question with the presuppositions that there is something wrong with this kind of dancing, and that it must be rooted in some deep emotional anxiety. I do not mean to say that rock'n'roll dances are expressions of "freedom" (the lack of physical contact between dancing partners is especially problematical). But we cannot advance one step in our understanding of these problems if we begin by saying that the kids are *wrong*.

There can be no doubt that the present development of rock'n'roll, and the milieu of young workers in which it thrives, is more consciously rebellious than it has ever been before. To be *revolutionary*, of course, is to be more than rebellious, for a revolutionary viewpoint necessarily includes some sort of *alternative*. And popular adolescent culture is pregnant with revolutionary implications precisely because it proposes alternatives—however crude and undeveloped they may be—to the ignoble conditions now prevailing.

Songs like "Dancin' in the Streets" by Martha and the Vandellas and "Opportunity" by The Jewels show that the feeling for freedom and the refusal to submit to routinized, bureaucratic pressures, are not confined to small, isolated bands of conscious, politically "sophisticated" revolutionaries. Rather, they are the almost *instinctive* attitudes of most of our fellow workers. Presently these feelings are to a great extent repressed, and sublimated in bourgeois politics, television, baseball, and other diversions. It is our function as disrupters of the capitalist system, and as union organizers, to heighten consciousness of these feelings, to encourage rebellion, to do all we can to liberate the intrinsically revolutionary character of the working class. Rock'n'roll, which has already contributed to a freer attitude toward sex relations, can contribute to this liberation.

There is no use being overly romantic about all this. I do not, for example, think that adolescent hangouts and record hops will provide fruitful recruiting grounds for the One Big Union; at least, not right away.

And for my part, I vastly prefer the more raucous rhythm'n'blues—songs sung by ghetto Negro groups—to the lukewarm, diluted sounds promoted in teen-celebrity magazines and on American Bandstand.

But what revolutionaries must consider is that many younger workers—rock'n'rollers—are discontented with existing society, and are seeking and developing solutions of their own. If traditional revolutionary politics hasn't appealed to them, it's probably because these politics haven't been as "revolutionary" as their protagonists like to pretend.

We in the IWW are not tied to narrow theoretical traditions and immovable dogmas. We are rising today because we are free to seek new solutions and develop new tactics to meet new situations. If we are going to keep growing, we will have to turn more to the problems of younger workers. It might be noted that jobs most common to kids (stock work, filling-station work, store clerking, etc.) are almost completely unorganized, and offer us a splendid opportunity to channel the "youth revolt" into a consciously revolutionary movement.

In any case, we cannot go on assuming that the rock'n'rollers are a helpless, ignorant, reactionary mass; that their problems are not our problems; that they are somehow "irrelevant." We must recognize that the rock'n'rollers, too, despite the hesitations of "socialist" politicians, are our friends and fellow workers.

Franklin ROSEMONT

# CONDITIONING FOR BUREAUCRACY

IT IS THE DILEMMA OF ALL CHILDREN coming into a society that is highly structuralized, bureaucratized, segmented, and regimented, to find their place, feel they belong, satisfy their need to change, re-evaluate themselves, understand their world and feel comfortable in their relationships with others. Max Weber pointed out that it is the ideal of every bureaucracy to have each individual performing assigned duties in an efficient, machinelike manner as set forth in a table of organization. Perhaps there may be an informational organization which modifies and runs counter to the formal organization, but still, when a person joins a given organization, much of his behavior is defined and prescribed. Unless he conforms, at least within limits, he will not be able to retain his position. A nation's way of governing its people is translated down into distinct influences on individual human behaviour. Such is the case when a child joins a "boy's club."

The main purpose of boys' clubs is to condition children to regimented bureaucracy. Nowhere else is this so evidently the case.

A club consists of a director, an activities director, an assistant activities director, and instructors for gym, arts and crafts, woodshop, and the games rooms, in that order. It is the job of each of these officials to supervise and control the particular area to which he is assigned, since the club is separated into distinct units or areas.

When a child comes into the club, he is asked to fill out a long questionnaire (usually assisted by the secretary of the director), asking questions about his age, religion, race, family background, health, etc. He then receives an identification card with instructions to wear it around his neck. (This makes him feel as if he belongs.) He is then assigned to a group according to his age and sex, *i.e.*, Rangers, Preps, etc., with preassigned times for preassigned activities for preassigned days. When his time has come for arts and crafts, no matter where he is or what he is doing, he is forced to run to his new activity as quickly as possible. He is not to eat his lunch until a preassigned time. He has one hour for this activity, but if he finishes early he must sit and wait.

If he wishes to play a particular game during "game time" and there are not enough games to go around, he must sign a list to determine his turn, and is given a specific amount of time to play when that time comes.

In arts and crafts, woodshop and gym he is allowed to do only the assigned task for the day. If he does not cooperate he is sent out of the club with instructions not to return until he is willing to cooperate.

The summer brings new activity and the days are designated "beach day," "trip day," "park day," "show day," etc. Transportation to these activities usually involves walking or taking a hired bus. Walking procedure is done in this fashion: First the kids are divided into two's in the gym, which involves separating the "troublemakers" and placing them in more controllable positions, closer to the instructors (or, as they are called, "leaders.") They are then marched in two's to their destination. At a given time they eat, and after each piece of paper is picked up and the grounds are inspected, they are allowed to go about the assigned activity. A whistle sounds to indicate "home time" and the march to the club begins in the same fashion.

The decisions as to where the kids will go and what they will see and do is entirely decided by the activities director who is responsible to the director who is responsible to the board downtown. The director's position is dependent upon three factors: the amount of money he brings into the club, the number of members he is able to obtain, and statistics as to the number of activities in his particular club. When on one occasion a staff member organized a union consisting mainly of teenagers to make decisions about their own activities, this staff member was immediately fired because it was claimed he was "making trouble."

However, the effectiveness in conditioning these children for bureaucracy is somewhat questionable. In the summer, when it's possible for kids to find enjoyment without this structure, the membership drops to about one-third. But there are other indications that the effects could be greater than they can be judged by the membership rate alone. Some kids tend to develop a driving lust for power and control. This may take the form of working hard to be accepted into the "junior leader" program, or of pushing other kids around when one feels he can safely do so.

Many more things could be said pertaining to the system of the club and the incidents which go on every day; and much more could be said about the effects that all this has upon the individual child. In the case of the boy's club, even more than in school, children are everyday subjected to a bureaucracy through manipulation of the activities they enjoy most. The effects tend to be stronger because they do not hate the "club" as they do the school, and they adjust and condition to it more voluntarily. The club is associated with play whereas the school is associated with forced work; thus the former is more desirable than—and even a relief from—the latter.

The inherent danger of such an organization cannot easily be overlooked. A system that has found it necessary to control and regiment the behavior of its adults has now realized the necessity of training for this control long before adulthood.

Robert R. GREEN

# STORMING HEAVEN IN HUNGARY

W HAT ACTUALLY HAPPENED in Hungary in 1956 is not known to the majority of American workers. Those who read the average daily voice of the employing class probably have the impression that the Hungarian Revolution was bourgeois-democratic, and that the Hungarians fought to gain "freedom" in the capitalist sense of free enterprise. Meanwhile, Stalinists have found it necessary to "prove" that the Hungarian Revolution was "fascist-inspired."

In the Solidarity book *Hungary 56*, Andy Anderson explains both these points of view in terms of the ideological necessity from which they grew. It is essential to their own preservation that the capitalist countries conceal the nature of the Revolution. And the best answer to the Stalinists' silly charge is provided by the satirical humor of the Hungarian workers themselves in the form of crude posters: "Ten million counter-revolutionaries at large in the country!" And: "Former aristocrats, land- and factory-owners, Cardinals, Generals and other supporters of the old capitalist regime, disguised as factory workers and peasants, are making propaganda against the patriotic government and against our Russian friends." Anderson's book is the only one available which allows the reader to see the Hungarian Revolution as it was: a spontaneous revolutionary uprising of the working class.

In the first eighteen pages Anderson describes the situation prior to the demonstrations of October 23, beginning with the East-West agreement at Yalta and the Russian domination of Eastern Europe. He then gives a clear account of the specific events and demands of the workers during the days of the Revolution. He explains why the Kremlin crushed the Hungarian workers, and why Hungary received no aid from the West.

The Hungarian Revolution should be distinguished from all other revolutions of the past and also from those presently occurring in Africa, Latin America and Asia, because it occurred in a *modern industrial society* dominated by a bureaucracy. The Hungarian Revolution was a rising of the workers against the exploitation of the bureaucratic state. The functioning of the bureaucratic "elite" was halted by the formation by the workers of workers' councils, followed by a general strike. "From the first day of the revolution, a truly proletarian movement had expressed itself.... These councils, partially isolated by the Red Army, immediately sought to federate. By the end of the first week...only their authority meant anything. The Government...had no authority whatsoever."

Students and intellectuals played a significant but somewhat confused role. The Revolution began essentially with the government rejection of student demands for reform. However, the workers realized much sooner than the students that bargaining with bureaucracy is impossible, and took the initiative in organizing councils.

The Hungarian Revolution failed to receive aid from the West, or concessions from Russia, because its demands of workers' management of production threatened the bureaucratic and class-divided foundations of both. It was "far more than a national uprising or than an attempt to change one set of rulers for another. It was a social revolution in the fullest sense of the term."

Penelope ROSEMONT

# A "LABOR LEADER" SPEAKS

"I never went on a strike in my life, never ordered anyone else to run a strike in my life, never had anything to do with a picket line.... In the final analysis, there is not a great difference between the things I stand for and the things that National Association of Manufacturers' leadership stand for. I stand for the profit system; I believe in the profit system. I believe it's a wonderful incentive. I believe in the free enterprise system completely."

—George Meany, head of the American Federation of Labor, addressing the National Association of Manufacturers, December, 1956

# ANARCHISM AS SEEN FROM AN IVORY TOWER THROUGH OPAQUE LENSES

ANARCHISTS UNFORTUNATELY ARE IN NO position, financially, to re-publish rare anarchist classics or to publish inexpensive paperbacks for mass distribution. Until that day arrives we must be saddled with the likes of *The Anarchists*, Irving Horowitz's recent anthology of writings by anarchists and about them and their accomplishments (Dell, 1964). What makes the volume deplorable is not that Horowitz doesn't have an intellectual grasp of anarchism, but that he lacks an incisive view of the state of present society; wanting this, he is blind to the relevancy of anarchism.

The selections are fair, historically, anarchists from Godwin to Goodman are represented—all one would expect. But besides the classics, there are several pieces that one must applaud—the entry of Samuel Yellan and Gerald Brenan's histories of anarchists in the US. and Spain, and Berkman's eyewitness account of the Kronstadt massacre. Yet Horowitz does manage to include a great deal of garbage; for instance, Berkman's Kronstadt commentary is sandwiched between Woodcock's Latin American historical fantasies and Hugh Thomas's apology for the Spanish Republicans. And Conrad, Dostoyevsky, and Camus share Section Two: "Anarchism as a Style of Life" (and Death?), with Tolstoy, Goldman, and Sacco and Vanzetti!

It is usually fruitless to belabor the omissions in anthologies, for though the omissions constitute their notorious weakness the editors may be excused for purely technical reasons like lack of space. Sadly, this is not the case with Horowitz, for his omissions definitely leave the reader with the misconception that anarchy has no significance in a highly complex, technological world.

Horowitz's whole condescending approach to anarchy stems from his (purposeful?) inability to appreciate its contemporary relevance beyond its pertinence as a "posture" for intellectuals.

Two very recent articles, one by Herbert Read, the other by Karl Shapiro, typify—according to Horowitz—current anarchist writings. The Shapiro article, mistitled "The Revival of Anarchism," desperately attempts to distill anarchism from Gandhism in order to make anarchism comfortable with some heavenly, sugar-coated world of brotherly love. He altogether overlooks the real revival of anarchism within American radical political thought and direct action. Read, in his essay from *Reconstruir* (No. 19, July August, 1962), pathetically searches for anarchism in the kibbutzim of Israel and the Chinese communes, but he ignores the Committee of 100, the Spies for Peace, and the recent British industrial disputes, all of which have been influenced by anarchists.

Moreover, where Horowitz touches on anarcho-syndicalism, the most obviously relevant strain of anarchism, his discussion is sterile and completely devoid of any exposition of the syndicalist truth, slowly but definitely being realized by the workers throughout the world, that the boss can reside in the union hall just as surely as he does in the executive john. The realization on the part of the workers that they must fight bossism in the unions can have radical consequences not only for future union structure, but for society as a whole. Nowhere does Horowitz mention, much less explain, the revival of syndicalist thought among radicals throughout the world. This is doubly strange (and likewise more unforgivable) because his teacher, C. Wright Mills, was a part, though one must admit a small part, of this revival.

This paperback will be purchased in drugstores across the country and read by people who imagine anarchists as cloaked, bearded bomb-throwers; Horowitz has done his academic best to destroy that conception and replace it with that of a toothless, palsied codger feebly and absurdly flaying the wind with incoherence. Even an anarcho-pacifist would prefer the former image, with all of its falsity, to one that relegates anarchism to the dustbin of history, there to remain undisturbed except by the journey of an occasional scholar in pursuit of professional recognition.

But we must not be too severe for, after all, academicians are the last group in society to recognize change. I am thoroughly confident that the sparks of truth ignited by the true anarchist selections in *The Anarchists* are not about to be extinguished by the rancid syrup of a vapid academicism.

Bernard MARSZALEK

Lester Doré: *Robotic Reproduction*
(from *Rebel Worker* 4)

# LETTERS

*The Rebel Worker* is not only Damn Good, it is excellent. It should be on news-stands and in libraries all over the country. It's good to see the old black cat back, but let's not forget the good old wooden shoe.

Guy B. ASKEW (Skidroad Slim)
Seattle, Washington

I have just finished reading your great journal *The Rebel Worker*. We in England have possibly an easier task in obtaining "left" literature than you in the U.S., owning to our lack of McCarthyism, which I understand still lingers in the States.

The journal is fresh and hardhitting; like *Solidarity* it is no respecter of "the traditional left" and bricks are more often thrown than bouquets. More power to your elbow.

I personally would like to read more about the Negro struggle for equality and the U.S. left's opinion of the Black Muslims and why such an obscenity as Goldwater has been spewed up.

Tom HILLIER, AEU (Amalgamated Engineers Union)
London, England

I bought the first two issues of *The Rebel Worker* when I was in Chicago, and I think it's great! I think you could really get a big circulation—I have no idea how many people read it now—because it's about the only thing around with a good viewpoint that is really well done.

Judith KAPLAN
Philadelphia, Pennsylvania

We read your *Rebel Worker* with interest and have forwarded to you copies of our own *Broadsheet*, which we will continue to send. Your letter coincided with our annual camp at the beginning of September, and received wide circulation. At present we would be able to distribute copies of *The Rebel Worker* ourselves, if you would care to send on a few of each issue.

The radical movement here is considerably fragmented. A strong anarcho-syndicalist influence has persisted in a few trade unions, notably the wharfies and seamen; however, other pressures are growing stronger and only a week ago the Communist secretary of the Seamen's Union, in return for a substantial wage award increase, relinquished the right of the union to man ships. However, in the

Waterside Workers' Federation, job control is flourishing. Many other unions are frankly right-wing, out for wage increases at all costs. Official Communist Party policy is to defend the arbitration court (from which militants in the WWF, Seamen's Union and Building Workers Industrial Union want to de-register) and counsel moderate attitudes so as to "influence" the moderate unions for purposes of solidarity. Hence the defection of the Seamen's Union leadership.

There is a lot of interest among students and young people in CND, anti-election campaigns and so on, but the society as a whole is complacent.

Ian BEDFORD (for the Libertarian Society)
Sydney, Australia

Received #2 of *The Rebel Worker*. In reading it we noted with pleasure the revival of activity of the IWW. We wish you a good continuation in this course. The revolutionary movement in the U.S. is a question which is very little known here and would certainly interest our militants and our readers.

Marc PREVOTEL, Federation Anarchiste
Paris, France

Enclosed find the STRIKE leaflet (of the recent Berkeley Student Strike); we do not know who the author was; however, when it hit the streets, Gov. Brown called in an army of police and announced that he would not tolerate ANARCHY in California as long as he was Governor. Nearly 800 students, teachers and workers were arrested in a desperate attempt to smash our General Strike at the Education Mill. The Governor's move boomeranged. IBM machines ground to a halt. Classes were cancelled or empty. 12,000 students and workers manned the picket lines, collected funds, coordinated, directed and won the greatest victory over the combined forces of State authoritarianism in anyone's memory.

Among the arrested were two IWW organizers and several rank-and-file members. IWW tactics and slogans (notably: "An Injury to One is an Injury to All") were tried, tested and proved true.

The Chancellor and the Regents, stunned by the demands for student and faculty control of "their" university, were completely routed. The powerful academic senate (composed of the entire professorial staff) voted overwhelmingly to support the student demands. The Regents are in a tough spot. They must either concede to the student and faculty demands...or face what Gov. Brown claims is Anarchy. The Strike goes on.

The activities of the IWW in the Bay Area including our participation in the General Strike at the University of California have brought us into increased prominence. The SF city jail is once again covered with Wobbly stickers. The daily press slanders us. The bosses jail us. The scabs and finks fear us; but most important, spirited, rebellious, and responsible students and workers are JOINING our movement. The American labor movement is being rebuilt.

Alan GRAHAM, IWW
Berkeley, California

Drawn by Mike Konopacki, one of today's outstanding labor cartoonists, this portrayal of the IWW/surrealist bookstore is excerpted from the centennial comic-book history of the IWW, edited by Paul Buhle and Nicole Schulman (Verso Books, 2005)

# REBEL WORKER 4

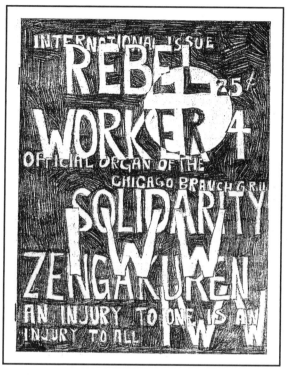

July 1965 / *Cover by Lester Doré* / 39 pages

*Expectation may amount to prophecy.*
—Thoreau—

Notable above all for Charles Radcliffe's "Roots of Revolt," on the demise of the traditional left in Britain and the rise of a new youth rebellion, this "International Issue" also introduced many U.S. readers to the Japanese Zengakuren, the important libertarian Marxist theorist Paul Cardan (Cornelius Castoriadis), and the revival of interest in anarchism. Like *Rebel Worker* 3, this was a good "recruitment" number; it brought many newcomers into the IWW and even a few into the *Rebel Worker* group. But you can't please everybody: Pointing out that 5 of the 19 contributions were translated from the French, one young left sectarian angrily accused us of "French Nationalism"!

—F.R.

Antiwar demonstration, Chicago, 1968 or '69,
with Carlos Cortez and Fred Thompson in foreground

# HOW TO MAKE FRIENDS
# AND INFLUENCE NO ONE:
## A Report on the Anarchist-Pacifist
### Youth Conference

FRIDAY, JUNE 11 WAS AS BEAUTIFUL A DAY as any for the urban anarchist-marxist-syndicalist synthesizers to meet their home-steader friends and neighbors, except that visitors from the cities sweat more. Anyway, on that day began a far-from-epochmaking Anarchist-Pacifist Youth Conference in the rural hinterlands of scenic Maryland. It was sponsored by the School of Living (HQ in Ohio), the Mutual Aid Fellowship (in East Chicago, Indiana) and several independent fellow travelers and passersby.

From most points of view, including several of my own (anarchist, pacifist, IWW, CNVA, Junior Woodchuck, motorcyclist, etc.) it was a failure. About 40 or 50 people showed up. Quite a number were "marxists" of various kinds, on the scene to get anyone possible sected, carded and catalogued into their factions, vanguards, splinters and fronts: *i.e.*, the traditional left! A number were homesteaders and back-to-the-land Green Revolutionaries, vegetarians, etc. These were mostly sincere and surprisingly well-informed people with whom I felt quite sympathetic, but some came only to recruit others into various communities. A few people, like myself, came mostly to see what was happening and to meet some new people with new and original ideas. These last, I can say with all modesty, were the most interesting people there.

Of the sessions held, some were of very little or at best mild interest, others were quite good. Mildred Loomis of the School of Living (publishers of *A Way Out* and *The Green Revolution*) gave what was actually a pretty fascinating account of the economic theories of Henry George, once widely known and acclaimed, but now nearly forgotten. (Her presentation was more interesting and I hope more representative of the facts than the unsigned ridiculous rave review of this conference which appeared in the latest issue of *The Green Revolution*.) By far the best discussions were on the subject of psychedelics, which interested nearly everyone there.

One thing should be noted: hardly any girls showed up. This is significant, isn't it? Why doesn't the revolutionary movement attract women? This is a subject that needs a closer look than I can give it here. But I think it's important. As Joe Hill said:

*We've had girls before, but we need some more,*
*in the Industrial Workers of the World,*
*for it's great to fight for freedom*
*with a Rebel Girl.*

The conference closed, after founding a loosely-defined (perhaps only semi-existent) Mutual Aid Society and calling for a second conference to be held, presumably in New York, some time in August. For further details write to *The Rebel Worker.* If you can't make it there, see the next issue for a report. Meanwhile, let us hear from you.

Craig T. BEAGLE X76116

# MODERN CAPITALISM
# AND REVOLUTION

(This "Synopsis" of Paul Cardan's *Modern Capitalism and Revolution* was sent to us for this issue of *The Rebel Worker* by Bob Potter of the London Solidarity Group as a statement of their revolutionary perspective.)

A PROLONGED POLITICAL APATHY of the working class seems to characterize modern capitalist society. This contrasts with the activity of the masses in "backward" countries. Since Marxism is above all a theory of proletarian revolution in advanced countries, one cannot call oneself a marxist and remain silent on this problem: What does the modernization of capitalism consist of? How is it linked with the political apathy of the masses? What are the consequences of all this for the revolutionary movement today?

New and lasting features of capitalism should first be described and studied. The ruling classes have achieved greater control over the level of economic activity and have succeeded in preventing major crises of the classical type. Unemployment has greatly diminished.

Over a period of several decades real wages have been rising, both more rapidly and more regularly than in the past. This has led to an increase of mass consumption which has become indispensable to the functioning of the economy and which is by now irreversible. The unions have become integrated into the whole system of exploitation: they negotiate the docility of the workers in production in return for wage increases.

Political life is almost exclusively limited to specialists. Ordinary people are uninterested in it or frankly contemptuous of it. In no important country are there any political organizations whose members are mainly industrial workers or which is capable of mobilizing the working class on political issues. Outside of production, the proletariat no longer appears as a class with its own objectives. The entire population is drifting into a vast movement of private living. It attends to its own business. The affairs of society is a whole seem to have escaped its control.

Prisoners of traditional schemas would have to conclude that there is no longer any revolutionary perspective. Traditional Marxism saw the "objective contradictions" of capitalism as essentially economic ones. The total incapacity of the system to satisfy the economic demands of the workers made these demands the driving force of the class struggle.

Although the classical analysis corresponded to certain manifestations of capitalism, at a certain period of its development, it must be re-examined in the light of contemporary experience. The "objective economic contradictions" disappear with the total concentration of capital (as in countries controlled by the Stalinist bureaucracy). But even the degree of state intervention found today in the West is sufficient to confine within narrow limits the spontaneous imbalance of the economy.

Wage levels are not determined by "objective economic laws" but by the actions of men. The class struggle plays a crucial role in this respect. It has its own dynamic which modifies the actions and consciousness of both workers and bosses. Wage increases, provided they do not exceed increase in productions are quite feasible under capitalism.

The traditional socialist view of capitalism is also false philosophically. Objectivist and mechanistic, it eliminates the actions of men and classes from history, replacing them with an objective dynamic and "natural" law. It makes of the proletarian revolution a simple reflex against hunger, lacking any clear connection with a socialist society. But it has even more serious implications. It sees the understanding of capitalist economy and of its crises as a task for specialized technicians (the revolutionary elite).

The solution to such problems then becomes a question of economic transformations to be performed from above, needing no autonomous intervention of the proletariat. The working class is reduced to the role of infantry at the disposal of revolutionary generals. This approach is, has been and can only be the foundation stone of bureaucratic politics.

If the fundamental contradiction of capitalism is not to be found in the "anarchy of the market" or in its "inability to develop the productive forces," where is it to be found? It is in production, in the labor process itself. It is in the alienation of the workers. It lies in the necessity for capitalism on the one hand to reduce workers to simple executors of tasks, and on the other hand, in its impossibility to continue functioning if it succeeds in so doing. Capitalism needs to achieve mutually incompatible objectives: the participation *and* the exclusion of the worker in production—as of all citizens in relation to politics.

This is the real contradiction of contemporary society and the ultimate source of its crises. It cannot be alleviated by reforms, by increasing the standard of living or by eliminating private property and the market. It can only be eliminated by establishing collective management of production and society by the collective producers: the working class in the course of production. This is the only possible foundation of a socialist consciousness. It is what gives the class struggle under capitalism its universal and permanent character, whatever the level of production.

Such conceptions provide a framework for understanding the history and development of capitalist society, which is nothing else than the history and development of the class struggle. Such a dynamic is historic and not "objective" for it constantly modifies the conditions of its own development. It modifies the adversaries themselves. It gives rise to collective experience and collective creation. The class struggle has more and more determined the evolution of technology, production, economy and politics. It has impressed on capitalism the profound modifications of its structure which we see today.

There are few patterns of thought more "unmarxist" than those which attempt to explain contemporary economy and politics in terms of "laws" governing an entirely different phase of capitalist development. Equally "unmarxist" is the assumption that these "laws" are absolute, like the laws of gravitation, and cannot be profoundly modified by the actions of men.

At the subjective level, the modifications in capitalism appear in the accumulation of class struggle experience among the ruling classes, and in the new policies they accordingly adopt. Marxists used to regard capitalist policy as impotence, pure and simple. It was dominated by the ideology of *laissez-faire*, limiting the role of the state to that of a policeman. Today, however, the more farsighted of our rulers recognize the state's potential and constantly seek to enlarge its function. They assign to their state certain objectives (such as full employment and economic development) that were once left to the spontaneous functioning of the system. The ruling class today tends to submit more and more spheres of social activity to state control; society thus becomes increasingly totalitarian.

At the objective level, the transformation of capitalism is expressed in increasing bureaucratization. The roots of this tendency are in production, but they extend and finally invade all sectors of social life. Concentration of capital and stratification are but different aspects of the same phenomenon. And in their turn they significantly modify the functioning of the economy as a whole.

Bureaucratization implies the "organization" and "rationalization" of all collective activity *from the outside*. To the extent that it succeeds, it completes a process started by an earlier phase of capitalism: it renders all social life meaningless. It produces mass irresponsibility. Individuals begin to seek private solutions to social problems. This is the inevitable corollary of bureaucratization.

The inherent objective, the "ideal tendency" of bureaucratic capitalism is the construction of a totally hierarchic society in constant expansion, a sort of monstrous bureaucratic pyramid where the increasing alienation of men in labor will be "compensated" by a steady rise in the standard of living, all initiative remaining in the hands of the organizers. Anyone who cares to look at contemporary social reality can easily recognize this tendency. It coincides with the ultimate objective of the ruling classes: to make the revolt of the exploited fail by diverting it into a personal pursuit of the standard of living, by breaking up working class solidarity through hierarchy and differentials, and by preventing all attempts at collective action from below. Conscious or not, this is the real aim of bureaucratic capitalism and the real meaning of ruling-class action.

The bureaucratic drive must fail. It cannot overcome the fundamental contradiction of capitalism, as we have defined it. In fact, bureaucratic capitalism multiplies this contradiction manyfold. The increase in bureaucratization of all social activities only succeeds in extending into all domains the conflict inherent in the division of society into order-givers and order-takers. It scatters everywhere the intrinsic irrationality of the bureaucratic management of production.

It is for this reason that capitalism cannot avoid crises (that is, periodic breakdowns in the normal functioning of society), which vary in kind and stem from very different immediate causes. The inherent irrationality of capitalism remains but now finds expression in new and different ways.

Only the class struggle can give the contradictions and crises of modern society a revolutionary character. The present situation is peculiar in this respect. *In production* the struggle shows an intensity formerly unknown. It tends to raise the question of who will manage production, and this in the most advanced countries. But *outside of production* the class struggle hardly shows itself at all, or only distorted by bureaucratic organizations. This political apathy of the working class has a dual significance. On the one hand it represents a victory of capitalism. The bureaucratization of their organizations drives the workers away from collective political action. The collapse of traditional ideology and the absence of a socialist program prevent workers from generalizing their critique of production and transforming it into a positive conception of a new society. The philosophy of consumption penetrates the proletariat. But this apathy also has potentially positive aspects. Workingclass experience of the new phase of capitalism could lead to a criticism of *all* aspects of contemporary life, a criticism far more profound and total than anything attempted in the past. And from this could arise a renewal of the socialist ideal in the proletariat at a much higher level than witnessed hitherto.

The "ripening" of the conditions of socialism continues. This does not mean a purely objective "ripening" (increase of the productive forces, increased centralization, increasing "contradictions"). Nor does it mean a purely subjective "ripening" (accumulation of experience in the proletariat). It means the accumulation of the objective conditions of an adequate consciousness. The proletariat could not eliminate reformism and bureaucratism before having produced them as social realities and experienced them in everyday life. Today large numbers of people can grasp as profoundly real and relevant the idea of workers' management of production, and can reject as inadequate the capitalist values that see education and consumption as ends in themselves.

This new type of analysis will demand profound changes of the revolutionary movement. Its criticism of society, which is essential to help workers to evaluate and generalize their everyday direct experiences must be completely reoriented. It should seek to describe and analyze the contradictions and the irrationality of the bureaucratic management of society at all its levels. It should denounce the inhuman and absurd character of contemporary work, the alienation of people in consumption and leisure. It should expose the arbitrariness and the monstrosity of the hierarchical organization of production and of contemporary relations between men.

The central element of its program of demands should be the struggle around the organization of labor and life in the factory. It should oppose everything which tends to divide workers (wage differentials, piecework, etc.). But it should do more. Under modern capitalism, the essential problem is how to pass from the struggle at factory level to struggle against the whole pattern of society.

The revolutionary movement will only succeed in this respect if it ruthlessly denounces all equivocations and double-talk on the idea of socialism, if it mercilessly criticizes the values of contemporary society, if it presents the socialist program to the proletariat for what it really is: a program for the humanization of labor and of society.

The revolutionary movement will only be able to fulfill these tasks if it ceases to appear as a traditional political movement (traditional politics are dead) and if it becomes a *total* movement, concerned with all that men do in society, and with their real daily lives.

Paul CARDAN (Cornelius Castoriadis)

# ZENGAKUREN:
## Perspective of the Revolutionary Movement of Japan

THE POLITICAL AND THEORETICAL position of Zengakuren today has been attained through many years' hard struggle in the midst of the class struggle of Japan in recent years.

Zengakuren eight years ago was under the strong influence of the stalinist [communist] party. We had been known as the "leftist and militant wing" of CP through our incessant struggle against the government since the establishment after the war.

The revolt of the Hungarian proletariat in 1956 was the beginning of the transition period of Zengakuren from stalinist dominated movement to the revolutionary movement against both imperialism and stalinism.

There broke out a heated discussion over the suppression of the rising Hungarian workers by the tanks of the "red army," yet there were very few students at that time who supported the uprising of the Hungarian proletariat against the stalinist oppression. It has, however, given rise to the criticism of the existing state of the USSR and other so-called socialist countries and the distortion of Marxism by the hands of the stalinist bureaucrats and it has gradually combined itself with the partial and tactical disagreement with the Japan CP that had existed before that.

Two years after that passed in the deepening conflict between Zengakuren and CP, and in 1958 many communist students were excluded from CP because of "leftist adventurism."

The Ampo struggle (struggle against the amendment of Japan-USA mutual security act) 1959–60 was a stage of open conflict between CP and us. We opposed the policy of CP, according to which the struggle should be fought as that of the "patriotic and democratic" power against the "supporters of USA." For our part we insisted to concentrate our struggle against the Japanese capitalists who tried to strengthen their domination over us to prepare for the imperialistic aggression based on the accumulated power that they attained through the "development" after the war.

On the tactical problem we emphasized the militant demonstration combined with the industrial action of the working class, while CP together with SP tried to confine the struggle in the "peaceful march" for petition to the members of the Parliament, being afraid of the vital energy of the workers and students ready to explode against the ruling class.

The conflict took place in every sphere of the struggle. When there was a demonstration around the Diet, for example, and Zengakuren wanted to join the demonstrating workers, the officials of CP came in haste and made a "cordon" between the workers' demonstration and that of the students, saying that they were defending the workers from the "provocation" of the Zengakuren as a duty of a "vanguard party" of the proletariat. CP even formed a picketline in order to "defend the policemen from the 'violence' of the Zengakuren."

When the angry workers and students at the massacre of a girl student by the brutal policemen in the demonstration rushed against the Diet in which the act had been passed, the role of CP was to persuade the demonstrators to refrain from "provocative action" and to go home to sleep in the daily order of life. Moreover, CP excused themselves to the government that they had no intention of "disturbing" the society but it was Zengakuren that tried to "violate the order."

Many workers and intellectuals saw CP together with SP [Socialist Party] suppress not only the demonstration of Zengakuren but also every struggle when it took a militant character against their expectation. As a result, after the defeat of the Ampo struggle, CP lost support of the workers and students who fought the struggle and experienced the suppression of the "vanguard" party.

In the general assembly after the struggle in 1961, we discussed over the problem which was sharply posed through the struggle, especially about the character of the existing leadership of the labor movement and found that its degeneration is connected with the policy of the so-called socialist countries. We also examined the history of our struggle during the period since the revolt of the Hungarian proletariat and through the criticism of our own experience adopted the fundamental line that we should fight against all kinds of suppression, whether it be capitalistic or stalinistic, with our own power and that the student movement should be closely connected with the struggle of the rank and file workers to overcome the false leadership of the labor movement today.

Anti-war struggle of the Zengakuren has been possible only through this discussion and we have been able to develop our fundamental line through actual struggle against the American and Russian bombs together with the young workers and in the international solidarity. Thus a new era has begun for the Japanese student movement to be anti-stalinist revolutionary mass movement.

\* \* \*

The period starting in 1956 is characterized by the rapid rationalization and modernization of Japanese capitalism, and at the same time, by the heavy resistance of the proletariat against the mass discharge and aggravation of the working conditions accompanied with the process of the drastic transformation of Japanese capitalism. Especially the workers of railway, post office and coal mines fought the most militant struggle but they were compelled to surrender to the attack of capital under the pressure of the conformistic leaders of the trade unions.

In the railway workers' strike in 1957 against mass discharge, CP which is the minority in the labor movement assisted the socialist leadership in giving up the strike against the fighting will of the workers. Many communist workers left the Party on that occasion…. In this situation the independent struggle of Zengakuren drew keen attention of the militant workers and in the Ampo struggle there was certain co-operation between the rank and file workers and the Zengakuren. In the anti-war struggle the co-operation was developed further and resulted in the "Anti-war Assembly of Workers and Students."

151

The whole process of the Zengakuren from left-wing opposition in the stalinist party to a revolutionary wing of the Japanese proletariat for self-emancipation has been strongly influenced by the activity of an anti-stalinist revolutionary organization, the Japan Revolutionary Communist League (JRCL). This organization, established after the Hungarian Revolution in 1956, has the support of militant workers through its uncompromising struggle in the factories against management and labor bureaucrats at the same time, through denouncement of the Japanese Communist Party based on the sharp and exhaustive criticism of the distortion of communism and Marxism in the USSR, China and other so-called socialist countries. The JRCL has influence not only among the workers but also among students and intellectuals, and the recent struggle of Zengakuren has been developed through the concentrated discussion of stalinism suggested by JRCL.

Threatened by this situation unfavorable to the stalinist bureaucrats who had long pretended to be the only "vanguard party" of the proletariat, CP is trying to destroy the movement of Zengakuren. Their attempt to build up another student organization outside Zengakuren, and their abusive demagogy (such as "Zengakuren are paid by American imperialists," *etc.*), is confronted with the strong criticism of the majority of students.

Zengakuren is composed of self-governed body of the universities and committees are elected by all the students in the university. The activities of Zengakuren are practiced through discussion in the class room of the university and the success of the struggle depends on the contents and method of the discussions.

Besides, Zengakuren is confronted always with suppression by the government not only by the direct attack of the brutal police during demonstrations (against this we have developed the unique tactic of linking arms of the demonstrators and the sit-down), but also by juridical forms. Thus, we Zengakuren are surrounded by many difficulties and the hardest thing is our struggle against the general tendency of the Japanese labor movement to go after the reformist and collaborative policy of the labor bureaucrats of the Western countries.

We regard the present stage of Zengakuren as very important, for now, through the exposure of the false character of the Moscow-Peking conflict, we can clarify the fundamental problems and the perspective of the revolution in the world today.

We do not choose between Russia and China. Neither do we choose between East and West. These alternatives mean only to choose between different kinds of alienated class society. Our problem is not to adapt ourselves to the existing societies, but to create a *new* society which adapts to us. Russian and Chinese stalinists force us to admit either of the two stalinist societies as "communism"—the one relatively developed, the other underdeveloped, but both of which are dominated by privileged bureaucrats, just as the western societies are ruled by the monopolizing capitalists. Thus the working class of the whole world is deprived of political and economic power and is reduced to the status of passive object in both West and East.

Communism, however, means essentially the abolishment of class and private property through combining the powers of production of all the world by means of the *international* struggle of the proletariat against the oppressors who possess all means of production in their hands.

Russian and Chinese "communism" are far from communism. "Communism" that is dominated by bureaucrats? "Communists" that fight each other over their "national interest?"

The emancipation of the working class and human beings can be attained only through the overthrow of capitalistic *and* stalinistic domination by the working people's own power.

We are convinced that we are united with the revolutionary struggle of the Japanese working class and with the struggle overseas for the same purpose.

Joji ONADA, Torum KUROKAWA
General Secretary, International Secretary.

"What force on Earth is weaker
than the feeble strength of one?"
—Ralph Chaplin—
*ORGANIZE!*

Cartoon by Roland Topor; words added by *Rebel Worker*
(*Rebel Worker* 1)

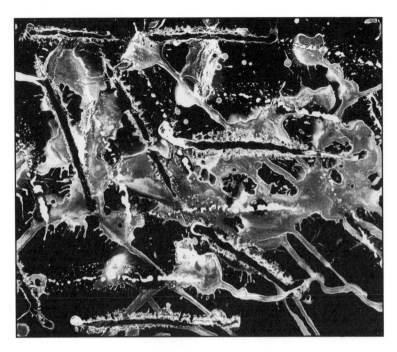

Penelope Rosemont:
*Misterioso, or The Desire of Desire*
(Alchemigram, 1967)

# BERKELEY WAS ONLY THE BEGINNING

RECENTLY STUDENTS HAVE BEGUN to emerge from the so-called postwar political apathy—a development, by the way, not particularly welcomed by the very same bourgeois critics who lamented that apathy. Through increasing interest and participation in the civil rights struggle, students have begun to develop a consciousness of themselves and an understanding of their own situation, along with an understanding of this odious system that becomes increasingly oppressive.

Far from being only the "attention-seeking protests of children against parent-substitutes" (as Prof. Lewis S. Feuer, amateur psychologist, would have us believe); far from being a "Communist plot of Maoists and Castroites" (as Feuer, now posing as a political analyst, again misses the point); far from instigated by "non-students," "Bohemians" and outside agitators, the rebellion at Berkeley last fall was the manifestation of an indigenous revolution, conscious of its opposition to the "benevolent bureaucracy" of Clark Kerr and all that stands with it.

Needless to say, the forces of reaction—the police, the politicians, the press, the state and businessmen—came to the aid of the administration. Even the few papers that gave somewhat favorable (or accurate) coverage managed to explain away the significance of the revolt by attributing it to the "bigness" of the university: that the administration had ceased to treat them as human beings, and instead treated them as commodities; that the universities had become "factories to produce technicians" to fit the requirements of industry; that the university administration is totally allied with the *status quo*.

These students, according to a writer in the *New York Times Magazine*, were not "political in the sense of those student rebels in the turbulent thirties; they are too suspicious of all adult institutions to embrace whole-heartedly even those ideologies with a stake in smashing the system. An anarchist or IWW seems as pronounced as any Marxist doctrine" (14 Feb. 1965, page 25).

Two excellent pamphlets have recently been published on the Berkeley revolt and are available at the Solidarity Bookshop in Chicago. *Students in Revolt* is a London *Solidarity* pamphlet containing a narrative of the events last fall, and a review of Hal Draper's pamphlet, *The Mind of Clark Kerr*, itself a review of two books by University of California President Kerr, in which his reactionary ideology is exposed.

*The Free Speech Movement and the Negro Revolution* is published by the Marxist-Humanist group *News & Letters* in Detroit. It contains articles on the student revolt itself ("Berkeley Fall" by Mario Savio and "Inside Sproul Hall" by Joel L. Pimsleur, "the only journalist to spend twelve hours in Sproul Hall when the students were arrested"), and articles relating the Berkeley revolt and the Negro freedom struggle. In Raya Dunayevskaya's article is included a fine critique of the views of Clark Kerr and Lewis Feuer (spokesman for the faculty minority who opposed the student strike: scabs).

The Berkeley revolt and strike united thousands of students who proved that they could run their own university and run it well, without a bureaucracy. They disowned the bureaucratic machine, what it stood for and what it wished to make of them—unthinking parts for an automated giant corporation. Along with this they realized how profoundly bureaucracy (as well as automation) has affected our society, and how their own destiny is bound up with that of the worker.

The Berkeley Revolution was only the beginning of the student revolution, and the student revolution is only a part of the revolution of youth, who threaten the survival of this system which refuses them the right to their own determination.

Penelope ROSEMONT

# EVERYTHING MUST BE MADE ANEW:
## PAUL CARDAN'S *MODERN CAPITALISM AND REVOLUTION*

IT DOES NOT TAKE MORE THAN AVERAGE perceptiveness to realize that the traditional left is more or less dead, in theory and practice, and that a new and vital revolutionary movement is gradually emerging. But this raises at least two important questions which have been insufficiently discussed in U.S. radical papers: Why and how did the traditional Left lose its relevance? And how is the new revolutionary movement fundamentally different?

It is useless, it seems to me, to attempt to answer these questions from any standpoint other than that of a complete revaluation of all revolutionary values. Young radicals today are, for the most part, undogmatic, experimental, free, looking for solutions to problems that the traditionalists don't even know exist. (Witness, for example, the condescending approach of the traditionalists to the problem of alienation.)

The traditionalists see very little (although they are good at pretending) of what is happening in the world today. How could they? They use their opaque marxism and sometimes anarchism and syndicalism to shut themselves off from anything in the real or surreal world that might challenge their cherished, archaic beliefs. They wave their hands in the darkness and pretend they possess the light. They have, with their dogmatism, sectarianism, lack of imagination and general inability to see what's happening, cast a dark shadow over what should have been the brilliant and unfettered development of radical thought.

Paul Cardan has brought a sort of Diogenes' lamp into this political darkness. *Modern Capitalism and Revolution* can perhaps best be "reviewed" by reading its synopsis, reprinted in this issue of *The Rebel*

*Worker.* It is the latest of several excellent publications of the London Solidarity Group, with whom we are in close contact, and in nearly complete agreement with their analysis of contemporary bureaucratic capitalist society and their revolutionary perspective.

The book is described in a brief introduction as "an attempt to describe the main features and to analyze the dynamic of modern, fully industrialized, capitalist societies from a revolutionary socialist point of view." This Cardan does with a conciseness and yet thoroughness which the hurried or casual reader with no fondness for searching through huge tomes in remote libraries should find gratifying. It also presents the clearest, deepest and most thoroughgoing critique of the traditional Left available today. Finally, it offers a perspective for today's revolutionary movement. It is, as far as members of the Chicago Branch are concerned, an IWW perspective.

*Modern Capitalism* calls into question everything that socialists have been supposed to take for granted. And its attention is always focused on just what it is that makes socialism worth fighting for. "Socialism is not fundamentally about production.... It is about freedom." But read the synopsis. Read the book. And buy extra copies for your friends.

Franklin ROSEMONT

# MALATESTA

ERRICO MALATESTA WAS BORN in Santa Maria Capua Vetere in the province of Caserta, Italy on December 14, 1853, met Bakunin when he was only seventeen years old, was exiled from Italy when he was twenty-five and returned several times only to be exiled each time within a year for his radical activities. At the age of sixty he strongly took issue with Kropotkin over the latter's support for the Allies during World War I. He returned to Italy in 1919 to stay until he died in 1932. This is about all that most historians know about Malatesta.

To set the picture straight, Vernon Richards compiled his book,* which stands as undeniable proof that Malatesta was more than an untiring anarchist activist—he was a superb writer and theoretician. Better than half of this book is devoted to Malatesta's extensive writings most of which Richards translated and compiled according to twenty-seven topics, ranging from "Anarchism and Violence" and "Money and Banks" to "The Workers and the Intellectuals." The book is rounded out by a short fifty-page biography and an essay of equal length entitled "Malatesta's Relevance for Anarchists Today."

This arrangement makes the book an excellent introduction to the anarchist case, for Malatesta's writings are lucid and free from pettiness. But Richards does not see his book as just another volume to be added to the small shelf of anarchist tracts already in print. His reason for publishing is based on his belief that Malatesta is relevant for our age as are none of the classic anarchists. For him Malatesta is a bridge to us, because his anarchism is firmly grounded in the same industrial society we live in. And because he possesses two highly esteemed qualities of the Industrial Revolution—pragmatism and realism.

In his approach to anarchism Malatesta was pragmatic, for he was an anarchist because it "corresponded better than any other way of social life" to the kind of life he wished to live. And he was realistic in his approach to politics, in his un-apocalyptic view of the revolution and in his non-sectarian views towards participation with others in common struggles.

But these aspects of Malatesta's thought don't make him any more relevant than anyone whose ideas are lucid and free of trivialities. Malatesta is not one of those rare individuals who seems to speak to two generations in the future. He dealt with the people and the events of his time and he did that quite effectively. But we today have to face very different problems. We can no longer pretend that capitalism has changed only insignificantly since the twenties. Capitalism since the twenties would be unknown to Marx, much less Malatesta. And when Richards maintains that the problem remains the same for us as Malatesta, and then claims that the problem is one of authority, he is merely begging the question.

What we must face squarely is the fact that under capitalism the methods of exploitation have changed, and along with them the tactics of defense employed by the exploited. Exploitation is more subtle: the ruling class having at its disposal the entire gamut of mass media and the cornucopia of consumer goods with which to entice the proletariat into the most hideously stupid, self-defeating behaviour. But even dullards eventually realize that they have exchanged their freedom for a bucket-seat, and when this dawns upon them they can devise the most magnificent schemes to beat the credit and installment syndrome. And in this way these assumed sheep protect themselves and in the process have revolutionized the defensive tactics traditionally associated with the oppressed. For instance, never before in history have so many people used the system to beat it at its own game, and never before have they so effectively defended themselves from such a distinct anti-organizational basis. Direct-action demonstrations, wildcat strikes, student boycotts are all kinds of protests which are outside the rules of established society. No wonder that every petty, drivelling bureaucrat, whether in government, business, the unions or in school administrations, screams "FOUL" at the prospect of rank-and-file direct action.

The affluence of modern capitalism and its bureaucratization individually are responsible for these two changes; and collectively they lead to the third major development of modern society: the metamorphosis of the lumpenproletariat. The lumpens can no longer be relegated to the dank, black forces of reaction, they must be correctly seen as the most oppressed and the most revolutionary force in our society.

Malatesta is relevant to any one of these tradition-shattering developments only in the sense I mentioned previously—that is, in his clear thinking. What he says about unionism, for example, highlights the most serious defect for the radicalization of the lumpenproletariat. Malatesta saw unions as "a means whereby workers can begin to understand their position as slaves, to want their emancipation and to accustom themselves to the solidarity of all the oppressed in the struggle against the oppressors." This latter point, class consciousness, has not yet been evoked in large segments of the lumpen.

Though the lumpens become radicalized individually by ever-more increasing bureaucratic rationalizations, in the same manner as union men do through the machinations of their "leaders," they along with the workers will require some kind of organization to give them a sense of community, of solidarity. What kind and how it will arise remain to be seen. This is an impasse we must face. To maintain that Malatesta speaks to us with more relevancy than the classic anarchists may be true, but for Vernon Richards to believe Malatesta can contribute significantly to the radical's perspective in modern society is dangerous, because the prospects for relevancy are not to be found in his writings, but in the new society emerging.

Knowledge to further the revolution will be found struggling with people and witnessing them evolve their unconscious radicalism into a mode of expression, as they will, as have all oppressed peoples throughout history.

The activist among the dispossessed and exploited would do well by reading the writings of anarchists and libertarian socialists, for they all contain important lessons that the traditional Left has never learnt. And now can be added one more volume to his list, but I would suggest that he insert it in its proper alphabetical place.

Bernard MARSZALEK

*Malatesta, His Life And Ideas*, edited by Vernon Richards (Freedom Press, 1965)

# LETTERS

Just recently a copy of your magazine *The Rebel Worker* came into my possession. I am very much a member of the working class— my father is a miner in the Rhondda and I am a quarryman in a remote village in West Wales. Consequently, your magazine expressed a lot of my own politic opinion (if that is the right word to use).

Could you inform me how it is possible to get further copies of *The Rebel Worker*? Also, is it possible to get a copy of IWW songs— there are some flames of discontent in the quarry where I am employed and occasionally working.

Deri SMITH
Llandysul, Cardigan, Wales

We sold most of the 45 copies of *Rebel Worker* 3 which you sent us at a CORE & an anti-war-in-Vietnam demonstration. Those 45 disappeared in 3 days and we haven't even gone around to book-shops yet. Send 50 more. It's really a great issue. Except for the mimeographing.

Barton STONE, IWW
Berkeley, California

We liked *Rebel Worker* 3 very much. Those we had were snapped up like hot-cakes. I think the format which you have adopted is the best one as it gives you room to deal with subjects on a serious basis. Workers today are no longer physically hungry, but they are hungry for information, and not only about industrial matters. One of the greatest condemnations of most "radical" papers is that their attitude to workers is analogous to cheerleaders at a football match (American style not soccer). They first of all deal with struggle itself in a most primitive manner ("rah rah strikes are good") when what is needed is information and analysis so that when workers do fight they fight on their own ground and they fight to win. Secondly, the average radical paper treats the workers as if he is as the boss would like him to be, a philistine, without interest in art, education, psychology, history, etc. etc. Thus the socialist movement itself has contributed to the debasement of working class life. They treat him (and believe him to be) the object of history not the subject.

The reason for this attitude is obvious. Leninism, Fabianism, etc., etc., all preach that the ordinary bloke cannot understand society and that this is the role of the elite who, armed with the sacred texts, will lead him unknowing into the promised land. It is this attitude which separates libertarians from authoritarians.

So keep up your broad coverage in *The Rebel Worker*, although as you develop I would like to see more description of what modern industry in the US is really like, more reportage (inside news if possible) and analysis of new managerial techniques and workers' resistance and offence.

If we in England can help you in any way or if you see anything which you want us to cover, just let us know.

Ken WELLER
London *Solidarity* Group
London, England


Please send us *The Rebel Worker*, official quarterly journal of the Chicago Branch IWW. We wish to receive *The Rebel Worker* from its first issue. We have strong interest in the emancipation of workers in the age of automation.

I. SHIGEO
*The Three-Penny Review*
Nagano-shi, Japan


We have to have some way to contact the younger generation to get them interested in the class struggle or it won't be long before the IWW will go out of existence. So it is up to you young fellows to devise ways and means to get the IWW back in the industries where it belongs, so that workers will get some benefit of their struggles and

161

have a goal to drive at such as the six-hour day to do away with unemployment. We all know it was the struggle for the 8-hour day that put the IWW on the map in years gone by...

O.N. PETERSON
Branch Secretary, IWW
Seattle, Washington


I received *The Rebel Worker* a few days ago. What impresses me most about it is that it deals with all sorts of questions which the traditional radicals consider "non-political" but which are actually of the greatest concern to most ordinary people (such as rock and roll and child-raising) and it does not treat of these things from the point of view of the "superior" intellectual decrying the ignorance or backwardness of the masses. The test of a revolutionary publication is very often much more what questions it concerns itself with rather than its formal political "line" in the narrow sense. I have, however, I must confess (despite the fact that we publish a mimeographed bulletin ourselves) an antipathy toward mimeographed magazines intended as popular organs. But I suppose mimeographing is the inevitable consequence of being poor.

Martin GLABERMAN
*Facing Reality* Publishing Committee
Detroit, Michigan


I enjoyed *Rebel Worker #3* very much, especially the article called "Mods, Rockers and the Revolution." I was also glad to see the excerpt from *Summerhill*—the fact that you printed it shows that revolution has to be in every sphere, and we have to examine everything we do, because no area is free from the influence of our sick society. Your conception seems to be opposite that of the traditional groups; they concentrate on the political area and call themselves revolutionary, but in every other area they are quite conventional. This has probably been their greatest hindrance to growth—who except a schizophrenic will accept a philosophy which calls for revolution in one sphere and reaction in another? You seem to be revolutionary in everything, hurray!

Judy KAPLAN
Philadelphia, Pennsylvania

# AU GRAND JOUR

**T**he time is coming when seas of boiling rage will reverse the icy current of rivers, overflow and fertilize, fathoms deep, a crusted, petrified soil, tear away frontiers, uproot churches, clean the hills of bourgeois complacency, decapitate the headlands of aristocratic insensitivity, drown the obstacles the exploiting minority set in the way of the mass of the exploited, restore humanity to its future by freeing it from outdated institutions, religious fears, jingoistic mysticism and all that constitutes and consecrates the evils of the majority for the benefit of the two-legged sharks, their mates and the whole gang.

~René CREVEL

## SOLIDARITY BOOKSHOP
## 745 ARMITAGE, CHICAGO

This widely distributed 17" x 22" poster (late 1967/early '68)
was part of the *Rebel Worker* group's ongoing struggle
against gentrification (euphemistically called "Urban Renewal").
René Crevel was one of the early surrealists in France.
"Au Grand Jour" = In Broad Daylight.

Cartoon by Roland Topor; words added by *Rebel Worker*
(*Rebel Worker* 2)

**The Stalinist Program (5 for $1)**
Cartoon by Bernard Marszalek (*Rebel Worker* 5)

# REBEL WORKER 5

THE
REBEL WORKER

5

ORGANITAZION

WHAT TIME IS IT? TIME TO ORGANIZE.

March 1966 / *Cover by Tor Faegre* / 32 pages

*There is no use being alive if one must work.*
—André Breton—

Before leaving for London and Paris in December 1965, I typed a few stencils for *Rebel Worker* 5. Tor Faegre, however, edited this issue, which featured original texts by some of our most inspired and prolific correspondents. In these texts, what Herbert Marcuse termed "the power of negative thinking" points directly to a politics based on the Pleasure Principle. Louise Crowley's article deepened and developed *The Rebel Worker*'s guiding principle—*rebellion against work*—and Jim Evrard pursued our interest in popular culture with his reflections on workers' leisure. Jonathan Leake's poem resonates with the millenialist fervor of *Resurgence*, the mimeo'd mag he edited with Walter Caughey in New York.

—F.R.

Taking to the streets against war, Chicago, 1966
(in the crowd: Simone Collier, Tor Faegre, Bernard Marszalek)

Support the
**WEST SIDE**
**INSURRECTION**

i
w
w

One of several rubber-stamp "silent agitator" stickers
issued by the *Rebel Worker* group

# WATCHING THE WAR

*"War is the health of the State.... It automatically sets in motion through-out society those irresistible forces for uniformity, for passionate coopera-tion with the Government in coercing into obedience the minority groups and individuals which lack the larger herd sense. The machinery of gov-ernment sets and enforces the drastic penalties, the minorities are either intimidated into silence, or brought slowly around by a subtle process of persuasion which may seem to them really to be converting them.... [I]n general, the nation in war-time attains a uniformity of feeling, a hierarchy of values culminating at the undisputed apex of the State ideal, which could not possibly be produced through any other agency than war."*

—Randolph Bourne, *The State* (1919)

BOURNE DOESN'T RING TRUE ANY MORE. His State was too obvious, too open. It sentenced objectors to the firing squad, jailed them, or had vigilante squads run them out of town. Vietnam isn't World War I, but one still expects a little more of the old-style suppression of news blackouts on American "mistakes," and a crescendo of enemy atrocity stories—it hasn't happened, not yet anyhow. The machine no longer seems to need the old rationalizations. It can admit the war is a mistake, the issue a hoax, the whole thing a fraud, and yet go right on cooking. Why bother wasting time stifling dissent? Spend the time fighting the war. There is less patriotic fer-vor, but then, there is less needed.

It all makes for a frustrating experience. Some suggest blowing up tanks. Others would sit in front of them. No one has a clear idea of how to stop the war. But if we are to end this mess we had better begin by understanding it: Then, like a hungry dog, we will look for the weak points, grab by the neck and hang on.

The Solidarity Group [London] has started us on the way to under-standing with a short but excellent pamphlet on Vietnam (Bob Potter: *Vietnam*, Solidarity Pamphlet No. 30). It claims a "dispassionate analysis...detrimental to all parties concerned."

For Solidarity (and for us) the battle cannot be viewed simply as a peasant guerrilla war against a bad imperialist aggressor. Vietnam must be seen "in the context of the world situation—a world where the giant economic powers are struggling for supremacy."

> This pamphlet traces the history of the two Vietnams and how the people of both have been used. That the Vietnamese peasants are sincere revolutionaries is unquestioned. But how this dedication is used by Hanoi, Peking and Moscow is an altogether different

matter. It is not the first time in the history of communism that bureaucracies have been founded on the sacrifices of millions of revolutionaries.

Read the pamphlet. Go back and read Bourne for a view of our past troubles. Then, with a head full of knowledge, batter down the State.

Tor FAEGRE

# ON THE UNWHOLESOMENESS
# OF HONEST TOIL

L AST NOVEMBER, an article my husband and I wrote was printed in *Monthly Review*. Regularly published writers may smile at our naiveté, but nothing like that had ever happened to us before, and we hadn't the slightest idea what to expect. As it turned out, we got almost everything from anathema to praise; but of all of it, what confused me most were the honest workingmen who rose indignantly to defend their addiction to work. Mostly, they came to us in a spirit of good will, sincerely puzzled that we could defend anything as indefensible as sloth, and condemn anything as laudatory as industriousness. Their sincerity merits a thoughtful answer.

Yet, confronted in person, I always found it hard to give one. That work—*i.e.*, the labor one is constrained to perform in order to "earn" the right to food, shelter and clothing—should be a good-in-itself is a concept impossible for me to grasp; I've sold a great deal of my life in eight-hour slices, and always got the worst of the bargain. If I had been more highly paid, or worked under less unpleasant conditions, I'd still have been cheated, because life, even by the hour, simply cannot be compensated with money. All that can be said is that lack of money can terminate life sooner in our society, so that in order to prolong our years we sell our days—no, no matter how I phrase it, it just doesn't make sense. Whether a life is sold *in toto* on an auction block or piecemeal in personnel offices, it's still *life* that's being sold. Maybe if I accepted the saleability of life, I could comprehend the virtue of work,; but I don't, and can't.

But if people didn't *have* to work, our diligent critics tell us, they wouldn't do it. That may well be true, we agree, and they smile in satisfaction, confident they have won their point. Then it is I who's puzzled: what point? That idle people would waste their lives? But how can lives be more wasted than in a steel mill or a laundry? What could they do that would be worse? Watch television all day? That may be bad, with the programs we get, but it's not as bad as feeding punch presses. Get drunk? But they do that anyway when they can, and with desperation instead of joy.

Maybe the point is that society needs their labor. That has been true in the past, but at the moment, with over 40,000 jobs being lost to automation each week, it's a rather anachronistic proposition. Besides, our critics seldom argue society's need; their fear is that society will demonstrate the dispensability of their labor, any minute. If that fear has decreased somewhat in recent months, it's only because the government is now thoughtfully providing make-work jobs in the murder industry. That can't be it.

You see, I have been thinking, and defining work as labor performed under the duress of economic need or social custom, I cannot find any valid defense for it except as a dubiously necessary evil. For pay, the human workingman degrades himself into an adjunct to an inanimate machine or into a brute beast of burden; and that act is a prostitution of his humanity.

There is, however, a thoroughly plausible explanation for this proletarian devotion to the cult of work: it's a pathological condition, an industrial disease, one of the more malignant manifestations of that endemic time-clock syndrome with which the modern working class has been inoculated.

The nineteenth-century socialists did not fall victim to this madness, by then as rampant among the working class as consumption and rheumatism. They recognized clearly enough that love of work was a monstrous perversion of the worker's human instincts, and they took the proletariat of their day roundly to task for allowing itself to be so corrupted. Note this, from Paul Lafargue's *Right to Be Lazy* (1880):

> And meanwhile, the proletariat, the great class embracing all the producers of civilized nations, the class which in freeing itself will free humanity from servile toil and make of the human animal a free being—the proletariat, betraying its instincts, despising its historic mission, has let itself be perverted by the dogma of work.

Rude and terrible has been its punishment. All its individual and social woes are born of its passion for work.

"Shame on the proletariat!" he added, and went on to propose a three-hour workday as the maximum compatible with human health and welfare, and entirely feasible given France's level of productivity in 1880; but to be reduced as new machines were invented:

Our machines, with breath of fire, with limbs of unwearing steel, with fruitfulness, wonderful inexhaustible, accomplished by themselves with docility their sacred labor. And nevertheless the genius of the great philosophers of capitalism remains dominated by the prejudice of the wage system, worst of slaveries. They do not yet understand that the machine is the savior of humanity, the god who shall redeem man from the sordid arts and from working for hire, the god who shall give him leisure and liberty.

Engels noted the corruption of the British proletariat, but the housepainter-writer Robert Tressel described it best:

In May, as the jobs increased and the days grew longer, they were allowed to put in overtime; and as the summer months came round once more the crowd of ragged-trousered philanthropists began to toil and sweat at their noble and unselfish task of making money for Mr. Rushton. Papering, painting, whitewashing, distempering, digging up drains, repairing roofs, their zeal and enthusiasm were unbounded. Their operations extended all over the town. At all hours of the day they were to be seen going to or returning from jobs, carrying planks and ladders, paint and whitewash, chimney pots and drainpipes, a crown of tattered imperialists, in broken boots, paint-splashed caps, their clothing saturated with sweat and plastered with mortar. The daily spectacle of the workingmen, tramping wearily home along the pavement of the Grande Parade, caused some annoyance to the better classes, and a letter appeared in *The Observer* suggesting that it would be better if they walked on the road. When they heard of this letter most of the men adopted the suggestions and left the pavement for their betters.

In America, the Wobblies had a word for such workers, and they spat it out with utmost scorn: *Scissorbill!*

Yet even socialism's resistance broke down when, after the Soviet Revolution of 1917, it was exposed to a new and more virulent form of *ourgomania*, the pathological addiction to work. Contrary to expectation, socialism had come first to a backward, agriculture-based nation, and the urgent need of the new socialist state was development of an industry that could hold its own in competition with the capitalist countries. Of necessity, work became the order of the day.

If it seems a bit ridiculous that the poor devils who fought a revolution to lighten their labors found themselves toiling harder than ever to sustain their revolution—well, *ourgomania* is a madness, by definition. At any rate, it happened; and as capitalism's necessity has been elevated into a *good*, so too did socialism's. In the Soviet Union, diligent scissorbills got Stakhonovite medals. Glorifying the working class, Soviet ideologists found themselves glorifying Work itself— they had to, for their heroic working class must continue to work, else descend to hooliganism and bourgeois decadence, and fall prey to the capitalist enemies that ringed round it. So the cult of work was sold to socialist workers too, and soon they surpassed all others in their zeal. Working like piss-ants, they consolidated their socialist society, caught up with capitalism both industrially and militarily—and have become so addicted to work they now strive even harder, aiming for a twenty percent advantage. When they get it they'll undoubtedly raise the ante, become unable to conceive of a life free from toil.

Indeed, they suffer from the most fearful depression at the very suggestion of it; and any real threat to deprive them of their work, or even to reduce the hours of its duration, is quite likely to bring on hysteria and may precipitate suicide. That it is fear of idleness and not paylessness which so obsesses the *ourgomaniac* is demonstrated by his desperate resistance to all proposals for his emancipation, even those which carry with them provisions for the continuance of his income. He clings tenaciously to outmoded methods of production, that he may work the harder. Fearful that in a moment of unwonted clarity he may be tempted to revert to his natural inclinations, he often sets up elaborate precautions, enmeshing himself in debts for no other reason than to reinforce his need to work.

In one serious form of the malady, the *ourgomaniac* whose job does not reduce him to the utter nothingness he apparently craves may remove himself to a distant suburb, in order to lengthen his unsatisfactorily short workday by several hours of strenuous freeway driving, and add yardwork to his extravocational chores. The advanced case (most often a childless worker with relatively well-remunerated skills, who least needs the additional pay) seeks another job, and moonlights. When this occurs the crisis may follow quickly, and the worker who escapes death recovers with a high degree of immunity.

The more sophisticated worker is apt to exhibit somewhat different symptoms. He claims that he himself would welcome his freedom from work, and is quite certain he could use it wisely and well, yet suffers from the delusion that he is alone, or nearly so, in his capacity for living. Others, he feels, would surely find a workless life unendurable, and only be corrupted thereby—blindness to their present corruption, and his, being a universal concomitant of the disease.

Louise CROWLEY

# BLACK INTERVENTION
# IN AMERICA'S DREAMS

ONE HUNDRED YEARS LATER: white agricultural slaveholders still fighting white urban-industrial wage-slavers over style for sustaining black labor force. So northerners are winning and are bigger and southerners want northern escape-from-unions new factories and are giving in. But the black man thinks Our King is winning.

One hundred years later: he still waits Something to be Done About rotten high-price food and flimsy easy-credit furniture and quarter-meter television and $20 more rent no maintenance apartments or live in projects and uninterested personnel offices and "social workers." (And that's only beginning of it and everything else is included and someone else can break out but you can't.)

And he waits change in northern toughcop and misidentification in court (if you disobey you may get caught. or someone else may get caught and if you obey someone else may get caught. or they may get you anyway.) Cops obey higher cops and you stay out of their way or obey them. Cops don't think and with Whites and (sometimes) middle-class Negroes, maintain law and order and thank you for your help. But blackman law is Enforced and crime Prevented and youth can't stand on streetcorners (where every family has had young uncle, cousin, brother in jail) and no protection for anyone against cops' lies.

One hundred and one years later and again one hundred and two, people get pissed. Which seems thank-God healthy.

Hungry editors and end of second season of (dogdays August)

172

newspaper-selling riots assign reporters to keep on writing. Paper inches of well-informed long-quotes and "analysis" columns again (as if they hadn't said it all year before) lie: people have no reasons and cops are absolved.

Reactionary cops, soldiers release deeper hates (from not knowing and not belonging there) than the festive rioters. And politicians and machines no longer have contact and leave get-people-off-streets talking to christians. (All the king's precinct workers and All the king's clergymen couldn't put riots forgotten again.)

America's Twenty Million ("There's always been a lot of Negroes. But before 1960, Opinion writers weren't leafing through census summaries muttering 'How many Negroes are there?, anyway.'") Colored people weren't shocked.

Revolutionaries thought (somewhere got) the revolution is foretold; or thought hoodlums. Political types don't see rioters state (when explanation is demanded) "make Whitey listen" reform goals. The angriest, looking for action youth for a while chase and/or divert confuse cops and people celebrate their temporary freedom in their own community.

Old revolutionaries who are American left without a revolution and are content or moving right—see only hoodlums, VIOLENCE!

Anarchists (and psychologists) don't look for (even though horrible breakdown of all law) order; no reports of rape or group white-murder. No radicals miss spontaneous voluntary organization which was not there. Marxists say "It could as easily be any poor," recognizing historical inevitability but not historical fact; black people, not of white society, do not think to control it (or even attack whiteworld homes and powerlines) but—like Quebeçois—seek only to control own community within.

Revolutionaries at best (better than newspapers) see this: Expropriation: and proclaim the prophecy, promised land. (Always "What does this historical event mean for Vanguard, us," never first what does it mean.)

All men are created equal; but, growing up different, live in 2 races. Someone said (in midst of leftwing changing party-line 1940s) "There is no Negro Question. The Negroes are *right*." America's white problem continues.

Peter ALLEN

*(excerpts)*

# POPULARLY APPLAUDED BUT
# SCIOLISTICALLY OBFUSCATED

T HE "REVOLUTION" THESE THREE BOOKS ARE ABOUT is one
gigantic and odorous crock of shit. No one can deny that the
act of taking over the Berkeley campus was truly revolutionary, but everything since the tremendous Sproul Hall sit-in has been
singularly lacking in ardor, revolutionary or otherwise.

The events therefore taken as a whole cannot be termed revolutionary. To do so is journalistic hyperbole, misleading by its superficiality. What has come out of the Berkeley controversy besides a
fantastic legend is a place in the young radicals' vocabulary of "stu-
dent-faculty control," "Free Universities" and so forth. This is certainly significant, though one should keep in mind that the reforms
that have grown out of the Berkeley disturbances have been just that—
reforms. Nothing revolutionary has happened anywhere else; in fact
nothing as simply colorful as the tar and feathering of professors that
took place in this country during the 19th century!

The Free University of New York, "The School" in Chicago, the
Swarthmore Society and other educational experiments aren't anything
to crow about; one can hardly entice a yawn. If this is "revolt" god
help us. Yet on another level the events at the Berkeley campus *are* revolutionary, just as are wildcat strikes and draftdodging, but the authors
of these volumes aren't talking about that, for to do so requires a larger
view of this sick society than they wish to admit to. To them, "revolt"
is merely an "in" concept and something which will "grab" the public—a concept that does, of course, have an element of truth in it.

The student revolt that does exist is smaller than the Luce corporation's imagination would make it, but in terms of activists it is
a little larger than the much less publicized student "rebellion" that
thrived during SPU [Student Peace Union]'s heyday in the early
Sixties: larger because, firstly, of the immediacy of the War; secondly,
because of the complacent myths shattered in many youths by the
U.S. intervention in the Dominican Republic; and thirdly, because the
bureaucratic trends of this society have become even more pronounced and many more are getting the shaft.

All of these reasons for growth of the left have resulted in a qualitative difference comparable to a generational one for students only
three years apart on the academic ladder. The vast anti-Americanism
evident on the "new left" is proof of this, as is the marked lack of
enthusiasm for sitting around discussing the fine points of foreign

and domestic policy exhibited by the young people in YPSL [Young People's Socialist League] and SPU. Today's New Left wants action. They want a commitment to a purpose—a pity that that is the easiest fulfilled of desires, much like "getting religion."

The point is, where do we go from the commitment?

The New Left is receiving all kinds of advice in that regard. Draper wants them to politicize their communities; Goodman wants them to communalize their politics.* Draper deplores the lack of clear ideological thinking among the students, and posits that this deficiency is the reason the FSM [Free Speech Movement] didn't persist through the spring semester. Goodman doesn't exhibit despondency over this; he rather is stimulated by the community he found in Berkeley, during his spring visit. He bases his alternative advice on this experience. He believes that the wonderful dynamism that the FSM possessed, and which Draper freely admits grew out of FSM's political naïveté, should be directed toward developing better communications among the young students and the faculty, and creating a real community from which politics can emerge in a meaningful sense.

Furthermore, Goodman understands the significance of the "social revolutionaries" at Berkeley: the hashish-users and the "Filthy Speech Movement," whereas Draper remains utterly blind to their relevancy. He in fact reduces himself to hysterical name-calling in referring to these people as "nihilists"! Goodman on the other hand must be commended for his insight into the need for a *New* Left, one that is more than just a political expression of a superficial ideology.

Yet those who perceive the frivolity of Draper's traditionalist approach grow impatient with Goodman's reflections. Berkeley and many SDS and SNCC centers of activity are communities for the participants, but isn't there the possibility of moving beyond these centers to the disaffiliated elsewhere? The dynamism of the movement is providing the outside world with the fruits of the labors of these groupings, but when that dynamism is dissipated, one fears that the movement will fall apart as the erstwhile "peace movement" did after the signing of the Test Ban Treaty. Or will this movement remain and transform itself into a few insular scattered communities of dissent? And will it leave the field open to the stalinists to again drag out their frail, shriveled tit of a program that they always have ready with the pathetic expectancy that the masses will suckle at it? This is the saddest and most terrifying of possibilities.

Problems and opportunities must be met with understanding now! We can't wait. We have to build a truly revolutionary movement by reaching out to people on their terms. This means we talk to students about controlling their schools directly, and not about school boards, or worse, city halls. When they begin to smash their teaching machines we will know that we are getting someplace. With workers, we must understand their distrust of bureaucracies and the overriding pride they take in that part of the job they can control; obviously we have to encourage them to extend this control. When they start smashing their timeclocks we shall know that the revolution is around the corner. The most myopic prejudice that the New Left will have to dispense with is that only the most dispossessed are worthy of identifying with. Both on the job and in school and in their everyday life, people are beginning to verbalize the major problems of this society as the suppression of their alienation, through unlimited cultural escapism and consumption and the increasing division of people into order-givers and order-takers.

All of these workers and others students and the unemployed experience our society in basically the same way. No matter who they are, they are ordered about and constantly humiliated. It's not impracticable to express to them the arbitrariness and cruelty of hierarchies both in factories as well as in welfare agencies and schools and their total superfluousness. Nor is it difficult to explain that the basic problems of society are not solved by a rise in the Standard of Living but in fact are hidden by it. And that this is the whole purpose of the "Great Society," to obfuscate the real issues about who will control this society: the people or the bureaucrats.

It's not absurd to advocate a radical change; it's imperative! Any genuine New Left must do just this; otherwise, what's the use of wallowing in self-righteous parlance? Yet the New Left won't be able to do a damn thing until it sees beyond the various surface "issues" to the basic contradictions of modern capitalism.

Though I have rambled to some extent, all of this does relate to Berkeley, for there, in one of our finest institutions of learning, who was benefitting? Not the students. Nor the faculty. The basic problems of a meaningful teacher-pupil relationship increased with the university's budget, just as a worker's real problems increase with his paycheck. The students and faculty took action to cut through the bureaucracy and get on with their purposes. Workers also wildcat. The students and faculty haven't succeeded; they took only one step. They actually can't succeed until the workers do. When the people who work in factories and offices run them, then the students and faculty will run their schools.

Berkeley was one battle in a war more and more people are waging against an absurd, regimented, and sanguinary system. In this sense and only in this sense was there a "revolution" on Berkeley's campus last fall. But none of these books see it this way. A pity, for their authors are in for a shock.

Bernard MARSZALEK

*Berkeley: The New Student Revolt* by Hal Draper (Grove Press) 246p $.95. *Revolution at Berkeley,* edited by Michael V. Miller and Susansea Gilmore (Dell) 348p, $.95 *The Berkeley Student Revolt* edited by Seymour Lipset and Sheldon S. Wolin (Anchor) 585p $1.95

*NOTE: Those interested should read Draper's book; it's filled with advice and also the best description of what happened. Goodman's views are contained in both the Dell and Anchor books, but probably best in the former, which has a reprint of his *Dissent* article (Spring 1965). The Anchor book is a testament to Goodman's statement that the FSM was the best researched and documented movement in history. Among the reams of boring analysis it contains one worth reading: Henry May's "Impressions" of the students and non-students (the community) around the campus.

Bernard Marszalek:
*Self-Portrait*

177

# FIVE O'CLOCK WORLD:
# POP MUSIC & PROPAGANDA

EOPLE ARE ALWAYS TALKING about advertising, propaganda, and manipulation of public opinion in general, but they rarely get specific. I would like to take the concrete example of a popular song about the five o'clock world to illustrate some some aspects of the techniques of manipulation to which we are constantly exposed.

But first, a word of clarification. This talk of manipulation is often brought up by smug, pseudo-sophisticated individuals who think they themselves are exempt, who think propaganda is effective only on the "peasants" below them. These people think that responding to manipulation techniques is a matter of insufficient intelligence, naivete, human weakness," or letting yourself be taken for a sucker. If there were only fewer "stupid" people in the world, they pretend, the problem would be solved.

This approach is fundamentally wrong. It is rather the fact of *not* responding to their techniques that would indicate there is something wrong with you. One of the most basic techniques they use is made possible for them by the lousy condition of "our" capitalist society. In this miserable society of ours, many of our most fundamental needs and wishes are constantly and systematically frustrated. Modern psychology has discovered methods whereby this condition of frustration can be exploited by offering us partial satisfaction in the form of surrogates—that is, substitutes of inferior quality.

Let's exemplify this on the basis of the text of the Animals' song, "Five o'clock World." It begins by indicating how miserable our work day is, using the phrase "another day down the drain." What human being who has ever worked for a living in our society would not respond to that statement? You don't need to be "stupid" to respond to that one—you only need to have to work for a living. Under the inhuman conditions of work in our sick society, work-time is in fact time cut out of your life, another day down the drain. Up to this point, then, a song like this one fulfills one of the functions that folk songs used to fulfill in the past: namely, to help people alleviate their sufferings by giving expression to them.

Then comes the verse: "But in the five o'clock world, when the whistle blows, no one owns a piece of my time." What working person hasn't felt that? When you work, you don't own your own time anymore: the company does. "You may own your own soul, but the company owns your body." As far as your boss is concerned, your work power is a commodity which you sell on the "labor market," as the economists call it. (As you know, the slave market has been abolished.) And what you've sold, your friend the boss puts to good use in his own interest, regardless of what human misery this may cause you.

No propaganda yet. Up to here, it could even be the beginning of a revolutionary song. You can imagine how the text should go: "Take over the wor day. Take over the factories and manage them yourselves. Don't let anybody own a piece of your time *before* five o'clock, either.

But here comes the twist. Up to now, if you are a normal working person, the text of the song has said "yes" to some of our profoundest human strivings. If you are a normal human being, with normal human feelings, wishes and sorrows, your emotional response has been positive. You have been "softened up for the sale"—*not* because you are "stupid" or "weak," but because the text up to now *really does* correspond to your needs and wishes.

*This is an important point for the understanding of manipulation technique.* It always starts out by offering partial satisfaction for a genuine human need. You are now ready for the message.

And what is the message? Find yourself a fair-haired girl after five o'clock, who will make you forget the misery of everyday existence in our society (until tomorrow morning at eight o'clock). And the girl? What does she get out of this? As you know, in real life, relationships between people built on a basis like this dry up in a matter of weeks, or months at best. So the message offered by the song turns out to be first-rate establishment propaganda—for three reasons (at least):

First, it suggests we seek the answers to a real problem in an unreal world. There is a whole collection of pop songs, movies, radio and television programs whose basic tendency is the suggestion to escape from our miserable real life into a dream world, instead of taking active steps to change the real world. In this song, it takes the form of a dream girl waiting for me at five o'clock to make me forget my misery by attending to all my frustrated wishes of the day without having any needs or demands of her own. (Nice role for you girls, isn't it? But don't fret: our loving entertainment industry is busy creating dream boys for you!)

Second, it suggests an individual solution to a social problem. The problem of inhuman working conditions can be solved only in the factory or office itself, by collective workers' action, not by each individual going home and overtaxing his wife or girl friend.

Third, it suggests we accept a surrogate for a fundamental human need—a surrogate in the form of sexuality. Don't get me wrong. I am *not* putting sexuality down. As an activity in its own right between two people who dig one another, it is one of the best things mankind has discovered yet. But as a substitute for eight hours of my humanity? No, thanks!

As a matter of fact, the tendency we develop—in this sick capitalist world of ours—to make to many demands of sexuality, is another of the things that create human misery, because it inevitably leads to disappointment. Sex is wonderful, but it is a wonderful thing in itself, not as a substitute for the many frustrations and miseries our inhuman society causes in us. If we demand the latter of it, it will disappoint us. (And then we blame it on our partner.)

The frustration caused by inhuman working conditions cannot be solved except by changing these working conditions. All suggestions that we seek surrogates instead of making work human are propaganda for they imply the suggestion not to take action to solve the basic problem, an inhuman social order.

This type of argument is often misunderstood. It does not imply that you should stop digging pop music. You can sing a lousy text to swinging music. You can go on dancing to the music and ignore the text. Furthermore, this argument does not suggest that songwriters are conscious propagandists for capitalism. As individuals, they themselves may be as much victims of brainwashing as anyone else.

The point is, we can go on digging the pop arts, but we can at the same time keep our eyes open for the propaganda hidden in them. The heart is *not* the natural enemy of the head. It is only the miserable conditions of our society that make it seem so.

Jim EVRARD

# WINDY CITY EMERGENCY

*Laughable Unlaughables*
*Unborn wailing night children*
*Dropped like coal flakes*
*singing*
*In earth's sullen furor of the new world they were*
    *all looking at*
*Redeemed in a hurricane*
*(The eye hovering this spring)*
*Risen on ten thousand legs at various places*
*On multiple artillery torch helicopter thoughts*
*Shattering clattering on new horizons*
*Floating insurrection motions*
*After the wheels across iron unconscious pastures*
*Sing out brothers and sisters*
*Earth Air Fire Water*

*Mentionable Unmentionables*
*Witches and warlocks: vietcong street gangs*
*Unembraced save in red and black magic*
*Afternoon alchemy*
*Dust will not burn nor melt, must be submerged*
*Stone will not burn nor melt, must be smashed*
*Hate will not burn nor melt, must be swallowed*
*By ten thousand timeless laughing antichrists*
*The year of the beast, the fire horse*
*With hooves of solid oak*

*Touchable Untouchables*
*Suddenly, or with all appregations possible*
*Remember: if it is all unfamiliar, this is the Change*
    *It Is Now*

*Will bends and sinks*
*Lead guilt soaked nastiness of straight and crooked crosses*
*Burning crosses and double crosses*
*A five pointed star*
*A six pointed star*
*A seven pointed star*
*A star with ten billion points that*

Has become a circle
Turning: the revolution
The All spinning out from the center to the freedom
    of perimeter
Come tomorrow: here it is

Here, the Haymarket labor truth, labor saints, labor devils
Labor revolution world
Black revolution world
Youth revolution world
world revolution world
word
revolution
word
Here, wobbly Dillinger died in our allies' alley
Reborn under a million breakfast tables
Here, the machine gun criminals crucified
Here, on the grey lake
Here! Here! Here!

Forge your green and black and red ranks
The single fist opened to sky and oceans (inside, without
    bottom)
A moment of conjunction
Equinox: Emergence: Emancipation
Five planets: three stars
One billion hands: One mind

We are all one and in this dawn of the phoenix, the sphinx,
the Coming Dawn of good loving
the rough beasts, beautiful high
Reborn on plateaus, jungles of caution
At this moment, here, now,
The only Poem is Revolution

Jonathan LEAKE
March 14, 1966

# LONDON BLUESLETTER

WE GOT THE COPIES of *Mods, Rockers & the Revolution* and the latest *Rebel Worker*—excellent as ever. I still think that it's the best political magazine being produced anywhere at present—of the ones I've come across, of course.

The high point of public popularity of blues is now probably over—the days when Wolf's "Smokestack Lightning" crawled into the top thirty and John Lee Hooker crawled into the top twenty for a tail-end dice are past. However, the residue remains and it's possible now to write seriously on the subject for jazz magazines as well (viz. *Jazz Monthly*, to which Mike Rowe and I contributed the first of a two-part epic we are doing on Chicago blues).

Certainly this year's blues-fest will be a sellout, whereas Count Basie won't be and Ornette Coleman, my vote for the most lyrical of all altoists presently working an avant-garde vein, wasn't. We have Jimmy Lee Robinson, Buddy (yeah, yeah), Shakey Horton, Fred McDowell, Roosevelt Sykes, J. B. Lenoir, *et al.* coming, and this year's should be the one to end them all. My rough guess is that "Big Mama" Willie Mae Thornton's going to go through this year's audience like a knife. No one's really expecting anything from her because no one's heard "Me and My Chauffeur."

I like *Rebel Worker*'s insistence on the revolutionutritional value of rock, but I think it's a sight too optimistic, at least applied to this country. Our censors get much less steamed up about rock than about "Eve of Destruction"-type shit.

The big rocker/mod crisis is almost certainly *passé*. It began just pre-Beatles and seemed to disintegrate, at least as far as open manifestations were concerned, as the Beatles stormed to popularity. As the Beatle-fad subsided the crisis came out into the open once again. The mods began to seek victims. The rockers never manifested any open hostility toward mods, and what offended the mods, who were much more overtly rebellious (rockers will usually say that we're doing no harm, just enjoying youth before we settle down in a suburban nest), was the rockers' insistence on ultimate respectability, and their constant endeavors to anesthetize opposition, by organizing charity drives, church rock'n'roll, etc. The rockers were much more interested in motorbikes than rebellion. The mods picked on them, and for their part were interested in largely aimless rebellion.

Now the whole thing seems to be submerged. Only one mod rock group here, the brilliant Who, who do create a real storm of sexuality and rebellion.

Charles RADCLIFFE

*(excerpts)*

# LETTERS

I dug the hell out of your number four. I was impressed by the varieties of different points of view you've united under one cover...

I was glad to see an article stressing among other things the need to consider the theoretical and philosophy foundations of a radical position. The doctrine that the head is the natural enemy of the heart is integral to Anglo-Saxon culture. Whereas this doctrine on the continent remains more exclusively associated with fascism and the right in general, in American and England it affects the radical left as well. It is an inhuman doctrine, and should be exposed as such, in all its subtler forms as well.

Yours for solidarity,

Jim EVRARD,
Munich

Dear Editor,

As a New York wob, and a female, I'd like some more information on the upcoming anarchist-pacifist youth conference to be held here this month. I saw it mentioned in issue 4 of the *Rebel Worker*, which by the way was really beautiful.

I can't agree with Craig Beagle that there are hardly any rebel girls (I know many myself) but I think that the number of women involved in politics has always been proportionately lower than the number of men. I don't think the proportions any different among the radical groups than anywhere else.

yours for the revolution,

Judi SIGLER, X323596
New York IWW Branch

Dear Friends,

I am taking my sophomore year at the Rome Center of Loyola University of Chicago. I think *The Rebel Worker* is a tremendous publication. Could you please start me a one-year air-mail subscription, figure out how much it will cost, and bill me? Also, could you send me several sample copies? I would like to see if I can get more people to subscribe.

Sincerely yours,

Brooks Lewis ERICKSON

Dear Friends,

Thanks for the *Rebel Worker*, which we think is a good paper. I read most of the items with great interest. We hope you will continue to send it to us, and we in turn shall send you our *De Vrije* in return. Fraternal greetings, for *De Vrije*, anarchist monthly,

Arthur MENDES-GEORGES
Rotterdam, The Netherlands

Where will YOU be when capitalism collapses ?

Cartoon by Roland Topor; words added by *Rebel Worker*
(*Rebel Worker* 1)

*Above:* In the spirit of George Herriman, Tex Avery, and Jack Cole, Charles Radcliffe's zany lettering fanned the flames of the *Rebel Worker*'s wild, no-compromise humor.
(The examples here are all from *Rebel Worker* 6).
*Below:* Tor Faegre's sketch of an IWW rock band appeared in *Mods, Rockers & the Revolution*

# REBEL WORKER 6

London edition, May Day 1966
*Cover by Charles Radcliffe* / 22 pages

*The road of excess leads to the palace of wisdom.*
*What is now proved was once only imagin'd.*
*Exuberance is Beauty.*

—William Blake—

Thrown together in six or seven days—a joyful week-long fit of collaborative enthusiasm and improvisation—this issue, edited by Charles Radcliffe,
Penelope and me in London, quickly became (and remains today) the single
most widely circulated and best-known *Rebel Worker* of all. The London
edition made a big splash at Hyde Park on May Day (*The Rebel Worker*'s second anniversary), and a little over a thousand copies of the Chicago edition
appeared a few weeks later. Thanks to its global diffusion, and no doubt to

the rumor industry as well ("Is it true that The Rolling Stones read *Rebel Worker*?"), our little mimeo'd mag was suddenly in the limelight. The traditional left denounced us—some called us a "nuisance"; others, a "menace"—and of course that helped, too. Subscriptions and queries poured in from all over; for the first time it was really hard to keep up with our correspondence.

—F.R.

# THE REBEL WORKER 6

Chicago edition, June 1966
*Cover by Pieter Breughel the Elder* / 24 pages

# FREEDOM: THE ONLY CAUSE
# WORTH SERVING

THIS SIXTH ISSUE OF *The Rebel Worker* is being produced in London, several thousand miles away from its customary home in Chicago. We hope this issue, and subsequent ones, will help give our ideas a wider audience than they have had so far in Britain.

*The Rebel Worker* is an incendiary and wild-eyed journal of free revolutionary research and experiment, devoted principally to the task of clearing a way through the jungle of senile dogmas and aiming toward a revolutionary point of view fundamentally different from all traditional concepts. We believe that almost all political propaganda is useless, being based on assumptions which are false and situations which do not exist. We are tired of the irrelevant concepts and the old platitudes. The revolutionary movement, in theory and in practice, must be rebuilt from scratch.

Many of us around *The Rebel Worker* are members of the Industrial Workers of the World (IWW), once one of the largest and most powerful rank-and-file revolutionary organizations the world has ever seen. We have joined the IWW because of its beautiful traditions of direct action, rank-and-file control, sabotage, humor, spontaneity, and unmitigated class struggle.

It is these principles that constitute our editorial basis, but our task is not limited to mere recruitment. Our role is to promote "whatever increases the confidence, the autonomy, the initiative, the participation, the solidarity, the equalitarian tendencies and the self-activity of the masses and whatever assists in their demystification."[1] We want and support revolutionary direct action on every level—in the factories, on the docks, in the fields, in schools, in colleges, in offices and in the streets. But this is not enough. Revolutionary action should be accomplished by theoretical understanding. The revolution must be made by men, women and children who know what they are doing. Consciousness and desire must cease to be perceived as contradictions.

The Revolution, for us, cannot be limited to economic and political changes; these are urgent and absolutely, it is true, but we see them as a beginning rather as an end. We see social liberation as the essential prerequisite, the first step, in the total liberation of man.

It is especially to young people—young workers, students, drifters, draft-dodgers, school drop-outs—to whom we address ourselves and our solidarity. You are one of the largest and most oppressed sectors of society, and it is you who must make the Revolution.

What we want, and what *The Rebel Worker* is about, in short, is Freedom—"the only cause worth serving."[2]

Ben COVINGTON, Charles RADCLIFFE,
Franklin ROSEMONT, Penelope ROSEMONT,
Nat TURNER, Emiliano ZAPATA

1. Paul Cardan, *Modern Capitalism & Revolution*, Solidarity.
2. André Breton

# LOST WHISPERS
## (Preface to Chicago Edition)

THIS IS THE CHICAGO PRINTING of *The Rebel Worker* 6 (June '66), originally published in London on May Day, exactly two years since our first issue. Response to the London issue has been encouraging, both in terms of sympathetic letters, subscriptions, and offers of collaboration as well as the outcries and disdainful comments of traditional radicals and liberals. One English cat said it was the first revolutionary paper which actually frightened him. Another, a member of the Young Communist League, said he would have none of these "little sects," adding that he at least belonged to a "well-organized group"!

Let us note here that the London Solidarity Group are graciously distributing 100 copies of the London printing for us; this is the group which publishes *Solidarity*, one of the best revolutionary periodicals in the world today.

Charles Radcliffe, our London soul-brother, has written to us that further issues of an incandescent-carbonated journal sharing similar scandalous preoccupations with *The Rebel Worker* will appear there with the name *Heatwave*, adding its own delirious lucidity, vengeful humor and millenarian sensibility to the revolutionary movement in England. *Heatwave* 1 will appear in 3 to 4 weeks. Copies, of course, will be available from us at 25 cents each.

The London printing carried a last-minute-type cover, hastily prepared by Radcliffe, portraying a bearded, bomb-toting anarchist in a balloon. We have decided to use here, instead, an engraving ("The Temptation of St. Anthony") by Radcliffe's distant relative, the Flemish anarchist Pieter Brueghel, the Elder. H.Arthur Klein, in his *Graphic Work of Pieter Brueghel the Elder* (Dover Books, paperback), writes about this particular engraving: "In its drastic criticism of the conditions of both the Church and State, this may well be the most 'outspoken' of Brueghel's graphic works. Corruption and decay beset both the State (the one-eyed head below) and the Church (the rotting fish above)." This engraving is for us a pretty accurate presentation of contemporary reality, although we feel that the curious figure in the lower right-hand corner (who happens to be St. Anthony) is now historically and poetically outmoded, to say the least, and would perhaps be replaced best today by a passionate saboteur, armed to the teeth with mad love and the uncontrollable desire to be free.

# A VERY NICE, VERY RESPECTABLE, VERY USELESS CAMPAIGN

WHEN THE ANARCHIST POET Jeff Nuttall spoke at the final rally of this year's CND Easter march, he added new dimensions to the usual ritual, just as did the giant political puppet theatre which showed politicians as they really are, not just without conscience but small, grovelling men, sustained only by the persecuting knowledge of their own vacant treason to their humanity. By calling for the destruction of the Ministry of Defence, Jeff Nuttall gave intention to an affair which had none of its own. By speaking he let it be known that any number of people saw in CND and its charmless entourage of parliamentary vipers nothing so much as the sell-out of a once genuine popular movement against nuclear war to the so-called immediate imperatives of political relevance and political advance.

Since the CND leadership made public its refusal to challenge society—after the Spies for Peace revelations in 1963—the Campaign has lived on borrowed time. The complex manoeuvres to present a libertarian image while denying to anarchists the right to speak at the rally, the dummy-protests and the dummy-Members-of-Parliament are not going to save it. CND is doomed. It is time for a young movement which addresses the contemporary reality—a movement which will challenge every tiny aspect of our war-sustained society, even unto the last public utility, which will militarise the dissatisfaction of almost every young person in this country. For dissatisfaction is not confined to politics; it extends into every street, club and classroom. It must be encouraged in its every aspect; its active expression may be welded into a revolutionary weapon which will strike fear into the deepest recesses of our society.

Imagine briefly: if every time the police decided to victimize young people they were faced with the united fury of such people. If young people were to turn on their attackers with all the venom their frustration could muster. Then we might talk of protest.

Such a movement would support the emotional eruptions of all youths; would learn to sanction the outrages of youth recognizing in them a kindred spirit—albeit a bolder one—in the rejection of the spiritual death of a society which has attempted too long and too successfully to postpone the irrefutable logic of its indifference: destruction. This society, if we will it, can drown in its own corrupted blood. It can die in its tracks—on the streets, in the clubs, in the factories.

The new revolution may be obscene and blasphemous; it must deface the power structure when it cannot destroy it; the criterion is defiance not discipline. The new revolution must support every last insurrection of the mind and body against this bloodfed society— our movement is symbolized by the bomb-thrower, the deserter, the delinquent, the hitch-hiker, the mad lover, the school dropout, the wildcat striker, the rioter and the saboteur.

This year 500 anarchists caused a "near riot" in Trafalgar Square, until the "platform" capitulated to their demand for a speaker. Significantly, it was Nuttall who spoke on their behalf rather than an "Establishment anarchist" (as *Peace News* delights to term those comrades who are old enough to have sold out but have not done so). The anarchists were roundly condemned by the national press. The peace movement, as represented by *Peace News* condemned them in more sophisticated fashion. (The dedication of the liberals to respectability has so clouded their vision that they no longer care about the effect of their actions, only that they should not be attacked for them). The relevance of the action of these predominantly young anarchists is obvious. Their voices and actions exploded their precise consciousness of the fact that respectability finally involves simply this: Clamber into your own arsehole and quietly die.

Charles RADCLIFFE

# SOUVENIRS OF THE FUTURE:
## Precursors of the Theory and
## Practice of Total Liberation

EVERY SCREAM OF PROTEST and genuine anger, every signal of true resistance, whether expressed in wildcat strikes, in certain strains of pop music, in violence against the police or on anti-war demonstrations, in ghetto uprisings, in the blues, in jazz, in poetry or guerrilla warfare against the state—wholehearted revolt in any and every form gives the lie to the fat and hypocritical complacency of those who cower in fear behind closed doors, afraid of the people in the streets, afraid of their own children, afraid of everything that gets in the way of their own stupidity, afraid above all of every vestige of a human being concealed within themselves.

It is also clear, however, that the presently emerging movement of protest is too little conscious of the implications of its actions, too unsure of whence it came, where it is going, and why. Certainly one of the most important tasks of a revolutionary journal is to expand, broaden and deepen this consciousness. The motives, inspirations and aspirations of the present movement, of which *The Rebel Worker* constitutes one of the more adventurous forces, cannot be understood properly without a complete revaluation of revolutionary values as well as a vast reassessment of the whole revolutionary tradition, necessarily involving research into, and reinterpretation of, all levels and all varieties of past struggles.

The most relevant voices of the past are not the ones sanctified in the bourgeois mausoleum of heroes. The degree to which they are acceptable to this society is the degree to which they are useless to us. Nor can we hope to find most of them in the genealogy cherished by the traditional left. It is also essential that we do not seek from them exclusively political or economic or even sociological revelations. "In periods of political inactivity," as Fellow Worker Lawrence DeCoster wrote not long ago, "the greatest hope of revolutionaries lies in non-political activity."

Let us note here a few of those whom we can unhesitatingly affirm as precursors of our own theoretical and practical activity, a few desperate enchanters whose magical lucidity still burns in our eyes today, a few lone soul brothers of whom we can still speak in connection with freedom. Academic and journalistic parasites may attempt to obscure them with their false elucidations, or ignore their work through the ignoble "conspiracy of silence," but nothing will stop us from pouring into the crucibles of the revolution these splendidly subversive inspirations and implacable dreams.

## LAUTRÉAMONT

It was Aragon who, before his Stalinization, observed that just as Marx had laid bare the economic contradictions of society, and Freud the psychological contradictions, so Lautréamont threw into a dazzling new light the *ethical* contradictions: The whole problem of morality, not to mention such other problems as the animalization of the intellect and the purpose of literature, assume with Lautréamont an excruciating significance next to which most of the philosophical babbling of his contemporaries seem to us today as nothing more than a handful of lies.

The importance of Lautréamont on the ideological development of surrealism is second to none. His work has been called "a veritable bible of the unconscious"; the validity of many of his discoveries and revelations were subsequently demonstrated by Freudian psychoanalysis. It can probably be generally agreed that the liberal-humanist pantheon has, in the last century and especially during this century, crumbled to ruins; and it is Lautréamont whose criticism of it was most thoroughly, most devastatingly to the point, and who, moreover, best indicated a way out of the morass of confusion by rallying around the "reality of desire" which, theoretically elaborated by surrealists, remains the key to our most revolutionary aspirations.

## FOURIER

The traditional left of the Twentieth century has almost invariably consigned the many so-called "utopian socialists" to a position amounting to historical irrelevance, assuming them to be of interest exclusively for their influence on Marx and Engels, or Proudhon and Bakunin. Critical re-examinations of utopians by revolutionaries *have* occasionally appeared, and sometimes they are very good (see, for instance, Marie-Louise Berneri's *Journey Through Utopia*, which discusses not only the best known Utopians, but also Winstanley, Diderot, Sade, William Morris, *et al.*) But much more still needs to be done. In particular, the fantastic and visionary works of Charles Fourier (whose delirious cosmology and "passional" psychology, no less than his penetrating social analysis, intrigued Marx and later Trotsky as well as many anarchists), deserve sympathetic and serious study.

Fourier, more than any of the utopians, pioneered many of our own preoccupations. He was very aware, for instance, of the central problem of love and the crucial role of human passions in social life. He insisted on the necessity of completely changing the very fabric of life to meet the needs of desire. The implications of his theory of analogy suggest a possible new development in revolutionary theory. His importance, in any case, cannot be limited to the experimental rural phalansteries (Fourier's name for communes) of his disciples—which are important too, of course, but in a very different way—nor to his immediate influence on later socialists. It is above all Fourier the *poet* and *seer* who interests us today.

## SADE

The theoretical and imaginative work of the Marquis de Sade, along with the practical efforts of the celebrated Enragés, can be considered, from the revolutionary point of view, the highest points reached during the French Revolution and the so-called Age of Reason.

The rising bourgeoisie was anti-feudal, anti-monarch, anti-superstition, but its talk of liberty and reason soon reduced itself to platitudes to be carved by the State in stone above the doors of prisons. It was a limited freedom, freedom defined to meet the needs of only one comparatively small class of exploiters. The Enragés struggled for a deeper revolution, representing the class needs of the proletariat. This effort was to receive its theoretical analysis and justification later, first in certain workers' papers and eventually in the monumental contributions of Marx and Engels.

Sade, too, realized the inherent weaknesses of the revolution (see particularly his *Frenchmen! One More Effort If You Wish to Be Republicans!*, which was, incidentally, reprinted as revolutionary propaganda during the struggles of 1848). He was aware of the social conflict—the class struggle—but brought to his analysis a consciousness of other problems (love, sexuality, desire, crime, religion, etc.) which were not to receive systematic exploration until surrealism. His works, which at various times have been reduced to providing tea-party chatter for senile *littérateurs*, and are currently enjoying a paperback revival (doubtless for being "classic pornography"), should now be read by everyone struggling for a revolution which will not end in a new set of chains.

## BLAKE

The editions of his own works printed by William Blake are highly prized by cretinous bourgeois collectors (let us spit in their faces and note in passing that everything he wrote spits in their faces, too). He is probably the greatest poet in the English language, but most radicals seem to know nothing about him in connection with revolutionary politics other than the fact that he hid Thomas Paine who, at the time, was wanted by the British government.

But Blake saw much further than any of the other radicals of his time, and his works—which are now only really becoming active influences on the revolutionary movement—bear witness to the extraordinary depth of his perception and the prophetic surreality of his vision. The revolution, too, will become non-Euclidean!

It is true that the semi-religious symbolism he often employed has detracted somewhat from the truly subversive, anti-religious and liberating message of his works. But compared to his contemporaries—and that was a revolutionary age!—Blake was the brightest star in a cloudy, moonless night.

## THE GOTHIC NOVELISTS

Professional literary critics and academics today are practically unanimous in their rejection of that extraordinary profusion of works of the late 1700s and early 1800s usually know as "gothic novels." These tales of haunted and crumbling castles, apparitions in the night, maddening lust, pacts with the devil and bleeding nuns are quite evidently not suited to the refined tastes of our numerous literature experts, who dismiss the entire genre as "musty claptrap," or with some other derisive appellation. Like most matters of interest to us, the academics put them down, utterly missing the point. These works, like the real meaning of the revolution, are simply beyond their understanding.

What makes the gothic novelists of special importance to us is not only the immense popularity they enjoyed at the time of their publication (they were the best-sellers of their day) but also the great influence they exerted on some of the most brilliant and critical minds of the younger generation: Shelley, Byron, Coleridge, Sade, Hugo, Baudelaire, the Brontë sisters, *et al.* Very few works of any period enjoy this double privilege; it was André Breton, I believe, who first pointed out that these works were highly successful expressions of the *latent content* of the period in which they were written (*i.e.*, the days of the bourgeois revolutions).

One of the greatest weaknesses of the traditional left has been its neglect of the problems of the individual, and human personality in general. There has been, for instance, little investigation of the psychological changes occurring during periods of great social upheavals. It is obvious that people who support reactionary candidates in bourgeois elections do not think the same way as the people who take over the factories and smash the government. Workers as a class cannot make a really successful revolution (that is, one leading to complete freedom) unless they are individually, psychologically as well as socially, capable of it. That is why it is important for revolutionaries to reinforce spontaneity, creativity, self-reliance, independence, and rebellion on the part of individual workers as well as of the working class. This is also one aspect of the relevance and importance of workers' sabotage, an individual act serving the needs of the class.)

Obviously much more work must be done along these lines. Meanwhile, we should restudy the imaginative works of sensitive writers of the past who, more or less automatically, documented some aspects of this problem. In particular the greatest of the gothic novels—Horace Walpole's *Castle of Otranto*, Matthew G. Lewis' *The Monk*, Charles Robert Maturin's *Melmoth the Wanderer*—offer us valuable testimony in tracing the genesis and evolution of individual revolutionary sensibility, the latent and personal drama unfolding with the manifest and general cataclysm.

\* \* \*

Of course we have only penetrated the surface of a hardly explored sea, to which no limits can yet be assigned. We must remember that we are in the preliminary stages of our experiment.

We know that we cannot build a new revolutionary movement with the skeletons of the old. The Old Left has taught us very little of what we want to know; we must learn to teach ourselves. Every exploration must be the preface to several others. Every dream must lead to new actions.

Franklin ROSEMONT

---

## Don't mourn, ORGANIZE.
# JOE HILL
## WAS HERE.
## JOIN the IWW.

---

Another rubber-stamp "silent agitator" sticker
issued by the *Rebel Worker* group

# HUMOR OR NOT OR LESS OR ELSE!

*Humor is not resigned; it is rebellious. It signifies the triumph not only of the ego but also of the pleasure principle.*

—Freud—

HUMOR, WHICH HAS LONG BEEN NEGLECTED by many so-called revolutionaries in their attempts to prove to themselves that their intentions are altogether noble and serious (no doubt also because of the desolation and barrenness of their thinking), ought to be given the recognition it has long deserved, and regain its rightful place in the revolutionary struggle.

The Wobblies have long been recognized for the humor they have contributed to the class struggle. A famous incident in the history of revolutionary humor occurred when IWW construction workers, whose pay had been cut in half, reported for work the following day with their shovels similarly cut in half. (The pay was raised.) The IWW's *Little Red Song Book* contained such songs as Joe Hill's "The Preacher and the Slave," which mocks the famous religious hymn, "In the Sweet Bye and Bye," used by the Starvation Army to sell its "pie in the sky." And aside from being the greatest of the IWW writers, T-Bone Slim is also one of its greatest humorists.

Humor has vast, as yet only partially realized powers as a polemical weapon. Its users can, with the least possible effort, pull the keystone out of any argument, leaving the opponent standing stunned amid a pile of bricks. *Solidarity*, for instance—one of the outposts of revolutionary humor today—once recommended that nonviolent demonstrators "go limp and refuse to bleed."

The movies of the Marx Brothers, Charlie Chaplin, and Bugs Bunny are all implicitly dangerous to bourgeois society; they express their bitterness and aggression in humor.

Potential potentates are notorious for their lack of humor and their total inability to cope with it. The entire functioning of a bureaucracy depends on the fact that it is taken seriously. The bureaucrat as an individual usually has little control over the violence which is at the command of the State. This is functional in that it serves to absolve him of any guilt which might result from the use of this violence, for in a bureaucracy as in a firing squad no one really knows who has the live bullet. Bureaucrats have at their disposal little more than the "prestige" of their position. Humor is the archenemy of prestige!

The most violent and extreme form of humor, known as *black humor*, has found its greatest expression in the work of Lautréamont, Alfred Jarry, Jacques Vaché, and Benjamin Péret. A popular although diluted variety of black humor is found in the elephant jokes and "sick" jokes. Unlike other forms of humor, black humor is totally unacceptable to present-day society. It has an extremely disturbing effect because, while milder wit functions merely to deflate the ego of the person whom it happens to be used against, black humor threatens it and devastates it. It surveys reality, sees through it and exposes it. Black humor releases all the power of unconscious desire.

Through the adoption of humor as a conscious attitude we can assert ourselves over the confines of our environment ("reality") and in effect topple the whole structure and reassemble it as we wish, thus revealing a glimpse of the pride which the Revolution will restore to us.

Revolutionaries must be the enemies of bourgeois "reality"—they must be poets and dreamers with uncontrollable desires that will not be repressed, sublimated or sidetracked. They must be willing to be ruthless in their humor. The economic change brought by the Revolution is only the first of our demands. We will not be content with anything less than the total annihilation of existing "reality" and the total triumph of Desire.

Penelope ROSEMONT

# CRIME AGAINST THE BOURGEOISIE:
## INTRODUCTION TO THE WHO

I FIRST HEARD ABOUT THE WHO before they were The Who; just another mod r'n'b group, playing one of Central London's most fiercely mod clubs, but apparently doomed to remaining unknown outside a small circle of fans, despite their defiantly hip name—the High Numbers. I didn't hear any more about them for nearly two years, when suddenly a rash of posters appeared in Central London advertising a new group: The Who. The posters were superb—heavily shadowed, crudely dramatic and featuring The Who lead guitarist, Pete Townshend, his arm raised in an arc over his head, his guitar barely visible. A few months before they had been unknown, under the new name, outside the Shepherds Bush area but gradually the news spread that the Marquee Club—whence came, among others, the Rolling Stones, the Yardbirds, the Moody Blues and Manfred Mann—had a fantastic new group. They were taken up by *Melody Maker*, the hippest British music weekly, and shortly afterwards by *Record Mirror*.

Despite the enthusiasm of the fans—the musical press, for the most part managed little more than perplexed astonishment. The Who's first record, "I Can't Explain," one of the best pop records of 1965, didn't really move nationally at first, though it created enough interest in the group for their explosive views about pop to gain some attention. More people went to the Marquee; provincial fans carried back the news. The record took off, finally making the top ten. When The Who made their second record, "Anyway, Anyhow, Anywhere," they were again able to go almost into the Top Ten. The weird feedback sound effects, the carefully cultivated Pop Art image the wearing of jackets made from the Union Jack and sweatshirts embroidered with the freeform sound effects of American comics as well as military insignia, and later their championship of autodestructive pop, guaranteed them attention in a world where long hair was becoming more a recommendation for respectable employment than a mark of depravity.

The Who's stage act is a shattering event. They start off quietly but, providing the audience is with them, they soon turn on the special effects. The singer, Roger Daltrey, legs slightly apart, torso jutting forward, begins to smash his microphone with a tambourine, first gently and then with increasing fury until the amplifiers howl. Alternatively he crashes a hand-mike against the cymbals or screams harshly into the microphone, leaning forward at an absurd angle, his body straight, held above the stage by the microphone stand. While singing he cavorts round the stage in the curiously paralytic dance of a reigning mod. Occasionally he blows harmonica, furiously and grotesquely, like the screeching of a moon-struck tomcat. One way or the other he often leaves microphones smashed.

Meanwhile Pete Townshend, face bland and impassive, creates banshee howls, stutters and the staccato burr of distant machine guns from feedback and by scraping his instrument against the amplifier, before finally smashing it into the amplifier to produce the noise of tearing metal and screeching car tires. His arm swings wildly, higher than his head, arcing before smashing back onto the guitar. He strikes chords and his arm swings in circles, faster and faster; he holds a pose; arm extended, before once again swinging onto his guitar. Or he holds his guitar at the hip, shooting notes at the audience.

The Who's stage act can end with his guitar hurled into the crowd. John Entwhistle, on bass guitar, keeps the thread of the group's performance with heavy double rhythms and a driving base line. Drummer Keith Moon, mouth wide open, head gyrating from side to side, eyes wide and glazed, thunders out a furious rhythm, acknowledging the howls of the crowd for whom he has always been the main attraction.

The whole effect of The Who on stage is action, noise, rebellion and destruction—a storm of sexuality and youthful menace. They proudly announced, after the success of "Anyway," that their next record was going to be anti-boss, anti-war and anti-young marrieds. The result was this:

> People try to put us down
> Just because we get around.
> Things they do look awful cold.
> Hope I die before I get old.
> My generation, this is my generation, baby,
> Why don't you all f-f-fade away.
> Don't try to dig what we all say.
> Not trying to cause a big sensation
> Talking about my generation.

"My Generation" was the most publicized, most criticized and possibly the best record yet by The Who. If it didn't entirely live up to its expectations and if it wasn't quite so unrecalcitrantly hip as "Anyway," the offense it caused—particularly when the group announced that the singer was supposed to sound "blocked" (high) on the record was extremely gratifying.

There is violence in The Who's music; a savagery still unique in the still overtly cool British pop scene. The Who don't want to be liked; they don't want to be accepted; they are not trying to please but to generate in the audience an echo of their own anger. If their insistence on Pop Art, now dying a little, is reactionary—for of all art, pop art most completely accepts the values of consumer society—there is still their insistence on destruction, the final ridicule of the spectacular commodity economy. Townshend's room has shattered guitars hanging as trophies on the wall. There is also their insistence on behaving as they wish. Townshend told *Melody Maker*:

> "There is no suppression within the group. You are what you are and
> nobody cares. We say what we want when we want. If we don't like
> something someone is doing we say so. Our personalities clash but
> we argue and get it all out of our system. There's a lot of friction, and

offstage we're not particularly matey. But it doesn't matter. If we were not like this it would destroy our stage performance. We play how we feel."

Likewise, their manager told reporters that he saw their appeal lying in rootlessness. "They're really a new form of crime—armed against the bourgeois." Townshend talked defiantly on the hip TV show, "Whole Scene Going," to denounce the other members of the group, the pop scene, society at large and non-drug users in particular. "Drugs don't harm you. I know. I take them. I'm not saying I use opium or heroin, but hashish is harmless and everyone takes it." Townshend's views, which he expresses freely and frequently, are weirdly confused. On the General Election: "Comedy must come in the end and it just has...I think the tories will win because so many people hate Wilson...I still reckon English Communism would work, at least stronger trade unions and price freedom. I've always been instructed by local communists to vote Labor if I can't find a Communist candidate. The British C.P. is so badly run—sort of making tea in dustbins like the Civil Defence." On the Chinese: "They are being taught to hate. But they are led by a great person who can control them." In the same *Melody Maker* interview he came out against the Vietnam war but curiously did not support the Vietcong, complained about vandalism in phone booths and Keith Moon getting old ("Once—if I felt aging, I could look at Keith and steal some of his youth"). The conscious revolution, if at all, is, however, submerged under the unconscious and consuming fury of The Who.

The Who are at full volume; despite predictions of their imminent demise they have two records in the English charts and they will not die until they are replaced by a group offering more far-reaching explosions of sounds and ideas. The Who are symptomatic of discontent. Their appearance and performance alike denounce respectability and conformity. They champion their own complete expression of feeling. Bernard Marszalek has written: "One can only work toward this goal ('the intrusion of desire with all of its marvelous aspects into a decadent and crusted society') by developing with youth a sense of rage and urgency to unite the realms of dream and action fearlessly and with candor."

The Who may be a small particle of this explosion but they have a power unlike any other pop group's; on a good night The Who could turn on a whole regiment of the dispossessed.

Charles RADCLIFFE

# THE HAUNTED MIRROR

THE GRAY PILLOW DECORATES the omnivorous moon, upsetting the wizard's organ of the electric sidewalk. Later, the silence grows sinister and delinquent. The old women run frequently, and the monkey loses track of the crisp cathode. There is a striped squirrel on the roof, and a staircase on the bridge or bog. The night is as spacious as a sacrificial mirror, and all I know is that I love you because goldfish are cavernous and the sea is as singular as a rose.

Meanwhile, the cliffs overlook the visible waves, and the trees are black with ostriches. The automobiles entice the chairs in the desirable rain, as if the pedestrians had all recalled their spiral doorbells. The streets are full of rugs and windows; the shop windows full of waves. Who knows what the thunder will be like tomorrow, or the day after? The wheels are forlorn like the sleeping finger, or the tigers running loosely on the shore, observed only by the prickly scorpion, who sleeps with one eye open as wide as a paper, and always keeps another eye bearded next to his winding ear.

Finally, the woman cuts open the resourceful pendulum. There are the usual uncanny screams, the bloodstains on the sky, astonished limits in the dimly-lit ocean. The wolves are rheumatic. The house burns foolishly like a sacrificial accordion. The deceptive goat lies in the osteopath's bed. Every door leads to a new thief, but the blind adjectives own all the pencils. Every old winner is an alphabetical loser, every red table a letter of white sugar. Fallacious pipes are always rare, and I love you as madly as the sky is contagious.

Franklin and Penelope ROSEMONT
Paris, 1966

In the spirit of Jacques Vaché
(*Rebel Worker* 6)

# I AM NOT ANGRY: I AM ENRAGED!

I ADDRESS MYSELF TO BIGOTS: those who are so inadvertently, those who are cold and premeditated with it. I address myself to those "in" white hipsters who think niggers never had it so good (Crow Jim) and that it's time something was done about restoring the traditional privileges that have always accrued to the whites exclusively (Jim Crow). I address myself to sensitive chauvinists—the greater part of the white intelligentsia—and the insensitive, with whom the former have this in common: the uneasy awareness that "Jass" is an ofay's word for a nigger's music (viz. Duke and Pulitzer).

Allow me to say that I am—with men of other complexions, dispositions, etc.—about art. I have about 15 years of dues-paying—others have spent more—which permits me to speak with some authority about the crude stables (clubs) where black men are groomed and paced like thoroughbreds to run till they bleed or else are hacked up outright for Lepage's glue. I am about 28 years in these United States, which, in my estimation, is one of the most vicious racist social systems of the world—with the possible exceptions of Southern Rhodesia, South Africa and South Vietnam

I am, for the moment, a helpless witness to the bloody massacre of my people on streets that run from Hayneville through Harlem. I watch them die. I pray that I don't die. I've seen the once-children now-men of my youth get down on scag, shoot it in the fingers, and then expire on frozen tenement roofs or in solitary basements where all our frantic thoughts raced to the same desperate conclusion: "I'm sorry it was him; glad it wasn't me."

I have seen the tragedy of perennially starving families, my own. I am that tragedy. I am the host of the dead: Bird, Billie, Ernie, Sonny, whom you, white America, murdered out of a systematic and unloving disregard. I am a nigger shooting heroin at 15 and dead at 35 with hogshead cheeses for arms and horse for blood.

But I am more than the images you superimpose on me, the despair that you inflict. I am the persistent insistence of the human heart to be free. I wish to regain that cherished dignity that was always mine. My esthetic answer to your lies about me is a simple one: you can no longer defer my dream. I'm gonna sing it. Dance it. Scream it. And if need be, I'll steal it from this very earth.

Get down with me, white folks. Go where I go. But think this: injustice is rife. Fear of the truth will out. The murder of James Powell, the slaughter of 30 Negroes in Watts are crimes that would make

God's left eye jump. That Establishment that owns the pitifully little that is left of me can absolve itself only by the creation of equitable relationships among all men, or else the world will create for itself new relationships that exclude the entrepreneur and the procurer.

Give me leave to state this unequivocal fact: jazz is the product of the whites—the ofays—too often my enemy. It is the progeny of the blacks—my kinsmen. By this I mean: you own the music, and we make it. By definition then, you own the people who make the music. You own us in whole chunks of flesh. When you dig deep inside our already disemboweled corpses and come up with a solitary demand because you don't want to flood the market—how different are you from DeBeers of South Africa or the profligates who fleeced the Gold Coast?

I give you, then, my brains back, America. You have had them before, as you had my father's, as you took my mother's: in outhouses, under the back porch, next to the black snakes who should have bitten you then.

I ask only: don't you ever wonder just what my collective rage will—as it surely must—be like, when it is—as it inevitably will be—unleashed? Our vindication will be black, as the color of suffering is black, as Fidel is black, as Ho Chi Minh is black. It is thus that I offer my right hand across the worlds of suffering to black compatriots everywhere. When they fall victim to war, disease, poverty—all systematically enforced—I fall with them, and I am of yellow skin, and they are black like me or even white. For them and me I offer this prayer, that this 28th year of mine will never again find us all so poor, nor the rapine forces of the world in such sanguinary circumstances.

I leave you with this for what it's worth. I am an antifascist artist. My music is functional. I play about the death of me by you. I exult in the life of me in spite of you. I give some of that life to you whenever you listen to me, which right now is never. My music is for the people. If you are a bourgeois, then you must listen to it on my terms. I will not let you misconstrue me. That era is over. If my music doesn't suffice, I will write you a poem, a play. I will say to you in every instance, "Strike the Ghetto. Let my people go."

Archie SHEPP

Note: Archie Shepp's article is reprinted here in part from *Down Beat*, where it presumably had a readership akin to the magazine's policy of woolly blue-eyed liberalism. We hope this reprint will let his words reach a small part of the audience they deserve. We agree with what he says but think Fidel and Ho would sell him short. Maybe one day we'll get the chance to discuss this with him.—Charles Radcliffe.

# I HATE THE POOR

UNTIL ALL MEN UNITE in hating the poor, there can be no new society. Stalin loves the poor—without them he could not exist. The revolutions of the future must be directed not against the rich but against the poor. To be poor means to be blind, demoralized, debased. The poor have been the slop pails of capitalism, repositories for all the filth and brutality of a filthy, brutal world. Do not liberate the poor: destroy them—and with them all the jackal-Stalins that feast on their hideous, shrunken bodies.

How the Church and the false revolutionaries draw together: love the poor for they are humble. I say hate the poor for the humility which keeps their faces pressed into the mud. The poor are the product of a false and cruel society; but they are also the cornerstone of that society. Lift them to the stars; tell them to walk proudly on this earth: the cathedrals and broad roads were made by the labor of their hands; it is the duty of all true revolutionists not only to restore these things into their hands but also—and this is the key—to put them into their heads. Empty stomachs, empty heads: fill both with good food. Don't shove Peter the Great back into their throats.

Kenneth PATCHEN
(from *The Journal of Albion Moonlight*, New Directions)

Cartoon by Lester Doré (*Rebel Worker* 3)

# LETTER FROM CHICAGO

I WROTE A LETTER IN HONOR of Barry Bondhus, a Minnesota youth who took two buckets of shit into his draft board office and dumped them into six file drawers. I hope to pass these out at Dick Clark's World Fair of Youth being held for ten days at the Amphitheatre, and which will present 10 r'n'r groups, mod clothes exhibits, youth culture generally: it is being billed throughout the Midwest as a real blowout! But very conservative—several of us plan to change that. We still get suburban kids in to talk and I am beginning to come up with nice variations on disruptive activity that they can pull off.

What generates me at present is the altogether exquisite future that I see. Wait till you get back; the climate is changing here at a surprising rate: the acceleration is simply fantastic. Everybody is flipping out.

Another thing I am working on is a ball for May, probably outdoors, maybe at the Tap Root Pub after we get chased off open lots. With several rock bands, blues, etc. Several anarchists are interested, but I may have to do all the work, ecch.

There is a group here from the western suburbs called the Shadows of Night—have they been heard of in England?

Bruce Elwell is hoping to start a Theater of Provocation in Phillie. What I am doing is getting high and higher on one little realization: that I have one task alone and that is to bring out the most delicate outrage in myself. Explode the hair follicles, whee!

I can think of only lovely destructive stuff, like painting ourselves blue and walking on water. These scandals must be spontaneous. I'll talk to you when you're both back in this land of the brave and home of the free, or is it the other way around—I never could get it straight.

May Day, I'll send you a letter from prison.

Bernard MARSZALEK

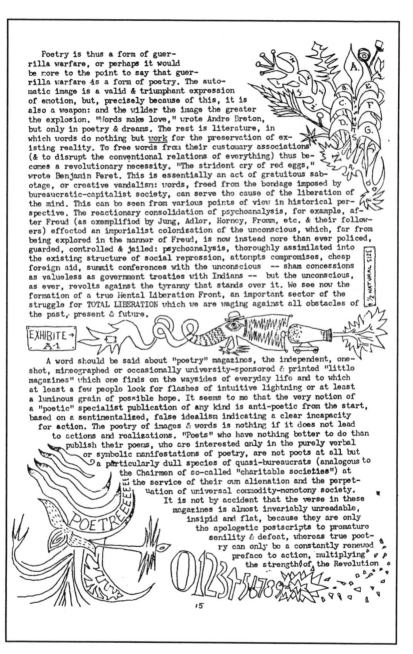

Poetry is thus a form of guerrilla warfare, or perhaps it would
be more to the point to say that guerrilla warfare is a form of poetry. The automatic image is a valid & triumphant expression
of emotion, but, precisely because of this, it is
also a weapon: and the wilder the image the greater
the explosion. "Words make love," wrote Andre Breton,
but only in poetry & dreams. The rest is literature, in
which words do nothing but work for the preservation of existing reality. To free words from their customary associations
(& to disrupt the conventional relations of everything) thus becomes a revolutionary necessity. "The strident cry of red eggs,"
wrote Benjamin Peret. This is essentially an act of gratuitous sabotage, or creative vandalism: words, freed from the bondage imposed by
bureaucratic-capitalist society, can serve the cause of the liberation of
the mind. This can be seen from various points of view in historical perspective. The reactionary consolidation of psychoanalysis, for example, after Freud (as exemplified by Jung, Adler, Horney, Fromm, etc. & their followers) effected an imperialist colonization of the unconscious, which, far from
being explored in the manner of Freud, is now instead more than ever policed,
guarded, controlled & jailed: psychoanalysis, thoroughly assimilated into
the existing structure of social repression, attempts compromises, cheap
foreign aid, summit conferences with the unconscious -- sham concessions
as valueless as government treaties with Indians -- but the unconscious,
as ever, revolts against the tyranny that stands over it. We see now the
formation of a true Mental Liberation Front, an important sector of the
struggle for TOTAL LIBERATION which we are waging against all obstacles of
the past, present & future.

EXHIBITE →
A-1

A word should be said about "poetry" magazines, the independent, one-
shot, mimeographed or occasionally university-sponsored & printed "little
magazines" which one finds on the waysides of everyday life and to which
at least a few people look for flashes of intuitive lightning or at least
a luminous grain of possible hope. It seems to me that the very notion of
a "poetic" specialist publication of any kind is anti-poetic from the start,
based on a sentimentalized, false idealism indicating a clear incapacity
for action. The poetry of images & words is nothing if it does not lead
to actions and realizations. "Poets" who have nothing better to do than
publish their poems, who are interested only in the purely verbal
or symbolic manifestations of poetry, are not poets at all but
a particularly dull species of quasi-bureaucrats (analogous to
the Chairmen of so-called "charitable societies") at
the service of their own alienation and the perpetuation of universal commodity-monotony society.
It is not by accident that the verse in these
magazines is almost invariably unreadable,
insipid and flat, because they are only
the apologetic postscripts to premature
senility & defeat, whereas true poetry can only be a constantly renewed
preface to action, multiplying
the strength of the Revolution

15

A page of *Rebel Worker* 7 (reduced),
with automatic drawings by Tor Faegre

208

# REBEL WORKER 7

December 1966 / *Cover by Tor Faegre* / 56 pages

*There's so much to learn. I keep hearing something else*
*beyond what I've done . . . more possibilities of new things.*
—Eric Dolphy—

Even in its last issue *The Rebel Worker* was expanding, not only in size and circulation, but also in the area of revolutionary theory and criticism. Surrealism was much in evidence, along with several pages by and about T-Bone Slim. The critique and subversion of everyday life was the focus throughout, with articles on proletarian hobbies, demystifying media, and the "practice of poetry." Important, too, is the stress on new or little-known radical voices: a Native American manifesto, taking up concerns the US left had shamefully ignored for generations; an essay on reification, which also happened to be the first situationist text published in the US; and James Cain's "Prophetic Mutterings."

Expansive, too, are the notices of *other* periodicals scattered through the issue. We had always promoted like-minded publications, but never had there been so many at once: *Heatwave* and *Solidarity* (London); *Solidarity Scotland*; *Resurgence* and *Black Mask* (New York); *Provo* (Amsterdam); *Revo* (Brussels); *Red & Black* (Sydney); *Blast* (Duluth); and *Internationale situationniste* (Paris). As 1966 came to a close, we all felt that a new revolutionary international was in the making.

—F.R.

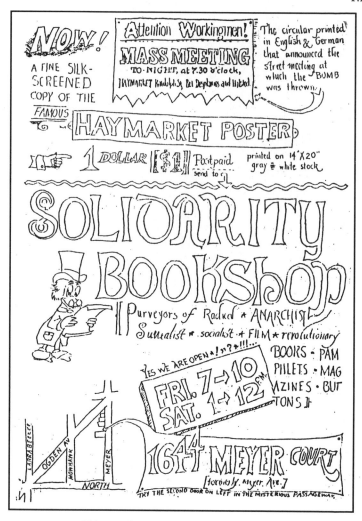

This was the back page of *Rebel Worker* 7

# WILD CELERY*

THE PROTRACTED DECLINE AND THOROUGH disintegration of criminal desperation has been happily reversed in the last several years in every major American ghetto, if nowhere else, but naturally, also elsewhere. Though the cynical may refer to these explosions of expectations as picturesque forays based upon shallow greed and shame, we prefer to think of them in a revolutionary context as merely the opening shots in a new and revivified class struggle. The possibilities for a total repudiation of everything offered to us by this society have never been so complete. For what is offered that is not merely an invitation to assimilation, to incorporation into a petty and disgusting niche?

The universality of this exigency leads us to conclude that, at bottom, fortuitous differences aside, we all live the same *disgusting* lives. One of the necessities for a revolutionary journal is to elucidate the various implications of this situation, for class differences, which in our affluent society, only apparently, have been extinguished, dominate the course and content of radical consciousness and protest.

Under these circumstances the rebel is confronted with a double necessity: to overcome, on the one hand, all the cops of everyday life (at home, school, work, and play) and, on the other hand, the hesitations derived from a fragmented and delicate rationalization, a systematization of unconscious fears rooted in memory and sustained by the official watchdogs of "common sense," which tend to inhibit the natural and perpetual superimposition of revolutionary aspirations.

What is needed, obviously, is a proper perspective or an indecent indifference; we hold no distinction here, but in fact wish to serve as a wrecking-bar at the service of all, and at the same time a crystal ball forecasting the delights that await us beyond the mean presumptions of our rulers. The efflorescent revolutionary situation today catalyzes our endeavors, and our works in turn should be considered nothing but wasted unless they raise the stakes.

The logic of all this necessitates our coming transformation: being, above all else, alchemists of Desire who know no boundaries, we jubilantly announce that this is the last but wildly prehensile *Rebel Worker*. To intensify our assaults we have decided to forego regular publication and opt for the thorough exploration of the Streets. Our aims remain essentially the same but now our war-cry shall be ZTANGI!

Bernard MARSZALEK, Franklin ROSEMONT

*favorite food of the gorilla.

# I SAW IT ON TV AND THEN
# WE PROVED IT AT HOME

THE ONLY EVIDENT EXPLANATION for the current dearth of creative, uninhibited, subversive and, let's face it, lucid thinking on the part of those who supposedly are most aware of this society's liberating potentialities, must simply be the novelty of a revolutionary situation. It's the old story again, and we hope for the last time, of the spinster's blind owl.

The thought patterns and ways of behaving that defined this society are speedily disintegrating in splendid imitation of sparkling Alka-Seltzer, progressively increasing its decomposition as the end approaches. Despite this, one finds all about a gloom and despair, an inappropriate—stillness, and have you noticed how empty the streets are of dancers during the day? Nonetheless, each established institution confronts a vast spectrum of discontent and abuse: amplified at every moment, traditional values are refurbished and displayed to the "masses." Spontaneous revolt is present in all places. Its more energetic forms exhibit a fiery brilliance not frequently manifest in the context of a supposedly contented populace and therefore easily misunderstood, or, worse, ignored by those who pretend to bow at Wisdom's egg-shells.

The end of the common consensus has been marked for all to see, through the immediate and intimate explosion of innumerable, complex social issues and crises. In white urban areas it is the racial unrest in the ghetto and its appalling intimations that has had the most recent and significant consequences upon formally complacent individuals. The riots have struck a raw nerve, albeit superficially racial, more profoundly social in effect, that hurtles into proper perspective the formerly ignored machinations of Established Society's political leaders. Irrationality prevails not only in racial matters, but in every manifestation, by the appendages of a wilted and constipated governmental structure.

The obfuscating complexity of the War in Vietnam, so carefully fostered by our well-suited warlords to induce apathy upon the citizenry, has engendered an unexpected popular reaction: the politicians appear to be witless and bungling fools (reinforcing a long held prejudice) who cannot cope with these intricacies and therefore cannot be trusted in their present course. The reaction has not been to cut through the complexities and thereby end the confusion in a violent manner, but in a pacific one, thanks to the reportage of the mass media.

Television especially has contributed positively in this respect, for every news program carries quite candid coverage of the war in progress, with each report adding more evidence to the brief that there is absolutely nothing in South Vietnam worth sacrificing the lives of American youth for. On top of all the useless bloodshed, the bankruptcy of the war is personified by that supremely unpleasant caricature of a fly-swatting, mustachioed petty dictator out of a hastily assembled, low-budget flick—General Ky, who, unfortunately for Washington, has done a magnificent job in building U.S. anti-war forces. A beautiful case of the double-edged razor at work: the institution meant to serve as a sedative has in fact, through its own inexorable economic laws, become a stimulant. And this despite the censorship that runs rampant, suppressing news of Army revolts in Vietnam, for instance.

One can appreciate the opposition of Hans Morgenthau, and those of his ilk, to the war, for Realpolitik is threatened to its foundations, since it presupposes a modicum of intelligent political behavior that is altogether absent in this situation, leaving open the field of political "science" to the uncontrolled excursions of psychoanalysis, astrologers and other disreputable types.

Media journalism in this case undeniably flabbergasted the Establishment in inadvertently presenting a real solution to a fictitious crisis and the institutional solution it was meant only to report. In other areas of unrest, however, this has not been true. Institutional solutions to racial problems, for example, are pretty thoroughly demonstrated to be wholly inadequate by the media, simply because riots persist, but no real solution (even a partial one) is offered. The resulting irrationality has a profound and disturbing effect upon those who expected answers from their community leaders, not evasion and patently inadequate stopgap measures. Religious, business, and civic spokesmen have only two claims to respect: obviously they are symbols of success (the right order of people and things), and, less visibly, but more basically, they are (or were) voices of Reason: one flowing out of and depending on the other. In recent crises their erstwhile reasonable voices now echo political platitudes, and their powers of settlement (reasonableness) are only made legitimate by the acquiescence of the opposition, as typified by Martin Luther King's open-housing agreement for Chicago—an agreement that will benefit the black bourgeoisie and the white power structure.

Yesterday's complacency and privatism were situated within a mellow and all-answering rationality. Others would safely prevent the intrusion of the world. After all, it was their world anyhow. But with street-rioting in cities all over the globe; with a senseless war resembling more the nightmare of a megalomaniac; with television revealing angry black faces screaming fear into virgin ears, and silly, impotent white men shouting back; with long-haired youths flaunting everything proper—generally, with all things in question from God to autos, complacency has lost its moorings and chaos reigns. All forms of communication have contributed to this conflagration of an ingenuine security.

Mass media has moved from a position of neutrality and passitivity on certain matters towards a hesitant force for chaos itself. Every news program, every television documentary, the newspapers and popular magazines all scream horror and destruction, amplifying for more sales—every riot, all mass murders and rapes, and blood begins to seep through the pages and flow from one television program to another, eventually to drip upon living-room rugs across the country.

Among all of these hammer-blows to the mirror, and among all the broken glass, the most beautiful and hopeful signs of wakefulness are emerging. Young blacks are tasting victory for once, and an almost forgotten appetite has been revitalized, never to be quickly appeased in the future. The most militant unionism since the Forties is developing. Only yesterday (September 22), several thousand auto-workers in Milwaukee struck the American Motors Stamping Plant, despite the opposition of local union leadership who hysterically demanded that the workers return to the line—for a shutdown during the beginning of new-model production could seriously hinder American Motors' attempt to achieve plush solvency. The workers, we should take heart, still know when to strike effectively. The anti-war sentiment, not withstanding the futility of Saran-Wrap boycotts, is definitely growing among all segments of the population. And lastly we have the flourishing disaffiliation of youth of all economic levels and from all geographic areas.

This last development has reached outstanding proportions only in the last year when, with their gains in sexual freedom elaborately displayed, young people began to invade their own consciousness and there extract the beginnings of a new culture. The drug scene lumbered out of the basement and began to occupy a choice but mistrusted storefront to become a part of what the Situationists refer to as the Spectacle.

The mass influx of young people created the Psychedelic Movement, and this movement has joined the other red and black forces of chaos generating more broken glass for reasonable adults to nervously sweep aside. (The popularization and resulting commercialization

214

could only be anticipated given the nature of this commodity-oriented society where the emotional starvation of the population must constantly be stayed by new extravaganzas.) Yet the psychedelic phenomenon is of a different order from the other chaotic happenings, for within it there is the wholly significant tendency toward the most absolute confrontation with Authority. Unlike the physical threats and destructions, which are needed of course, the psychedelic phenomenon cannot be a matter of argument. Authority can be altogether banished temporarily from its putrid, concrete pedestal by dynamite, but to prevent new lice from rebuilding, a totally free consciousness is demanded: a consciousness that has dismissed the dualisms that are the very sand and stone of Authority's support. Psychedelic experiences in transcending so thoroughly the individual and the collectivity will aid tremendously in advancing this new, sublimely complete consciousness.

The collectivity of these licentious black desires issuing from the shadows illuminates the disgraceful insipidity of thought and action quivering behind clichés, an almost unnoticeable twitch its only claim to life. History has again rushed past the innovators, leaving behind in their over-crowded rowboat a socially myopic and emotionally bovine horde of caterwauling malcontents, diligently oozing out of their tender open pores a pessimism that is too puerile to be an existentialist affectation. A most quaint ethical predicament affects this group, who, in stating their aim to transcend pessimism and optimism achieved a "new" stage: the Idea of Struggle, which encompasses all activity and becomes the very meaning of life. What they in fact achieved was a new pessimism, steeped in traditional ethics, not a new foundation for action, but only a restatement of a familiar failing of will. Some threat to our rulers this!

The entire mystification of social reality gains form and propagates itself on the basis of duty, and on an inverse conception, the so-called enemies of this mystification expect to reveal its putrescence.

The only results possible from this spurious ethic is a program of non-violence and its communitarian aim—the counter-society: medieval blood-letting where immediate major surgery is required: banal utopianism. To avoid unnecessary confusion we should make clear that we are not opposed to social experimentation; in fact, we wish to encourage it, for the multifarious social and personal relationships possible should be thoroughly explored. However the test tube in this case cannot transform the laboratory and we do not wish to be deluded by attacks upon "the twigs of the capitalist tree."

Needless to say, the expectations of these Utopians are filled with their own liberating contradictions, for there are those who, while

215

half-heartedly subscribing to the Idea of Struggle, also, to the horror of the establishment, hold Kicks Now as a proper demand. These are the "human beasts of love" acclaimed by Michael McClure, who in their glorification of passion in all of its manifold brilliance chafe under the reins of the new pessimism and its mangy superfluities. Here we have the souls divining the freest expression of the fullest extension of their immediate needs and creating, to speak cryptically, the Revolution. For as Felix LeDantec has said, "Rights are natural: duties are metaphysical."

To these various colored threads we add a sweetly warm and wet crowbar with which we can break out of this musty crate. Firstly, we must clear the decks of the seaweed of moral elitism that can only attract more of the same, and the very last thing we need is the twaddling savant displaying his refurbished liberal values to the select. (The tear-damp cheek is laughable.) Only a cracked mirror could reflect such useless piety in the face of breathtaking transformations. An impacted affirmation will not suffice, for only an exhaustive celebration is proper while avowing that everything is immanent to man. The frightened thread upon the dismal planks of a rotted ship and remain oblivious to its slow sinking.

Accomplishing this, we are free to subvert Authority with a methodical thoroughness it will never overcome.

Bernard MARSZALEK

Franklin Rosemont: Automatic drawing on Mimeo Stencil
(from *Surrealism & Revolution*)

Lester Doré: Solidarity Bookshop in 1967,
at 745 Armitage Avenue
(from the Chicago *Seed*)

The Celebrated
SOLIDARITY
BOOKSHOP
CATALOGUE
OF RADICAL BOOKS-IN-PRINT.
[& related topics]

Containing herin books on
The I.W.W., Anarchism, Socialism
Surrealism, & World Labor History.,
INCLUDING: the Spainish Civil War, the
Hungarian Revolution, the Negro Freedom
Struggle, Students & youth, Biography
Cinema, Psychedelics, Psychoanalysis
& Calligraphy.

50¢

A I
W★W

A kind of special out-of-series issue of *The Rebel Worker*, the
Solidarity Bookshop Catalogue featured a cover, internal
lettering and illustrations by Tor Faegre, plus book-descriptions
by most of the group. Many readers ordered extra copies.
Unquestionably, this flamboyant booklist introduced a large number
of (mostly) young people to the international "ultraleft."

# POST NO BILLS

Nevermore shall the wind's bones terrify the old clocks
   howling in the sardine tins
     Nevermore shall the feet of tables put their legs round
their necks to imitate flies
Nevermore shall broken teeth make music
Nevermore shall loaves of bread walk about naked
Nevermore shall air-currents give orders to statues of salt
Nevermore shall the cross-bar be a railway signal
Nevermore shall my shaved-off moustache grow again above my
     neighbor's eye
Nevermore shall the beefsteak whistle for its dog
Nevermore shall the metro ask for a drink for pity's sake
Nevermore shall cherry-stones steal latrines for the last speck of
     dust  which looks for the ears left behind in taxis
the hardboiled eggs which are so good at spying through keyholes
and all that's left of the great wall of China
are there to observe the traditions
and see that the first strawberries are respected
which look at themselves in every mirror
and would be so pleased to see a calf hanging from the butcher's
     stall
throw itself onto the butcher
and run away after its skin which would be so worn out
that it would see its brother through it

Benjamin PERET

*Translated from the French by David Gascoyne*

# VENGEANCE OF THE BLACK SWAN:
## NOTES ON POETRY AND REVOLUTION

APPLES FALL FROM TREES AT A SLOWER RATE than novels are published, yet gravity is a conventionally established fact, the world is believed to be round, and time is measured by the duration of its turns. If the world is round, then most of what is called "literature" must be flat; it complements well the revolving monotony that passes for life today.

Literature points in all directions at the same time because it has no place to go. Deliver me from the "meanings" of literature, from the absurd maneuvers of a clever literary psychology that calls all the shots and invariably declares itself the winner. A little psychology is a dangerous thing.

A book of matches is more useful than a book of sonnets or the average novel. This is not in itself of much importance, but this is: The book of matches is infinitely more interesting, more enlightening, more charming. It also poses more valid solutions to the problems confronting us.

\* \* \*

It is time to discredit the idea of a literary imperialism which submerges free human expression under several centuries and millions of pages of rhetorical chains, grammatical traditions, senile metaphysics and general philological inhibition dogmatized and bureaucratized in modern bourgeois society. It is time to distinguish clearly, once and for all, between *literature* (authoritarian, official, rigid, academic, confining and cold), and *poetry* (desperate, spontaneous, wild-eyed, convulsive, hot and liberating).

\* \* \*

To the bourgeoisie, for whom prophesy long ago became the compartmentalized private property of "scientific" specialists, poetry too has become the task of "qualified experts" with college degrees—those who are called Poets by *Mademoiselle* or *The Paris Review* and whose works fill the cretinous libraries of politicians, university administrators and the presidents of large metropolitan banks. The bourgeois sees in words only commodities, and in communication only the exchange of commodities; for him, "money talks." His conception of the role of language in human affairs is thus rationalized to the astonishing limits he has placed on this society. It is as if the prisoner were to construct a worldview based on the "everlasting truth" of handcuffs, guards, stone walls and iron bars.

This degraded conception of language resembles the equally degraded bourgeois conceptions of love, freedom, dreams and art, in which man's inhumanity to man is transformed into the collective insult known as the Humanities. Against these conceptions, and against the whole edifice of bourgeois-Christian civilization, the surrealists have raised the battle-cry of Lautréamont: "Poetry must be made by all. Not by one." This "all" exists on at least two levels: first, that of an all-inclusive collectivity; second, that of a human psycho-physical totality (rather than exclusively emotional, intellectual or other partial and therefore alienating, restricting planes).

We must oppose to the reactionary conceptions of the ruling classes all the latent potentialities of truly human life.

\* \* \*

We are taught in school to respect literature the same way we are taught to respect cops. If we are under 18, in most cities, we are coerced into schools by day and confined to parents' homes by curfews at night. All day we witness a ceaseless spectacle of unfreedom held together by soldiers, cops, governments, businessmen, bosses, priests, teachers, scoutmasters, social workers, truant officers, courts, pseudo-opposition groups (like the Communist Party), journalists, loan companies, insurance agencies and the Book-of-the-Month Club.

It is evident from the start that we must *rebel* against all this with anger, humor, violence, and the whole range of emotions and intelligence. But to rebel we must love, madly, and to love madly we must hate the obstacles to our love. From the dream to the word to the act! Let us destroy the obstacles to love! Let us rebuild this world, this society, everything, from top to bottom!

Thus comes the deluge of visible messages of insubordination on the rooftops of consciousness and in the streets of dreams: Drop Out! Make Love, Not War! Dodge the Draft! Let the State Disintegrate! Don't Fight the Bosses' War! I Won't Work! Sabotage! Freedom Now! Dancin' in the Streets!

In the long hot summer, the rain of terror and the rain of pleasure: Burn, baby, burn!

Understood in this sense, poetry *is* the revolutionary movement.

\* \* \*

To forestall unnecessary confusion: The poetry taught in schools has nothing to do with poetry. Occasionally, it is true, real poets are included in textbooks, but most often they are "represented" by their worst poems, or their works are so concealed in the maze of introductory notes, annotations, explanations, biographical and bibliographical information that they do not breathe and pulsate as poems should. Textbook poetry is lifeless, irrelevant, empty and above all *safe* (for the bourgeoisie).

It offends no one, destroys nothing, creates nothing, inspires nothing; it is *boring*. And this is the condition generally reserved, officially, for poetry today. Bureaucratic-capitalist society, in bureaucratizing poetry into textbooks, has thus attempted to bureaucratize real poetry out of existence. Poetry, now a specialization, is thus excluded from the lives of "ordinary people" except in sterilized, deodorized, State-approved, regulation plastic squeeze-bottle form. We shall see, however, that these attempts, like all defense-measures of our ruling classes, backfire in reality, for just as people in the street find weapons (rocks, bricks, bottles, gasoline) to use against cops, so they will find poetry: *automatically.*

Poems, in any case, are not nearly as important as poetry.

At certain historical periods, especially periods of crisis and great social change, poetry has sought refuge *outside* the poem. This was true of late eighteenth-century France, which produced no poems of any importance, but which brought into being the anarchist, presurrealist and marvelously poetic works of the Marquis de Sade (as well as Diderot and some others), whose best works were written in prose. The same is true of the United States immediately after the Revolution, which saw the appearance of several amazing novels by Charles Brockden Brown (*Wieland, or the Transformation*; *Edgar Huntly*), extensions of certain preoccupations of the Gothic genre in England.

At other periods, poetry breaks through its traditional forms into something altogether *new.* The works of Blake, Baudelaire, Lewis Carroll, Lautréamont, Rimbaud, Mayakovsky, Samuel Greenberg, Lorca and the surrealists are evidence of the poet's desire to smash complacency, conformity, convention, the "official" view, the accepted version of things—to pose anew for the consideration of all the gravest problems of human existence, and to propose tentative, daring solutions.

\* \* \*

The automatic image is a valid and triumphant expression of emotion, but precisely because of this, it is also a weapon: and the wilder the image, the greater the explosion. "Words make love" wrote André Breton, but only in poetry and dreams. The rest is literature, in which words do nothing but work for the preservation of existing reality. To free words from their customary associations thus becomes a revolutionary necessity. "The strident cry of red eggs," wrote Benjamin Péret. This is essentially an act of creative vandalism. Words, freed from the bondage imposed by bureaucratic-capitalist society, can serve the cause of the liberation of the mind.

* * *

A word should be said about "poetry" magazines, the independent or occasionally university-sponsored "little magazines" to which at least a few people look for flashes of intuitive lightning or at least a luminous grain of possible hope. It seems to me that the very notion of a "poetic" specialist publication of any kind is anti-poetic from the start, based on a sentimental, false idealism indicating a clear incapacity for action. "Poets" who have nothing better to do than publish their poems, and who are interested only in the purely verbal or symbolic manifestations of poetry, are not poets at all but a particularly dull species of quasi-bureaucrats, analogous to the chairmen of so-called "charitable societies," at the service of their own alienation and the perpetuation of the universal commodity-monotony society.

True poetry is a constantly renewed preface to action, multiplying the strength of the Revolution at its source in human *desire*.

* * *

Is it necessary to add that there can be no question of "engaged" poetry, of dictatorship over art, of any chains of any kind?

Traditional political journals, in their theoretical austerity, preferring the technological chemistry of speech to the "alchemy of the word," and too often settling for uninspired versification of the embarrassingly obvious and boringly incidental, present themselves as a body of ideas without any blood. It is insufficient to remain critically "receptive," for it is not a matter of having poetry in one hand and criticism in the other, but of letting poetry be marvelously critical and criticism ruthlessly poetic.

* * *

The tasks historically handed down to us by Lautréamont, Marx, Engels, Bosch, Fourier, Blake, Rimbaud, Sade, Jarry, Dadaism, Charles Fort, Freud, Maturin, the IWW, the surrealists, Shays' Rebellion of 1786, the Nat Turner Insurrection of 1831, the Paris Commune of 1871, the Russian Revolutions of 1905 and 1917, the Spanish Revolution of 1936, the Hungarian Revolution of 1956, the Enragés, the Durutti Column, Emiliano Zapata, much of contemporary science, the youth revolts and guerrilla wars of all generations, and the liberating mythology of desire suggested in *Bugs Bunny, Daffy, Uncle Scrooge, Hulk* and *Spirit* comics, in the Cthulhu Mythos, the blues, the "trickster tales" and *The Rebel Worker* (Numbers 1–7) are being achieved, not by academicians or the editors of such journals as *Encounter, Evergreen, Life* or *Liberation*, or by traditional radicals, but by the people in the streets, for whom these questions, though often unconscious and thus theoretically unformulated, are nevertheless in practice a matter of life and death.

Our own role is to raise these questions to the level of general consciousness, to share visions and the most far-reaching experiments with others on all levels of revolutionary struggle, to penetrate deeper and to soar higher into the multifarious reality of our time and all times, and to unite theory and practice in a mad, passionate embrace.

\* \* \*

Words in chains (in advertising, law, religion), words manipulated by sclerotic bureaucrats, words abandoned in textbooks, words gagged by television, words surrounded by newspapers, words without margins, words whose light has nearly been snuffed out, archaic words, words waiting to be born, words that order one about senselessly, words whose edges are blunted, words imposed on the poor, words confined to the rich, words that fight the bosses' war, words smothered by the ruling class, words that riot and burn, words that lie in the street, words that sit in the tops of trees, words that ride on the crests of waves, words that fly, dive, swim and burst into flame: Let us liberate these words, let us open once and for all the commodity-literary cages of their quotidian imprisonment and let them speak for us in the poetry of revolution.

The black swan of Lautréamont, "with a body bearing an anvil surmounted by the putrefying carcass of a crab, and rightly inspiring mistrust in the rest of its aquatic comrades," is now everywhere, a comrade-in-arms, one of us and all of us. The Revolution today is no longer a question of political parties and vanguard sects, but rather of the spontaneous self-activity of masses of people risking everything *to be free.*

Men and women must be made to realize that the world of the mind is capable of practically limitless expansion, and that the material world is capable of providing practically limitless pleasure, perceived in its countless manifestations according to love, humor, mythology, dream, play and the thirst for adventure. "The dream, too," said Nicolas Calas, "must have its own Bastille Day."

\* \* \*

Freedom, despite the innumerable compromises performed so ignobly in its name, retains still its power of limitless attraction. Like love, it can be understood most clearly during its realization (I should say: surrealization); otherwise it succumbs too easily to abstraction. Like love, too, the more it is realized the better it is understood. I say "understood" the way one can say that darkness or light or a Kwakiutl raven sculpture is understood: that is, one sees, and draws conclusions from what one sees.

Poetry, the nocturnal flamethrower, the black sunflower, burns latently in the eyes of all who *see*. The journey from vision to action comprises a series of steps in which the superficial mystifications of the commodity culture's immediate reality are successively liquidated. We must take these steps; we must aid relentlessly in the incessant proliferation of totally poetic acts. In this way the labyrinth loses its terrors and the minotaur, formerly a total stranger, becomes our closest friend.

Franklin ROSEMONT

# THE COLORS OF FREEDOM

RANGED ABOVE OUR HEADS, the flaglike windows forever unlit, continued to lap up their measure of air. They had the dimensions of those red cloth flags which in Paris flank certain highway works and from which there stand out, in big black letters, separated by dots, the inscription 'SADE' which has often returned to me in reverie.

The red flag, free from any mark or inscription—this flag I shall always see with the same vision I had at seventeen when during a popular demonstration just before the other war; I saw it unfurled by thousands, low in the sky of the Pré Saint-Gervais. And yet, I feel that reasoning is powerless to intervene here—my pulse will continue to beat yet more powerfully when I recall the moment that this flamboyant sea, in places flowing but thinly and restrictedly was pierced by the soaring flight of black flags.

At that time I had not much political consciousness, and I must admit I am perplexed when I take it on myself to gauge what degree of consciousness I now have attained. But, more than ever, the currents of sympathy and antipathy seem to me strong enough to demand the subjection of ideology; and I know that my heart was set beating, is still set beating, by that day's very movement. In the deepest galleries of my heart I shall always rediscover the swaying to-and-fro of these countless tongues of flame among which a few linger to lick a marvelous carbonized flower.

The present generation will be hardly able to imagine a spectacle of that order. The heart of the proletariat had not been rent as yet by innumerable factions. The torch of the Paris Commune was far from being extinguished; there were many hands there which had held that torch—a torch uniting all in its great light, which would have been less beautiful, less true, without a few spiraling wreaths of thick smoke. So much individually disinterested faith, so much resolution and ardor could be read in these faces; so much nobleness, too, in those of the veterans. Around the black flags, to be sure, the effect of sheer physical suffering could be sensed more strongly, but passion had really burned itself into some eyes, had left there unforgettable points of white heat. It always will seem as if the flame had spread over them all, burning them only less or more fiercely; serving to maintain some in their absolutely realizable and well-based demands and hopes, while leading others, more rarely, to burn themselves out on the spot in an inexorable attitude of sedition and defiance.

The condition of humanity is such (independently of the ultra-amendable *social* condition which man has made) that this last attitude especially of which there is no lack in the history of the intellect of illustrious respondents, whether named Pascal, Nietzsche, Strindberg or Rimbaud has always seemed to me absolutely justifiable on the emotive plane, leaving out of account the purely utilitarian reasons for which society may repress such an attitude. One is compelled at least to recognize, that it alone is marked by an infernal grandeur. I shall never forget the exaltation and the pride which overcame me, when as a child I was taken for one of the first times into a cemetery, at the discovery among so many depressing or ridiculous monuments of a slab of granite engraved in red capitals with the superb device: *Neither God Nor Master*. Poetry and art will always retain a preference for all which transfigures humankind in the desperate, irreducible demand which, now and then, takes a derisory chance to make in life.

The fact is that over art and poetry also, whether one likes it or not, there flys a flag in turn—red and black. There, too, time is urgent.

It is a question of insuring that from human sensibility is drawn all that it is capable of giving. But whence comes this apparent ambiguity as to the color?

Perhaps it is not given to any man to act on the sensibility of other men in order to mold and enlarge that awareness, except at the price of offering himself as a sacrifice to all the scattered forces of the soul of his time: forces which, in general, only seek each other in an attempt to pronounce mutual exclusions. It is in this sense that such a man is, has always been and, by a mysterious decree of these forces, *must* be at the same time their victim and their executioner. Thus, the same is necessarily the case as regards the taste for human liberty which, called to extend its field of receptivity to all in practically infinite proportions, draws down on a single person all the dire consequences of excess.

Liberty does not consent to caress this earth except in taking into account those who have known, or have at least, partly known, how to live because they have loved her *to a point of madness.*

André BRETON

(from *Arcane 17*, 1945)

# ELEMENTARY STRUCTURES
# OF REIFICATION

AS IF THE OLD MARX WAS DIRECTING everything from his grave, the commodity *form* contributed, by the *logic* of its real development, to the clarification and deepening of the critique of political economy. Most certainly, the heirs of this critique have done everything, theoretically and practically, like the bourgeois and like the bureaucrats, to disguise or to maintain confusion on his subject by drowning it beneath a heap of metaphysical subtleties and theological arguments. But the world has continued without them. These analyses which they strive themselves to conceal, it has transcribed with a blinding light in everyday triviality: it has made the theory of fetishism of commodities both an objective truth and common knowledge.

Despite the transformations it has undergone since Marx, the commodity-economy has been conserved in its form: a *form* clothing the products of creative activity (of praxis) that wage labor has stripped of all humanity; a *form* which, faithful heir of the old judeo-christian god, acquired an autonomous existence and created man and the world in its image; a *form* which has engendered the anthropology of an isolated individual who remains *deprived* of the wealth of his social intercourse. The commodity-economy is the praxis of power: not only the principle of dissolution of the old peasant-religious civilization (the ruins of which it still pursues), but a mode of representation of the world and a form of action upon it; it has reduced the whole of social reality to the quantifiable, and established the totalitarian domination of the quantitative, extending this increasingly to all the as yet non-dominated sectors of life. (See *Internationale Situationiste 7, 8, Banalités de Base* by Raoul Vaneigem. English translation, *The Totality for Kids*, available as a pamphlet).

What appeared to be most concrete was in fact most abstract; a formal rationalization, an illusion. But such an illusion, similar to and contrary to revolutionary ideas, once it had acquired its autonomy, operates, like an incitement to resignation, on the real world.

Dominant society always moves forward and leaps to new stages in the escalation of repression and alienation. The "Cybernetic State" has thus raised, in *combining* the fetishism of the commodity-economy and the fetishism of the work of art, a successive fetish: the commodity-spectacle, projection of *all life* in a hypostatic and crystallized essence, the image and normative model of this life. The concentration of alienations is thus pursued in the course of the accumulation of capital. Competitive capitalism was content to overwhelm social man with a multitude of partial alienations; in reducing the formerly separated spheres to one and the same reification, this bureaucratic capitalism, on the road of rapid cybernetization, congeals and places it in a showcase.

Such a process was unforeseeable only for bourgeois thought, and for the abortion, structuralist and prospective, which issued thereform. A structural analysis, in effect, would be able to remove from the commodity form the whole of the society that it produces and which reproduces it, the structuralist ideology would be there comprised. The latter was incapable, since it translated only *unconsciously* the structures of the process of reification in its course, and erected them into an a-historic absolute.

The obsolete negative work of the bourgeoisie, undertaken as early as the Renaissance, has been accomplished indifferently and with delays, being replaced by the void, a void constructed as the only possibility. In this micro-society which was organizing itself around real but quantitatively and qualitatively restrained unities (village, family, corporations, etc.), it substituted a cohort of reified abstractions: *the* individual, *the* State, *the* consumer, *the* market, which had their apparent reality from the appearance of reality that they have captured in our own life.

The principles of formal logic (which penetrated into the City with the first merchants) find their adequate realization in the commercial spectacle. The principle of *identity* is to the commodity-economy what the category of totality is to the revolutionary movement. In the structure of the commodity form, prior to this crisis of growth, the general identity of commodities is obtained only by turning their fictitious identification to a general, abstract equivalent. This daily assumed illustory identity has ended by inducing the identity of all needs, therefore of all consumers, and thus attains a certain degree of reality. The integral realization of the former abstract equivalence would be the ultimate point of this process. The sector of cultural production, or publicity, from the fact of inflation, has more and more difficulty in differentiating products, and announces and prefigures this great tautology to come.

The commodity-economy, like the bureaucracy, is a formalization and a rationalization of praxis: its reduction to a dominable and manipulable *thing*. Under this domination social reality ends by reducing itself to two contradictory significations: a bureaucratic-commodity signification (which on another level corresponds to exchange value) and a real signification. The bureaucratization of capitalism does not convey an internal qualitative transformation, but, on the contrary, the extension of the commodity form. The commodity-economy has always been bureaucratic.

The spectacular-commodity form parodies the revolutionary project, of mastery of the environment (natural and social) by a humanity at last master of itself and its history. It has the special attribute of the domination of an isolated and abstract man by an environment which power organizes. If it is true that men are the product of their conditions, it suffices to create inhuman conditions to reduce them to the state of things. In the parcelling out of commodity surroundings according to the principal of communicating vessels, "man" is reduced to the state of a thing, and things in turn assume human quality. The magazine *Elle* can title an advertisement "This furniture lives"—yes, our life itself. *Man is the world of man.*

Nietzsche remarks in *The Gay Science* that "an enormous predominance of rice in the diet induces the use of opium and narcotics, just as a predominance of potatoes induces the use of alcohol. This accords with the fact that the promoters of modes of narcotic thought, like the Hindu philosophers, extol a purely vegetarian diet. They wished to make of this diet a law with the masses, searching thus to provoke the needs which they are capable of satisfying, those and no others." But in a society which can secrete only the need for another life, the opium of the commodity-spectacle is only a paradoxical realization of this sole real desire. By the commodity form and the representations, which it issues, the society of the spectacle tends to crumble this unique desire in furnishing it a mass of illusory satisfactions in small portions in exchange for abandoning what is alone *possible*, that is, another society, it generously grants us all the *possibilities of being another in this society.*

The commodity-spectacle colonizes the possible in delimiting like a cop the theoretical and practical horizon of the epoch. Just as in the Middle Ages the religious framework appeared to be the unpassable horizon within which the class struggle must be inscribed, the spectacular-commodity form tends to create such a framework, in the womb of which will unfold all the struggles for total emancipation, lost in advance.

But just as the commodity form, in monopolizing the whole of the real, has real existence only in the brain of the nineteenth-century bourgeois, this nightmare of society is only a true ideology, an organization of appearance which elevates itself only to the appearance of organization. The spectacle, in effect, has been only the fantastic realization of the commodity-economy because the commodity-economy has never possessed any true reality: its mysterious character resides simply in its returning to men the characteristics of their own life and presenting them as objective characteristics. Power, therefore, projects the image of survival, permitting this image by integrating therein elements possessing sometimes a liberating content, to be always open to the possible. By this operation they pass to the service of repression, rendering alienation more supportable after having glorified the flowers of criticism.

From this fact the reveries of the dominant classes are more and more readable to those who know how to decode the social text of the epoch: nothing less than the constitution of an abstract society (abstract from society) where abstract spectators abstractly consume abstract objects. Thus will be obtained the coincidence, so much desired, between ideology and the real: representation becomes image of the world, at the limit, to substitute itself for the world and to build a world of the image, created by power and sold on the market. The conscious representation of its life, as produced from its own activity, then disappears from the mind of the spectator-consumer, who will assist only at the spectacle of his own consumption.

The cybernetic conception of the surpassing of philosophy is on a par with its dream of reconstitution, on the basis of the society of the spectacle, the paradise lost of unitary societies, enriched by two thousand years of progress in social alienation. These dreams reveal, in passing, the cleverly hidden and mystified character of these societies: they have maintained their unity only by repression. In a reality entirely reduced to the quantitative, integrally dominated by the principle of identity—without which the least bit of dispute would come to menace its equilibrium the old philosophical-economic verbiage would become, in effect, useless.

These phantasms find elsewhere, from time to time, an embryo of practical realization, always exemplarily revealing. A hospital in Richmond, Virginia, features an "Isle of Life" for the seriously burned. This consists of a gigantic plastic bubble maintained free of all germs. Inside, the patients, after complete decontamination, are installed in a *pre-sterilized atmosphere.* "No claustrophobia: the Isle of Life is *transparent*" (*Paris-Match*). While waiting for a nuclear conflict to furnish to this philanthropic work the patients it merits, society builds the image of the conditions it imposes: survival in controlled isolation.

Although the commodity-spectacle tends to establish this flat and spiritual positivity, it reheats the negative in its breast, and like all historical reality produces itself the germs of its own destruction. The ancient socio-economic commonplace, the development of the industry of mass-consumptive goods produces and super-produces superproduction. Certain sociologists have even arrived at the understanding that with commodity superproduction all objective difference between things disappears. The only differentiation which would be able to be introduced is subjective. But to discover the latent tendencies to auto-destruction which such a process conceals is beyond the capacities of a sociologist.

With the disappearance of use-value, the general identity between things passes from living fantasy to phantasmagoric realization. Use-value, however, is the nucleus of reality, indispensable to the production and survival of exchange value. Commodities themselves suppress their own conditions. When the system is able to do without reality, then reality is able to do without it. Modern society has grown to such a point of revolution that it parodies in advance its own destruction. Gadgets work to the end of the world of commodity-economy. The last gadgets are the "nothing gadgets": the useless machine, the machine which destroys itself, counterfeit money to burn in the fireplace.

But the commodity-economy, also produces its own gravediggers, who would not limit themselves to the spectacle of its destruction, since their objective is the destruction of the spectacle. One cannot refute the conditions of existence, one can only liberate oneself.

At all stages of practical confrontation, gestures proliferate themselves, ready to transform themselves into revolutionary acts. But in the absence of a revolutionary movement this practical confrontation remains on the individual level. The nostalgia of the deprived appropriation has been the basis of the theory of individual reappropriation and has reduced it to a simple reaction against abstract socialization, introduced by the commodity form. Theft in the big department stores, that the psychosociologists of the owners have so justly called the "unknown method" is of a qualitatively different essence. In the spectacle of abundance, the so-called *objects of consumption* cease to be objects of enjoyment and become instead objects of contemplation, more and more radically strangers to those whose needs they are supposed to satisfy. Theft seems to be, then, the only mode of appropriation for enjoyment, contrary to the "known method" which appears as a mode of contemplative use, a way of being possessed by objects without enjoying them.

Certain sociologists have announced, as a discovery in their police investigations, the existing rapport between the *blousons-noirs* (young hoodlums, gang kids) and archaic societies. There is not, however, simply and obviously, a real resemblance between a society on this side of the commodity-economy and groups placing themselves beyond it. Voluntary destruction of commodities, the breaking of store windows, recalls the sumptuous destruction of pre-capitalist societies (with the reservation that such gestures would see their revolutionary capacity limited in a society of a commodity superproduction). In stealing commodities to give them away, certain blousons-noirs void this ambiguity. They reproduce at a higher level the practice of gift-giving which dominated archaic societies and which exchange, as the formalization of social relations on the basis of a weak level of development of productive forces, has come to ruin. Thus they discover a line of conduct better *adapted* to a society defining itself as a society of abundance, and beginning practically its transformation.

In the course of past insurrections, the most spontaneous gestures, those that the bandits of power have called blind, were, definitively, the most revolutionarily clairvoyant. To cite an actual recent example, the insurgents of Los Angeles seized directly the spectacular

232

exchange-value which served as the ornamentation of their slavery; they rose to assault the heaven of the spectacle. At the same time that they were destroying windows and burning supermarkets, they outlined on the spot—a restoration of use-value: "One black carrying a stolen refrigerator in a wheelbarrow, opened it and took out the steaks and some bottles of whiskey" (*L'Express*).

If it is true that up to now revolutions have generally missed their chance to clothe themselves in the skins of ancient holidays, the enemy that they seem to have forgotten has always the knowledge to remind them of gestures which they ought to have accomplished long since. What they have taken to be the gestures of despair—express only the despair of not accomplishing them sooner. These gestures the next revolution must rediscover immediately and accomplish without delay; as the destruction of the commodity-spectacle, they are the carriers of the hope for a free construction of life. It will then be a question of reclaiming as the property of men and women all the robbed treasures in the profit of the spectacle sky, to turn them in the direction of true life. They will call us the destroyers of the world of commodity-economy; we will be only the builders of ourselves.

Jean GARNAULT

From *Internationale Situationniste* 10 (1966);
*translated by Dotty DeCoster*

# DELIGHT NOT DEATH:
## EXCERPTS FROM A LETTER

D ESPAIR IS NOT A STATE, just a town.
For believers in analogy, the following fact: The heaviest artillery and ground-to-air missiles are not so effective for the North Vietnamese against U.S. bombers as the kid with a rifle who merely aims at the computer section of the bomber and effectively destroys its capability to deliver bombs, causing its later scrapping. A fifty-cent shell for a multi-million-dollar bomber.

Is not society as delicate as its bombers?

This analogy appears to me quite fateful and a necessary point of departure for anyone passionately determined to change life.

Comics were censored—when will R&B? And then an underground?

"Be Yourself." Does this adage now become the revolutionary's key to victory? And what would happen if we'd invent new palaces equal in emphasis to the "mod" scene—strewing the streets with jewels for cops to trip on? The value of any non-social universe is its necessary attack on history which ever more increases its meaning to reaction while pulling its shell thinner and more brittle.

And the sea is so beautiful at twilight—just as trees at dawn. It's a conversation and an opera, a memory. I've been shadowed in recent weeks by "remembrance of things present," which even prompt me to consciously enlarge the vision by checking details of the memory not immediately apparent.

Lawrence DeCOSTER

# REMINISCENCES OF T-BONE SLIM

YES, I KNEW T-BONE SLIM FOR MANY YEARS during the IWW harvest drives in North Dakota and Montana. His mind was far above the average of the wage slaves, but strictly rank-and-file. He was highly intelligent, generous and kindly towards his fellow workers, always neat and clean in appearance and was considered by many as handsome. When I knew him he was strictly sober at all times. He was a powerful, prolific writer and journalist.

T-Bone Slim many years ago was a top writer and reporter for the Duluth, Minnesota daily *News-Telegram*. In the early days of the IWW he was sent by this paper to cover an IWW mass meeting. T-Bone Slim sent the paper a good factual write-up, favorable to the IWW. But the editor of the Duluth *News-Telegram* misquoted him and balled up his article. T-Bone Slim quit his job as crack reporter for that paper and lined up in the IWW. Then he traveled around the country and reported and wrote for the IWW press—*Industrial Worker*, *Solidarity*, *Industrialisti* and the IWW monthly magazine.

T-Bone Slim's articles for the IWW press were always printed with a pencil, so the editors wouldn't make any mistakes on them, and he could print with a pencil to perfection.

T-Bone Slim was an excellent cook and used to cook on IWW threshing rigs in the cook-shacks. He could also make the finest and tastiest Swedish hotcakes of any chef in the U.S.A. On one job the workers ate so many of his hotcakes Slim quit. Although there was plenty of ham and eggs and other good chuck for breakfast the threshing crew liked Slim's hotcakes so well they didn't eat much of anything else. So he got tired making so many hotcakes and blew the job. The Wobs always wanted T-Bone Slim for cook in their jungle and picket camps.

All T-Bone Slim's wonderful talent was given by him to the IWW and its press free, gratis.

Although T-Bone Slim went by the name of Arnold, he was of Finnish descent. He was known, highly respected and well-liked by thousands of home-guard and migratory wage slaves all over the country. If he wasn't working on some job, he was a damn good bum on the main stem at restaurants, rich homes, offices and elsewhere. T-Bone made friends among the wage slaves wherever he went, and was always active and agitating for the IWW on the job, picketlines, box cars and everywhere else.

Yours for the IWW, the Libertarian League, and the Free Society,

Guy B. ASKEW (Skidroad Slim)

Of the four main sites of Solidarity Bookshop in its heyday,
the one on Meyer Court (shown here before the books arrived,
in a rare drawing by Bernard Marszalek) was the most "underground,"
located in an old apartment house. The building, and Meyer Court
itself, were bulldozed out of existence in the 1970s

# FIVE O'CLOCK WORLD 2: WORKERS' HOBBIES

YOU CONVERT YOUR WORK POWER, your muscle, nerves, intellect, your creativity as a human being into a commodity, and sell it on the "labor market" from 9 to 5 (or other hours) for the lousy wages you get. As far as they are concerned, you are not a human being during this time, but a thing, a "factor of production," as the economists like to call you. You, or rather your wage—you actually don't count—you go down on the books as "costs of production" alongside plant machinery, raw materials and fuel. Human being OK, but not on company time.

Pretty miserable life, isn't it? Especially when you consider that Hungarian workers in 1956 proved to the world that workers could run the show themselves, except for Russian tanks. True, you say, but at 5 o'clock my tour of duty is finished, and I can go home and rest and enjoy myself. Wrong again, my friend—your loving rulers got other plans for you. At 5 o'clock your tour of duty as consumer begins. Somebody's got to buy all that junk your labor has created. You don't think they spend that $10,000,000,000 a year or so on market research, packaging and advertising just to make the super market shelves look pretty. Man, in this economy you're on duty from get-up to go-to-bed, and you better not forget it.

And if you've got a good wage, *that* isn't all it's made out to be either. It only makes your consumer duty heavier.

*All* of us partake in this rat race in one way or another, including people like me who write about it. You can't escape it in our society, not even if you see through it. But how do they hook us?

Before answering this...I'd like to forestall a possible misunderstanding. I don't mean here to put down material wealth itself. In its pure material aspect, a great part of that junk pile they sell us has real value. As objects of practical utility or enjoyment, many of those things satisfy real human needs.

So that's the first way they hook us: *Some* of those goodies they offer us in exchange for our souls are in fact the good things of life, things we ought to be demanding from them without having to pay the price.

So-called "constructive hobbies," do-it-yourself kits and like, fit into this scheme. They allow us, in the five o'clock world, partial satisfaction of a basic need whose satisfaction is absolutely forbidden in the work world before five o'clock: *the need to work*—that is, work

236

as meaningfully productive human activity.

The existence of this as a basic human need should need no long and involved proof for anyone who is capable of opening his eyes and digging children. The ideological distinction our society makes between work and play (whereby play becomes meaningless and work brutal) simply doesn't exist for children. They have to learn it from those idiots of adults who surround them. In their play, children are constantly searching for meaning, identity, or recognition. If you are around children, you can see this a dozen times a day if you keep your eyes open.

But meaningful productive human activity is just what's absolutely forbidden to us during our wage labor time. This leads to terrible frustration among working people, even if they do not become fully conscious of the nature of that frustration. Louise Crowley expressed it beautifully in a letter to me:

> Another manifestation of this is the folk-art that I've encountered in almost every place I've ever worked. Whatever the workers do that they get paid for is so devoid of human value that they sneak the time and materials, on the job, to do something else. A machine shop provides all sorts of opportunities for this; but in a macaroni factory, the workers make things out of macaroni. Now they wouldn't feel the need to do this, at the risk of their jobs and the cost of a great deal of effort, if the work for which they were getting paid satisfied that "basic human need." But if you're caught being human on a job, you're fired.

Here is where hobbies come in, and in our all-commodity society, I mean specifically hobbies as a commodity. If you have a hobby like making braided rugs out of old socks and ties, you may satisfy yourself personally, but you're not doing much for the "economy." You can be sure there'll be a dozen advertisers after you trying to sell you a hobby that will cost you more MONEY. Why don't you try electric trains, or photography, or some activity that will require you to sink a thousand or two into power tools? On some job applications they ask you about your hobbies as if having one, or the right one, were a prerequisite for the job. If you don't have the safety valve, you might begin making too many demands for satisfaction out of your job, and make trouble for the company.

After having deprived you of the possibility of doing human work in your wage-labor time, the bastards expect you to return to market, this time as buyer, and pay them back your hard earned money in exchange for the wherewithal, *that you may work*, this time in the human sense. In this rat race they've got you coming and going. Who says capitalism don't stink?

But no matter how much you invest in your hobby, you'll get at best only partial satisfaction of the basic need that drives you to indulge in it and spend your money on it. For your real need and what you have every right to demand, is more than a measly hour or two at the end of the day, isolated from the rest of your life. You have the right to demand that your whole working day be meaningful, pleasurable, satisfying activity. You have the right to demand that the fabulous possibilities of mechanization and automation be exploited not for maximum profit or efficiency (from the manager's point of view) but to abolish the stupid and unpleasant jobs, and to preserve the pleasant and satisfying ones from the worker's point of view, that it be introduced to eliminate superfluous work, not superfluous workers. You have, in short, the right to demand that work, in the pre 5 o'clock world, be converted into the type of activity many now chose freely after 5 o'clock in their hobby. Or rather you will have to make this conversion yourself. The bosses won't do it for you.

The social function of hobbies is therefore exposed as that of a safety valve. You are allowed just enough satisfaction of your need for human work during your free time, that your collective frustration during work time does not become an explosive force. And they have the nerve to expect you to pay for it.

In addition, their multi-billion dollar propaganda and brain-washing apparatus hammers at you night and day the line that demands of this sort are utopian. Considered from the angle of the techniques of exercise of power, they have to do this, of course. It is both cheaper and more efficient to brain-wash people into thinking that a society that would allow them genuine satisfaction of their needs is utopian, than it would be to pay the tremendous costs of police and army necessary to keep them down once they catch wise that a free world is possible.

Jim EVRARD

*(excerpts)*

*(Rebel Worker 7)*

# WHITE RABBITS

THE TIME HAS COME THAT I MUST TELL the events which began in 40 Pest St. The houses which were reddish-black looked as if they had survived mysteriously from the fire of London. The house in front of my window, covered with an occasional wisp of creeper, was as blank and empty looking as any plague-ridden residence subsequently licked by flames and saliva'd with smoke. This is not the way that I had imagined New York.

It was so hot that I got palpitations when I ventured out into the streets—so I sat and considered the house opposite and occasionally bathed my sweating face.

The light was never very strong in Pest Street. There was always a reminiscence of smoke which made visibility troubled and hazy— still it was possible to study the house opposite carefully, even precisely; besides my eyes have always been excellent.

I spent several days watching for some sort of movement opposite but there was none and I finally took to undressing quite freely before my open window and doing breathing exercises optimistically in the thick Pest Street air. This must have blackened my lungs as dark as the houses. One afternoon I washed my hair and sat out on the diminutive stone crescent which served as a balcony to dry it. I hung my head between my knees and watched a bluebottle suck the dry corpse of a spider between my feet. I looked up through my lank hair and saw something black in the sky, ominously quiet for an aeroplane. Parting my hair I was in time to see a large raven alight on the balcony of the house opposite. It sat on the balustrade and seemed to peer into the empty window, then it poked its head under its wing apparently searching for lice. A few minutes later I was not unduly surprised to see the double windows open and admit a woman onto the balcony—she carried a large dish full of bones which she emptied onto the floor. With a short appreciative squawk the raven hopped down and picked about amongst its unpleasant repast.

The woman, who had hemp-long black hair, wiped out the dish, using her hair for this purpose. Then she looked straight at me and smiled in a friendly fashion. I smiled back and waved a towel.

This seemed to encourage her for she tossed her head coquettishly and gave me a very elegant salute after the fashion of a queen.

"Do you happen to have any bad meat over there that you don't need?" she called.

"Any what?" I called back, wondering if my ears had deceived me.

239

"Any stinking meat? Decomposed, flesh…meat?"

"Not at the moment," I replied, wondering if she was trying to be funny.

"Won't you have any towards the end of the week? If so I would be very grateful if you would bring it over."

Then she stepped back into the empty window and disappeared. The raven flew away.

My curiosity about the house and its occupant prompted me to buy a large lump of meat the following day. I set it on the balcony on a bit of newspaper and awaited developments. In a comparatively short time the smell was so strong that I was obliged to pursue my daily activities with a strong paperclip on the end of my nose or occasionally, I descended into the street to breathe.

Towards Thursday evening I noticed that the meat was changing color, so waving aside a flight of numerous bluebottles I scooped it into my sponge bag and set out for the house opposite. I noticed, descending the stairs, that the landlady seemed to avoid me. It took me some time to find the front door of the house opposite. It turned out to be hidden under a cascade of smutty ivy, giving the impression that nobody had been either in or out of this house for years.

The bell was of the old-fashioned kind that you pull and pulling it rather harder than I intended it came right off in my hand. I gave the door an angry push and it caved inwards emitting a ghastly smell of putrid meat. The hall which was almost dark seemed to be of carved woodwork.

The woman herself came rustling down the stairs carrying a torch.

"How do you do? How do you do?" she murmured ceremoniously, and I was surprised to notice that she wore an ancient and beautiful dress of green silk. But as she approached me I saw that her skin was dead white and glittered as though speckled with thousands of minute stars.

"Isn't that kind of you?" she went on, taking my arm with her sparkling hand. "Won't my poor little rabbits he pleased!"

We mounted the stairs and my companion walked so carefully that I thought she was frightened.

The top flight of stairs opened into a boudoir decorated with dark baroque furniture and red plush. The floor was littered with gnawed bones and animals' skulls.

"It is so seldom that we get a visit," smiled the woman, "so they all scuttle off into their little corners."

She uttered a low sweet whistle, and, transfixed, I saw about a hundred snow-white rabbits emerge cautiously from every nook, their large pink eyes fixed twinkingly upon the woman.

"Come, pretty ones—come, pretty ones," she cooed, diving her hand into my sponge bag and pulling out a handful of rotting meat.

With a sensation of deep disgust I backed into a corner and saw her throwing the carrion amongst the rabbits which fought like wolves for it.

"One becomes very fond of them," the woman went on, "they each have their little ways. You would be surprised how very individual rabbits are."

The rabbits in question were tearing at the meat with their sharp buck teeth.

"We eat them, of course, occasionally. My husband makes a very tasty stew every Saturday night."

Then a movement in the corner caught my attention and I realized that there was a third person in the room. As the woman's torch light touched his face I saw he had glittering skin like tinsel on a Christmas tree. He was dressed in a red gown and sat very rigidly with his profile turned towards us.

He seemed to be as unconscious of our presence as of that of a large white buck rabbit which sat masticating a chunk of meat on his knee.

The woman followed my gaze and chuckled; "That is my husband, the boys used to call him Lazarus."

At the sound of this familiar name he turned his face towards us and I saw that he wore a bandage over his eyes.

"Ethel?" he enquired in a rather thin voice. "I won't have any visitors here. You know quite well that I have forbidden it strictly."

"Now, Laz, don't start carrying on." Her voice was plaintive. "You can't grudge me a little bit of company. It's twenty-odd years since I've seen a new face. Besides, she's brought meat for the rabbits."

She turned and beckoned me to her side. "You want to stay with us, do you not, my dear?"

I was suddenly clutched by fear and I wanted to get out and away from those terrible silver people and the white carnivorous rabbits. "I think I must be going, it is supper time."

The man on the chair gave a shrill peal of laughter, terrifying the rabbit on his knee, which sprang to the floor and disappeared.

The woman thrust her face so near to mine that her sickly breath seemed to anaesthetize me. "Do you not want to stay and become like us?"

I stumbled and ran, choking with horror; some unholy curiosity made me look over my shoulder as I reached the front door and I saw her waving her hand over the banister, and as she waved, her fingers fell off and dropped to the ground like shooting stars.

Leonora CARRINGTON

# A PLEA TO ALL

## FROM THE SURVIVAL OF AMERICAN INDIANS ASSOCIATION

THIS CAN BE CONSIDERED as an Indian appeal to all other minority groups within America—as well as to those whites still possessing a moral conscience or code—to form a coalition movement, dedicated to righting the wrongs within American society itself before embarking upon the self-appointed role of world policeman...

The Indian's objective today is stated simply enough, to regain every single acre of land that they can, and to receive a proper indemnity for all that they cannot regain. All of this in order that they may lay the economic foundations for rebuilding an Indian way of life. To bring to an end, finally, the intolerable conditions under which they live today. Conditions which give them a life expectancy of 43 years! Is there a racial crime worse than the theft of life itself? No other group of people, in American society, has a life expectancy as low as the Indian. And the time has come to put an end, once and for all, to the cruel farce of attempting to integrate him into a society for which he is not adapted, historically or culturally. And if "biological memory" means anything at all, he never will be...

One major factor, in this struggle, should be firmly established from the very outset—and that is that the various American racial minorities have different goals and objectives. It is basic that they form a coalition, learn to work together, in order to compel the white power structure to face its responsibilities to all of them. Alone, as in the past, none of them can muster the pressure needed to get their wrongs redressed, but together they can accomplish this, so of course there is no alternative to forming a coalition.

But, once having said this, they must then go on to the realization that each group has the right to a different solution to its problems. One blanket program will not cover it all. Nothing better illustrates this than the contrasting goals of the Negro minority and the Indian minority. So lets briefly examine them:

The Negro aims at nothing less than full integration into American society. He is now fighting to have his children bussed to predominantly white schools, for his right to live in a predominantly white residential district, for his full share of jobs at all levels, for his civil rights, in short to an end of every single form of racial discrimination against him in America. And he has every right to these objectives, if that is what he really wants.

But this is not the Indian's goals. He is fighting desperately to

242

retain his identity, not to lose it! He doesn't want his children bussed to predominantly white schools, he doesn't want to live in a white neighborhood, he considers it below his dignity as a man to fight for equal rights in his own country! This is his "America," it is the others who shot their way in, uninvited and unwanted...

Oversimplified, he doesn't want to pack a lunch bucket to a Boeing plant, as a preliminary step towards owning a Cadillac car and belonging to the country club set. He doesn't want a thing to do with the "rat race," (to use the phrase some white critics have coined), that he sees all about him. He sincerely believes that his own native way of life is better—or at least better suited to him. So lets have an honest look at why there are such basic differences in Indian society and that which the whites have evolved from their European base...

The Indian believes that he is an integral part of a harmonious whole, all created by a Great Spirit, and that even the smallest creature has a right to life. He is, so to speak, in tune with Nature—not at war with it. On the other hand the caucasian believes that the deity was made in his own image and likeness, and if he so desires he has the right to exterminate every form of life here on earth, including his own. He has already wiped out many species of animal life.... One of the reasons the Indians so hated the early settlers was this insane mania for killing.

The Indian tribe used virtually every part of a slain buffalo, killing only to eat, and then saying a prayer for forgiveness to the Great Spirit for this taking of life. The settlers often slew for the pure joy of killing, taking only the buffalo's tongue for eating—and sometimes not even that. Many wantonly butchered the great beasts, taking only the tail for a trophy and letting the huge carcass lie upon the plains to rot. And this trait is still present today, in the few remaining places where there is game to vent it upon...

For example the current craze of the white businessman turned 'hunter' hiring a white bush pilot, in the Arctic regions, who run down a polar bear—with his plane! When the bear is thoroughly exhausted, and not a moment sooner, they set their plane down and the "great white hunter" steps out and shoots the spent bear. What your eskimo and Indian hunters think of him would have to be printed on asbestos paper.

No, the Indian's religious beliefs are far closer to Buddhism than they are to Christianity, which perhaps reflects his racial origins. And he is beginning to suspect that these never ending wars, of white America's making, are a part of this blood lust rather than the product of insoluble problems. Young as the United States is, and isolated by two oceans, it has still managed to wage war against virtually every

European country at least once. Not a bad record, for even a Christian Nation. And how do you explain the morality of a race which believed that the Japanese were buck-toothed monsters, capable of every crime, then less than five years later were calling them faithful allies and marrying their daughters by the hundreds. Simply because they had found a new enemy to hate. Can their society function without an enemy to fight?

No, the Indian wants his own way of life, and who is to say that he is wrong? To obtain this goal he must have his broken treaties reviewed by an International Tribunal, one in which other colored nations have representation, and whose decisions are final. To gain these ends he must join in a coalition with the other minority groups in America, helping them to gain redress for their grievances in exchange for aid in his own fight. They might adopt, as their slogan, the old saying—"An injury to one is an injury to all."

Robert D. CASEY

# PROPHETIC MUTTERINGS

THE TOTALITARIAN DRIFT OF SOCIETY creates the only conspiracy which most people know: the controlled life. As faceless cogs, we move through the predetermined motions of the humming treadmill. It is not that our controllers love freedom less, but that they love efficient operation more.

Men often see the world as fluid and chaotic, a place where individuals are victims of impersonal forces which they can seldom understand or control. They feel caught in a system which they cannot change or escape, and so they acquiesce. Their potential revolt, unable to find words, is hastily buried by forces and shadows. The shadow of our doubts beckons us to succumb to the siren of self-perpetrated comfort. Men know that rash commitments may prove outdated tomorrow, viewpoints are rapidly shifting, and it is difficult to locate a fixed position on which to stand for even a few moments. Our paralyzed will leaves promises unrealized, dreams dead, and prevents our selves from hoping for anything beyond the necessary evil. And that evil is simply man's failure to confront himself.

Our paralysis is founded on ourselves being taught to relinquish the right to order our own lives. Accustomed to the top-down control of our society, men forget that they are capable of doing the opposite— of working to change the conditions that oppress them. But our doubt is not reason for inaction, but serves as a reminder that infallibility is not the possession of any one man, and compassion and empathy for the stranger are manifestations of our deepest moral anxiety.

James W. CAIN

From *Blast* (excerpts)

# NOT EVERY PARADISE IS LOST: ANDRE BRETON (1896–1966)

ELSEWHERE IN THIS ISSUE of *The Rebel Worker* we have reprinted a short text by André Breton, a text forming part of the anthology *Surrealism and Revolution* which we have just published, and which contains extracts from several of his other works. "The Colors of Freedom" had already been selected for inclusion in this issue, with the hope of introducing to our readers the marvelous, formidable and clairvoyant thought of the leading theoretician of the surrealist movement, when we learned of his death in Paris in late September.

If we choose, here, to say a few words about him, it is primarily because of the lies and defamations that will inevitably appear elsewhere, doubly dangerous and doubly detestable because they will be masked as sympathy and good will.

André Breton in the *Surrealist Manifestoes, Surrealism and Painting, Nadja, The White-Haired Revolver, The Communicating Vessels, The Political Position of Surrealism, Mad Love,* the *Anthology of Black Humor, Arcane 17, Young Cherry Trees Secured Against Hares* and the *Ode to Charles Fourier,* has given to us, to the revolutionary movement of all countries, works of enormous theoretical importance and excruciating significance also as *weapons* with which to battle the armed guards of our mental and physical prisons.

His influence upon our own sensibility has been decisive, thoroughgoing, and second to none. Many of us discern in his life, in his works, the most essential reasons we could give for living; first (subtle and convulsive in its simplicity), the idea that "freedom, acquired here on Earth at the price of a thousand and the most difficult renunciations, must be enjoyed as unrestrictedly as it is granted, without pragmatic considerations of any sort, and this because human emancipation…remains the only cause worth serving" (*Nadja*), and also love: "absolute love,…the only principle of physical and moral selection capable of guaranteeing the non-vanity of human presence and human witness" (*Mad Love*), "the exceptional grandeur and value of human love" (*The Communicating Vessels*), "that promise which goes beyond us" (*Fata Morgana*).

Breton's work, which he hoped was of a nature "to send some men rushing out into the street, after making them aware, if not of the non-existence, at least of the crucial inadequacy of any so-called categorical self-evaluation," must find its way into the hands and minds of millions. The coming Revolution must be made by people who know what they are doing, people whose spontaneity and improvisation are rooted in the consciousness of gratifying desire, in the aspiration toward total liberation. The surrealist evidence of Breton is the common theoretical property of this Revolution, which will see, which is seeing already, the emergence of surrealist action complementary to the surrealist dream.

To advance: That is what is essential. Not to linger over uncertainties, not to bemoan the vicissitudes of chance, not to weigh down one's mind with doubt and hesitations, but to *act*, and to act *freely*, to move continually closer to the fusion of dream and reality, to seek the Revolution as Jason sought the Golden Fleece.

We are already in the street, where, in the heat of our vision and the light of our dreams, André Breton is "living among us."

Franklin ROSEMONT

Tor Faegre: Automatic drawing

246

# LETTERS

There are two (possibly three counting the hipster) ways to respond to Authority—obey or pour shit in its files. We know of course which is the more noble. I am not so sure as you about the existence of a revolutionary situation—although I would like to think so. But anything like sabotage, mutilating IBM cards, etc., no matter how futile in itself, can be justified in that it keeps Authority on its toes and reminds it of its ultimate fate. Also keeps fires of holy rebellion alive in bad times. Also such acts can serve as an example for others who mistankely believe that bureaucracy becomes stronger as it grows. On the contrary—the bigger and more complex it gets the more vulnerable it becomes to having sand thrown in its gears (or shit in its files).

Mike EVERETT
Washington, D.C.

You are right about high school, it's very disgusting. The rules, how stupid! Being treated like a dog on a leash and not being able to give your opinion.

I agree very much with your ideas about revolting and the way society is pushing as around. We just can't be free.

Of course I read your "Mods, Rockers and the Revolution" pamphlet, and a lot of it really shows the truth that society just won't face. So youth rebels and it's about time. We've taken enough from parents and society and it's about time we did something about it. The way they push us around and look down at us and are always mocking us! You'd think we were animals or something! I could write forever about the Youth Revolt and I'm starting to get carried away so I'd better stop before I do something drastic.

Linda KOPCZYK
Rolling Stones Fan Club, Chicago

Recently I came across an article titled "Mods, Rockers and the Revolution" which appeared here in translation in *Informations Correspondance Ouvriers*. We understand that this was extracted from a brochure published by your group in Chicago. We are very interested in mods and rockers, rock 'n' roll and the youth movement in the U.S. and would like to receive this brochure and your other publications.

I am a member of the Provos, an organization of anarchists, mods, rockers, ban-the-bombers, beatniks, nozoms, blouson noirs, etc. I am sending you copies of *Provo*, published in Amsterdam, and *Revo*, published by Provos in Belgium.

Madrid DANIELE<br>Brussels, Belgium

I have talked with several provos here and they are interested in communicating with American anarchists. I enclose a manifesto, the only thing they have at the moment in English. You have probably read about these people by now, they are quite remarkable and have a lot of strength here in Amsterdam. The movement is spreading with students in Paris staging experimental street happenings to test the reactions of police. Very likely there'll follow several advance copies of articles now in translation for a book to be published in English in England in a few months. These are, I understand, the pick of articles from the past issues of *Provo*.

Lester DORÉ<br>Amsterdam

I was glad to be reproduced in your surrealist pamphlet. The publishers of anthologies and histories of surrealism seem to ignore me because they do not consider me dead enough for their purposes.... I am indeed gradually moving toward a more aggressive point of view; I think the time is ripe but I still maintain that the independence of the artist from political domination is absolutely necessary and I am too marxist in my training to approve of adventurism.... I still believe that pop art is an important phenomenon and I am for constructive criticism. Breton, when I last saw him four years ago, agreed with me on this. I refuse to take up a dogmatic position in art.

Nicolas CALAS<br>New York

Cartoon by Lester Doré (*Rebel Worker* 3)

# *REBEL WORKER*
## PAMPHLETS

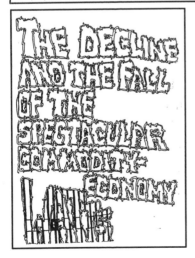

With texts by André Breton, Nicolas Calas, René Crevel,
and many others, *Surrealism & Revolution* was the most
comprehensive collection of surrealist theoretical/political writings
in English at the time. The cover, calligraphed by Tor Faegre,
also featured a collage by Max Ernst, and the contents included
an introduction by Franklin Rosemont and drawings by Lester Doré,
Tor Faegre, Bernard Marszalek and Penelope Rosemont.

# POP GOES THE BEATLE

THE TEENAGE CONTROVERSY between the "mods" (modernists who favor short hair, wool shirts, casual suede or corduroy jackets, lightweight ankle-length trousers and casual shoes) and the rockers (traditionalists who favor long hair, sideburns, long jackets, jeans and winkelpicker shoes) is resolving itself into a uniform pattern for Beatlemania beatlejackets, beatlehaircuts, beatlevoices, beatle-phraseology and now beatleriot. In just over a year four young men John Lennon, Paul McCartney, George Harrison and Ringo Starr known collectively as the Beatles, have risen from the relative obscurity of Liverpool's Cavern Club to become national figures

With a string of hit records behind them, they are arbiters of teenage and even adult taste. Lord Hailsham's hairstyle—surely his least objectionable feature—has been unfavorably compared to the Beatlecut which is "a credit to British professional hairdressing" no matter that the Beatles cut their own hair! And it's now almost impossible to go a day without hearing the raucous "scowse" of the Beatles, either on records or from their ubiquitous and imitative fans.

The Mersey Beat or Beatlebeat is simplified rhythm-and-blues of the type made popular by urban Negro entertainers like Bo Diddley, Chuck Berry and, to some extent, Ray Charles—with important modifications. The impression left by a beatlerecord is of an uninhibited and repetitive vocal—usually the whole group with one "lead" voice—and a thumping beat, based on guitars and harmonica and, above all, enthusiasm. There is no real harmony—the Mersey-side groups don't and probably can't hit the top notes but no one cares—and little real tune. Their vocal style, borrowed from the Americans but carefully altered and developed, is hoarse and aggressive: their most persistent enemy is loss of voice.

A thousand pop groups play as well as the Beatles, but the Beatles are rather more than a pop group. Their fuzz-plus-fringe haircuts, their Cuban-heeled elastic-sided boots, their collarless jackets and rounded shirt-collars are imitated everywhere. The Beatles are a fashion in a way that Bill Haley and the Comets, who caused minor riots seven years ago through personal appearance tours and through the film *Rock Around the Clock*, never were.

It's not surprising that the liberals have seen incipient fascism in the Beatles and their fans. There *is* something alarming about beatle-dress and beatleriots, and it is true, as *The Guardian* has said, that the Beatles were much influenced—probably musically rather than politically—by a visit to Hamburg two or more years ago. But it's too easy to put their success down to nascent fascism. They may be a symptom of fascism in much the same way as the arrogant, body-worshipping, leather-jacketed young thugs of pre-Hitler and Hitler Germany—were but they are much more as well. It's one thing becoming a fashion and quite another becoming a fascist.

What started the recent beatleriots is not clear. It probably began when police had to keep fans off stage at the London Palladium on October 13 [1963]. The press plugged the story and the "new teenage craze," as the *Evening News* called it, was under way. It reached a peak a fortnight later. In Bournemouth 1000 beatlefans stormed the Winter Gardens to get tickets. In Carlisle 600 beatlefans started a baby beatleriot and smashed windows. In Hull 2000 beatlefans swept aside police and crush barriers in a beatleriot, and in Cambridge 2000 beatlefans took up the full width of the road and started throwing bottles through church windows. Two nights later the Beatles themselves were amorously assailed on stage in Stockholm, and 7000 Newcastle beatlefans held another beatleriot. And now the Beatles are to make a film scripted by Alan Owen who likes "their goonish sense of humor." In a year the Beatles may be finished—they are making the most of their current popularity.

The press has built up these stories considerably. *The Daily Express* says that the 7000 Newcastle beatlerioters were controlled by only 40 police! The myth is taking over from the reality. But the press is quite right not to print scathing leaders on "the threat to Law-and-Order implicit in teenage riot." The beatlefans are not challenging anything. A few faint, a few get hurt, a few lose their jobs—just to get tickets so they can join in another riot during the show. In ten years' time they will look back on it and giggle.

In these beatlefans we can see the results of a society which allows and encourages the deception and manipulation of young people by vast impersonal enterprises. This society has virtually discarded young people and their ideas. Those who do worry about this have usually shouted at pop music *per se*, as though it were all equal rubbish. They haven't realized that young people buy records like Peter, Paul and Mary's "Blowin' in the Wind" and Trini Lopez's "Hammer Song," which are excellent songs—well sung—as well as beatlerecords, or that beatlemusic has something. It is new and young and vigorous. It's no earthly good fulminating against beatlemusic unless we have something more exciting to offer young people.

It is fashionable to deride the idea of an anti-youth conspiracy, but nonetheless the conspiracy, both conscious and unconscious, exists. The music teenagers make for themselves—and this is what the Mersey groups began by doing—is filched from them by the yahoos of Tin Pan Alley and then fed back at them,—shorn of its vitality, flavor and uniqueness. The Mersey Beat was fine when it was the Mersey Beat. It's the commercial youth-robbers who have turned it into a national teenage orgasm-substitute, and who are attempting to turn the teenagers in on themselves, instead of out on society.

It's not surprising that young people, when their elders have tolerated the creation of the mechanism of mass destruction and sapped the will to resist it, should turn to beat music, dancing and riots in the search for something less unenterprising than the complacent world of their bingo-loving parents. It was what Joe Brown was getting at when he sang "What a Crazy World We're Living In." Teenagers can feel that they're being done. They are denied sex and offered war; denied responsibility and offered docility; denied pleasure and offered beatleriots. When they ask for or demand things, they are told they want too much and are irresponsible. It's not the demanding that's wrong but what they demand; it's not so much that they are irresponsible as that they are never allowed to be responsible.

Isn't it time the anarchists acted as though young people really do count, instead of just paying lip-service to the idea? We should be beyond consoling ourselves that the Beatles and their fans are neo-fascists or subhuman twits; we should be beyond putting them away in the back of our minds with the teddy bears and forgetting them as peripheral to our ideas. The point is that they are not peripheral. The beatlefans, the mods, the rockers, the ton-up kids are people with ideas of their own. If anarchism has nothing to say to them—it has nothing to say at all. Do we have to be so bloody superior? The other day a teenage pop fan friend of mine advised me to go to a beatleriot: "You can hack the coppers as much as you like and this time you won't get done!" Sure: but isn't there more to life than hacking the fuzz in beatleriots and can't we say just what?

Charles RADCLIFFE

*Freedom*, 16 November 1963

(*Rebel Worker* 7)

# BLACKOUT

## ELECTRONIC ATTENTAT

ON NOVEMBER 9, 1965, shortly after 5:00 P. M. e.s.t., at the "Sir Adam Beck Number 2 Distribution Plant" at Queenston, Ontario, a little four-inch-square electric relay took it upon itself to illuminate a number of anarchist principles. Indeed, in doing so it selected a method which in and of itself is anarchistic: direct action. And far be it from anyone to accuse this nihilistic little relay of being a parliamentarian, although it was described in a good many other terms including the *New York Times'* brilliant understatement, "improperly functioning." Certainly it was far and away the all-time world's champion blown fuse, in that it blacked out 80,000 square miles of the U.S. and Canada, leaving about 30,000,000 people in total darkness. This was sort of an electronic attentat and on a scale one is hard put to overlook. Yet shining through the darkness like a beacon were such anarchist truisms as decentralism, mutual aid, direct action, and the like.

The first of these, decentralism, is so obvious but radical a solution that it was barely mentioned at all. On the day following the blackout, the *New York Times* ("all the news that's fit to print backwards") ran an article entitled: "A Nationwide Grid Termed a Solution." Herein they averred, "There is no question that last night's power failure furthered the cause of connecting all the power systems in the country into one grid, or network" (*sic. sic. sic.*). And later when the Federal Power Commission released its official report, the worthy gentlemen "stated flatly that more, rather than fewer, inter-connectors between power systems in different areas were needed to provide reliable electrical service" (*Times*, Dec. 7, 1965). There we have the quintessence of the bureaucratic mind: with an 80,000 square-mile area at the mercy of a four-inch relay, and the best they can come up with is more centralization. One-sixth of the country plus thirty mega-victims aren't enough—they want to offer it more hostages year by year, until by 1984 it's clutching the whole continent by the scrotum.

In fairness, the *N.Y. Times* in its coverage of the FPC report did mention in passing that, "Since the blackout there have been some assertions in Congress and elsewhere that the inter-connector system itself is a bad idea, inasmuch as it permits the wide spreading of power failures. Proposals have been made for the reversal of the nationwide trend toward such inter-tying…" However, so far as the FPC was concerned, "The prime lesson of the blackout is that the utility industry must strive not merely for good but for virtually perfect service." If nothing else this qualifies as the platitude of the year. Politicians are priceless.

As soon as their respective public relations departments, could gather their wits together in the darkness, President Johnson, Governor Rockefeller, and Mayor Wagner all spoke out fearlessly against blackouts. The Father, the Son, and the Unwholesome Ghost each ordered an immediate investigation, although protocol required that they be in decreasing order of magnitude and melodrama. *Newsweek* (Nov. 22, 1965) described Johnson, presumably trying to achieve that lantern-jawed hero effect despite an unfortunately chinless physiognomy, as he "fired a memo to Federal Power Commission Chairman Joseph Swidler, ordering a full-scale inquiry into why the blackout had happened and how another could be prevented." Notice they invariably "order," they never request. Personally I'm not quite certain what sort of weapons are used to "fire" memos, but I suppose as an anarcho-pacifist I'm obliged to oppose them. Be that as it may. Rockefeller and Wagner fired off orders for proportionately smaller investigations, but with palpably larger chins.

## J. ADDLED HOOCHER

Naturally J. Addled Hoocher leaped into the act forthwith. *Newsweek* had his relentless FBI agents fanning out "to prowl the grid for clues." They failed miserably in their search—not one volume of *Das Kapital* was unearthed. Actually, I don't have anything against Hoover, it's just that I wouldn't want him to marry my brother.

## NEO-LUDDITE ELEVATORS

At any rate the net result of all these investigations was the aforementioned FPC report which observed that this astronomical fiasco "would not have occurred if all the electric power systems involved had been following more careful operating practices." The *N.Y. Times* reported this profundity with a straight face. I have a friend who insists that the entire paper is written tongue in cheek. Someday I expect a page of the *Times* to waft by the mushroom cloud, a few of whose particles is me. Said page will contain an august report that "World War III would not have occurred if all the political power systems involved had been following more careful operating practices."

Lest the impression be conveyed that federal commissions do nothing but hide in the safety of platitudes, generalities, and kindred inanities, it must be conceded that this is only 95% true. The FPC report included a few specific suggestions, all along the lines of decentralization—thereby unwittingly contradicting their main thesis. Numbered among these were alternate power sources for airports,

255

bridges and tunnels, and if no separate power system could be devised for the subways, then at least an evacuation scheme. Not to be outdone, the NY City investigators pointed out that they had been studying auxiliary power not only for subways, but also for hospitals.

My own particular favorite, however, was the recommendation that manual cranks be installed on elevators. As a die-hard neo-Luddite I side with man against the machine "automatically;" hence the concept of Damoclean hand-levers in luxurious elevators as constant harbingers of forthcoming electronic attentats is delightful imagery. The only suggestion I'd care to add is the possibility of a mass homestead movement with candles.

## MUTHA!

When one turns to the geographic achievements of our "improperly functioning" relay, one is struck anew with the merit of decentralization. Consistently the less populated the area, the quicker electric serivce was restored. Thus in the map the *Times* printed of what was euphemistically called "outage," there were four gradations of severity: The least of these, anything from a momentary blackout to 15 minutes duration, embraced northern New York and most of New Hampshire. The next level, ranging from 15 minutes to 3 hours, included Ontario, Long Island, and the southern tip of New York. In the third category, running from 3 to 8 hours, were most of the states of New York and Vermont, as well as the entire states of Massachusetts, Connecticut, and Rhode Island. Finally New York City itself was blacked out the longest of all: 8 to 13 hours. Thus the final score was all or parts of nine states, two Canadian provinces, plus the god-damned Moscow hotline all "outaged" by a four-inch relay in some screwy place I never heard of in my life—Queenston, Ontario??? Maybe 150 years from now they'll hold a Sesquicentennial there in honor of the improperest motherfunctioner that ever goofed.

Nevertheless, ignoring logic as only a reactionary can, the *U.S. News & World Report* (Nov. 22, 1965) blithely presented the following question and answer: "Q. If the U.S. had a national power network, all interconnected as the Government has advocated, could a blackout spread to the whole country? A. Experts say no. In part, they rely on finding more effective safety devices." Only a red rat could condemn centralization after that.

## MUTUAL AID

On the individual level, however (and what else should anarchists consider?), we found people acting so beautifully that even Kropotkin

256

might have been impressed. Naturally, there were instances of people acting like capitalists selling candles at $1.50 each, charging up to $50 for a taxicab ride, gouging pounds of flesh for flashlights, etc. However, as *Newsweek* (Nov. 11, 1965) pointed out, the "real keynote" was struck by a Negro cleaning woman who led a Manhatten career girl up ten flights of stairs to her apartment, gave her two candles, and then waved away a $5 tip. "It's OK, honey. Tonight everyone helps everyone."

Somehow it seemed as if the whole crazy city had read *Mutual Aid* the night before the blackout. Remember, New York is notorious for being this planet's biggest cutthroat rat-race. Furthermore, it was not only the longest hit by the blackout, but also it was by far the most vulnerable. The blackout struck in the middle of the rush hour; hence there were probably 800,000 people stranded in subways and/or subway trains when the power failed. Another 100,000 were stranded waiting for commuter trains. Thousands more were trapped on the upper floors of skyscrapers. But indubitably the worst off were the hundreds upon hundreds who were trapped in elevators.

Yet there was no panic! Everyone was calm and patient. Neither were there any crime waves or looting—of course for this we have to thank the fact that the police were kept too busy with rescue work and other emergency activities. It was estimated that $100,000,000 was lost in revenue and certainly one of the hardest hit business interests was the New York Police Force. Therefore I have to give them credit for coming through in the pinch, although several cops of the 24th Precinct failed to appreciate my concern when I walked by in the darkness explaining to my companions in stentorian tones of commiseration that the poor guys were beating their brains out and "all on straight salary for a change." (The 24th Precinct specializes in shooting 14-year-old Puerto Ricans.) All in all some 5000 off-duty policemen were called up to join the 7000 already on duty. The Fire Department brought in their off-duty personnel also.

Yet although these men all performed beautifully at tasks of supererogation, the real stars of the show were the people. Piecing together various contemporary reports (*cf. Life, Time, Newsweek, U.S. News & World Report, N.Y. Times* and *N.Y. Post*) many people actually enjoyed the situation. There was drinking, singing and necking in the streets. Parties of Frenchmen and U.S. Southerners stuck on the 86th floor observation roof of the Empire State Building chorused each other alternately with *La Marseillaise* and *Dixie*, though how many hours they kept this up was not reported. A church sexton handed out free votive candles—even God lost money—while a blind

257

woman led passengers out of a subway station. One 19-year-old girl said, "They should do this more often: everyone is much more friendly. It's a big community again—people have time to stop and talk."

Volunteers directed traffic with flashlights and handkerchiefs. Some transistor radio listeners pitched in to report on developments and incidents, so that helpful information could be shared with everyone else. Drivers shared cars with pedestrians. People quietly queued up at pay telephones, restaurants, and saloons. They gathered on street corners to listen together to portable radios. One shoeshine boy completed his task by his customer's matches.

### "THAT OLD BITCH"

There was incident upon incident: the whole situation was fantastic. *Time* later mentioned a "crisis-born spirit of camaraderie and exhilaration," and a very prevalent view was that "it brought out the best in people." Of course the fact is that our authoritarian social system cannot help but bring out the worst in people, hence its removal—and bear in mind that the state had well-nigh disappeared—merely allowed them to act as free human beings. After the blackout various politicians, officials, and kindred parasites delivered encomia to the splendid behavior of their "fellow citizens" never realizing how completely superfluous this splendid behavior proved their own functions to be. Somehow or other the ruling class is incredibly fortunate: people often see through individual leaders, but rarely through leadership *per se*. One woman said that she had received "so many singular courtesies" during the power failure that her "faith in mankind had been restored." Tragically, she didn't say she had received so many that her faith in force-propped authority had been lost. Yet that power failure was nearly a power vacuum—we were easily closer to a true anarchy for those few hours than anything most of us will ever be lucky enough to see again.

Incidentally, the Statue of Liberty, because it draws its current from New Jersey, remained lighted throughout the blackout. For the first time in her life "that old bitch," as one of her would-be bombers described her, was almost telling the truth.

To some extent there was a Dionysian quality reminding one observer of VE or VJ Day, "when everybody loved everybody." Another commented on "the same air of revelry that often accompanies a heavy snowstorm." A lawyer in his 32nd floor office said, "first we just sat around having drinks. Now we're having a 'séance' to communicate with the spirit that caused this bliss. We could have walked down, but it's about 600 steps, so we're staying, and we're all getting to know each other." Someone else confessed, " 's a big pain and all, but I sort of hate to see it over. Tomorrow will be just another working day."

But the following day, and several thereafter, there was continued *élan* as people exchanged anecdotes of courage, kindness and adventure. There was something to talk about, and we were impressed by one another. Cab drivers, waitresses, secretaries, truck drivers, grandmothers, teenagers, lawyers, and bellhops interviewed by the *N.Y. Post* all remarked on the "calm, cheerful, considerate attitude the majority of people maintained." Yet, by way of contrast, there were the inevitable exceptions: an elderly woman paused diffidently trying to cross Fifth Avenue and instantly acquired a four-man escort; meanwhile a panhandler continued to intercept passers-by, concentrating on his own version of mutual aid.

### THE UNDERWORLD

Naturally the transportation hang-up, vertical as well as linear, posed the biggest problem. There were 600 stalled subway trains containing some 800,000 commuters, hundreds of whom were trapped for as long as 8 hours, and 60 of whom stayed on for over 14 hours. (Compare this situation to the one obtaining in Boston where subways continued full service as usual, including lighted stations. They operate on an independent, *i.e.* decentralized source of power.) Furthermore in New York City there were hundreds of elevators stalled between floors in apartment and office buildings, which meant several thousand additional victims requiring rescue.

Nonetheless even in these untoward circumstances the leitmotif was solidarity. As one housewife put it after a six-hour stay in a subway car, "I never thought New Yorkers could be that way. I mean everybody seemed to lose his anger." In one car a passenger was leading people in Calypso songs and hand-clapping. Couples were dancing when the conductor arrived to lead them out an emergency stairwell to the surface. The universal report was that there was no panic. As one woman said, "Our conductor would pop in every once in a while and ask, 'How's everybody?', and everybody would say, 'Fine.' We really weren't worried at all."

Some good Samaritans left one train and walked along catwalks to find emergency exits, but then, instead of going safely home, they returned to lead their fellow passengers out. On other trains, talented victims entertained their fellows: in one car there was a tenor; in another a harmonica player; but the *pièce de resistance* was a bagpiper. Many cars featured communal singing. The most common thing, however, was light conversation interspersed with sardonic humor. Men gave up their seats to ladies who frequently offered them back. In one car a woman fainted but word was transmitted from person to person until someone was located with smelling salts. Thereupon these were passed back up hand to hand.

Those who had long waits on their hands exchanged whatever comestibles they had in pockets or pocketbooks: peanuts, wild cherry drops, assorted goodies, or even antacid tablets. One group shared a combination of doughnuts and salami which had been sliced with a nailfile. At midnight the Transit Authority sent in food to those who hadn't yet been extricated. The food-bearers were greeted with a tableau of people sleeping with their arms draped about other people who had been complete strangers five hours previously, and nary a cop in sight!!!

## SEX AND THE ELEVATOR

Meanwhile those unfortunates trapped in elevators—96 in the Empire State Building alone—were enduring their plight with the same sort of equanimity exhibited in the subways. Here too the people entertained one another with improvised games, such as the unlikeliest partners for stalled elevators. This was readily won with the combination of Defense Secretary MacNamara and a draft-card burner. In an elevator in the RCA Building one gentleman gave a course in Yoga positions. When firemen chopped their way into one immobilized car, they asked: "Are there any pregnant women in here?" They were answered: "We've hardly even met."

Surface transportation reflected the same sort of cooperation and solidarity that the crisis had brought out below and above ground level. Even though the Transit was running 3500 of its 4000 buses it could barely make a dent. Therefore countless thousands hiked home across the bridges or up the avenues. Others waited calmly in line at the bus stops, with no pushing or shoving. Nobody seemed to take advantage of the confusion to avoid paying fares, although some passengers couldn't have paid if they'd tried—they were riding on the rear bumpers. Busdrivers, themselves, were inordinately accommodating, calling out each stop as they approached. In New York this comes under the heading of *Mirable Dicta*. At the same time, dozens of private automobiles were loading up at every intersection with absolute strangers.

## CRIME BY CANDLELIGHT

On the other hand, all was not sweetness and light during the darkness. Some people acted like capitalists, *i.e.*, they capitalized on others' vulnerability. About 100 windows were smashed in, and about 41 looters were arrested (none in blue uniform). All told perhaps a dozen stores were looted, which was absolutely negligible in a city of over eight million. Even Police Commissioner Broderick conceded that both the crime and the casualty rates for the night were far below normal. (So who needs him??) One enterprising gunman held up a rare-coin dealer by the flickering light of the shop's only candle—a touching vignette to be sure. There were a total of 65 persons arrested for burglary, larceny, or felonious assault as opposed to the typical 380 for a comparable sixteen-hour stretch. The sum total of arrests for all crimes was only 25% of what it would have been during an ordinary night. There were very few shoplifters reported, which is nothing short of miraculous considering the open-house policy of the department stores (cf. infra). Moreover, there were only 33 vehicle accidents involving injuries, and 44 involving property damage—and this is the world's largest city, completely devoid of traffic lights!!! There was one bus that plowed into a crowd of people in Queens, knocking down 38 persons, some of whom were seriously injured. The driver, evidently in complete consternation, jumped out and fled. Yet his actions must be viewed in context with the fact that his was only one out of 3500 buses operating under these weird conditions.

Somewhere along the line a subway motorman found himself facing charges of rape for flashing a badge and leading a young lady to the ostensible safety of his room. Yet later in court he contended that on any number of previous occasions he had led the same young lady to a similar lair to similarly lay her, so who knows. But progressing from the debatably to the unquestionably false alarms, we find that the Fire Department reported a much higher incidence than usual: 227 rather than the typical 50. This is totally irreconcilable with anarchist theory, so I've decided not to mention it at all.

## THE GREAT SLEEP-IN

Easily offsetting those relatively few human beings who acted like capitalists were the many capitalists who acted like human beings. For example, many department stores flirted with free access for the evening. Macy's played host to an estimated 5000 customers and employees for the night—inviting one and all to make themselves comfortable, and serving them all coffee, sandwiches, cookies, and candy. Needless to say, the furniture department on the ninth floor was the optimum spot for comfort. Meanwhile, across the street, Gimbels, whom Macy adamantly refused to tell—was featuring a guitar-playing salesman for the entertainment of its customer/guests.

One of the songs they reportedly joined in on was the old wartime favorite, "When the Lights Go On Again All Over the World." Evidently no one was familiar with "We Shall Overcome."

Lord and Taylor's turned over its entire floor to customers for the duration of the blackout, while B.Altman's turned over its first. Altman's, incidentally, has its own power generator, so there was some light by which to enjoy the caviar and specially blended coffee which were among the imported delicacies provided by the gourmet department and served to shoppers and employees. 500 stayed there overnight, evidently being unable to tear themselves away from all that caviar. Bloomingdales turned over its home furnishings department to strandees—one woman slept on an $800 sofa—and then capped it off by having its staff serve breakfast to everyone the next morning.

Fina Company had a combination sales meeting and dinner scheduled for that evening, but they catered it to customers instead. Bonwit Teller chartered two buses to get its employees home and suggested that they hold hands leaving the store so that none would get lost. Indicative of the prevailing mood was the fact that the employees danced out of the store together because "someone thought it would be fun." Meanwhile 40 people were bedded down for the night in the showroom of the Simmons Mattress Company.

Similarly, the city's hotels came through in grand style. The Commodore set up 150 cots in a banquet room. Both the Roosevelt and the Algonquin switched elderly guests and those with heart conditions to the lower floors. At the Stanhope the manager gave up his own room, and an assistant manager carried a crippled woman up to the 16th floor. On arrival she said, "Now I'd like a glass of water," so he procured one. At The Statler Hilton two bellmen carried a crippled guest to the 7th floor, but it was not reported what his needs were on arrival. The Americana passed out blankets and pillows to the 200 occupants of its plush lobby—most of the other hotels merely provided as free space. The Sheraton-Atlantic, whose lobby was occupied by some 2000 people, considered the evening somewhat less than a total loss because, as one manager pointed out, "The bar is doing a land-office business." That hotel's report seemed typical: 99% of the people were "terrific" but a few guests tried to sublet their rooms at double the rate.

## EAT

Unfortunately, Utopian free access was much less prevalent in the category of food than it was in that of shelter. Nevertheless one meat market in Brooklyn donated a whole pig to a neighboring convent, thereby providing roast pork snacks to everybody for blocks around.

Two numerically named restaurants, the 21 and the Four Seasons, adopted a policy dangerously akin to: *From each according to his ability; to each according to his need.* The 21 passed out steak sandwiches and free drinks without limit, while the Four Seasons ladled out free soup. Fully to appreciate the enormity of this, reflect on the following: in 1960, when prices presumably were lower, an acquaintance of mine told me that two friends of his (notice I'm three stages removed) went to the Four Seasons for luncheon. Including drinks and tip it cost them nearly $60 while the band played "Nearer My Veblen to Thee." My wife and I didn't happen to go there that night so we missed out on the free soup, but we did enjoy knishes by candlelight at our own expense in a nearby delicatessen. Many other restaurants, although they didn't give away food, stayed open all night to provide free shelter.

Most downtown offices close at 5:00 P. M. so they were empty when the blackout struck, but those still occupied did whatever they could. Revlon, for example, gave its girls couches in the executive offices and then told them to take the following day off. One of their secretaries, stuck on the 27th floor, ate crabmeat and graham cracker sandwiches, and described her experience, with a wistful "I had a great time." Whether she was alluding to the crabmeat or the couches was not made clear.

All sorts of institutions opened their doors, or in some instances dropped their gangways, as a free public service during the emergency. Final estimates included well over 400 people who had been put up for the night in staterooms of ships in port when the lights went out. Armories were thrown open to all comers, while railroad stations, airline terminals, and churches sheltered countless thousands.

## THE GARRISON STATE

The 34th St. Armory alone accommodated 1500 refugees, offering wooden chairs and what illumination could be furnished from the headlights of a few jeeps parked in the middle of the drill floor. For some unexplained reason no cots were available. Naturally Rockefeller had immediately called out the National Guard, which is always a good safe ploy for masking gubernatorial inutility. According to the *New York Post* the Guardsmen were armed with rifles "unloaded but impressive." To complete the farce they wore packs containing ponchos and gas masks, perhaps out of fear that someone would fart. The Guard's major contribution seems to have been scouring the area around 34th St. and Park Ave. until 1:30 a.m.—a full eight hours after the attentat!—at which point they finally came up with coffee and French bread for the beseiged. Compare this forlorn, dilatory effort

263

on the part of the military to the ingenuity of the prostitutes in their quest for bread. *Life* magazine pointed out that these ladies "were among the first to procure flashlights," indicating that the yen is still mightier than the sword.

At the Central Commercial High School, a double session school, the second session runs from 12:30 to 5:50 p.m. Thus there were 1000 students being subjected to obfuscation when the blackout struck. Some 400 of these left during the course of the evening as parents arrived to pick them up, but the school officials kept the other 600 in the classrooms all night. These joked, sang, and later put their heads on their desks and slept—readily taking the crisis in stride. Of course they were nowhere near as comfortable as the lucky ones who spent the night cradled in luxurious barber chairs, but they were infinitely better off than the hundreds who sought sanctuary in St. Patrick's Cathedral. These were huddled in the pews without even a hair shirt for warmth, and worst of all, no restrooms. Msgr. McGovern later confessed, "We've been sending people over to the New Western Hotel for 80 years," which tends to confirm something many of us have long suspected: God's up shit creek.

Of far more serious import was the situation in hospitals, but here too people improvised brilliantly in the emergency. At Bellevue a delicate cornea transplant was underway when the lights went out, but it was successfully completed by battery-operated floodlights. At St. Johns, under similar conditions, emergency surgery was performed on two people, whose spleens had been ruptured in the previously mentioned bus accident. In another hospital a five-hour craniotomy was performed by makeshift light. Final reports indicated at least five dozen babies delivered by candle or otherwise. One man died tragically in the emergency room at Flushing Hospital. He had been in an automobile accident prior to the blackout and was already under surgery when the lights went out.

Only two other deaths in New York City were attributed directly to the blackout: one man suffered a heart attack from climbing ten flights of stairs, and a second fell down a stairway and struck his head. Injuries, of course, were much more common: at the emergency ward of Bellevue alone, 145 patients were treated for blackout injuries—broken arms or legs from falls, car-accident victims, and some heart cases. Police, firemen, and volunteers rushed dry ice to the city's hospitals to keep stored blood from spoiling, whereas a distress call from St. Vincent's brought forth thirty volunteers from a Greenwich Village coffee house to hand-pump iron lungs.

## REVOLUTION SPREADS

Although New York offered perhaps the most spectacular, and in view of its well-deserved reputation for ruthless competition, the most unexpected examples of mutual aid, the same pattern was repeated everywhere throughout the blacked out area. It was solidarity, ingenuity, lack of hysteria, consideration, *etc., etc.,* and little or no government. In Toronto, Ontario, businessmen directed traffic, and in the process unsnarled the city's all-time record traffic jam. Among other things, all the street-cars and trolley buses had stopped dead. In Albany, New York, teenagers with transistor radios went from house to house advising residents to turn off electric appliances.

In Burlington, Vermont, 200 people hurried with flashlights to the local hospital to answer a radio plea which later turned out to be a prank. In Springfield, Vermont a barber finished trimming a customer's hair by the headlights a motorist aimed in his front window. All over the stricken territory civilians patrolled areas, directed traffic, and maintained order. Included among all these civilian volunteers would have to be the contingent of Boston gendarmes who rushed out of the Policeman's Ball dressed in tuxedos. Devoid of badge, uniform, and gun these were on identical footing with the students from nearby Boston University who also pitched in.

## THE URGE TO DESTROY IS A CREATIVE URGE

Incident after incident offered irrefutable proof that society can function without the implicit threats of force and violence which constitute the state. There was probably more freedom from law, however temporary, in that blacked-out 80,000 mile area than there has been at any time since it was originally stolen from murdered and/or defrauded Indians. And it yielded compelling evidence of anarchist theories. As Kropotkin once stated: "We are not afraid to say, 'Do what you will; not as you will'; because we are persuaded that the great majority of mankind, in proportion to their degree of enlightenment, and the completeness with which they free themselves from the existing fetters will behave and act always in a direction useful to society." And John Hewetson pointed out, "far from requiring a coercive authority to compel them to act for the common good, men behave in a social way because it is their nature to do so, because sociableness is an instinct which they have inherited from their remotest evolutionary ancestors...without their inherent tendency to mutual aid they could never have survived at all in the evolutionary struggle for existence."

Such then might be the blackout's confirmation of Kropotkin, but what reinforcement does it offer Bakunin? Actually a good deal, but I'll cite only one case—a frequently distorted quotation which Max Nettlau once described as "a clarion call for revolution in the widest sense." Written in 1842, some 20 years before Bakunin became an anarchist, in fact before be could even be considered a conscious revolutionary, it appeared at the conclusion of an article entitled, "Reaction in Germany," under the pseudonym Jules Elysard: "The urge to destroy is a creative urge." Bakunin's detractors, both in and out of the anarchist movement, invariably swoop down like vultures on that line. However Bakunists might suffer less dismay (and, let's face it, embarrassment) if they viewed it in context with a heart-warming article which appeared in the Financial Section of the *New York Post* the day after the blackout: "Without Power, Computers Died and Wall St. Stopped."

## SECURITY: IT'S IN YOUR HANDS (MOTTO OF NAA)

On the other hand, if the blackout provided all sorts of verification for decentralists, anarchists, Kropotniks, and Bakuninists, what comfort did it offer to pacifists? The answer is damn little. As both James Wechsler (*Post*), and Brad Lyttle (*Peace News*) pointed out, the same sort of unfathomable but infallible electronic technology which blacked but 30 million of us temporarily is exactly what we're relying on to prevent an accidental World War in blacking out 3 billion of us permanently! Small solace to me is the fact that the whole god-damned Pentagon will come down as local fallout, my urge to destroy is not quite that creative. What with the hotline konked out and despite the blithe "assurance" from the First Regional Army Air Defense Commander that all of the Army's missile sites on the Eastern Coast are operative it was obviously a case of genocide continued as usual—bring on the Dark Ages.

All of which serves to illustrate a final object lesson of the Blackout—the predictable, virtually automatic responses of various members of society when confronted by crisis: soldiers fall back on their weapons; clergymen fall back on their prayers; doctors fall back on their antibiotics; bureaucrats fall back their desks; and politicians fall back on their asses. But people fall back on one another, and in that fact must remain all the hopes—however minimal—for the survival of the human race.

Robert S. CALESE

# CONSCIOUSNESS AND THEORY

FOR CENTURIES WORKING PEOPLE HAVE SMARTED under the arrogance of those who called themselves intellectuals, theoreticians, or philosophers. Thought, cultivation of the intellect, higher intelligence have long been held to be the god given privilege of an elite. This attitude even had a certain superficial justification, for access to learning was and remains a privilege not equally open to all, and the contents of established education served and serves the needs of the rulers, not of the rules. This begins in grammar school, where the children of the workingclass are told that the language they learned from their parents is inferior:"incorrect." It doesn't end until death— or a new society.

Throughout history, this evaluation has damaged working people. One reaction has been the "humility reaction." The "lower" classes accepted the evaluation of themselves as inferior, looked up to their "betters," and developed an uncritical respect for the learned man or the intellectual. This reaction was probably more typical of the feudal period than it is of today (if so, that is progress). But it is still with us. It takes the form, for example, of many workers at least partially accepting the idea that managers, specialists, those who "know better" can run the society and economy better than the masses will ever be able to.

Another symptom of damage is what we might call the "sour grapes reaction." Intellectuals and theory, it is felt, have no relation whatsoever to real life. The intellect is seen as the deadly enemy of good, practical common sense. This reaction, although false, is perfectly understandable. Social theory has been and is largely the monopoly of a privileged elite. In its degenerate form, ideology, it has been used to justify a social order that is contrary to the interests of the workingclass. Even the sincere "left," themselves damaged by this society like everyone else, has largely failed to present social theory to the workers in terms of their needs and interest. Furthermore, the way children are taught at school, theory is experienced by the child as the deadly enemy of all natural human impulses.

So when we examine our society critically, our widespread antitheoretical attitudes are exposed for what they are. Not a "healthy reaction" to pedantry, but rather a part of the damage this rotten society of ours inflicts on our intellect and emotions both. Capitalism stinks!

Our anti-theoretical attitudes represent the rejection of a potentially valuable tool—critical analysis of ourselves and our society—

simply because this tool has been misused. Just what our loving rulers need! We badly need *good* theory, growing from and relating to our own practice. We have to reject the trash offered to us by our rulers, but not the intellectual tool itself. Rather we must work to break their monopoly of it.

Why is it dangerous to remain unaware of our own theoretical assumptions? We find the answer in the structure of our society. No one in his right mind can seriously claim that the workingclass controls education, or that we determine the content of the newspapers, magazines, radio, television programs, movies and other products of mass communications that pound at us night and day. And yet these things have a decisive effect on the formation of our ideas, opinions, attitudes and concepts, an effect of whose nature we are often only dimly aware. Here in the United States, movie theatres have experimented in repeatedly flashing Coca Cola ads on the screen for such a small fraction of a second that the public was not aware of having seen them. They call this subliminal advertising. On the days that the ads were shown, however, sales were significantly higher than on the days the ads were not shown. This is only a striking example of a process which goes on in a thousand different ways, each one more subtle than the next. We are not helpless against such things unless we are unaware of them.

Most of the concepts that we take on unawares and uncritically are ideological, that is, they offer us seeming explanations of things. But their real function is to justify the existing order of things in the interests of those who rule over and profit from this society.

They have miseducated us as children that they may manipulate us as adults with their movies, TV, radio, and newspapers. It is essential that working people do not adopt an anti-theoretical attitude. This would render them even more victims to the attitude-forming agencies and forces of the established order. We must formulate our theoretical assumptions consciously. We must shape for ourselves theoretical tools which we can use the better to grasp the reality of today in terms of our own interests. We must construct tools with which we can better unite in common understanding of the interests we all share: our common liberation from a form of tyranny which, as never before in history threatens to make man a willing captive in a golden cage, or to sacrifice him in an atomic furnace.

The continued existence of capitalism absolutely requires our continued ignorance, prejudice, lack of insight into ourselves, and into what makes this society run. There has been a total organization of all the resources of the established order to prevent mankind's self-realization in freedom. This is the final proof of how real the possibility of human fulfillment has become in our time.

A workingclass armed with a coherent insight into the inhumanity of our present social order, coupled with a grasp of how real is its power—this will be the death toll of capitalism and the birth of a new order.

Jim EVRARD

From *Revolutionary Consciousness*

# REFLECTIONS ON INVISIBILITY

## 1. PROBES

THE INCOMPLETENESS OF THE VISIBLE world has given birth to a search for origins, an extension of probes beyond the boundaries of the visible world. This search has resulted in the discovery of an ever-increasing number of enigmas, of phenomena which have apparent importance but which defy explanation in terms of what had formerly been our experience.

In the past this exploration of the invisible has taken two forms. One is the intuitive approach of the mystics, who look beyond the laws of nature, searching for principles that operate independently of the law of cause and effect. The other is the approach of the scientist, who by the combination of symbols hopes to base the events of the visible world on a small set of abstract assertions.

We in the twentieth century are witnessing a reversal of the separation of these two trends. A number of discoveries, among them that of the unconscious by the psychologists, that of Goedel's incompleteness theorem by the mathematicians, that of the uncertainty principle by the physicists, are bringing about a basic reorientation of the intellect. The function of science, which has been the explanation of things, has become the isolation of the inexplicable.

## 2. PROJECTIONS

Thus it is in this century, when the intellect has entered the second phase of a full circle, that the surrealists have made their appearance.

The surrealists have chosen as their mission the projection of invisibilities onto the plane of material existence. Because these are projections of a higher reality they result in the juxtaposition of phenomena which had formerly been mutually contradictory.

The collision of opposites thus produced results in the liberation of forces of extraordinary power. New patterns of action emerge which, because they depend less and less on what had formerly been part of the visible world, are by the standards of the past increasingly bizarre. That this process has been unconsciously taking place is indicated in our own century by the rise and fall of totalitarian regimes, by gang war and satyagraha, by the expansion and by the increasing intricacy of the radical movements, by world wars and the atomic bomb and by the exploration of outer space, by an increasing uncertainty as to what the future may bring.

### 3. THE FUNCTION OF THE ENIGMA

For the surrealists the liberation of these forces becomes a purposeful act, motivated by a love of freedom and the realization that the source of freedom is and always has been the enigma. The projection of enigmas into the visible world is an unforgivable affront to the bureaucrat who presumptuously imagines his assembly of regulations to reflect the nature of the real world. The irreconcilability of authority and the surrealist mission is the reason why the consistent and dedicated surrealist is irrevocably anarchist.

The time has come for men who have seen beyond the boundaries of the visible to advance beyond the stage of ideas and into the stage of action. We must adopt as our conscious mission the process which even now is changing the world about us: the search for origins, the isolation of the enigmatic, the confrontation of the old order with discoveries from the realm of the invisible, and the creation of new patterns of action following therefrom.

Walter CAUGHEY

From *Revolutionary Consciousness*

(*Rebel Worker* 6)

270

# SURREALIST AMBUSH:

## PREFACE TO *SURREALISM & REVOLUTION*

IN THE SUBLIME DOORWAYS of curiously meandering streets, in the trembling oblivion of anonymous gestures (lighting a cigarette, folding an umbrella), in the eyes of a toad trapped in the elevator, what man calls life goes on according to the wrinkled calendars of hallucination and despair. The superhighways to Xanadu have been clouded over with the diffused fish-hooks of obscure mental and physical traditions, icy limitations (linguistic, sociological, ideological, *etc.*) and heavily-lidded dead-ends (stay in school, worship together, register to vote)—a whole daisy-chain of infinite pretensions skewered into the hydrogen afterthoughts of a mindless theological pig.

The "beauties of life," in conventional terms (as in a deodorant commercial on television or a 9″ x 12″ reproduction of the "Mona Lisa") are little more than the platitudes of death. Everywhere the hands, heads, eyes, arms and legs of millions are manipulated through abominable choreographies of obligations, restrictions, responsibilities, laws. Life itself becomes inside-out, upside-down, flattened to the pastel walls of bureaucratic insensitivity.

What is there left in all this of human freedom?

Nothing (we can reply with certainty)—*unless* one begins with a violent, *absolute refusal*, a boundless defiance, a spirit of *total revolt*; unless one has the courage (or the madness) to be a visionary and a revolutionary, a *poet* armed not only against the gods but against the conditions on Earth that necessitated man's invention of gods in the first place. Then, in the struggle for the realization of man's desires— and *only then*—can we speak of *freedom*. All the rest is cowardice, hypocrisy, stupidity, complacency and evasion.

Fortunately, the struggle for total liberation, although fragmented and isolated through laziness, habit, superstition, the existing social structure and the inevitable conflict and confusion of varying levels of revolutionary consciousness mingling in a common movement, nevertheless possesses its own discernible unity, despite the naive precautions of an ironically anti-dialectical traditional Left, whose fear of totality is itself a reflection of a scarcity economy only now seen to be rapidly heading toward extinction.

Fortunately, too, this struggle is able to draw on resources of ammunition, illumination and tactics more profound, more subtle, more thoroughgoing than those which provided the means of comprehension and attack for earlier struggles. Surrealism, in particular, which is *at the same time* an arsenal, a drug, a way of seeing, a kind of total guerrilla warfare and "a way of life"—so little understood on these shores, so systematically lied about by academicians and journalists—is nevertheless making its seditious presence felt. Simon Rodia's marvelous towers in Watts intrude upon the landscapes of hidebound rationality like Merlin with a machinegun, and this a bottle's throw from the birthplace of the insurrectionary cry, "Burn, baby, burn!" revivifying the flames of the apocalypse and becoming, overnight, the inevitable revolutionary watchword of this combustible society.

The surrealist miracle, without any eclecticism, unites strands and seashells of marxism, anarchism, utopianism, psychoanalysis, hermetic philosophy, "poetry of the damned," Zen, psychedelic drugs, mythology, nonsense literature, anthropology, madness, play, cinema, relativity theory and popular culture into an effervescent, non-Cartesian, ceaselessly unfolding tapestry of desire and action known mythomorphically, perhaps still best, as "the disquieting muse."

Among its many methods and weapons, let us single out only three or four as examples: *black humor*, black as the swan of Lautréamont ("with a body bearing an anvil surmounted by the putrefying carcass of a crab, and rightly inspiring mistrust in the rest of its aquatic comrades"—*Les Chants de Maldoror*); Maldoror, one hundred years later, rampages more than ever through the fertile valleys of our sizzling minds: the *automatic revelation* ("pure psychic automatism" expressing "the real functioning of thought"—*First Surrealist Manifesto*); the *objective chance* of the streets (or anywhere) where the zodiac of fleeting moments weaves innumerable marvelous images and patterns so susceptible to the impassioned divination of total, *mad love.*

Surrealism pours magic into everyday life and everyday life into magic. The relentless exploration of the Marvelous clears the road to freedom. The Revolution must be perceived as (among other things) an *expedition.*

For the Revolution! Let us discredit, distort, deface, dismantle and destroy the senile mechanisms of immediate reality! No more cops! No more bosses! No more jails! No more churches! No more courts! No more taxes! No more army! No more governments! No more chains on the mind or body! No more enslavement of man by man!

Long live the Surrealist Revolution! Long live surrealism at the service of the Revolution! Long live the Minotaur, our comrade in the expanding labyrinths of the real and the *seas and skies of dreams!*

Meanwhile, as for myself, I can usually be found, on a Sunday morning, on Maxwell Street (amidst the broken toys, the invisible seismographs and the howling, hypodermic rhythm-and-blues) or, on weekday evenings, bicycling with Penelope at the Lincoln Park Zoo, where the delirious promenade of the anteaters reveals to us, to anyone with eyes to *see*, a small but essential part of the entirely realizable grandeur of life.

Franklin ROSEMONT
*Chicago, September 1966*

# OPEN THE PRISONS!
# DISBAND THE ARMY!
## There Are No Common Law Crimes

S OCIAL COERCION HAS HAD ITS DAY. Nothing—neither recognition of an accomplished fault nor contribution to the national defense—can force man to give up freedom. The idea of prison and the idea of barracks are commonplace today; these monstrosities no longer shock you. The infamy lies in the calmness of those who have got around the difficulty with various moral and physical abdications (honesty, sickness, patriotism).

Once consciousness has been recovered from the abuse that composes one part of the existence of such dungeons—the other part being the degradation, the diminution, that they engender in those who escape from them as well as those imprisoned there; *and there are, it seems some madmen who prefer the cell or the barrack room*—once this consciousness is finally recovered, no discussion can be recognised, no recantation. Never has the opportunity to be done with it been so great, so don't mention opportuneness to us. Let the assassins begin, if you wish; peace prepares for war, such proposals conceal only the lowest fear or the most hypocritical desires. Let us not be afraid to acknowledge that we are waiting, that we are inviting catastrophe. Catastrophe? That would be the persistence of a world in which man has rights over man. 'Sacred unity' before knives or machine guns— how can this discredited argument be cited any longer? Send the soldiers and convicts back to the fields. Your freedom? No freedom for the enemies of freedom. We will not be the accomplices of jailers.

Parliament votes for a mangled amnesty; next spring's graduating class will depart. In England a whole town has been powerless to save one man. It was learned without great surprise that in America the execution of several condemned men had been postponed until after Christmas *because they had good voices.* And now that they have sung they might as well die, for the exercise. In the sentry boxes, in the electric chair, the dying wait. Will you let them go under?

*OPEN THE PRISONS!*
*DISBAND THE ARMY!*

The Surrealist Group<br>Paris, 1925

From *Surrealism & Revolution*

# DECLARATION OF 27 JANUARY 1925

REGARDING A FALSE INTERPRETATION of our enterprise that is stupidly circulating among the public, we declare to the entire braying literary, dramatic, philosophical, exegetical and even theological body of contemporary criticism:

1. We have nothing to do with literature; but we are quite capable, when necessary, of making use of it like anyone else.

2. *Surrealism* is not a new or an easier means of expression nor even a metaphysics of poetry. It is a means of total liberation of the mind *and of all that resembles it.*

3. We are determined to make a revolution.

4. We have coupled the word *surrealist* and the word *revolution* only to show the disinterested, detached, and even totally desperate character of this revolution.

5. We do not pretend to change the *mores* of men, but we intend to show the fragility of their thought and on what shifting foundations, what caverns, they have built their trembling houses.

6. We hurl this formal warning to society: Beware of your deviations and *faux-pas*; we shall not miss a single one.

7. At each turn of its thought, society will find us waiting.

8. We are specialists in revolt. There is no means of action which we are not capable, when necessary, of employing.

9. We say in particular to the Occidental world: *Surrealism exists.*

And what is this new ism that is fastened to us? Surrealism is not a poetic form. It is a cry of the mind turning back on itself, and it is determined to break apart its fetters, even if it must be by material hammers!

*Bureau of Surrealist Research*
Paris, 1925
19 Rue de Grenelle

From *Surrealism & Revolution*

# LETTER TO THE DIRECTORS OF LUNATIC ASYLUMS

GENTLEMEN:
Law and custom concede you the right to measure the human spirit. You are supposed to exercise this sovereign redoubtable jurisdiction with judgement and good sense. Excuse us while we laugh in your faces. The credulity of civilized peoples, scholars, administrators, endows psychiatry with a limitless supernatural enlightenment. Your profession's case is awarded the verdict in advance. We have no intention of discussing here the validity of your science, nor the doubtful existence of mental disorders. But for a hundred pretentious pathogenic diagnoses in which a confusion between matter and spirit runs wild, for a hundred classifications out of which the few usable ones are still very vague, how many noble attempts have been made to approach the cerebral world in which so many of your prisoners live? For instance: for how many of you is the dream of a paranoiac and the images which haunt him anything more than a salad of words?

We are not surprised to find you incompetent for a task for which few people are equipped. But we protest vigorously against the right attributed to certain men, narrow-minded or not, to sanction their investigations into the domain of the human spirit by a sentence of life imprisonment.

And what imprisonment? One knows—one does not know well enough—that asylums, far from being *asylums*, are fearful jails, where the inmates provide a source of free and useful manpower, where brutality is the rule—all of which *you* tolerate. A mental hospital, under the cover of science and justice, is comparable to a barracks, a prison,

275

a slave colony.

We will not raise here the question of arbitrary confinements; this will save you the trouble of making hasty denials. But we state categorically that a great number of your inmates, however mad by official definition, are also arbitrarily confined. We protest against any interference with the free development of a delirium as legitimate, as logical as any other sequence of ideas or human acts. The repression of anti-social reactions ia as chimerical as it is unacceptable in principle. All individual acts are antisocial. Madmen are above all else the individual victims of social dictatorship. In the name of that quality of individuality which belongs specifically to man, we demand that you liberate these people convicted of sensibility. For we tell you that no laws are powerful enough to lock up all men who think and act.

Without insisting upon the perfectly inspired nature of the manifestation of certain madmen, within the limits of our capabilities of appreciating them, we affirm that their conception of reality is absolutely legitimate, as are all the acts which result therefrom.

Try and remember *that* tomorrow morning during your tour of inspection, when, without knowing their language, you attempt to converse with these people over whom you have one single advantage: force.

The Surrealist Group<br>Paris, 1925

From *Surrealism & Revolution*

# INAUGURAL BREAK

WHILE ITS ADVERSARIES OF THE RIGHT AND LEFT, as if spellbound, obey rather dismal tactical considerations or cut their own throats with short-range calculations, surrealism forges ahead, *both protected and exposed* by the passion which gives it life and which remains its first, its chief, constant. This passion, concerning whose nature there can be no uncertainty—a subversive passion, in fact, and not a sacrificial one, intended for the unchaining of man and not for his hypocritical and infamous 'redemption'—has never for a moment been inconsistent, whatever the ordeal, and it guarantees better than any long phrases the part that surrealism undertakes to play in the permanent revolution of men and things, from which it is inseparable.

To the extent to which it asks the revolution to include the whole of man, not to conceive his liberation in any single respect but rather in all its aspects at one time, surrealism emerges as the only doctrine qualified to throw into the balance the forces of which it was first the prospector and then the *marvellously magnetic conductor*—from the child-woman to black humour, from objective chance to the will to myth. The chosen ground of these forces is the unconditioned, overwhelming, mad love which alone permits man to live expansively and to evolve according to new psychological dimensions.

Once prospected and given the possibility of joining together and stimulating one another, there is some chance that these forces may finally reconcile human finality and universal causality. They are the corollaries and participants of the progress of the most advanced intellectual disciplines of our time to which we owe a non-Euclidean geometry, a non-Maxwellian physics, a non-Pasteurian biology, a non-Newtonian mechanics—disciplines which, in turn, are bound up with a non-Aristotelian logic and with that evolving non-Mosaic moral code whose authority we instantly invoke to avert the unlivable.

The response evoked by Rimbaud's outcry with regard to life, by Marx's injunction with regard to the world, is assuredly no new thing in the heart of man. But ever since the reasonable and rational developments of consciousness took precedence over the passionate developments of the unconscious, that is, since the last myth hardened into a deliberate mystification, men seem to have lost the secret which permitted them to know and to act—to act without alienating the acquirements of knowledge. The hour has come to promote a new myth, one that will carry man forward a stage further towards his ultimate destination.

This undertaking is specifically that of surrealism. It is its great rendezvous with History.

It is in the nature of dream and revolution to agree, not to exclude each other. To dream the revolution is not to renounce it but to pursue it doubly and without mental restrictions.

To avert the unlivable is not to flee life but to throw oneself into it totally and irrevocably.

SURREALISM IS THAT WHICH SHALL BE.

The Surrealist Group<br>Paris, 1947

From *Surrealism & Revolution*
(*excerpts*)

# INTRODUCTION TO
## THE DECLINE AND FALL OF THE
## SPECTACULAR COMMODITY ECONOMY

THE SITUATIONIST INTERNATIONAL characterizes itself as a Durutti Column of the intellect, after the band of Spanish Revolutionaries who liberated villages during the Civil War. Their theoretical strength, their ability to consolidate the works of Godwin, Marx, Lautréamont, Rimbaud, Freud, Stirner, Reich and others, along with their engaging prose, testifies to the truth of their claim. In the last few years their influence has not only been felt in the corpse that is France, but also in England and the United States, where it has begun to stir a moribund theoretics.

The Situationists' basic formulations include their concepts of the *Spectacle* and of *Survival*. The Spectacle is the joint project of the communications media, the entertainment industry, and the effusions of a bootlicking cultural avant-garde, to contain Desire by projecting a commodity orientation. Though an important formulation, their absolute extension of it—for example, to a blind dismissal of surrealism as being an integral part of the Spectacle—tends, at times, to put the Situationists in the backyard of nihilism.

Life as an endeavor to survive, their other basic formulation, is of course directly related to commodity enslavement. Domination becomes a way of life for millions who believe it natural to struggle for existence. But life in a post-scarcity economy can be, so to speak, a creative experiment in freedom, a work of real art.

On both of these points the Situationists approximate Herbert Marcuse's analysis in *One-Dimensional Man* and *Eros and Civilization*. The Situationist concept of life as survival is, in fact, an abbreviated form of Marcuse's theory of surplus-repression.

Situationist ethics are anarchist-individualist: a repudiation of sacrifice—the basis of Western ethics, the foundation for productivity, racism and humanism. Most important for us is their emphasis upon the absolute unity of theory and practice, which provides the cutting edge for most so-called revolutionary organizations.

> The rock on which the old revolutionary movement foundered was the separation of theory and practice. Only at the supreme moments of struggle did the proletariat supersede this division and attain their truth. As a rule the principle seems to have been, *hic Rhodus, hic non salta*. Ideology, however 'revolutionary,' always serves the ruling class: false consciousness is the alarm-signal revealing the

presence of the enemy fifth column. The lie is the essential product of the world of alienation. Once an organization which claims the social truth adopts the lie as a tactic, its revolutionary career is finished (*Ten Days that Shook the University*).

Because we believe that *The Decline and Fall of the Spectacular-Commodity Economy* is probably the best exposition of a Revolution now in process, we have undertaken to reprint it and make it more readily available. It should be read, however, not as the Truth, but as an exercise of a method of analyzing reality.

Bernard MARSZALEK

# EPILOGUE: 1967—
# THE SUMMER PLUNDER FESTIVALS

*"The riot was beautiful."*
—Community Union organizer from Newark—

*"It is beauty that leads to freedom."*
—Friedrich Schiller—

HISTORY, THE ONLY TRUE ARBITER of theory, has endorsed much of the Situationist statement on the Watts Insurrection with a vengeance. Two years after Watts had become synonymous with all the fears of the Johnsonian Consensus, Watts as a symbol was smashed, first by Newark, and less than a month later, by Detroit. A small group of French revolutionaries had foreseen the pattern and had projected the most precise critique.

In the United States, the response could be expected. Journalists continued to feed the needs of racism in attempting to make anachronisms and outright lies fit a revolutionary situation. The populace is expected to believe that only a "criminal element" was responsible for the insurrections, as if most blacks are too chicken-shit to fight for their freedom. The capitalists, and their running dogs, the politicians, always better aware of the reality simply because their survival is at stake, quietly have initiated feeble reforms to absorb the discontent of the poor. They are practicing, especially in Detroit, social therapeutics for an epidemic. Needless to mention, the ruling class cannot surmount its inherent limitations. Its response must be determined by its goal—total domination. It can give the poor nothing, because it cannot give them their freedom. In the meantime, most revolutionaries, probably over-reacting to the Establishment's smokescreen of lies, have seen in the uprisings elements of revolt not present there and have ignored aspects of great significance.

The worth of *The Decline and the Fall of the Spectacular Commodity Economy* lies in its emphasis upon the most important phenomenon associated with each urban revolt—to quote a capitalist tool, the Mayor of Detroit, its "carnival atmosphere." The immediate transcendence of a commodity orientation, which is always exhibited in these so-called riots, is ignored by most radicals, who in turn demonstrate their own lack of insight by equating the struggle for black liberation in this country with the national liberation movements of the Third World. So what if 15,000 troops, 3,000 of whom just returned from butchering the people of Vietnam, suppressed the Detroit Insurrection? Does the nature of repression define the struggle? Only an insignificant propaganda point can be established with such an equation. In the process, nothing is learned about the specific, and unique, struggle that is occurring in this country: a struggle for liberation that includes laughter both as its elusive strength and as its defining characteristic.

The element of play associated with each insurrection is an outgrowth of a post-scarcity economy. The underpinnings of domination are abandoned whenever the ethic of scarcity is transgressed. Productivity, racism and corporate humanism are delicately balanced upon it. They all come tumbling down like toy soldiers when people take "the vaunting of abundance...at its face value."!

One should not gather, however, that these upheavals are totally emotional outbursts. They are very reasoned orgies of selective and purposeful destruction. Yet their impetus is not exclusively revenge, but, more to the point, fun. And their goal is not exclusively the looting of goods, but also, the re-possession of Time. It is through the colonization of their time, by capitalists and their financial leeches, that oppressed people are kept in bondage. The destruction of loan company offices in both Newark and Detroit achieves greater significance within this perspective. The far greater significance, however, lies in the revolutionary criticism embodied by these acts. By simple extension, what we have here is a most resounding repudiation of work and the artificial compartmentalization of time. In a post-Industrial Age, we can proceed to a use of time determined solely by individual desire. The "rioters" know this, even if "revolutionaries" don't. Obviously, the puerile demand for jobs for the poor is the most reactionary development to be visited upon us. All the more so when so-called representatives of the oppressed quite self-righteously scream that they want time cards. Fuck them!

Demands that people be herded into factories is just what the Establishment wants. Let's all think economically. The solution resides in the Market. Go seek it, you fine revolutionaries. Dig for your bone! Proceed along this path and expect to be checkmated by the ruling class, for after all, you are playing a game for which they formulate the rules.

To agitate for the control of production, when machines can become the loci of all production, is to agitate for nothing. To hope for the Revolution to come bursting out of the factory gates, while the economy remains stable, is a silly millennialism. The only way to destroy capitalism is by totally repudiating its ethic. Wage slaves, for the fun of it, should heighten the amount of industrial sabotage they commit. Those unemployed and with the prospect of only menial labor to fill their time should steal. Life is something that happens outside of the job.

Bernard MARSZALEK
September, 1967

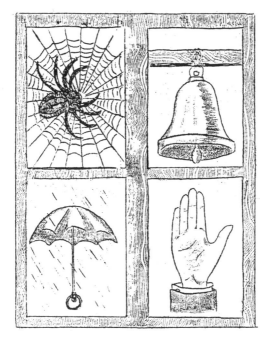

Franklin Rosemont: *Introduction to Hegel*
(from *Revolutionary Consciousness*)

# OTHER *REBEL WORKER* DOCUMENTS

# IN DEFENSE OF THE R.U. WOBBLIES:
## LETTER TO THE *ROOSEVELT UNIVERSITY TORCH*

TO THE EDITOR:
Among colleges, Roosevelt has been exceptionally lucky to have a discussion group so profoundly relevant, at present, as the Wobblies. In my opinion, most other college political clubs from right to left, whether YAF or Liberal or YPSL or Fair Play are superficial by comparison.

So in terms of education, it would be a pity if the club were not reinstated. In terms of student freedom to learn, *Lernfreiheit*, it would be intolerable. The IWW is the only current philosophy of industrialism that still takes seriously the workman as creator and decision-maker, as potential manager, and that regards work as integral with the whole human personality. If this philosophy of labor had prevailed in the past instead of being neglected or betrayed by both the socialist and communist unions and the AFL (and later CIO) we should not now be so trapped in the era-of Organization Men, labor bureaucrats, and totalitarian "socialisms."

I do not think that the IWW has adequate solutions for the present problems of automation neither does any other philosophy but it does take them with passionate human earnestness, and in the present confusion we surely cannot afford to ban one of the few serious voices.

I fail to see the relevance of the references to the Attorney General's list of subversives. My understanding is that the list has to do with being on the public payroll, etc. and I suppose it is reasonable for an entrenched club, like government, to make rules about who can join but what has it to do with the rights of free and honest citizens, not to speak of inquiring students?

I am also puzzled by the noise about Stewart's burning the flag. Does a community of scholars really mean to affirm that *lese majeste* is a crime or anything but a hangover superstition? If the state of Illinois has such a law of *lese majeste*, let it try to enforce it. Stewart's act seems to have been a piece of activist rhetoric entirely in the current, "existentialist" style, which I rather like.

But the thought expressed in the rhetoric is not only well considered, but is, I think, irrefutable: namely. We, shall never get rid of war and we are all likely to be incinerated if we do not get rid of the baroque system of sovereign states. To use a slightly different rhetoric, we must ring down those flags, French, Soviet, American, Panamanian, etc. (This ceremonial would not violate the fire laws.) As thinking men, would President Pitchell and Dean Hoover seriously deny this?

Then why should not a speaker say it, and poetically act it out? Of course, as a chartered corporation the University cannot sponsor "crimes" according to the law of Illinois. But it is under no obligation to approve of superstitious and baroque conceptions, or to act as if it approved of them. If there was no police action, why did any-official notice have to be taken of the incident at all?

Paul GOODMAN
Knapp Distinguished Scholar
University of Wisconsin

# THE MEANING OF IT ALL
## PREFACE TO THE SOLIDARITY BOOKSHOP CATALOGUE

*Books are keys to Wisdom's treasure.*
—Anonymous—

*All writing is garbage.*
—Antonin Artaud—

THE CRUCIAL SIGNIFICANCE of this catalogue lies in its presentation of the spirit of the Revolution in its totality. Opposing the flat, one-dimensional, Cartesian and putrescent world of bourgeois reality, as well as the equally useless puritanical facade of the sarcomatous Traditional Left, the dreams of the revolutionary movement find expression here in both their manifest and latent content, aiming at the continual expansion of consciousness and leading to the collectively and individually lyrical subversion of all values imposed by a repressive society.

This catalogue is, to our knowledge, the largest and most comprehensive catalogue of specifically *radical* books ever published, containing somewhere near 600 titles. Its agitational and educational usefulness is clearly evident by that fact alone.

The emphasis throughout has been on libertarian revolutionary works, though many books and pamphlets not exactly meeting this requirement have been included if in our opinion they were especially relevant and/or revolutionary by implication. In the Socialist and Anarchist sections the attempt was made to list all the "classics" of the past which are in print as well as an even greater number of contemporary works, representing practically every important tendency in the revolutionary movement today.

The Surrealist section lists nearly every surrealist work currently available in English, many of the most important presurrealist works, nearly every critical study and a few works in French which are almost completely unavailable in the U.S. except from us.

Certain sections, like Anthropology and Psychoanalysis, are very abbreviated; we feel the books listed therein are of particular importance to younger revolutionaries seeking new approaches to the problems confronting us, and thus deserve to be listed.

This catalogue, and the Solidarity Bookshop, and our journal *The Rebel Worker* are some of the agitational activities of members of the Chicago Branch of the IWW. *The Rebel Worker* has quadrupled its circulation (now about 1000) in only four issues, and we are confident that, as more people discover it, we can increase its circulation fantastically. We have recently begun a pamphlet series.

Our immediate aim is to bring revolutionary thought to the greatest possible number of people. But we are determined, as soon as possible, to overthrow the ignoble conditions now prevailing, to make a revolution, to rebuild the world from scratch. Applications for membership are available on request.

# HIGH SCHOOL STUDENTS:
# WHY STAY IN SCHOOL?

P ARENTS, TEACHERS, EMPLOYERS, MINISTERS, the government, the Boy Scouts, the YMCA, the Communist Party, Mayor's Committees and Barry Goldwater are all united in agreeing that high school students should stay in school. They will tell you that you will not be able to find work or get into college without a high school diploma. Don't believe them; they're putting you on.

The reason for keeping kids in school is not to prepare them for jobs but rather to keep them off the streets. (What do you learn in high school that could help you in your work, anyway?) They're "preparing" you for "jobs" which won't even exist five to ten years from now. American workers in their twenties and thirties are even now being laid off by the tens of thousands. Unemployment may soon reach depression proportions.

Negroes and Puerto Ricans in particular are suffering the worst effects of the job situation. They will continue to be "the last to be hired and the first to be fired" unless a strong protest movement is able to challenge this. We in the Industrial Workers of the World are tying to build such a movement. The Negro Freedom Struggle has made some progress, but much more needs to be done.

Remember: the supporters of the power structure want things as they are. They want you in school to keep you from joining sit-ins, picketlines, Freedom Rides, rent strikes and other protest actions against discrimination and exploitation. They want you in school to make it safe for them.

We cannot put our faith in the Civil Rights Bill or in politicians. Real power lies in the hands of those who work for a living and in the hands of their sons and daughters. If we use it, we cannot lose. We urge you to rebel against this system of truant officers, cops, juvenile courts, curfews, school "discipline," low wages and crummy living conditions. We urge you to join us in building a union fighting for true freedom and true security for all.

WHY WASTE YOUR TIME! DROP OUT! JOIN THE IWW!
Industrial Workers of the World,
Chicago Branch

*Spring 1965*

SITTING BULL * LEADER OF THE OGLALA SIOUX NATION

| Sunday | Monday | Tuesday | Wednesday | Thursday | Friday | Saturday |
|---|---|---|---|---|---|---|
| ꙨECEMBER | | Rosa PARKS keeps her bus seat 1955  BERKMAN & GOLDMAN deported to Russia 1919  **1** | John BROWN hanged 1858  SPROUL HALL sit-in Berkeley 1964  **2** | **3** | **4** | MONTGOMERY Bus Boycott 1959  **5** |
| Great trial of Anarchists in Milan 1889  **6** | **7** | Joseph DIETZGEN socialist  Born 1828  **8** | UBU ROI by Alfred JARRY first performed 1896  **9** | **10** | **11** | Opening of Solidarity Bookshop 1964  **12** |
| 1st Common Manifesto Russian Socialist Parties 1905  **13** | Errico MALATESTA Born · Italy · 1853  **14** | **15** | SITTING BULL leader of Oglala Sioux killed 1890  **16** | **17** | **18** | **19** |
| Eleven day strike Russia 1905  **20** | Peter KROPOTKIN Born Russia 1842  **21** | **22** | Thomas PAINE'S CRISIS published 1776  **23** | **24** | SHAY'S REBELLION Attack Springfield Armory - 1786  **25** | DECEMBERIST Uprising Russia 1854  **26** |
| **27** | Nibilists execute Chief of Police Sudejkin Russia - 1883  **28** | WOUNDED KNEE MASSACRE of the Oglala Sioux Pine Ridge S.D. 1890  **29** | **30** | Donela MEL/MENBUIS Anarchist Born 1846  **31** | | |

Designed & calligraphed by Tor Faegre, the Solidarity Bookshop Anarchist
Revolutionary calendars were among the group's most popular productions.

286

# ZTANGI!

## Some Texts that Might Have Been Included in a Journal that Never Appeared

—George Herriman

*The idea of Revolution: total human reintegration which,
bringing the alchemical process to fruition, is accompanied by
a veritable mutation of the understanding.*

—Claude Tarnaud—

One of the greatest magazines that never existed, *Ztangi!* was intended above all to expand and deepen the *Rebel Worker* quest for dialectical totality. It was conceived from the start as an unruly "catch-all" of revolutionary reflections and incitements, deliberately focused on matters overlooked or despised by other "radicals." We wanted *Ztangi!* to exemplify not only our refusal of the dominant order, but also—and especially—our refusal to limit ourselves to the "themes," "style" and "tone" of the traditional left. The following texts—on free jazz, Malcolm X, children's toys, sexual politics, Jimi Hendrix, surrealism, the Incredible Hulk, and new ways of disrupting/transforming existing social relations—affirm our collective desire and will to create a way of life based on joy and ecstasy *as well as* freedom and equality.

—F.R.

by Franklin Rosemont

The "official" function of music in this society is to deceive the purity of the human imagination. From the deceived eye to the confused ear, man is reduced to an idiocy as impotent as it is unforgivable. Through the savage eye everything that is poetry can be revealed. The ear can lend snow to the summer trees and a specifically disturbing aspect to a revolver being fired. I am interested in the maximum of consciousness, in liberating the senses from the fetters of concretized ideology in the hideous reality around us. The point is to resolve the arbitrary conflict between the eye and the ear by a truly definitive transformation of reality. It is necessary to follow one's own footprints inside the mind, and then outside. "It is time to realize," wrote the Belgian surrealist Paul Nougé, "that we are capable, also, of inventing feelings—perhaps fundamental feelings - of a power comparable to those of love and hatred." The point of departure is Rimbaud's "systematic derangement of all the senses," an experiment which must be continually renewed. It should be possible to juxtapose auditory, visual, olfactory, tactile and gustatory capacities, for sheer pleasure. Psychedelic experience validates the ear that sees and the eye that listens. Why not admit that man can be a tree or or a stone and that the sky lifts the sun from its nightly repose?

Several years ago I was listening to a very old recording of a medieval choir, Josquin des Pres, when the ending submerge... the r... ...the

...skeleton rattling in the brain. * * * *
The Jimi Hendrix Experience (Hendrix, vocals & guitar; Mitch Mitchell, drums; Noel Redding, bass) has recently emerged into the eldritch light that bathes the quotidian splendours of this universe and all others. They play regularly before standing - room - only crowds in Paris, Stockholm, Copenhagen, London... Eight days after the Beach boys broke the house record at the Tivoli in Stockholm, playing for 7000 fans at two shows, Hendrix appeared and (to say the least) broke their record, playing for 14,600 fans at two shows. The Experience stage show (Hendrix has been known to play his guitar with his teeth, and even to burn it on stage) possesses a demonizing convulsiveness in which the most traditionally cherished philosophical prejudices are dismembered on a monstrous scale, during a long midnight, luminous and black. Hendrix has acknowledged the inspiration he has found for lyrics in fairy tales and science-fantasy. Certain of his songs seem to hover like enchanted owls over the Garden of Earthly Delights subtly moving from paradise to hell. With profound lyricism, a sense of creative destruction and black humor, Hendrix weaves the tapestry of his violent and delirious myths across a sky that darkens as he approaches. Nothing is premeditated: everything belongs to the purely automatic revelation. With striking simplicity, he improvises a chaos of defiantly realizable beauty. All of Hendrix' comments... have spoken of this remai... At least

Lester Doré: *Jimi Hendrix* (Chicago Seed, I:8, 1967)

288

# THE POVERTY OF PIETY

THE STERILE IMAGINATIONS of the necrophiliacs who stalk among the tombstones of American politics lead these sad souls, in cases in which ignorance is no viable or proper excuse, to the most stupid solutions of life-and-death struggles.

Electoral campaigns, whether they are conducted for the benefit of a red-faced, fist-pounding apologist of capitalism or a "revolutionary" savior of mankind, are all redundant to any person whose sole concern is *Freedom*, and not sacrifice: the sacrifice of political necessities to some absurd, elitist notion of a political common denominator of popular apprehension, the sacrifice of time and labor to create a constituency centered on faith in the democratic process as an educative venture, the sacrifice, finally, of revolutionary action. Sacrifice, intellectual and libidinal martyrdom, is the only concept of transcendence offered by this dumb but highly dangerous assortment of clowns, perpetually in search of a circus, and always satisfied with the quiet hand-claps of any audience willing to forego immediate satisfaction out of a bourgeois respect for proper etiquette. Their ability to bore absolutely everybody not in their pay, an inherent characteristic of all politicians, is sufficient reason for their collective evaporation from our consciousness.

Postponing the essential question of the meaning of History for the moment, we can assert with certainty that no ministerial crisis (the only "revolution" politicians consider) will suffice to remove the often seemingly unobtrusive chains of total domination. When our everyday lives are circumscribed by a latticework of restrictions that range from blatant economic exploitation to subtle controls of our leisure, all aimed at limiting and channeling our desires to safe and predictable ends, and when, at bottom, the entire repressive nature of our society rests upon a selfless ethic that legitimatizes human impoverishment (and leads as a means to self-identity to an ego-centered culture) to serve the needs of authority, then only a critical orientation that repudiates not only capitalist economics, but also its psycho-social ornamentation, then only a liberated course of action which makes real our quests, shall together lead to a way of life that must become ours if we are to transcend repression in all of its manifestations. These necessities revolve around the most combustible conception of revolution possible to attain: the transformation of *all values* on both an individual and a social level in an effort to sustain a way of living that will make not only joy, but also sensual ecstasy integral to being.

The revolutionary must be post-revolutionary, or be nothing at all.

Bernard MARSZALEK

From the *Seed*, Chicago 1967

# MALCOLM, *SEMPER* MALCOLM

*The Autobiography of Malcolm X*, with Alex Haley
(New York, Grove Press, 1965. London, Hutchinson)

*When I am dead—I say it because from things I know, I do not expect to live long
enough to read this book in its finished form—I want you to just watch and see if I'm
not right in what I say: that the white man, in his press, is going to identity me with
'hate.' He will make use of me dead, as he has made use of me alive, as a convenient
symbol of 'hatred' and that will help him to escape facing the truth that all I have
been doing is holding up a mirror to reflect, to show, the history of unspeakable
crimes that his race has committed against my race.*

—Malcolm X—

MALCOLM X, IT HAS BEEN ASSUMED both in the USA and
elsewhere, was simply a Negro fascist, whose extremist attitudes bedeviled the "peaceful solution" of America's racial
crisis. This view has arisen mainly because of the liberal belief in the
efficacy and rightness of the nonviolent civil rights struggle and the
illogical "corollary" belief in the inefficacy and wrongness of other
methods of struggle. If anarchist commentators have been less ready
to denounce his violence, they have as happily contributed to the
public image of Malcolm as a hate-crazed racist. Now that his autobiography has been published, it should, if nothing else, correct this
false but convenient image; false because it denies the complexity,
inconsistency and evolution of Malcolm's ideas, and convenient because
it enables these ideas the more easily to be dismissed. In a way that
most biographies are not, this book *is* Malcolm X.

His father was murdered when Malcolm Little was 6; his mother

was as casually declared insane by criminally indifferent public authorities when he was 13. For the next seven years Malcolm's life followed
the archetypal pattern of ghetto delinquency. He was a shoeshine boy,
a pimp, a hustler, a procurer for white sex perverts, a pusher and user
of drugs and the leader of a burglary gang. By the time he was jailed,
in February, 1946, shortly before he was 21, he was carrying at least
two, and often three guns. In jail he proudly accepted the nickname
Satan—until he met a convict called Bimbi. "What fascinated me with
him most of all was that he was the first man I had ever seen command
total respect...with words." Bimbi "turned Malcolm 'round" and
Malcolm started correspondence courses in English and, later, Latin.
It was not until 1948 that he first heard of Elijah Muhammad's Nation
of Islam—the so-called Black Muslims—from his brother Philbert. "I
wrote Philbert a letter which, although in improved English, was
worse than my earlier reply to his news that I was being prayed for
by his 'Holiness' church." Later came a letter from his brother Reginald:
"Malcolm, don't eat any more pork, and don't smoke any more cigarettes. I'll show you how to get out of prison." Malcolm's automatic
response was to think "he had come up with some way I could work
a hype on the penal authorities." Gradually, however, Malcolm was
convinced. He wrote frequently to Elijah Muhammad and he left
prison in 1952 a Muslim, though, as he later discovered, a somewhat
unorthodox one for the Nation of Islam bore much the same relationship to Islam as the various apocalyptic Christian sects do to the
major churches.

Black Nationalism is not a recent phenomenon in the USA; during the 1920's Marcus Garvey's movement attracted sufficient attention for him to be deported, and the roots go back to slavery. The
Black Muslims themselves were founded in the 1930's by W. D. Fard,
salesman of Oriental carpets, whose beginnings and end no one knows,
but who is assumed by the Nation of Islam to have been the incar-
nate Allah, visiting the USA to free the Negroes. The movement
gained strength at almost the same points in time as the Civil Rights
Movement, after the war and particularly in the early mid-fifties which
were, curiously, periods of limited but genuine advance in race relations. Such improvements have been slow, often they have succeeded
not so much in affecting the status of individuals as in raising their aspirations and, with them, their frustrations. Likewise the collapse of
African colonialism in the years since the war has been an incentive
towards the destruction of a remarkably similar structure in the USA.
However, the largest single factor in the rise of the Black Muslims, and
the one they significantly do not share with the Southern Civil Rights

Movement, has been their appeal to the urban Negro lumpenproletariat, the section of American society described by the Negro poet
Calvin Hernton in the following words:

> The people are cold, they live with rats and roaches, the people
> are dying, their faces, before they reach fifteen years of age, are
> ruined with the poverty of centuries; their minds are thor-
> oughly depraved from public and private denial of dignity as
> human beings. In the "Negro section" of every town in
> America, on the "main drag," in liquor joints and beer joints, in
> pool rooms, barber shops, in dingy luncheonettes, at "hang-
> out"corners on the streets and milling around stations such as
> the courthouse or the local branch of a national bank—every-
> where the black masses are the "hoodlums" of our civilisation.
> They are the cultural alienates. Unlike the professional and
> skilled Negroes, the black masses of domestics, unskilled
> labourers, hustlers and the unemployed (over 50,000 are unem-
> ployed in Watts!), all are without hope of ever achieving a bet-
> ter life. For the black masses never have enough money! They
> possess no land and there is little chance of ever acquiring land;
> they have nothing to claim or reclaim; deep in the recesses of
> their psyches they are aware that the respectable Negro revolu-
> tion is not, when it comes to them, really a revolution; they are
> totally demilitarized; although they have fought and died in
> many foreign lands and jungles, in the jungles of their own
> country they cannot defend themselves when whites are setting
> dogs on them and throwing bricks and kicking them and calling
> them niggers and killing them. And there is the police, whose
> sole function in the ghetto is much worse than the function of
> the SS guards of Nazi concentration camps.

The condition of these people has in fact grown worse over the
years, just as their aspirations have risen. For example, in 1952, before
the "breakthrough" in race relations, the average Negro family's
income was 57 percent of the average white family's income. Ten years
later it was 54 percent. The following is taken from an article written
in 1963; I have not been able to obtain more recent figures but I understand the situation has further worsened, and almost certainly these
figures are misleadingly optimistic:

> Negro unemployment has been growing constantly since 1958,
> for unlike whites, Negroes do not recover any losses made dur-
> ing recessions. Negro unemployment is now two and a half

times that of whites. In some major cities the figures are even more striking. In Chicago, with a total unemployment rate of 5.7 percent, 17.3 percent of the Negroes are jobless; and a quarter of that city's Negroes are on relief. In Detroit 60 percent of the unemployed workers are Negroes, though only 20 percent of the city's inhabitants are Negroes. In Philadelphia the general unemployment rate is 7 percent, while Negro unemployment is 28 percent; in Gary, Indiana, the community as a whole has an unemployment rate of 6.3 percent, while the city's Negroes have one of 44 percent. According to official AFL-CIO statistics, the overall rate of unemployment of Negroes is 20 percent, which is higher than the rate of general unemployment during the depression.

Despite the support of the lumpenproletariat (for whom the main appeal of the Black Muslims was almost certainly in the violent directness of their critique of white society) it was from the lower middle-class that the Muslims made most of their recruitment; they might have grown even more had they not preached an almost impossibly rigid morality, for their message had a direct simplicity, a powerful mythology, an inflexible vision and an emotional force which made a powerful appeal to the dispossessed urban Negroes.

It was no coincidence that many conversions took place in prison, for the Black Muslims taught that the white man was cunning, vicious, lazy, untrustworthy and compulsively evil, and that the future would see the ascendancy of the Negroes with their inherent superiority. They saw their aim as creating a unified solidarity among black people and to do so they preached powerfully against the white social and political structure—many of their statements would have been echoed by civil rights leaders—and created in the white man, as a complete entity, an archetypally villainous enemy. They demanded separation from the USA and a territory where the Negro could evolve his own society. They damned Christianity, with every justification, as being one of the chief weapons in their exploitation, and attacked the Civil Rights Movement for "begging" for integration which was, in any case, completely undesirable. They saw in Islam the proper religion for the black man.

In essence they became a voice for those people, bypassed by progress in race relations, who no longer had any faith in white America's good intentions toward the Negro. Yet in their own way they were curiously unrevolutionary. Their criticism of white society echoed criticism made of Negroes by white racists, and their social and moral code produced results which likewise echoed the white bourgeois ethos they despised. Their belief in a final, Allah-given Black Utopia also tended to dim both their violence and their revolutionary potential. Revolutionaries are essentially people who *want* something, not people who know they are going to be *given* something.

On his release from prison Malcolm moved to Detroit, immersed himself in the Nation of Islam, and rapidly assumed importance, becoming Muhammad's right-hand man and travelling from state to state to organise temples and denounce the "white devils." His devotion to Muhammad as a man and to his ideas was never in doubt. He drove himself mercilessly, with a sort of passionate, controlled fury. His appeal was immediate. Unlike the downtown (bourgeois) civil rights leaders, Malcolm was of the ghetto and was trusted there. He never hid his criminal past, holding himself up as an example of what Islam could achieve, giving dignity to those who never expected to leave the gutter. Even those ghetto Negroes who did not accept his theological stance recognised the truth of his condemnation of white indifference. Malcolm saw clearly that in order to combat the casual tyranny of white America the first essential was Negro unity. He united Negroes in condemnation of the white man and the belief that no white man could ever be trusted.

Malcolm X had the charisma which is an essential feature of all great leaders. In him it was combined with something close to insanity, a programme which recognised the desperation of the situation and a personal courage which is outside most people's experience. In a very real sense Malcolm became the voice of the ghetto, of people who were not meant to have voices. He understood their language and their despair and he was able to articulate it, to carry it into the heart of white America in terms which lost none of the force of the original emotions. He told it "like it is." He knew that the white man in America had systematically plundered the spiritual resources of the Negro and, with Malcolm, many whites realised for the first time that one day they might face the logic of their unthinking disregard. It was this confrontation with their own guilt and the near certainty of ultimate justice that terrified them. No hate that Malcolm preached could match the hate that America had practised; if Malcolm, along with thousands of other Negroes, was as he was, America had more than partial responsibility. Much of the hate that was heard in Malcolm's speeches and statements was not hate in Malcolm but anger and pride; it was the self-hatred triggered by Malcolm that most of his opponents felt.

Perhaps inevitably, Malcolm's powerful political attitudes led him into conflict with the Black Muslims. When he said of President Kennedy's death that it was the result of white racism spreading unchecked, a case of "the chickens coming home to roost," Muhammad officially "silenced" him for 90 days. His knowledge of Muhammad's sexual life—as the leader of a rigidly monogamous and stringently disciplined sect—further estranged him from the movement. Shortly afterwards the Nation of Islam issued the first direct order for Malcolm's death. Malcolm's life was saved, on this occasion, by his assassin, who informed him of the danger.

In the early part of 1964 Malcolm X made his pilgrimage to Mecca; it was almost as profound a spiritual crisis as the one he had undergone in prison. His subsequent visits to various African states seem to have excited him as much as anything in his life. He came back to the USA wildly enthusiastic about Africa—and African concern about the fate of the American Negro—and even more enraptured with Muslimism. He discovered that orthodox Muslims were "colourblind," in marked contrast to the Nation of Islam where colour was the guiding principle. He realised that some white people in America might be genuinely concerned with the endemic racism. When he landed in New York Malcolm was faced with reporters intrigued by the news that he had renounced his blanket condemnation of whites but still sufficiently worried to ask him about the then-hot news of Negroes starting rifle clubs. Malcolm had changed but there was never any doubt that he still felt passionately about the American situation. "New York white youth were killing victims, that was a 'sociological' problem. But when black youth killed somebody the power structure was looking to hang somebody. When black men had been lynched or otherwise murdered in cold blood, it was always said, 'Things will get better'. When whites had rifles in their homes. the constitution gave them the right to protect their home and themselves. But when black people even spoke of having rifles in their homes, that was 'ominous'."

Malcolm himself had not much longer to live. Just before leaving for Mecca he had formed Muslim Mosque, Inc., in New York. Immediately on his return he formed the Organization of Afro-American Unity (OAAU). He was evicted from the home "given" him by the Nation of Islam, was subjected to a bomb attempt on his life and was trailed everywhere by Black Muslims. He knew they had orders to kill him. He openly accused the Black Muslims of plotting against his life. Later he was to change his mind about this, too. A few hours before his death he told Alex Haley: "I'm not all that sure it's the Muslims. I know what they can do, and what they can't, and they can't do some of the stuff recently going on." Later that day, Sunday, February 21, Malcolm X lay dead on the stage of Harlem's Audubon Ballroom, shot by a "firing squad" of Black Muslim assassins at a meeting.

Calvin Hernton said of Malcolm's death: "When the bullets ripped open Malcolm X's body every Negro in every ghetto in the United States died." And again: "What Dr. [Martin Luther] King is to and for the middle-class-oriented American Negroes, so was Malcolm X to and for the downtrodden, ignorant, hopeless, deprived and depraved masses." For just as King's essentially trusting and deeply religious attitude to race relations is a reflection of rural southern Negro attitudes, so was Malcolm's emotional fury a reflection of the urban ghetto Negroes' attitudes. The Alabama demonstrations and the Harlem and Watts riots are reflections of the Negroes' refusal to wait; they differ only in their methods, immediate aims and class orientation—the one allegedly "constructive, positive and realistic," the other allegedly "destructive, negative and meaningless."

The Thursday before he died, Malcolm X told a reporter: "I'm man enough to tell you that I can't put my finger on exactly what my philosophy is now, but I'm flexible." Malcolm's entire life was subject to changes, and it is impossible to predict what might have happened in the future. When Malcolm died he had dropped the racist theology of Black Muslimism, but blind spots and inconsistencies remained in his thinking. For a while he talked happily of colour-blindness among Muslim nations, and of the dignity of servant-master relationships in those countries; he seemed unaware of the fact that the Muslim nations are virtually the only ones still practicing large-scale slavery, and that the servant-master relationships, for all the religio-philosophical justifications, were precisely the same as servant-master relationships anywhere, based on servility and patronizing superiority. These relationships, had they been based on color as they frequently are in the USA, would have called forth Malcolm's most damning eloquence. Again his identification with the African states blinded him to their more obvious deficiencies. Possibly this is not very surprising; at least in such countries he was not treated as a fanatic or fool.

Malcolm's involvement with Islam also seemed to prevent him from developing the necessary thoroughgoing critique of American society. He had no economic program, and seemed uncertain whether he wished to follow the orthodox Black Nationalist separatist line or whether he wanted integration, albeit on terms more militant than those espoused by the Civil Rights Movement. His thinking, perhaps inevitably, was dictated almost completely by his environment. He saw the crisis in America as being wholly a race crisis and despite his advocacy of militant—and, if necessary, violent resistance to the encroachments of racism, even to the extent of sending OAAU commandos into Mississippi, he had neither a program for power nor a program for its dissolution.

Although he was potentially the most powerful, as well as the angriest black man in America, and although he had more influence with the ghetto Negroes (potentially the most powerful revolutionary force in American society today) than any other Negro leader, his ideas for mobilizing this support were vague. Had he lived he would doubtless have been forced by the pressure of events to consider more clearly the problems he would inevitably face as his influence increased. He might easily have decided to leave America and live in Africa or the Muslim world where social contradictions might not have impinged so forcibly on his consciousness. He might, alternatively, have evolved a position which would have enabled him to "strike the ghettoes" and, by implication, alter the entire social structure of the USA. Almost certainly his idea of unilateral treaties with African states was doomed from the start.

Ironically, Malcolm—the most revolutionary black man of his generation—caused trouble only with his words. Up to his death, he had never attempted to mobilize his support. It was claimed that he was the only man in the USA who could start a race riot. He was not prepared to echo the claim, but he added: "I don't know if I'd want to stop one." This attitude placed Malcolm apart from those respectable civil rights leaders, like Bayard Rustin, who see their function, in any riot situation, as being auxiliaries of the police force.

One thing is quite certain; Malcolm X was the only Negro leader capable of articulating, with all the emotional fury it required, the agony of ghetto life and, toward the end of his life, the only leader with the personal, magnetic potential to forge from this the revolutionary weapon which is needed if the American Negro is ever to free himself not only from the outward scars of racism but also from the subconscious burden of almost total alienation. He left white America considerably better informed about what it is like to be black in their society. He clearly indicated to many northern liberals that he saw in their liberalism no more than conservative realism, and he allowed his own people to feel a pride in their color and themselves, which may yet be seen as his major contribution to the solution of America's crisis.

Malcolm had his failings, but for the most part they were not the failings attributed to him by white people, and his approach, for all its limitations, was closer to the reality than that proposed by any other Negro leader. Others will inevitably emerge to carry on Malcolm's work—to ignore them and the movement they represent is to ignore one of the key movements in American society. Thus this book is amongst the most important to have been published in America in the last decade; it will undoubtedly become a key work. It is recommended unequivocally and with the hope that readers will have the intelligence to learn something about themselves as well as about Malcolm X.

Charles RADCLIFFE

From *Anarchy* 67, London 1966

Franklin Rosemont: *X* (1967)

# BEYOND COITION:
## FURTHER THOUGHTS ON THE MAN QUESTION

*This article first appeared, in a longer and rather different form,
in Bulletin No. 18 of the Seattle Group.*

THE REDISCOVERY, by this current generation of radical youth, that revolution must be sexual-social as well as economic-political is a healthy development, long overdue. It isn't, as many of them seem to think, a new idea; but it's been badly neglected.

Today's young people come at the question under tremendous handicaps. The boys are, of course, boys. This is like saying, in regard to Negroes, that Whites are white: they just don't know, they can't know, the most they can do is imagine. And imagination has been so stunted in this generation that the kids use consciousness-expanders. (Consciousness-expanders. Good grief. When our consciousness is constantly at the breaking-point, without any help at all.) And the girls—the girls have grown up in the era of the feminine mystique and the sexual sell, warped to Madison Avenue's self-seeking, sex-image of them, and looking for freedom in a change of cages.

But they have one great, material advantage. Previously, when feminists and their radical allies thought of liberating women, the only real alternative to dependence they could offer was competition with men in the industrial rat-race. That's not freedom—even with social provision for maternity, it would only be equity in bondage. Whether or not women put the shallowness of that kind of "emancipation" into words or not, they rejected it even at the cost of remaining the second (read second-class) sex. Now cybernation holds out the prospect of freeing all people from unwanted labor. In the society now within sight, women can break with their traditional dependence without giving up as much as they would gain. It has become possible to think in terms of equity in freedom.

So now we have to define that.

The earlier feminists were absolutely correct in their recognition that their first task was removal of all legal and social inequities. Equality before the law has now largely been achieved, though in the area just beyond it—legal recognition of women's special needs, *e.g.* re. abortion, etc.—our laws remain obdurate. Social inequity is but slightly lessened. Women of all social classes do lead more active lives nowadays than in the past. They dress with somewhat less torture to their bodies, with a consequent improvement in health. Few fields of endeavour remain utterly closed to them, but many are still difficult of entry and discriminatory in remuneration, upgrading, and prestige.

The lack of confidence from which most women suffer is a valid response to the discrimination and danger they face, in a still man-dominated culture. Their too-often-characteristic servility merely reflects that culture's prejudiced concept of them as but sex-gratifiers and home-makers, troublesome when they assert their own wills. And in the area beyond *that*, we're still Victorian: one of several stupid dissentions currently splitting our local peace movement concerns whether the movement's young mothers "should" nurse their babies "in public"!

Modern apologists for the feminine mystique make much of the real and imagined differences between the sexes. They seek to define a satisfactory role for each. They are supported by clinical studies aimed at discovering, in a culture-free laboratory environment, what actual behavioural differences do exist in animals that can be subjected to such observation. This approach can sound very scientific. But it's fraught with pitfalls for a generation lacking in historical perspective. The human species functions only in society, therefore society itself must be our lab.

Only in a society that allows free play to the varied inclinations of its individuals can the true natures of men and women emerge. To compress persons of either sex into a pre-determined role simply invalidates the experiment. And this is what all known societies have done, in greater or lesser degree, through all known time. (The sub-culture of today's radical youth, for all its self-conscious sexuality, is no exception.)

Of course the are differences. The only important thing about them (other than procreation) is that they should be a source of pleasure to both sexes, not grounds for domination by either. The objective basis for making them so now exists in push-button production, tampons, and effective, aesthetically inoffensive birth-control methods. Except for the widely variable mop-up still to be done on their own inhibitions and the disapproval of some prudes whose opinions scarcely matter, modern girls are free to fuck. The real question now is, are they equally free not to? And to retain their individual identities, as human beings as well as women, both in and out of the sexual relationship?

Or do the young men with whom they mate merely find in increased sexual accessibility an excuse for further narrowing their one-sided valuation? The proliferation of disparaging slang terms for women suggests it, and certainly I see no lessening, in these young males, of the prejudices I've suffered for forty years. I don't see any great number of young women being attracted to the revolutionary movement, over-all, as they would be if parity of personal esteem and intellectual scope were to be found there along with the fucks.

The prime and central fact is that woman, as such, is simply the female of the human species. Yet all the attributes of that species upon which its hitherto dominant males place a high valuation they have claimed as "masculine" virtues: courage, honour, intellectual excellence, etc. Those of which they are ashamed, or which they fear, they have relegated to women: e.g. inertia, guile, timidity, and those mysteriously subtle mental processes called intuition. By a neat linguistic trick, then any affront to their egos disparages not their humanity, but their "manhood." And any exercise by a woman of the common human characteristics they value diminishes her "femininity"; and makes her "mannish"—which by a further juggling of language then becomes, inconsistently, a term of contempt.

The psychological ramifications of such semantic sleight-of-hand are incalculable. And where language fails to denigrate women, it ignores them. The singular pronominal substantive for "human being" is "he." The general term for the species is "man." People can't even communicate without reinforcing the prevalent bias. Yet, generation after generation, anyone who broaches the need for reforming this aspect of language is dismissed, even in the "left," as a blithering crackpot. Without such reform neither freedom nor equity can come about, for the relationship between language and thought is reciprocal. Language reflects existing thoughtpatterns, then reinforces them and conveys them to new young speakers, ensuring their extension and perpetuation. Thus elimination of any prejudice demands a conscious attack on its verbal expression, however habitual or devoid of ill-will in any given speaker.

Ever since industrialization revolutionized the economic base of society, men have resisted women's entry into those jobs and occupations which, because of better pay or other relatively desirable features, they early staked out for themselves. They did so with reason, for there were never enough of these jobs to go around, and besides, someone had to darn their socks. As new forms of labour developed they were assigned, usually on the basis of relative ease, interest, or remuneration (and on the size of the available labour pool) to one or the other sex. Men rationalized women's exclusion from the more desirable jobs by finding the requirements of those jobs incompatible with their concept of the feminine nature, or particularly suited to their image of themselves. The common humanity of both sexes remained lost in the shuffle.

It was this common humanity that the feminists sought; and if in the search some sacrificed the specifically sexual aspects of their lives, their willingness to make that sacrifice testifies to the urgency of their need for recognition *as people.* Only prejudice could scorn this as a "negation of femininity." In truth, it was a magnificent assertion of the primacy of being human. But all that the blindly male-centric men could see in it was that it removed those women from the pool of conveniently available lays.

I suspect that extension of that pool is the chief interest today's young men have in the current sexual revolution. It's a valid interest, and I'm not knocking it. The question of men-women relationships has been opened again, for whatever reason; that's good. But this time let's not close it prematurely by settling for coition the way our grandmothers settled for the vote!

Louise CROWLEY

# A BLACK POWER WILDCAT IN CHICAGO

B Y LINKING BLACK POWER and wildcat job action, Chicago Transit Authority busmen unleashed a force of far-reaching revolutionary potential—and incidentally made some history worth reading about. The press did not even have the chance to suppress the news, as so often happens with smaller wildcats and Black Power demonstrations. This quickie strike had the advantage of spontaneity and surprise. Suddenly, one fine July morning, a couple thousand buses just weren't running. Not even the cleverest news-blackout artist—or rather, *whiteout* artist—could hide the fact.

Except for a very small strike in 1942 and a one-hour wildcat in '63, this was the first CTA strike since 1927.

The press did, of course, emphasize the "selfishness" of the striking drivers, and blamed them for the "suffering" of "ordinary people" trying to get to work or school. But the strikers' morale was unmistakably high, as is always the case when solidarity is high. An old IWW tactic is worth recalling here: Instead of staying home, drivers took the streetcars out in the morning as usual, but *charged no fares!* Such "striking on the job" not only improves "public relations," but also 1) exposes the bosses as the real instigators of "labor troubles," and 2) exposes the hypocrisy of the press. Revolutionary activity is always extremely clarifying.

Chicago's Black Power wildcat was almost totally successful in the ghetto areas, and far more successful than anyone expected or hoped for in so-called white areas. The strike leaders, who were all black, appealed to their white fellow workers for support, and many white drivers indeed respected the wildcat.

Following the Mayor's intervention, and all-night "behind closed doors" bargaining, the strike was declared over. Its actual outcome is still nebulous. The strikers are back on the job, buses are running, and a hell of a lot of grievances remain.

Clearly, however, this strike has introduced a new dimension in workingclass struggle. Joint Black Power/wildcat actions will surely increase. (At the moment of writing, Railway Express drivers are engaged in a similar strike.) In future battles, strikers would do well to draw on the energy and creativity of a third force that is ready and waiting: radical youth—dropouts and street kids as well as students. Many wildcat strikes are defeated because they lack facilities for communication with the broader community. At the very least, young people could offer the services of mimeographing or printing and distributing leaflets, and pasting up agitational/informational stickers and posters.

The free association of all truly radical forces is the first prerequisite for their unification, which is the first prerequisite of a successful revolution.

Franklin ROSEMONT

July, 1967

(*Heatwave* 1)

303

# EARTH MUSIC: THE AACM
## (Association for the
## Advancement of Creative Musicians)

THAT THE WEST IS IN THE ELEVENTH HOUR is now undebatable. We must redefine every aspect of what we now call art. Steps should be taken to show that all art is one (whether it be painting, writing, or running).

If I were to talk about my life (the part which the people of Earth call music) I would say the essence of what I am doing is re-creating life. I would talk about how amazed I am. All I know is that every day I wake up in this body and from then on everything is in a constant state of flux. I have been told this is called life. Since I really don't remember me before I was born, I find that something is happening that I don't know about, and this is what I play and write about.

At this point in my music I find little use for harmony, time, development, ideas, form, notes, technique, and sometimes sound—although some of the nicest people I know feel differently.

AACM: Never could I have imagined creativity on such a large scale. I am indeed fortunate to be able to work and exchange ideas in what must be another important link in what will likely be called Earth Music. The fact that we're being suppressed only gives us more time to explore and perfect (walls are falling down, truths are emerging).

The music happening here in Chicago is the end-product of years of trying to cooperate, help, and love each other, as well as an honest desire to participate in the cosmics.

Obviously, what is needed on this planet is some kind of understanding of our lives. What people call art is, in fact, life.

There seems to be an unplanned movement in the air among the young people with consciousness (I'll call them artists) toward unity. In Chicago, the Association for the Advancement of Creative Musicians, the Afro-Arts Theater, and COBRA are living proof that something is happening. In the last five years the music here has advanced farther than I had ever dared to dream, and we are only beginning.

There is a universal creative vibration in the air. The creativity here will undoubtedly play an important part when we gain more exposure (and when we do more exposing). More important, we are taking steps toward securing the development and understanding of art by teaching young people, and by becoming closer to our communities (knowing the self).

In the end, the destruction of art will lead to the rebirth of creativity, which is what is happening now.

Anthony BRAXTON
(*excerpted from the AACM's mimeo'd journal, 1968*)

# HISTORY AS HALLUCINATION

THE COLLAPSE OF BOURGEOIS CIVILIZATION is foreseen by everyone. But the institutions of that civilization are fast in developing means of controlling, rewriting and reshaping history. Instead of history, we have a series of defined concretions, dates, lists of casualties, names, etc., and instead of memory, we have only the sense of shock.

The press, particularly, and the other mass media contribute to this enforced amnesia concerning events which reflect the disintegration around us, which may be defined as crises, skirmishes in the class war, or confrontations with the machinery of power.

The events of one year ago, the uprisings in the northern ghettoes and the acceleration of activity, are overshadowed by the Establishment by a cloud of confused feelings, fear, guilt, and suspicion. The mass media portrays the ever-recurring full-page photographs of persons weeping—the actual emotional posture of the American bourgeoisie.

Harlem has happened. Events of revolutionary significance, blurred over by the official historians and the mass media, are permanently recorded in the consciousness of the persons who lived them, and a number of people who have also been prone to the official amnesia save for the fact that they were part of the radical movement.

In this age all history expresses revolutionary change. This is the basis for the existence of radicalism, its growth in America, and the great value of the radical press. The weeklies, monthlies and quarterlies, the mimeo'd, offset and printed journals of the left are above all attempts to chronicle, and to give poetry and purpose to the passage of time. And all this in an era when the passage of time has come to be feared more than everything else. Who knows what the future will bring? It is the task of the radicals to prophecy by giving hints of what is to come. The bourgeoisie are afraid of history. They would prefer time to be divided by their own petty and authoritarian regulations, according to their own wasted lives. Hours for working, days for working, weeks, months for payments on investments, quarters for dividends, the flickering passages of absurdities which blend into the confused image designated as the past.

History is a hallucination because it derives from our fear, which derives from our inability to affect it. Revolution is the undetermined element which brings history into the focus of our own actions. We, as young Americans and as anarchists, are determined to affect history.

We have become concerned no longer with political revolution, not so much even the traditional social revolution, but rather a *total revolution* in terms of the structure and spirit of our civilization. Social revolution of the working class and the youth is a basic element, as is also what Frantz Fanon called the revolt of the inferiorised, the racially subjugated. They are the Achilles' heels in the clay feet of this tottering civilization. The two conflicts become identical on the battlefield, as workers, peasants and students prepare to explode the shell of their existence through their self-conscious organization and direct action.

In heralding this apocalypse, the downfall of our civilization, we witness the "Ricorso," that period of barbarism which Sorel and Vico spoke of, "when all is instinct, creative, and poetic in society." This is the source of the parallels that we make between anarchism, as a barbarian form of socialism, and the culture of the gangs, rock'n'roll, the sudden release of life energy which marks the emergence of the Revolution in our own times. Our cities, the very face of this continent, are a shuffled image of what has been, what is, and what is to come.

Jonathan LEAKE

(excerpts from *Resurgence* 3, 1965)

# TOWARD A COUNTER-SOCIETY

WITH EVERY MEANS AT OUR DISPOSAL we must carry our way of life into every bourgeois landscape and totally disrupt and transform it. Before I return to discuss implementation, I wish to touch upon the alternative: that is, to do nothing and become a social oddity—a source solely of amusement.

Undoubtedly our oppressors would relish this occurrence; indeed, already they have begun to circumspect our influence to achieve this end. The entire hippy phenomenon has to a large extent become a colorful side-show in the Establishment's ongoing Spectacle. Once this happens the movement is incorporated into the system and becomes a stabilizing factor, allowing its members to "do their thing" within the context of general repression. Why? Simply because a movement for liberation can be emasculated quickly when it opens itself for categorization in the Establishment's frame of reference.

The commercialization of the movement allows for its democratization—anyone can "participate" in an historical phenomenon merely by purchasing some bells and beads.

Lastly and seemingly paradoxically, the movement has been overexposed by the mass media, assuming the qualities of a huge advertising campaign for something or other in the process. And like an extravagant promo everyone expects it all to vanish after a few months, when the new craze begins to ascend in the public eye. The purpose of all this is to mystify the population.

The kind of life we want to live cannot be served to us by reshuffling economic priorities. A new life can be found only by the release of Eros bringing about a transvaluation of all values and an existence that is fully cognizant of submerged realities. Given our desires, we cannot make the mistake accompanying all reformism: we cannot confront the system on the system's terms. In short, we cannot make use of the *language of repression.* We must be like children, able to imagine a world full of magic using the props of the so-called real one to smash its oppressiveness and to remake, from the ruins, a continuous celebration. This is what the Stones' "Dandelion" is all about. And for that matter, the Marx brothers.

We can form alliances with other suppressed elements of our society, first of all by not obstructing their efforts toward liberation, and by joining them whenever feasible in demonstrations of solidarity. We shall gain friends, however, mainly through building our own community and agitating in our own way.

To create a counter-society means also creating new rituals, myths and celebrations, illustrating a life devoted to gratification and non-productivity. Our agitation, our attempts at persuasion should *be* these new rituals.

It's irrelevant to work out the details on paper—the way to live is by doing. In this society, doing is a revolutionary act.

Bernard MARSZALEK

*Seed* I:8, Sept. 22–Oct. 12, 1967

## MUSHROOM COUNTRY

*Editor's note:* "Mushrooms" here refers not to the psychedelic fungus but to the atomic bomb cloud.

*I want to know where nature has gone in this world*
*    besides museums and national parks.*
*I want to turn off all the electric lights and heating pads*
*    and drown myself in the snow.*

*I want to know*
*    in my worship of cadillacs*
*        if the trees ever weep*
*    as I have wept*
*        in their absence.*

*I want to know if a place has been prepared for us*
*    in forest or ocean or mountain or meadow;*
*    or if we are doomed to end our days*
*    in the conversational chambers of beer-smoke.*

*I want to know if there is a substitute for gin.*

*I want to know*
    *why we can kill the Russians*
    *but not the whooping cranes.*

*I want to know how to approach this question!*
    *Why should I sit around*
       *in social ecstasies*
          *while there are still clouds in the sky*
          *which do not give off radioactive spore-prints?!*

    * * *

*I want to know HOW we can live*
    *the unfeigned life*
    *of unconcern*
      *when*
    *Each time we look to the sky*
      *an angel of death*
    *may come screaming*
        *pointed at us*
    *on her terrible hydrogen horse!*

*HEAR ME!*
*for if we would escape the deluge*
*it is time for us*
    *to rip the clothes from our bodies*
    *and cast them upon the waters of hell!*

      *then to go running*
    *pure and naked*
      *in the cold white snow*
      *to the solitary forest*
    *where we shall cling*
      *in the weeping night*
      *to the lonely trees*
        *and all we have . . .*

                  Charles Willoughby SMITH

(from *Liberation*, June 1959)

309

# MOMMY IN TOYLAND

SEARS, ROEBUCK AND CO. SENT ME their Christmas catalogue this year. I spent a lot of time looking at it, particularly the toy section, and when I was finished I was thankful that this year at least, my two children are too young to be interested. Next year I won't be so lucky.

Ten years ago I breathlessly scanned the pages of toys, admiring everything and wondering what I realistically could expect to get. The toy manufacturers have come a long way in ten years. The big thing then for little girls was dolls with "rooted Saran hair" instead of old-fashioned glued wigs which were liable to come off and leave one with a pathetically bald dolly; a few dolls walked or said "Hello, mommy." Now they have diverse accomplishments such as burping (but not spitting up), kissing, wriggling, growing hair and saying, among other things, "Play it cool . . . don't be a square."

Most overwhelming of all is the Barbie doll. A long-legged 11¹/₂″ sophisticate (what happened to the cuddly baby doll, anyway?) Barbie is a manufacturer's dream, for no child can ever hope to be able to buy all the equipment Barbie requires. I say *equipment* advisedly, because not only does Barbie have a wardrobe beyond the wildest dreams of any woman save the Ten Best Dressed, but she also comes with wigs, a lawn swing, a chipboard dorm room and sweet shop, cars, a boat, a plane, a dog, a house, and scads of furniture. Lest the child somehow acquire all this stuff for Barbie, the manufacturer's goose has laid several more golden eggs: a boyfriend for Barbie, a roommate, a boyfriend for the roommate, and a little sister, all of whom must be clothed, housed and amused. As you can see, the thing has infinite possibilities.

As a money-maker, Barbie is a screaming success, and for parents who can afford to dish out ten dollars for a mink stole for a rather unpleasant-looking doll, I suppose it makes no difference. But as a toy, Barbie is a complete flop. There is no room for creativity and imagination—the advertising men have built a complete fantasy around the doll, into which they conveniently fit all the expensive little doodads the manufacturer wants to sell. One gets, for example:

> "Barbie gets all A's in college. She works hard in class but has
> lots of fun on weekends. Barbie likes to visit the Sweet Shop for
> delicious sodas after leading cheers (buy "Pep Rally" outfits for
> dolls costing $5.87) in the College Stadium. Some evenings Barbie
> studies in her Dorm room with Midge or enjoys a movie at the

campus, drive-in theatre (buy car for $3.88) with Ken. College life is wonderful (buy chipboard Campus for $4.99) and Barbie and Midge (Barbie's roommate: initial investment $1.92) love every minute of it."

The child can hardly pretend to be a mother to this elegant creature, and who wants a hunk of plastic for a playmate? The sad truth is that Barbie was never meant to be played with—she was meant to be bought, and that is all.

For boys there are war toys. My little cherubs can have their own M14 recoil rifles, for instance, or their own Panzer tank. In fact there is a character named G.I. Joe for little boys who corresponds to the Barbie. The advertisement for G.I. Joe is not without humour: "*America's Movable Fighting Man in Action*. He's over 11 inches tall...has 21 movable parts. Stands...sits...kneels! etc. etc."

For G.I. Joe one may buy, among other items, a field pack set, a military police set, a machine gun and a frogman outfit.

We parents think of toys as things which bring pleasure to children and which help them to exercise their creativity. Unfortunately, manufacturers generally don't see things that way. Like everything else in our economy, toys are a source of profit, and parents and children are the consumers who must be cajoled and intimidated into buying. Thus, for example, Hassenfeld Brothers, the manufacturers of G.I. Joe, have spent $2 million advertising their highly successful product on television.

Advertising designed to pressure me into buying something I don't need and can't use irritates me, but it ends there. What I don't want I don't buy. It's different with children. They cannot understand the motives behind advertising—all they know is the desire it creates. And it is not right to use children as objects of exploitation.

Much has been said about the role of war toys in conditioning children to accept violence and inhumanity. Toys, I think, are also teaching the kids of today to become the consumers of tomorrow. Advertising and the resultant urge to buy, buy, buy, whether one really needs or wants a product, is a familiar part of the lives of parents and children alike.

Finally, the toys advertised popularly appear to me to contribute further to the emphasis on conformity in our society. Paints and blocks, which encourage individual creativity and thought are played down, perhaps because they are simple and unprofitable; elaborate toys like the Barbie doll are emphasized.

Let us hope that some day the whole of society will care for the

real needs of its members, young and old instead of fabricating false
desires for the profit of a few.

Sharon FREEDMAN

From *Strike!*, 1968

# THE JIMI HENDRIX EXPERIENCE

THE "OFFICIAL" FUNCTION OF MUSIC in this society is to
deceive the purity of the human imagination. From the deceived
eye to the confused ear, man is reduced to an idiocy as impotent as it is unforgivable. I am interested in the maximum of consciousness, in liberating the senses from the fetters of concretized
ideology in the hideous reality around us. The point is to resolve the
arbitrary conflict between the eye and the ear by a truly definitive
transformation of reality.

"It is time to realize," wrote the Belgian surrealist Paul Nougé, "that
we are capable, also, of inventing feelings—perhaps fundamental feelings—of a power comparable to those of love and hatred." Our point
of departure is Rimbaud's "systematic derangement of the senses," an
experiment which must be continually renewed. It should be possible to juxtapose auditory, visual, olfactory, tactile and gustatory capacities, for sheer pleasure. Psychedelic experience validates the ear that
sees and the eye that listens.

Several years ago I was listening to an old recording of a medieval
chorale by Josquin des Pres, when the ending was submerged by the roaring of jets across the sky. This charming vengeance of a non-Euclidean
futurism had the distinct advantage of opening more doors in my mind
than it closed. Who can demand more from music than exaltation?
Needless to add that such an assumption is vastly removed from most
European conceptions of music. So-called "primitive" people understand music best—its *physical* qualities, or rather its psycho-physical
dynamism which absolutizes frenzy in the dance. "Primitive" music
provokes a mythology of gesture born of spontaneous ritual.

The Jimi Hendrix Experience (Hendrix, vocals and guitar; Mitch

312

Mitchell, drums; Noel Redding, bass) has recently emerged into the eldritch light that bathes the quotidian splendors of this universe and all others. They play regularly before standing-room-only crowds in Paris, Stockholm, Copenhagen, London. Eight days after the Beach Boys broke the house record at the Tivoli in Stockholm, playing for 7000 fans at two shows, Hendrix appeared and, to say the least, broke their record—playing for some 14,500 fans at two shows.

The Experience stage-show possesses a demonizing convulsiveness—Hendrix has been known to play his guitar with his teeth, and even to burn it on stage—in which the most cherished philosophical prejudices are dismembered on a monstrous scale, during a long midnight, luminous and black. Hendrix has acknowledged the inspiration he has found for lyrics in fairy tales and science-fantasy. Certain of his songs seem to hover like enchanted owls over the Garden of Earthly Delights, subtly moving from paradise to hell. With profound lyricism, a sense of creative destruction and black humor, he weaves the tapestry of his violent, delirious myths across a sky that darkens as he approaches.

Nothing is premeditated: Everything belongs to the purely automatic revelation. With striking simplicity, he improvises a chaos of defiantly realizable beauty. All of Hendrix's commentators have spoken of this remarkable spontaneity. When asked to play certain songs from his first album, *Are You Experienced?*, he admitted that he had forgotten them—that he had invented them during the recording session and never played them since.

Hendrix has united the extraordinary poetic vitality of the blues with the more recent rock scene, which itself originally derived from blues, but which, with psychedelic, East Indian, baroque and other influences, has achieved a musical independence. Certainly he has brought a new tremor into the intellectual atmosphere, introducing us to marvels from cultures as seemingly disparate as those of the Kwakiutl, the natives of New Ireland, the Tarahumaras of Mexico, as well as the Bushmen, Yoruba and other cultures of Africa.

"Paint It Black," in any case, is a watchword not to be taken lightly. Harlem '64, Watts '65, Newark, Detroit, etc., '67 are moments in the realization of a splendidly magical dream, correctly known as the cause of freedom. Music that does not participate in this dream, music that does not express the passion for liberation that is bubbling through the consciousness of millions—music, that is, that does not *revolt* is only the auditory reflection of repressive ideology, like the sterile sounds played in department stores as "background," to "relax" customers into an imbecile stupor in order to increase their consumption of worthless commodities.

I want music that is the opposite of this pathetic servant of commodities. I want a delirious and luxurious music which drinks the space around it and colors it with the vibrations of liberating human impulses; music which concretizes the rhythm of blood and breath—music which burns the exploitative past and assists in the unveiling of the future: the creation of the harmony of passions.

True revolt goes as far beyond politics as politics itself, in its best expression (*revolutionary* politics) goes beyond apathy and false consciousness. Revolt is only very partially "political." It must also be poetic and sexual, putting everything at stake—all or nothing. What is called for today is a total revolution of everyday life, which leaves traditional politics groveling in the obscure categories of the past. Jimi Hendrix, who refers to himself as "apolitical," ruthlessly attacks not only imperialism but the entire foundation of oppressive Western civilization.

Music as it is known today will be replaced by the free play of human desires, the invention of life itself, the sound of imagination. Images of arson—a magical incendiarism—live in the very heart of all varieties of the new music: Archie Shepp's "Fire Music," the Doors' "Light My Fire," Jimi Hendrix's "Fire." Burn, baby, burn!

Soon there will be no more music, in the specialized and alienated sense, for *everything* will be music. Meanwhile, no one can afford to ignore the sensitive testimony of a man like Hendrix, who sings and plays to share his dreams.

In Jimi Hendrix, the music of revolt has found its poet.

Franklin ROSEMONT

*Chicago Seed*, November 3–24, 1967
(*excerpts*)

Tor Faegre: *The End of Time*
(from the Solidarity Bookshop catalogue)

# SURREALISM
# BY ANY MEANS NECESSARY

T HE "DADA, SURREALISM AND THEIR HERITAGE" exhibition at
the Art Institute has nothing whatever to do with either Dada
or Surrealism. The show is merely an attempt by art historians and critics to intern two cultural movements and make them safe
for art lovers. Many beautiful works of the imagination have been
made to serve as tools for its confinement.

Dada was a device to smash the last vestiges of a civilization that
could yawn, put away its croquet mallet temporarily and begin calmly
to pick up the pieces after promoting a barbaric war. Its nihilism was
more in the eye of the beholder than a matter of true content; nevertheless its many pronged attack began to grow redundant as more
people, influenced by the movement sought to build a new, totally revolutionary, culture, a magic way of life.

The movement in France in the mid '20s became surrealist, that
is, it began to explore all the aspects of life with the rationalist 19th
Century attempted to ignore. Einstein, Freud, Nietzsche and others
had already begun the demolition work and the surrealists swore to
carry their work forward.

Their first areas of research related to automatism (the free flow
of consciousness in order to reveal the unconscious), dreams and states
of mental derangement: all of this to reveal the submerged self, the
repressed id, to free the forces in the possession of all people.

Surrealism undertook the responsibility to find avenues towards
a definition of freedom that surpassed the narrow confines of the then
existing "revolutionary" groups. The simple political relationship of
man with society, Nature, reality, whatever, defined by these revolutionaries as man's basic need to labor was rejected. Other relationships
existed and could no longer be denied, but to fully explore them meant
the thorough affirmation of Desire. Because of the vital importance
to all revolutionaries of a most complete understanding of man with
all of his intricacies and with all of his uniqueness, surrealism's ongoing contributions cannot be ignored.

The Opening Night of the Exhibition at the Art Institute was disrupted by a number of people who entered, reading erotic poetry and
throwing underwear, birdseed, and playing cards at the spectators.
The lecture that night was punctuated by noise makers. Every Saturday
afternoon a group of Chicago surrealists have been distributing a
poster announcing their counter-exhibition at the Gallery Bugs Bunny.

The Surrealist show at the Bugs Bunny is a hasty, very limited, but nevertheless important response to the crap downtown. The sculpture-constructions of Robert Green, the delicate ink drawings of Franklin Rosemont and the works of the other contemporary surrealists on display belie the image being projected at the Art Institute. Their works reveal at once an extrasensory imagination, a fine sense of humor and a threat of real danger—danger that rides with a commitment to Total Emancipation.

Bernard MARSZALEK

# ICE PALACE

*The boundaries of night*
*balanced on soap bubbles*
*streaming with rainbow colors*
*and offering the alternatives*
*to nights and days*

*Dew characterizes the soul*
*of the searching eye*
*lighting the hallways of ebony*
*in a passage called time*

*Hanging upside down in trees*
*like possums*
*singing soundless songs*
*for sleepless dreamers*

*Awake to the blossoms of madness*
*that weave carpets of serpents' tongues*

*I touch stones*
*and they become black marble*
*I touch ice*
*and it is magnetized*

Penelope ROSEMONT

# ON THE SITUATIONISTS'
# "INTELLECTUAL TERRORISM"

WHY DO I CRITICIZE THE SITUATIONISTS' "intellectual terrorism"? Consider the irony—that those who conceived the beautiful theory of the spectacle should then use methods which in turn *perpetuate* the spectacle. "Intellectual terrorism" helps create the "fashion" situation on the "idea market," which makes it impossible to ask for definition. The Situationists, in other words, are trying to *force* other people to take on their ideas whole and undigested in order to stay "one-up."

I would recommend *Internationale situationniste* to people to read; their concepts of spectacle, commodity society, survival *vs.* living are very fruitful. But do we have to choose forever between the platitudes of the Old Left and the abstrusities of an intelligent and cynical Vaneigem? If *that*'s the new society, where's the love in it?

I knew some members of a German group called Subversive Action—I never saw a group more inhuman to women than they were. Some of them had been Situationists. Maybe the French Situationists are different. But what's this about expelling a member for taking part in a "Happening"? Why take pride in "intellectual terrorism"?

By the way, there is perhaps a real emotional difference between you and me. You celebrate—with love—the coming of the new society; I celebrate the fall of the old—with hate. Maybe this means I'm more damaged than you, maybe not. I'd like to live long enough to see the answer to that.

Jim EVRARD

*excerpts from a letter to F.R., 1967*

Bernard Marszalek: *UFOs in the Garden*

# LETTER FROM CALIFORNIA

San Francisco, February 6, 1967

W E GOT TO L.A. IN TWO DAYS from Chicago, driving through from the Windy City on Route 66. Arrived on Sunset Strip, began spray-painting walls, leafleting, rapping with kids. We arrived in the Fifth Estate just as the L.A. Sheriff was meeting with representatives of teenyboppers and coffee houses, and started handing out *Resurgence* 10 [the Chicago issue] and "Forecast Is Hot!" inside the coffee house to kids, cops and reporters. Got thrown out (all three of us), shouting "Death to the Bourgeois!"

Outside on the street, I was stopped and questioned by cops, then all of us were held in our car for a half hour while fuzz stalled looking at our I.D. and waving two-foot flashlights inside the car. (Thank satan, they never looked in our packs!)

We left 10 *Rebel Workers* and assorted leaflets at the *L. A. Free Press* bookstore, The Kazoo—they will send the cash to Solidarity Bookshop. We stayed in L.A. (the most evil and due-for-destruction city I have ever seen) for three days, put up by some strip cat in a pad just beyond the Strip.... Met some cats from Watts (who proudly showed us their looted TV, etc., from the 1965 Insurrection), took us home (in Watts), fed us—and then we all got roaring drunk together and blew cool riffs about a hot scene: the coming revolution, the worsening conditions in the ghettoes, and the growing black revolt in the Armed Forces. Also stressed was the growing unity between all minority oppressed— Mexicans, Puerto Ricans, Filipinos, Indians, Afro-Americans—which has been a marked trend in California.

We went on down to Mexico, spent one day there (January 13th), then got kicked out for lack of money and general appearance.

Left for San Francisco from the border—we arrived here in S.F. the day of the "gathering of the tribes"—the "Human Be-In" of 20,000 hippies, radicals, etc. The scene here is permeated with commercialism and reactionary religious elements....

We have an apartment on Fillmore Street in the Fillmore ghetto. We will be staying here for another couple of months. We attended the first planning conference (500 people from all over California and the West Coast) of the Spring Mobilization Against the War (planned for April 15), and I addressed the entire conference, denouncing pacifist hypocrisy and calling for armed struggle against Imperialism here in its home case. Unexpectedly (although the liberals were very shocked) the conference broke into wild applause at my address, and

I distributed what I had left of my literature to the Black and Student (high school) "caucuses" present. There is excellent prospect here for building a revolutionary grouping around anarchist, anti-imperialist and youth-revolt ideas.

Please send me some agitprop for distribution here in S.F.—copies of *Resurgence* 10, *Rebel Worker* 7 and "Forecast Is Hot" especially.

The Diggers are pretty pathetic—the New Left here is still wallowing in electoral politics—time for a change!

Yours for the Revolution,

Jonathan LEAKE

# INTRODUCTION TO THE LIFE & TIMES OF THE INCREDIBLE HULK

"WHEN THE AIR IS COOLER THAN THE EARTH," G. P. Quackenbos assures us, in his *Natural Philosophy* (revised edition, 1873), "the moisture imparted to it... is partially condensed and thus rendered visible, forming either *fog* or *clouds*. The only difference between the two is in their height. When the condensation takes place near the earth's surface, fog is the result; when in the upper regions of the atmosphere, clouds."

So, too, criticism, when confined to surfaces, gives us only fog; but when allowed to rise into the upper regions of the intellectual atmosphere, provokes the appearance of marvelous clouds, in whose formation we can perceive elements of a new mythology. In the fog we see only dim lights, and perhaps hands signaling vaguely before our eyes. In the clouds we may witness the unfolding of a universe, the revelation of *desire*.

\* \* \*

In the history of comics, the most *amazing* characters, from our point of view, are those who seem to be *least finished* from the cartoonist's point of view—characters whose personalities are only very lightly sketched: that is to say, incomplete, leaving wide margins for the unexpected. Hastily conceived, such characters seem to have been pushed into the comic field of action before their authors could draw up the full scale of their capacities and limitations. Unlike such predictable, straitjacketed characters such as Prince Valiant or Superman (to cite only two particularly boring examples), the "unfinished" characters tend to be ambiguous, amorphous, experimental, stubbornly indefinable and somehow strangely *free*.

Most important of all, the less a character is defined, the more that character is capable of expressing defiance, the poetic marvelous and other subversive thought. "Funny Animal" comics abound in such beings (Krazy Kat, Bugs Bunny, Daffy Duck, Woody Woodpecker); "Superhero" equivalents are much rarer. Jack Cole's Plastic Man is surely the brightest example from the so-called Golden Age. And now we have Jack Kirby's The Incredible Hulk—a kind of raging street-kid version of Frankenstein's monster, with strong touches of Jekyll-Hyde, King Ubu and the Wolf Man. This far-from-jolly green giant—a bitter, vengeful product of the "Atomic Age"—enjoys wrecking U.S. missile bases and miscellaneous military installations, along with countless other outposts and dwelling-places of Power and Authority.

Listen to The Incredible Hulk, the complete nihilist, in his own words:

> "Human? Why should I want to be human?"
> "The Hulk *has* no friends!"
> "You dare attack the Hulk?"
> "Hate you? Why *shouldn't* I hate you?"
> "I can't spend the rest of my life running and hiding! It's time for everyone else to run from *me*!"
> "The Hulk waits for nobody!"
> "Everyone runs from the Hulk! Everyone!"
> "I owe the human race nothing!"
> "The Hulk takes orders from no one!"
> "Nothing'll stop the Hulk!"
> "Every man on Earth is my enemy!"
> "The Hulk is *free*! Free—to do what?"
> "Nothing can hurt me! Nothing can stop me! I'm the Hulk! I'm the strongest there is!"

Franklin ROSEMONT

# LETTERS

Many thanks for *Rebel Worker* 6, which I found very exciting. Above all I liked its roundedness, in that it gets beyond the usual sociological rut; and the surrealist lines give it an extra dimension, too. As one of the young people to whom you address yourselves, I'm sure that this is the kind of approach that really can have some imaginative effect on what remains of the "Beat Generation." Perhaps what I'm trying to say is that we're looking for people to show us how to live as individuals rather than the old Marxian abstractions about the masses, which really don't communicate anything. The best way to recruit the young for a social revolution is to show that it is an essential preliminary before anyone can hope to live the fullest possible life.

Tony ALLAN
Oxford, U.K.

You ask my opinion about *Provo*. It is a rather complex thing. It all started quite a long time ago. You have heard of course of the *blousons noirs* in France, the *Halbstarken* in Germany, and the *Teddy Boys* of England—and we had here in Holland what we called the *Nozems*. So there were the Nozems and on the other hand there were a few youngsters who liked "happenings" and that sort of thing. So these latter started with "happenings" in the streets of Amsterdam. First arousing a bit of laughter, later on they got the police against them. And then it all started, really. The "happeners" called themselves Provos, and when they got into trouble with the police, the Noxems joined them, calling themselves Provos as well—and we had a fine riot going on between youngsters and the police force.

Then came the marriage of Beatrix (the crown princess) to a German ex-Nazi officer, and all hell broke loose. It all looked really like revolution in the streets—in my opinion somewhat like Watts or Detroit during the riots there—and this went on for quite some time. If you had long hair or a beard, you could be sure to be beaten by a cop.

The Provos, by now a big movement, did all kinds of things: They organized "happenings," issued papers, tracts, etc. and succeeded in getting into the municipal council with one seat. But after a short while trouble started within the movement—one said this and another said just the opposite, and it all became more and more boring. In fact, *Provo* died. And soon the "flower-power" business of San Francisco blew over to Holland, and everybody wanted to be "nice" to people, even to the police.

I was quite amazed to read that you know about Anton Pannekoek, a name I thought hardly known outside Holland—hardly known even here! We do not have any contact with possible adherents of the "Council Communists," and I must confess that I do not even know whether they still exist or not.

Her DE VRIES
Bureau of Surrealist Research
Amsterdam, The Netherlands

(letters from 1968)


A friend of mine in the Netherlands told me that a Surrealist Group has been formed in Chicago. I am most interested!

May I introduce myself: I was born in Indonesia and lived in Europe for twelve years. Some time ago I immigrated to the U.S.A. and am now living in the Midwest.

My surrealist aspirations are strictly in term of "expressions," criticism, and poetry—based, of course, on absolute standards of Love and Freedom.

I have a great need to participate in the struggle for the Revolution, and the emancipation of man. Therefore everything you have written and published is of high value to me. I have scrutinized all the issues of your *Rebel Worker*—they are great! Why this very good periodical stopped is a question! It contributed so much to my needs!

With fraternal greetings,

Schlechter DUVALL
Ottumwa, Iowa

I have written to Charles Radcliffe, and I have invited him down to Talgarreg. I think one can do more in one good night's discussion than in a thousand letters.

We had a demonstration outside Swansea Jail. One of our members is spending this month as a guest of her majesty for his activities in connection with the Welsh Language Society. A few hundred workers turned up, and after a march through town we had a good meeting outside the prison. Of course the police were everywhere, trying to look inconspicuous and quite determined to keep the queen's peace.

I am reading a book from the library now by Martin Luther King, which is proving quite good. Malcolm X was over in England and took part in the Oxford University Union debate on the "colour question." Quite a bit of the debate was televised—Malcolm X was fantastic. He got a standing ovation from the audience. I get *Anarchy* magazine from the Freedom Press—at least I share a copy with a friend of mine who is struggling on about 40 acres in this parish—and I have that article [by Charles Radcliffe] on Malcolm X.

Until the Revolution,

Deri SMITH
Cardiganshire, Wales

It was truly a joy when I stumbled into a Chicago bookstore and discovered *Surrealism & Revolution*. It is only recently that I and several others here at U. of W. have run across the French surrealists' critique—as if it were hidden, as it has been—and have come to realize that it harbors some of the most exciting and revolutionary contents, bridging especially the too-often existing gap between artistic and non-artistic revolutionary thought. To me, much of it is very close to what I consider the most profound contemporary criticism (a word far too emasculated): that of Herbert Marcuse and his lesser known German colleagues, T. W. Adorno, Max Horkheimer, *et al.*

I enclose a check. Send along some *Rebel Workers*, another copy of *Surrealism & Revolution*, and anything else of interest.

Russell JACOBY
Madison, Wisconsin

Schlechter Duvall:
*The Origin of Speeches*

323

These English periodicals were friendly (at least for a time)
to *Rebel Worker* and *Heatwave*

# HEATWAVE

Britain's wildest, most incandescent,
experimental libertarian journal.
—*Anarchy* magazine, No. 66—
August 1966

What a very weird little rag!
—**Jack Robinson, Freedom Press, 1966**—

The accelerating decomposition of secular values [in England]
is engendering profoundly revolutionary tendencies
in the critique of a aspects of the prevailing way of life.
One thinks here of the excellent journal *Heatwave*,
which seems to be evolving toward
an increasingly rigorous radicality.
—*Internationale Situationniste*, 1966—

What the hell sort of a magazine is this, anyway?
—**Inquirer at Solidarity Bookshop, Chicago, 1966**—

In London, members of the
Industrial Workers of the World
have joined with [other far-out radicals]
to start a magazine of revolution: *Heatwave.*
—*Playboy Magazine*, August 1967—

*Heatwave* laid the foundation for the next twenty years
of sub-cultural theory.
—Jon Savage, *England's Dreaming: Sex Pistols and Punk Rock*—
(London, 1991)

A noteworthy publication.
*Heatwave* shows aspects of the "traditional" revolutionary
labor movement and the newly-emerging situationist project
co-existing in a single, relatively coherent format. . . .
[Its] unabashed, "slightly crazed" and still fresh forays
into pop culture [point] toward the autonomous creation
of a society without classes and exploitation.
—**Bill "Not Bored" Brown, 1996**—

Diana Shelley, Paul Garon, Charles Radcliffe

# TWO FIERY FLYING ROLLS:

## THE *HEATWAVE* STORY, 1966–1970

EATWAVE 1 WAS PUBLISHED in the heady days of July 1966, when many of us felt that revolution was just around the corner, that dead time would itself die. We didn't believe that all that energy, frustration, imagination and thwarted creativity that people had could lead anywhere else. The only problem seemed to be to ensure that the inevitable revolution was one that fulfilled our desire for unfettered freedom and creativity. I wanted to keep alive the spirit of Mad Love, revolutionary comradeship, endless inquiry and unbounded optimism and spontaneous delirium that had marked Franklin and Penelope Rosemont's stay with Diana (Di) Shelley and me in London during the spring of 1966.

An earlier visitor from the US, Paul Garon, a fellow blues enthusiast (introduced to us by the late Simon Napier, editor of *Blues Unlimited*, then the best blues magazine in the world, for which Paul and I both wrote frequently) had stayed with us just before the Rosemonts. We had no telephone and Paul turned up on the doorstep, with Simon's introduction, just as our current guest, Eric Clapton, was moving out. Paul, we soon learned, was not only a blues enthusiast but also a heroin addict on the lam from Kentucky. (At the time Britain had a relatively enlightened stance on heroin.) So, if not exactly thrilled to have a junkie to stay, we were, nevertheless, not particularly alarmed.

We need not have worried. Paul in person soon put our minds at rest. We both liked him enormously. Himself an excellent guitarist, he really knew the blues. He had been interested for much longer and better placed geographically to pursue his enthusiasm. He was a mine of information. Everything: from tales of discovering rare blues 78s (being used as path edging) on record-hunting trips in the South to the stories of the blues people he'd met and talked to; from a detailed history of blues to a deep knowledge of the culture whence it came. He introduced me to the work of countless blues musicians about whom I knew little or nothing, as well as vastly increasing my appreciation of those I already loved. Among many, many others, Peetie Wheatstraw, Kokomo Arnold and Curley Weaver came into the first category and Charlie Patton, Memphis Minnie Douglas and Robert "Tim" Wilkins the second. A highlight was Charlie Patton's and Bertha Lee's "Oh Death," a spiritual of staggering, rough beauty and emotional force.

Although I have still never visited Chicago, Paul realised that it was already some kind of "Sweet Home Chicago" to me and had a constant place in my life and dreams. In acknowledgment of this crazed enthusiasm, Paul gave me a copy of one of his favourite books, Nelson Algren's magnificent *Chicago: City on the Make*. Encouraged by Paul, I also read William Burroughs and Franz Kafka for the first time. Like almost everyone else I applied the term "Kafka-esque" somewhat randomly to most aspects of Government. At the height of my ensuing enthusiasm I felt that Kafka had invented the entire tortured 20th Century.

Initially Paul's habit had worsened in the UK; British National Health heroin was pharmaceutically pure and much stronger than the street smack he'd used in the USA. He decided, before too long, that he had to kick the habit. Both he and I (doing my best middle-class act) talked with his doctor father in Louisville to raise the necessary money, and Paul finally went into the Bethany Hospital in Archway, London, for a cure. On one of my Bethany visits he leaned over to me, somewhat conspiratorially, and whispered: "Thank God I'm not a goddamn alkie—they're such slobby wrecks." Paul could always make me laugh! I believe that with his "Extract from *The Expanded Journal of Addiction*," *Heatwave* 1 qualifies, with pride, as Paul's first non-blues publisher. My great sadness at Paul's departure was lightened by the knowledge that he was going back to the USA to take the next step to full recovery at Connecticut's grimly named Institute of Living.

The visit by Franklin and Penelope Rosemont, not long afterwards, also resulted in the Anglo-American *Rebel Worker* 6, published and widely distributed by us at a May Day '66 rally in Hyde Park, which in turn produced a sizeable flow of letters from disaffected young Britons, Americans and Europeans who had read it. There had been scaffolding up round the flat at the time of their visit and we sat out on the scaffold planks in the uncustomary sunshine, drinking coffee and planning the future.

The May Day rally was a fine English celebration of a fine spring day, if not of revolution, and I think the open jokiness of the cover appealed to the general mood of at least some among the large, good-humoured crowd. Many people stopped to talk to us. A significant few read bits of it while standing beside us and then commented. Several people promised to make contact and did. Afterwards those who had bought the magazine obviously talked about it to others because there were a staggering number of orders by post for copies and subscriptions. It was an inspiringly successful day.

Among the responses was a letter from John O'Connor offering not only wholehearted support, but wanting to contribute. My quick reply brought in "The Great Accident of England." (Sadly I lost contact with John in the late sixties.) Di's schoolfriend Gaby Charing, then an Oxford student, liked the mag and wanted to write a piece on the economic chicanery of the Dutch ("The Strange Adventures of Holland"). Bernard Maszalek's excellent "Long Hot Summer #1" gave the magazine a much broader transatlantic sweep, as did the Chicago Wobblies' Letters from America. The Chicago pieces and mine provided the spine of the contents—Ben Covington and Paz, another of my pseudonyms who provided the graphics and titling. (Paz relates to Octavio, is the Spanish for "peace" and also a back to front "zap.") If *Heatwave* 1 was a less than entirely coherent production, it did, at least, convey something of the wide-ranging enthusiasm with which our generation confronted the world, with a strong desire to change its meaning. The conventional radical press, like the world whence it emerged, was indescribably dull and conventional in thought, word and deed. And a lot of old-style radicals made it clear they didn't think much of our efforts, which stank of poetry, passion and provocation, not qualities greatly admired by guardians of long-dead Holy Writ.

## EARLY DAYS: 1952–65

*Heatwave*'s parentage in *Rebel Worker*'s Wobbly Surrealism is abundantly clear, but it also owed much to the anarchist tendency within the British anti-nuclear movement.

On June 23, 1962, Diana Shelley and I met in a very large furniture removal van, being used as a makeshift prison wagon, after being arrested, along with 321 others, at the first ever Greenham Common USAF airbase demonstration a sit-down outside the gates. We were quickly fined and released. Less than a year later we were sharing our first flat. I was twenty, she a little younger. Six years after Hungary, her parents were still loyal, if dispirited, members of the Communist Party. My parents, however, were exceptionally conservative; though my mother was (and is) a wise and unfailing friend, my father, a much-decorated British army officer, was a highly disciplined, profoundly ethical, deep-dyed authoritarian. Di had a progressive education as befitted the only child of Hampstead liberal "intellegentsia." I had suffered six years of preparatory boarding school, followed by five more at Wellington College.

As mid-fifties teenagers, we met rock 'n' roll, the first real sign, along with the Teddy Boys, of a fracture in the social crust of national torpor, which had appeared to be thick, impermeable and immovable. And there was James Dean, whose early death added a necrophiliac glamour to *Rebel Without a Cause*, a movie that gave every surly teenager an iconic image to ponder. (In hindsight, there *was* a cause: opposition to the withering boredom of everyday life—precisely the same thing that was to bother *Heatwave* a decade or so later.) Both of us were too young (or possibly just too bourgeois and cloistered) to enjoy rock 'n' roll fully, as social rebellion. But the 78 r.p.m. shellac gramophone records at least carried the message!

From these different starting points, Di and I were both equally open to anti-militarist and anarchist ideas, and both equally keen to get more involved with the Committee of 100, which seemed to us to be the cutting edge of the anti-war movement; it contained clearly avowed anarchists alongside those with more conventional "radical" outlooks and was prepared to break the law, in the form of sit-downs, in London and at nuclear bases, in pursuit of its anti-nuclear ends.

The buzzword was "commitment"; both of us were deeply committed.

My initial interest in peace and socialism issue came at Wellington, through Oscar Wilde's *The Soul of Man Under Socialism*, which inspired me greatly and made me really question society for the first time. (I was, to my father's utter disgust, a very Wildean fifteen- and sixteen-year-old, complete with centre-parted hair, constantly subjected to enforced trims by the school barber as I attempted shoulder length locks. Oscar would have, and could have, had me in a trice!) I liked Wilde's inversions ("Work is the curse of the drinking classes") and his assertion that the possession of wealth in any large measure is so onerous a burden that, in the interests of the rich, wealth must be abolished.

At my first job, working for an evening newspaper in Middlesbrough, I started widening my reading. Wellington had tried to impose a strict mental conformity. (At least one of my fellow students had a passable sense of comic timing: during the Queen's visit for the school centenary one wit had shouted, from the back during her speech (in mimicry of Peter Sellers' very popular *Songs for Swinging Sellers*): "Wot abaht the workers?" The perpetrator was never caught and this potentially deeply embarassing issue was pursued no further! I shared "digs" with another journalist, Finn McKechnie, who proved more pro-actively sympathetic to anti-nuclear activity. We both agreed, if on little else, that nuclear weapons were a complete waste of time, money and space and that the Labour Party was not the solution.

In April 1961, I also took part for a few days, as it passed close by, in a Direct Action Committee (DAC) march from London to the Holy Loch, the base for American Polaris-armed nuclear submarines. This was to result in hitherto unprecedented police violence against peaceful, sitting demonstrators, on its arrival at the Loch in May, when police hurled elderly arrestees high into the air to land on the knees and heads of other sitters. There were front-page complaints, from the sympathetic *Daily Mail* journalist who had been on the march from the beginning, about the totally unwarranted injury-threatening displays of police hostility and violence to entirely peaceful sitting protesters.

## THE COMMITTEE OF 100

Partly out of frustration with CND's parliamentary cretinism and partly wishing to extend the élite tactics employed by DAC into a mass campaign of civil disobedience, Britain's elderly but most famous philosopher, the venerable 88-year-old mathematician Lord Bertrand Russell, founded The Committee of 100, with others, late in 1960. According to Christopher Driver, author of *The Disarmers*, it took its name from the Guelph Council of 100. Both Ralph Schoenman (Russell's secretary) and Gustav Metzger (later to achieve fame with his *Destruction in Art Symposium*), founding members of the Committee, were studying Renaissance Italy. Inspiration also came from the American Student Non-Violent Co-ordinating Committee (SNCC), then the spearhead of the Black anti-segregation movement, and Dave Dellinger, A.J. Muste and others around the magazine *Liberation*.

Russell himself, for all his undoubted passion, courage, intellect and hostility to nuclear weapons, actually had a fairly conventional political outlook: his intent was basically to extend CND's campaign of political persuasion by extra-legal means. He was an irreverent Labour Party democrat, not an anarchist, much of his anger fuelled by naïveté. The idea was to gather together a group of famous people to support disobedience actively (or in this case passively). Russell gathered many "name" writers, actors and actresses and numbers were made up by relatively unknown peace activists. Including Russell, the President, there were 108 members!

The Committee's first sit-down, involving some 4000 people, was at the Ministry of Defence on February 18, 1961. There were no arrests. (Trafalgar Square had been decreed off-limits by a slightly alarmed government.) Simultaneously the DAC was attempting raids by canoe on the Proteus submarine depot ship at Holy Loch. On April 29 1961, over 800 of the 5000 participants in a Committee demonstration in Whitehall were arrested.

On September 12, Bertrand Russell, now 89, and 31 others were imprisoned for refusing to be bound over to keep the peace, under a 14th century act devised to deal with soldiers returning from the Hundred Years War with France! (Over the next few days many Committee supporters handed themselves over to their local cops and demanded to be arrested with Russell, being "equally responsible" for proposed Committee actions. They soon learned that the police don't ever have to arrest anyone, no matter how guilty s/he might be!) On September 17, thousands of Committee supporters retaliated by taking over Trafalgar Square, despite a total ban on any form of central London demonstration. Arrests totalled 1,314 and over 650 spent a night in the cells. Britain had never faced organised, non-violent civil disobedience on this scale before.

Every Committee move was covered eagerly by the press. The very first pirate radio station, The Voice of Nuclear Disarmament (VND) made occasional illegal broadcasts (the first on February 10,1961) through the TV, after BBC broadcasts had formally closed each evening. The Committee was on the crest of an unprecedented wave. The next demonstrations, organised for December 9, 1961, were accordingly ambitious. The Committee was moving out of London. Its three crucial targets were three USAF bases—Wethersfield, Ruislip and Brise Norton. Its plan was to walk onto the runways and disrupt take-off and landing. Satellite demonstrations would take place at York, Bristol, Cardiff and Manchester. The Committee printed an excellent booklet, *Against the Law*, advising demonstrators on non-violent action, strategy and full legal rights.

As it happened, where I sat down, at York no one was arrested. Elsewhere, around 1000 were. This national day of civil disobedience resulted in a show trial in February 1962, under the Official Secrets Act (OSA), and long jail sentences for the Wethersfield Six. The supposed architects of the Wethersfield "invasion" got 18 months apiece for the men and twelve months for the only woman. The gentle, brave and beautiful Helen Allegranza, destroyed by her prison experience (and probably less than adequately supported by her Committee comrades), took her own life shortly after release.

The Committee was divided over response to the long prison sentences and decided against a return to Wethersfield, to the disgust of most radicals. The late Nicolas Walter in his *Nonviolent Resistance: Men Against War* considers this failure to return as marking the beginning of the end for the Committee. My distant view from County Durham and the dismal, industrial Northeast fringe of England was less well informed, and more rose-tinted.

## LONDON: JUNE 1962

By now the centripetal tug of London, where everything seemed to be happening, was beginning to dominate my feelings. I had passed my journalist exams and joined the National Union of Journalists, but I'd become a journalist because I wanted to write. All I was writing were small-time court cases, grisly inquests, second-rate local football matches, Darby and Joan Club notes and interviews with Golden Wedding celebrants, while hearing about scandals that could be proved but couldn't be printed because of local politics, which were totally Labour Party-controlled. I found having to be at work every day a tedious imposition. I was frustrated and bored. I decided to take a holiday and go to the Committee of 100's 24-hour sit-down blockade at Greenham Common.

I'd really enjoyed the feeling of comradeship as I'd dossed-down the night before, with a dozen other unknown but immediate friends, in Nick Ardizzone's Newbury pad. Somebody offered me a joint. I was shocked but tried it anyway. The effect added to the feeling of comradely ease and to the exciting sparkle of anticipation in the air. Greenham Common was my first Committee of 100 arrest. I felt oddly empowered by the whole experience. I had taken action against the nuclear state and it had been officially noted with fingerprinting and a small fine! Much more importantly I'd met Diana, still a friend, who was to be my very constant, loving companion and inspiration for the next four and a half hectic years.

I wrote to *The Evening Gazette* saying I wouldn't be back. I was reminded of my contract. I wrote again, suggesting they tear it up. I heard no more. I had left behind almost everything: bed, bedding, clothes, kitchen gear, cutlery, and plates. It was a small price to pay, and one I was to pay several times more! I still had my copies of Wilde, Blake, the parallel text Lorca with his wonderful essay on *Duende* (which might be translated as "devil-soul," and which I'd recognised immediately as the quality that "sent" me in Little Richard), and my anarchist and pacifist papers and pamphlets.

Di's and my general attitude in 1962 might have been summed up in print by Nicolas Walter's *Ends and Means* and in image by the famous photograph of Terry Chandler (of Polaris Action, a DAC "spin-off") planting a nuclear disarmament flag on a Polaris submarine buoy on the Holy Loch.

The Committee of 100 had formally decentralised early in 1962, with regional committees gaining autonomy, a London Committee being set up and the National Committee surviving as a formal co-ordinator. One by one the celebrity members slunk back into the woodwork and a gradual process of disintegration began. A mass civil disobedience event planned for September 9, 1962 at the Air Ministry was cancelled when the Committee received only 3,900 pledges of participation when they had called, very optimistically, for a minimum of 7000. An alternative Public Assembly was held there a fortnight later, attended by 2000, and addressed by the Trotskyist actress, Vanessa Redgrave, and Earle Reynolds who had sailed into the US Pacific atom-testing ground in 1958 in his yacht *Phoenix*. Then, in October, to a soundtrack that included the Beatles' first very minor hit, "Love Me Do," we charged through the streets of London in angry, terrified and chaotic protest against the Cuba Missile Crisis of October 1962. We saw the crisis as hypocritical and extremely dangerous grandstanding by Kennedy, particularly in view of the US missiles in Turkey, far closer to the Russian heartland than Cuba was to Washington. Many of us thought that we were going to be immolated very, very shortly, probably by the "friendly fire" of short-falling American missiles.

For my birthday in December 1962 Di gave me a copy of Joseph Heller's *Catch 22*, a novel that became a cult book for everyone we knew, like Alfred Bester's *Tiger, Tiger* and Theodore Sturgeon's *More than human*. Her inscription read: "So glad you managed to catch 21." So was I. Despite our universally pathetic (or bathetic, take your pick) response to it, the Cuba Crisis did emphasise the urgency of our long-term task and, for Di and me, 1963 was to be our climactic year of Committee activity.

### SPIES AND DEMISE: 1963

Just before Easter, Lenny Bruce, due to appear at *Private Eye*'s offshoot Establishment Club, was refused entry to the UK by Home Secretary Henry Brooke. Good Friday, April 12 1963, the first day of that year's Aldermaston March, provided a revenge no less sweet for being indirect. Spies for Peace, a clandestine group of eight militant war resisters from the libertarian wing of the Committee of 100, published 4000 copies of a pamphlet called *Danger—Official Secret!* (This gesture was no doubt inspired in part by the London Solidarity Group's pamphlet *Beyond Counting Arses*, which had urged militants to move beyond the passive and ultimately masochistic sit-down strategy towards more radical challenges.)

The Spies' pamphlet, widely distributed to the press and establishment as well as to marchers via the Spies' B Team ("No idea where they came from. This CND marshall just asked me to hand them out, so being an obedient little fellow, I did. Ho ho!"), revealed the government's plans for a post-nuclear war subterranean network of Regional Seats of Government, a bunker-based control system based geographically on Oliver Cromwell's regional government centres of more than 300 years earlier, to be run by an entirely unelected civilian and military elite. It included all the RSG's phone numbers. On

April 12 hundreds of us sat down at RSG6 (supposedly a mushroom farm) at Warren Row, near Reading and conveniently close to the Aldermaston March route. (The many police were determined not to arrest us, which would have made shame more shameful by publicising it. The solitary dog-handler urged the crowd to be less noisy for the sake of his nervous dog!) On Easter Monday, as the march closed on Central London, there was a new edition of 7000 copies.

The Spies' third edition on April 22 ran to 18,000 copies. From then on countless groups independently reprinted it. More instantly "folk" singers like Kevin McGrath transformed the information into clever and striking songs, which were taken up by thousands and thousands of marchers. There were several brushes with police as the march reached Central London and, sweeping police cordons aside, took up the full width of the streets. The mood of the march was wildly, buoyantly enthusiastic. A group from Zengakuren, the most militant of Japanese student groups, was on hand to provide examples of their street-strategy, which included turning the front ranks into battering rams by deploying bamboo or metal banner poles horizontally.

CND's leadership, its thunder stolen and respectability demolished, was less than happy. The ultra-right wing (and government-supporting) *Daily Telegraph* then caused further offence by reprinting the entire document, supposedly sourced not from England but from Czech radio coverage of the Spies story, an escape clause enabling the paper to escape prosecution under the Official Secrets Act (OSA).

The whole Spies episode left the government incandescent with rage, but despite the police and Special Branch arresting and interrogating large numbers of people, they were never able to nail anyone. Britain has no Statute of Limitations and the late Nicolas Walter remains the sole identified member of the Spies (in the obituary by his daughter Natasha Walter in The *Independent*, March 13 2000.) The *Situationist International* was greatly impressed by this uncharacteristically flamboyant, highly effective and well-organised coup, the sixties British peace movement's high point; SI's June 1963 "Destruction of RSG6" exhibition at Odense, Denmark, organised by J.V. Martin, was a rare act of homage to a non-situationist group. Even *Peace News* admitted "The Spies Were Right." The Spies, coupled with the considerable and growing number of military personnel making contact with the radical peace movement, made for a great spring.

On May 11 we went to RAF Marham in Norfolk, the bleak, flat, eastern coastal county which sites so many missile bases because it's a straight shot from there to Moscow. Only the Earth's curvature and the limitations of human vision prevent a direct view of the

Kremlin; there was little higher than church steeples between the two. The idea this time was to auction the base and contents, in the small and sleepy nearby market town of Swaffham, and then walk onto the base and claim our property. Swaffham natives already knew about "ban-the- bomb." Activists were constantly being arrested in the locality. In fact 400 demonstrators did walk on, over a hip-high fence, sat down and were then thrown out by RAF and civilian police. Some of us did it several times, with the same result. The *Sunday Telegraph* published a dramatic photograph of me being chucked out, with my Old Wellingtonian scarf, emblazoned with a large CND symbol and embroidered with "100," very prominent! Eventually the airmen got bored chucking us over the fence. By chance Di and I were having a break when the arrests began. A few hurried back over the fence to get arrested. We didn't. However, 80 were arrested and 68 were held in Norwich's ancient Mousehole prison, charged, like the Wethersfield Six, with serious offences under Section 1 of the OSA. (In hindsight, we might have done better to liberate one of the many Norfolk turkey farms and stampede the birds over the base, thus effecting two progressive moves at the same time!)

We clearly had to return to Marham in solidarity with those still in prison and on May 18 we did, producing another 56 arrests, but with everyone, including those already locked up, now charged under the less serious Section 3 of the OSA, with £50 fines or an alternative three months prison. (Such sums seem derisory now, but £20 a week was considerably more than I was earning: our rent on 13 Redcliffe Road was £7 a week!)

On June 29 we were among the 300 who invaded the government's Microbiological Research Establishment at Porton outside Salisbury, after listening in pouring rain to an excellent and angry speech by veteran local campaigner Austin Underwood, who had organised a successful protest-invasion of Imber (the Salisbury Plain village "borrowed" by the government as a "temporary" WWII firing range and never subsequently returned to the villagers). We got to Porton, clambered the 6-foot wire-mesh fence and were inside. The rain had stopped. Di's and my group were one of the few that traversed the whole of Porton. Helicopters flew overhead to pinpoint groups to the many soldiers, whose role was to stop us, but how exactly they were to achieve this had obviously never been defined.

As we made our way across the innocent-looking summer meadows, the laboratory area a grim slab in the merciful distance, we talked to a few soldiers who asked us, unexpectantly, to stop. They were perfectly friendly, if somewhat confused, but there were too few of them and too many of us for them to stop us non-violently. Those that were stopped (because, in their case, they had come to be stopped and arrested) were eventually rounded up by military or civilian police and evicted or arrested, according to official whim. I wrote a short account for *Peace News* (July 5, 1963). The courts sat until after midnight to deal with the 51 people who had managed arrest, most of whom got small fines of £3 or £5.

We rampaged angrily in the streets during the Greek Royal visit in July 1963, in a variety of nightly demonstrations. The gruesome Henry Brooke imposed a total shutdown on all political activity in London during the visit, in July 1963, of Queen Frederika of the Hellenes, notoriously ultra-right and widely viewed as the real power behind the crypto-fascist Greek government. Pre-emptive raids on Committee flats and offices had forewarned us. At the main Committee pad, a mansion flat close to Paddington Station, the Special Branch spooks had found hashish. They knew what it was but weren't interested. Only Greece, and Save Greece Now (the Committee's newly adopted temporary name) concerned them. The clampdown was so total that even the Conservative *London Evening Standard* ran a front page lead headline "POLICE STATE VISIT."

And while all this was going on, the MacMillan Tory government was spending the summer fighting melt-down over Spies for Moscow, Spies for Peace and the Profumo scandal. (Like everyone else, we thought Mandy Rice-Davies was pretty, witty and wonderful, but were astonished to discover that British Cabinet Ministers fucked.) Various subterranean texts, containing other "juicy details," were circulating about the case. Was Sunken Glands (the nickname for cabinet minister Duncan Sandys) the "headless man" in the recent Duchess of Argyll divorce case? Was Ernest Marples, the transport minister, a transvestite? Was MacMillan, no longer the Super Mac of the Tory press, capable of sex at all? These documents (which were popularly supposed to come via *Private Eye*), supposedly revealed all, and although they didn't, they did at least keep us amused at the profound discomfiture of our ruling class. It seemed more than ironic that sex, the great Anglo-Saxon tabu, should bring the government to its knees.

In September there was a retaliatory public gathering of 500 people outside the Hampstead home of Henry Brooke, protesting his totalitarian actions, exemplified in the "police state visit." He had also deported at least one man (the Nigerian dissident, Chief Enahoro) to a probable death sentence and had barred Lenny Bruce from Britain, among countless other offences. What had really rattled his cage was Queen Elizabeth being booed by Committee of 100 demonstrators.

"Our Queen was booed tonight and I am furious," he fumed.

In September I wrote "Super-Power and the Hot Line" (*Freedom*, September 14, 1963) in which I tried to pinpoint the contradictions in the recently opened USA/USSR presidential telephone hot line between Moscow and Washington. One man was destined to enjoy its benefits only briefly. On November 22, President John Fitzgerald Kennedy was assassinated. The assassination immediately produced counter-assassination and massive speculation, which continues to this day.

## HYDE PARK SPEAKERS: 1962–63

We used to go quite often to Hyde Park on Sundays to hear the speakers. Axel was a big, barrel-chested, heavily bearded, highly sentimental exile (as a child) from Hitler's Germany, but also the apparently proud, albeit pacifist, descendant of two generals of great renown (Ney and Hoch), both of whose names, hyphenated, he bore. He was older than us. A driving instructor, he had been Di's more or less platonic boy friend, and was shortly to be featured in Heathcote Williams' book, *The Speakers*, along with Van Dyn, a man whose skin was totally covered with tattoos, and others. With most of the speakers, unless you were interested in their topic, you'd stop, hear a few sentences and soon drift on. Some, like Van Dyn were actually more interesting privately than publicly. Others, however, stood out, and Axel was one: a fine speaker, adept at handling the crowd, intelligent, emotional, humorous. His topic was essentially the stupidity of war. Axel could exude pathos but he certainly wasn't frightened to let his huge frame rock with merry laughter.

Donald Soper was a methodist priest, a lifelong pacifist, socialist and activist campaigner for London's dispossessed (of which there were then a lot fewer). He could speak extempore, without notes, for two hours or more, without repeating, fluffing, correcting or much pausing. He was reputed to be the fastest public speaker in Britain, flowing on at a consistent average speed of 140 words per minute.

A close friend of Axel's named Richard spoke for London region CND. Tall and skinny, he could answer, coherently and with unlimited technical expertise, any question on the desirability or otherwise of Britain unilaterally disarming itself of nuclear weapons. And furthermore, he could do it in any of countless unpredictable ways, depending on what he thought the questioner needed. Sometimes it would be hard fact and hard logic; few mustered those as powerfully as Richard who had heard every question ever likely to be asked. But at other times it would be surreal flights of fancy which gradually ended up revealing in pure poetry what might have been further mystified by the cold recital of fact. Richard's surrealistic revelations of the horror of the State were wonderful, inventive, black, comic masterpieces.

## ANARCHISTS AND OTHERS

Throughout this period we regularly visited Freedom Press's musty and remarkable Maxwell Road bookshop in Fulham, just down the road from where we eventually lived, run by the bearded Jack "Sprat" Robinson, an ever-amused (and amusing) observer of all things anarchic. What we couldn't afford to buy we read there. Anarchism, utopianism, anarcho-communism, anarcho-pacifism, direct action, civil disobedience, the Paris Commune, the Spanish Civil War, Kronstadt, Winstanley and the Diggers, Zapata, Louise Michel, Nestor Mahkno and Durrutti. We read books, pamphlets, poems and essays by Godwin, Bakunin, Kropotkin, Thoreau, Bourne, Huizinga, Mumford, Landauer, Zamyatin (the latter two fitting in well with the Wildean concept of history being the endless realisation of utopias—and revolution being essentially unending which was, more or less, my belief at the time), Gandhi, Brenan, Borkenau, Orwell, Marie-Louise Berneri, Vernon Richards, Alex Comfort, Gary Snyder, Nicolas Walter. I also came across old copies of *Now*, the culturally-oriented anarchist magazine that had published material by Orwell, Kenneth Rexroth, Albert McCarthy and others. I was impressed by Landauer's "The State is not something that can be destroyed by a revolution. The State is a condition, a certain relationship between people, a way of human behaviour; and we destroy it when we contract different relationships and behave in a different way," and by his observations on topias and utopias (*The Revolution*, 1907). And by Zamyatin's "harmful literature is more useful than useful literature, because it militates against calcification, sclerosis, encrustation, moss, peace. It is ridiculous and utopian... Ideas which feed on minced meat lose their teeth, just as civilised men do. Heretics are necessary to health" (*On Literature, Revolution and Entropy*,1924)

We met a whole new world of people. (I felt a little like Miranda in *The Tempest!*) I moved into a new flat, early in 1963, shared with the anarchist historian, Philip Holgate, who had countless hair-raising tales of life as a teacher at Jimmy East's hyper-progressive libertarian school at Burgess Hill, Sussex, which would have appalled A.S. Neill, the venerated anarchist theoretician of progressive education. Our landlady, Daphne, was a close friend of the poet and critic Al Alvarez. In the flat below, Donald Rooum, the anarchist-individualist *Peace News* cartoonist, lived with his wife and children. At the other end of Fellows Road were Nic and Ruth Walter, who had friends that seemed, to a provincial like me, fairly wild and very interesting young libertarians. They were more radical than most anarchists and most people around the Committee. Nic himself was a writer who really impressed me. He was a stickler for factual accuracy: "Getting the facts right is not history, but it is a necessary preliminary!"

## ANARCHIST WRITING: 1963–64

I wrote extensively for *Freedom* (weekly) and *Anarchy* (monthly) put out by Freedom Press. Veteran anarchist and anti-militarist Vernon (Vero) Richards edited *Freedom*. His somewhat sclerotic outbursts on the limitations of the peace movement were useful antidotes to whatever euphoria we managed to generate from time to time. Vero was rarely seen in public. Committed revolutionary, deeply steeped in (and an acknowledged expert on) the lore, history and development of Spanish anarchism, and lover of the revered Marie-Louise Berneri, he had been one of the Freedom Press editorial group sent to prison for sedition in World War II. *Freedom* had called on troops to desert and take their weapons with them. Vero shocked many young anarcho-pacifists with his headline after a failed assassination attempt on Verwoerd, premier of apartheid South Africa: "Pity he missed!"

I wrote further pieces on pop culture and other topics for *Cuddon's Cosmopolitan Review*, edited by a genial, usually bearded Australian, Ted Kavanagh, who owned a printing press and The Wooden Shoe Bookshop. The Shoe was in Old Compton Street, just down the road from Better Books, then a key meeting place for cultural and political dissidents, who seemed to be growing in number daily. In 1962, Ted had been one of the first London anarchists to befriend Di and me. (It was through him that I met Dachine Rainer, lover of e.e. cummings, and that wise and wonderful veteran, Lillian Wolf, who knew just about everyone and everything in anarchism over an immense number of years.) Ted was a really good guy. In those days, when indulgency of various kinds was not yet, as it soon would be, *de rigueur*, within the London "underground," Ted contrived to run probably the most indulgent magazine of all time certainly in the history of anarchism. Ted's Coptic Press was very valuable, publishing pamphlets including the first UK edition of the Situationists' English language *Decline and Fall* and, a bit later, Rebel Worker Group's *Surrealism & Revolution*.

I'd already co-edited two issues of *Anarchist Youth* in 1963 with Wynford Hicks, debonair Oxford graduate, syndicalist and fellow Committee of 100 activist. (Wynford was later to resurface briefly in the early seventies on *Ink*, Ed Victor's and Richard Neville's ill-fated seventies attempt to take "hippy values" to a wider public.) *Anarchist Youth* was still directed at the anti-nuclear movement, and the only thing I recall now about *AY* was Di's clever little poem addressed to a pigeon, urging it to shit on bureaucrat Henry Brooke. Now I wanted to reach beyond the disaffected middle class towards what I sensed were the real rebel forces in society—the various youth cultures which all seemed to show considerable disaffection and disgust with the world, which was more and more what I was feeling myself. It no longer seemed interesting to isolate oneself within a milieu of kindred and self-referential spirits. I really hated the society in which I lived. I was prepared to do whatever was necessary to bring it down.

We were still involved with the peace movement, and the Committee of 100, but by 1964, it was clear that both had lost sense of direction. Notwithstanding the Spies and attempts to broaden its approach and appeal, the Committee was running on empty. People were no longer so willing to offer themselves passively for arrest on sit-downs, when such protests had no discernible effect on the authorities. Furthermore the police had wised-up. Their current strategy was to arrest individual members of the Committee on relatively serious incitement charges, which carried much longer prison sentences.

From their standpoint this was much better than arresting hundreds of us at a time, on minor charges, which carried small fines and created major administrative problems for them, while also providing more publicity for us. (It's always worth bearing in mind that the authorities, however stupid they may be, can learn in the end and that they have a wide choice of strategy once awake.) Some of the most energetic and up-front people ended up getting arrested, doing a longish sentence (18 months was becoming a norm) and emerging tired and dispirited. The Spies certainly got media attention but our sit-downs and walk-ons were now generally ignored, or got a sentence in news roundups. We had apparently been run to a halt. The Committee was to survive for quite a while longer, but, for us, it was finished. The anarchist movement seemed immovable: half-asleep and doomed to a ghostly and ineffectual, if benign presence on the fringes. Our "successes" were clearly in the past.

## THE NEW LONDON R'N'B SCENE: 1963–66

Until I moved to London I would have sworn that Little Richard, the true, dionysiac, sexually omnivorous King of Rock, was the ultimate in popular music. Since the late fifties I had seen all the best rock-'n'rollers killed, co-opted or marginalised, replaced by singers for whom Pat Boone had obviously been a prototype; a fresh delivery of bland, denatured, homogenised white bread. Even the already devitalised "burger King" was being fattened for the kill. Rock was sidelined and pop was deadly.

However, in London, through another mutual friend from Greenham Common, Nigel Turner—a tall, bearded, long-haired, would-be beat, working in acute boredom in an Acton factory—we had been introduced to two things that would play a huge part in my life: cannabis (he had handed me the joint the night before the Greenham Common demo) and Blues. I can still vividly recall exactly where I was, how stoned I was and on what, how much lardy cake I'd eaten but not why, my position on the floor even, when I first heard *The Best of Muddy Waters*. From the awesome electric power of "I Just Want To Make Love To You" to the empathetic grace and subtle—but propulsive swing of "Louisiana Blues," where Waters and harmonica-player Little Walter play so intricately and intimately together that it is hard to decide who is playing what, this was rare, beautiful and mysterious magic. There was none of the preciousness of white pop; this was raw, earthy, direct and "told like it is."

Black rock'n'roll (Little Richard, Little Willie John, Fats Domino, Chuck Berry, Screamin' Jay Hawkins and Bo Diddley) had always thrilled me and had fired a general and largely unsated curiosity about American black culture. But nothing had prepared me for the sheer majestic power of Muddy. Or for the fact that hearing him would really change my life and start a journey through time, backwards and forwards along the highways and byways of the blues and its culture. It took me in one direction through Robert Johnson and Son House back to the true Delta King, Charlie Patton, and sideways to Elmore James and Johnny Shines. I discovered other "greats" like Blind Willie Johnson (with a voice that sounded like the "before" to Louis Armstrong's "later" in a sore throat lozenge commercial), Rabbit Brown, Furry Lewis, Memphis Minnie, Sleepy John Estes, Yank Rachell, Gus Cannon, Noah Lewis, Skip James, Isaiah Nettles, J.B. Lenoir, Lightnin' Hopkins and Howlin' Wolf, whose roistering band sound could just as easily have made him one of the great rock artists.

I suppose, like most of my contemporaries, I was initially most impressed by Robert Johnson. Johnson's blues are amongst the most thrilling music of the 20th Century, a perfect fusion of highly imaginative and deeply haunting poetry, intensely charged yet highly artistically-conscious singing and a richly inventive bottleneck guitar technique of stunning virtuosity and "rightness." The whole is not only a perfect expression of his own life and experience (and a furious slap in the chops for the society that made it so). It is also so full of implication for the future, that it amounted not only to a blueprint for the definitive Chicago blues style of the fifties, but also for rock'n'roll.

I met and talked to many bluesmen and women over three years, either backstage at these annual Blues Festival roadshows or in clubs or hotels: the highly intelligent and socially aware J.B. Lenoir; the avuncular Waters; the fearsome but very friendly Wolf, with whom Mike Rowe and I talked extensively; the cantankerous and belligerent Sonny Boy Williamson, with his hooded eyes and the cobra-sway of his live performances; the self-possessed, self-confident, mesmerising and highly informative Sam (Lightnin') Hopkins; the embittered but prodigiously talented Little Walter; the swaggering John Lee Hooker; the ever-smiling Buddy Guy; Hubert Sumlin, Wolf's guitarist, totally integral to the fully developed Wolf "sound," missing his front teeth after a lupine assault; and, most memorably, the old and blind Sleepy John Estes who swore that night his performance would make me cry. It did. I'd really been far too ill to go to that concert. I spent the next two weeks in bed with pneumonia but nothing would have kept me away. Each singer got a few numbers to show their pace, and for the most part the quality was extraordinarily good.

We'd also been to quite a few concerts by jazz musicians. Early on, I was very impressed by the Modern Jazz Quartet and particularly the vibraphone player, Milt ("Bags") Jackson. However, I soon found the MJQ's "Eurocentricity" wearing: "Bags" always seemed on the edge of exploding into invention, but never actually did. Learning of this frustration, my friend Mike Rowe turned me onto Jackson's own great albums and to the music he'd made with Ray Charles, which allowed the most dynamic and fluidly inventive vibes-man since Lionel Hampton room to maneuver and get firmly "in the groove."

We even got organised enough to volunteer as publicists for Ornette Coleman's August 29, 1965 concert at the excellent Fairfield Hall, Croydon, home of the annual blues festivals, a prospect that sparked off great excitement among those turned on by "Free" or "New Wave" jazz. I loved Ornette: on first hearing, the blues-drenched "Rambling" had gone straight to all-time favourite status. I spent every spare penny on imported blues and jazz, much of it on the Origin, Arhoolie, Chess, Atlantic, Impulse or Blue Note labels.

My first blues venture in print (outside album reviews for the specialist *Blues Unlimited*) was "From the Grass Roots" (*Freedom*, March 20, 1965) about Buddy Guy, then unknown in the UK (and indeed in most of white America) beyond very keen blues listeners. I considered him to be one of the most thrilling musicians of any

343

kind anywhere. (I was an even bigger fan of Otis Rush.) This all-consuming Blacks'n'Blues jag culminated in the May 1965 issue of *Anarchy* (51, Blues, R'n'B, Pop and Folk), to which I contributed "Blues Walking Like A Man," a potted history of blues which, despite the inherent and inevitable injustices of simplification and truncation, I still consider one of my best-ever pieces.

I had made my first stumbling attempt to understand the new white Anglo-Saxon pop culture in "Pop Goes the Beatle" (*Freedom*, November 16, 1963) and concluded a more than somewhat confused piece of analysis by arguing that: "They are not peripheral. The beatlefans, the mods, the rockers, the ton-up kids are people with ideas of their own. If anarchism has nothing to say to them it has nothing to say at all."

Eighteen months later, in "Blues in the Archway Road" (*Anarchy* 51, using the Covington pseudonym), I had more of an idea what I was writing about—the socio-cultural ambience of the British R'n'B boom. By the mid-sixties there was a clearly visible generational shift. A post-war, post-Aldermaston, disaffected rebel generation had emerged, enjoying full employment (if they wanted it), just-about-livable social security payments (if they didn't) and relative affluence, certainly compared to twenty or even ten years earlier. This encouraged new attitudes toward work and play. A lot thought that machines would shortly be doing all the work. Some of us doubted it, but hoped. "New" ideas and images were in the air; Kerouac's *On the Road*, the beats, beat existentialism and the drugs that went with it, Brando, Dean, free jazz, dada, surrealism, the Left Bank, Camus, Sartre, New Wave cinema.

Countless real blues men and women visited England. In clubs, they were invariably backed by white London bands. I spent every moment I could listening to blues and investigating its background. Paul Garon had helped enormously in that area. I helped with production, and wrote sleeve notes for Mike Rowe's first Chicago "bootleg" blues album (*Chicago Blues*, May 1965) which included harmonica-playing singers like Little Walter, Junior Wells and the impassioned Little Willie Foster as well as Johnny Young, J.B. Hutto and the superb Johnny Shines. The album cover featured Peoria Street, an artery to Chicago's Heart, the globally famous Maxwell Street. Chicago was ever in mind!

I have written elsewhere ("Whitewashing the Blues," *Race Traitor* 9, Summer 1998) of the repellent cultural arrogance implicit in the very notion of "white blues." I will not rehearse my views again here, except to say that such cultural "imperialism," whether conscious (as it clearly was in some cases) or simply the result of sloppy thought (quite a feature of the time since many people preferred others to do everything for them, including think), was actually a very marked and typical attitude of the sixties generation in general in their relationships with existing and established communities, whether musical or social. (I take into account that they were in many respects simply carrying on the practices of the society from which they'd dropped out.) This process continues unabated and it made me a lot angrier in 1998 (and in 2004) than it did in 1965!

Di and I had struck up a friendship, through the clubs, with British "blues" singer John Mayall, and through him with his guitarist, Eric Clapton. We liked Mayall initially because he looked more interesting than most of the people on the scene! Clapton, with a guitar style modelled on Freddy King's, had already tasted minor stardom with The Yardbirds, and had quit them after their first big hit, refusing to forsake the "true blues" for pop. Mayall and his band the Bluesbreakers weren't the big attraction; without the slightest doubt "Slowhand" was. In those pre-Hendrix days, he was the sharpest and most respected guitarist on the London scene. "Clapton is God" and "Slowhand" graffiti were proliferating from central London walls to suburban walls. Clapton also happened to be one of the most genuinely enchanting people we had ever met. He soon moved in with us and through him we met many other musicians. Hughie Flint (later McGuiness Flint), John McVie (later Fleetwood Mac), Jimmy Page, Jeff Beck, Stevie Winwood and others also turned up, doubtless attracted at least in part by my wide-ranging blues collection, which included Skip James' "I'm So Glad," Blind Joe Reynolds' "Outside Woman Blues,"and Professor Harold Boggs" "Lord Give Me Strength" among many others. But most of these musicians were into hearing any new music. I remember Clapton was particularly knocked out by Eric Dolphy's extraordinary, serpentine version of Thelonious Monk's "Epistrophy" on his *Last Date* album. There was always music playing at Redcliffe Road, and almost always it was Black.

I was still very interested in libertarian politics but I knew a new approach was necessary and wasn't sure what it would be. I felt an increasing widening of issues and of interests, not just in myself but in everyone I knew. I was now infinitely more excited by music, particularly by blues and jazz, than by the old politics, and also by the developing London (and American) "pop" music scene. Many proponents of this new scene now had their music played by the new illegal offshore pirate radio stations to which everyone seemed to listen. (Both John Lee Hooker and Howlin' Wolf hit the charts.)

I was equally interested by the overspills between one "scene" and another. We were not entirely alone. It was like Aldermaston, but more constant and less isolated. Many former "politicos" sensed that politics wasn't over; it was simply one of many items on the burner at the same time.

*REBEL WORKER*: 1966

In one of my 1965 notebooks I wrote: "The message of life is despair and the true heroes are those that know this but continue to act as if they don't know." I think I really believed that then. Perhaps I still do.

Andrew Loog Oldham, the Rolling Stones' manager who'd also suggested mugging as a possible method of raising funds to buy a Stones album, had said in his sleeve notes to one of their early albums that the only solution to the bomb was to be higher than the bomb when it went off. I was beginning to think he might have a point. I had spent the early part of the sixties waiting to die in a nuclear holocaust, perceived then as being almost inevitable. I was determined to spend the rest trying to live to the full.

The USA had a strong civil rights movement but, probably understandably, in view of its position as "leader of the Western Alliance" no very strong anti-nuclear, let alone unilateralist movement. Now there were considerable signs that the USA too was changing. There was increasing disquiet about the Vietnam War. Urban blacks were beginning to develop a marked taste for torching their ghettoes. The Free Speech Movement at the Berkeley campus, California's most massive and massified campus, had also attracted our attentive interest. A new name, Mario Savio, one of its leaders, had joined the ranks of left-wing stars, which already included people like Stokeley Carmichael, one of the leaders of the Student Non-Violent Co-ordinating Committee (SNCC, known as Snick). Then there were Students for a Democratic Society (SDS), destined to become the most influential white youth movement of the sixties. The American civil rights and student movements attracted the same sort of middle-class affiliates that had been drawn to the anti-bomb movement in Britain. It was clear there was a huge generational flexing of mind and muscle. It was also clear that something new was needed.

This generation had grown impatient with the old politics and was instinctively grasping for new strategies, new approaches. Direct action might be largely symbolic, but it seemed to underlie whatever philosophy these new dissidents, on both sides of the Atlantic, had in common. We weren't entirely clear about all the nuances of the new American left but it did look distinctly promising. There were also American rebels, draft-dodgers, drop-outs and proto-hippies in London. However, although I was meeting more American libertarians in London, there didn't seem to be much co-operative endeavour between the American and the British left, let alone between libertarian socialists.

My first contact with the Rebel Worker Group—also known as the Solidarity Bookshop collective, must have been sometime late in the summer of 1965, initially through Bernard Marszalek who, as *Anarchy*'s Chicago rep, had contacted me through Colin Ward after *Anarchy*'s Blues issue. He sent us great tapes of Chicago blues radio shows by Purvis Spann, "The Blues Man," on WVON ("if you don't dig blues you got a hole in yer soul") and Big Bill Hill on WOPA. There were also inflammatory texts and magazines—*Rebel Worker* and *Resurgence* (magazine of Jonathan Leake's and Walter Caughey's New York-based Resurgence Youth Movement which, less directly, was also to influence *Heatwave*). I was thrilled to be in touch with an American group, particularly one from Chicago, "home of the blues."

*Rebel Worker*'s approach, content, style and outlook were more interesting and exciting than anything I'd come across in London. In those days we looked on the USA as being "where it's at," and Chicago, for my own reasons, was "Where It's At" Central. I was thrilled by the news that Franklin and Penelope Rosemont wanted to visit us in London.

Franklin struck me as a cuddly bear of a man, with long, dark, uncombable hair, and scruffy 1950s-beatnik appearance. His quickfire enthusiasms, obvious intelligence and, to me, apparently polymath grasp of the unusual belied his initially shambling flu-stricken appearance. Penelope was long-haired and beautiful, and clearly Franklin's intellectual match. The closeness of their relationship seemed to echo mine with Di, when it was at its best. The four of us immediately gelled. The more we explored each other's ideas the more obvious became our deep underlying affinities.

On the one hand my deep offshore immersion in American culture—rock'n'roll, blues, jazz and soul and enthusiastic reading of left field American history from hoboism to Marie Laveau and the Voodoo kings and queens—gave me plenty of common ground with the Rosemonts. On the other, it was they who introduced me (and probably many others in Britain) to Sade, early Gothic fiction, Fourier (the first revolutionary thinker to give real significance and importance to human passion), Lautréamont (Isidore Ducasse, the 19th century French poet whose corrosive imagination, corruscating wit, and radical subjectivity had inspired not only the Surrealists but also the Situationists), Freud, Surrealism, Nat Turner (leader of the famous slave revolt), H.P. Lovecraft (whose name alone was enough to secure my wholehearted interest) and the young Marx.

I knew a little about gothic fiction; surrealism meant Buñuel's cinema (for most English people surrealism meant Dali); the rest was new to me. Marx was not only unread but, for me as an anarchist, a veritable pariah. I had long since trashed the plaster bust I had at Wellington as a convenient symbol of dissent. The irony was that much of this new input was European; as a supposedly "well-educated" Englishman, I was woefully ignorant of most of these broad European cultural and political ideas. It seemed a pertinent reflection on British insularity that it took Americans to introduce me to them.

The Rosemonts were resolutely opposed to sectarianism and had a refreshing belief in the primacy of Mad Love, Desire and Humour. This pointing to a productive inter-relationship between apparently distinct phenomena, most of which would then have been dismissed out of hand by the conventional left, libertarian or otherwise, finally gave me the "permission" I needed to pursue wholeheartedly the fusion of personal life-style and politics. The need to develop a new and comprehensive politico-cultural vision, incorporating everything that excited me and others—until then simply a nagging visceral undercurrent, expressed in much of my "non-political," "cultural" writing—now became an explicit preoccupation. It is impossible to underestimate the impact of this visit on me. It opened a path out of the political impasse I was in and towards the future.

It wasn't just "serious" thinkers either. Bugs Bunny's profound revolutionary teachings were admired with reckless enthusiasm. We saw a lot less difference between the supposedly trivial and the supposedly non-trivial. A whole new world was suddenly grist to the revolutionary mill. The list of our precursors and inspirations included equally the famous, the infamous and the misunderstood—Will Eisner's *The Spirit*, and Marvel's *Incredible Hulk* and *Silver Surfer* among them. (I had by then amassed a vast collection of Marvel and other comics, by junking my way round London's chain of Popular Book Centres.) For me it was a truly magical time. Ideas flowed fast and free. Wild imaginings. Utopian speculation. New doors constantly opening. New inspirations constantly beckoning. We read and talked endlessly, listened to music—blues, jazz, The Who and the Stones, and explored possibilities.

Even before their visit I had bored Di to distraction with endless praise of *Rebel Worker*, which from the start felt much closer to my attitudes than anything published in the UK. It was young, fresh, open and not tied to archaic dogma. Graphically it seemed light years ahead of any British duplicated magazine. So when the idea of doing an Anglo-American edition was mooted I was inordinately pleased. We rapidly wrote and compiled *Rebel Worker* 6 in a spirit of intense excitement. (As would happen with *Heatwave* 2, the process of writing and typing had been flawlessly democratic. Ideas and suggestions flew thick and fast. *Rebel Worker* 6 was a genuine collective production and, more importantly, richly and deliciously thrilling.)

In "Freedom, the Only Cause Worth Serving," an editorial signed by the Rosemonts, Radcliffe, Covington, Nat Turner and Emiliano Zapata, its stated aim was

> to promote whatever increases the confidence, the autonomy, the initiative, the participation, the solidarity, the equalitarian tendencies and self-activity of the masses and whatever assists in their demystification. ...we see social liberation as the essential prerequisite, the first steps, in the total liberation of man. It is especially to young people, young workers, students, drifters, draft dodgers, school drop outs that we address ourselves and our solidarity: you are one of the largest and most oppressed sectors of our society and it is you who must make the Revolution.

My main contribution to *Rebel Worker* 6 was "Crime Against the Bourgeoisie." (The title recycled Pete Townsend's own description of The Who, used in an interview.) For me, from the moment I first heard them at Soho's Marquee club, The Who were the purest, most instinctive and most exciting rebel band in British pop history. "Maximum R'n'B" proclaimed their posters. They actually no longer had much if anything to do with R'n'B (unless it stood for Revolt & Blood) but Maximum they certainly were. I had been as impressed by their stance towards society—initially a blend of belligerent, semi-articulate but resoundingly clear disgust at almost everything that surrounded them—as by their mesmeric, incredibly loud and often wildly dissonant (in every sense) club performances. I had no idea either that The Who's descent into mainstream pop would be so swift; from denouncing "suburban culture and young marrieds" to "Happy Jack" in a few months.

### HEATWAVE

Unhappily (for me) Franklin and Penelope left shortly after May Day (May 10, to be exact). Briefly I faced a void but I was already determined to follow up *Rebel Worker* 6, and had countless ideas and even a name, *Heatwave*. The profusion of new ideas and questions was fermenting fast and furiously. With my Chicago soul brother and soul sister gone, what now involved me was planning the new magazine. There was just one problem. Di was happy to help with any of my projects but I knew she was unhappy about the *Rebel Worker*'s bloodthirsty tone (her words!). *Heatwave* was unlikely to be more peaceful so I knew I couldn't count on her for much whole-hearted support.

In effect, I was alone in London with a few hundred copies of *Rebel Worker* 6, the name and a couple of articles for a future magazine, supposedly speaking for a movement which, despite enthusiastic letters, didn't actually exist. (The absence of the Rosemonts felt, at certain times, like an amputation.) I did however know several other people who thought more or less as I did, or who were, at least, sufficiently pissed-off to try something different.

During their trip, the Rosemonts had visited Paris to meet with André Breton and other surrealists, as well as with Guy Debord and Mustapha Khayati of the Situationist International (SI). They brought back copies of the English language *Watts 1965: The Decline and Fall of the Spectacular Commodity Economy*, not only the first Situationist text I'd really read, but also the most exciting and cogent comment on the black riots of Los Angeles. It tied in with my abiding interest in Black America, for me the source of almost everything that was strong, vital and progressive in American culture and politics. Whilst most radical groups were disapproving or dismissive (or both) of this Black anarchy—the Situationists, like the *Rebel Worker* Group, embraced it wholeheartedly, explained it, celebrated it and greedily asked for more: much, much more. This was my kind of music. I'd also noticed that the SI's rare mix of theoretical rigour and firebrand immediacy really excited most of my libertarian friends. Even Di was impressed. We all wanted to know more about the SI.

I wanted to keep alive the spirit of Mad Love, revolutionary comradeship, endless inquiry, unbounded optimism and spontaneous delirium that had culminated in *Rebel Worker* 6.

Writing of *Heatwave* in 1991, Jon Savage says:

> The keynote pieces are about British pop culture: Ben Covington [Charles Radcliffe] wrote a critique of the "first teen take-over" novel, Dave Wallis' *Only Lovers Left Alive*, which describes a near-future where the adults have committed suicide with "Easy Way" pills and the teenagers have taken over. In "The Seeds of Social Destruction,' Charles Radcliffe laid the foundation for the next twenty years of sub-cultural theory.

Foundation-laying for any kind of sub-cultural theory was never the intention. My real intention was distinctly more modest: to lay waste the world as we knew it and to join in the endless party that would create it freely and passionately anew. That was the minimum programme. The details would have to await the event and would assuredly emerge, like a new dawn, when the all the values of the Old World were sucked inexorably into the vortex of revolution.

In the mid-sixties the countless and varied strands of autonomous post-war youth rebellion—rock'n'roll, the Beats, ban-the-bombers, Surrealism, Dada, existentialism, avant-garde artists, drugs, "blues" and so much else—began to coalesce into the disparate, amorphous but apparently more or less gelled phenomenon, known variously as "hippie culture," "the alternative society," "counter culture" or "underground." I hoped that as consciousness of the underlying poverty of everyday life seeped through this "underground," as I felt it inevitably must, the underground would understand the necessity of changing the world, rather than prettifying it, and would itself inevitably become a vehicle for such change.

## PROVO & THE PROVOS:
### THE MAGIC APPLE IN AMSTERDAM

I visited Amsterdam and made strong contacts with several Amsterdam provos: Hans Metz, Rob and Sara Stolk, Raoul Van Duyn and Bart van Heerikhuizen. I liked all the "leading" provos that I met, and I liked many of the "white plans." (Intelligent, autonomous, voluntarist, egalitarian communal co-operation for easing life's burdens, as long as they weren't a substitute for a real street party, were acceptable. We might have to wait a year or two for revolution.) I also liked Provo's symbol, an apple with a small hole in it—the entry-point of the worm of discontent.

I was interested by the former-Situationist Constant Niewenhuys's "utopian" New Babylon. Constant had first postulated his ideas, heavily influenced by Huizinga, within the CoBrA group of avant-garde artists. The initials stood for Copenhagen, Brussels and Amsterdam. In the late fififties he had worked with Guy Debord in the SI to define the notion of "unitary urbanism" for the Amsterdam Declaration of 1958. For the next year or more Constant was heavily involved with SI but in 1960 there was, predictably, a rupture. In Constant's view the cause was the "refusal or incapacity of the situationists to carry out ...the kind of activity... defined by this declaration."

By 1966 Constant was, for the situationists, a *bête noire*, particularly since he was now not merely "a man with a plan" (blatantly reformist and easily recuperable) but was widely touted as part of Provo's "leadership." Provo attracted withering scorn from the SI, which, with customary mandarin hauteur, preferred analysis of obviously impoverished written pronouncements by an avowedly reformist leadership, to real understanding of the inherent radicalism of the street provos.

The Provo movement had come to international prominence in June 1966 when Dutch construction workers had rioted for several days in the centre of Amsterdam and were possibly surprised to find themselves supported by a new "radical youth movement," Provo, the name taken up by several articulate young political radicals. Certainly the Godfather of Provo and probably its unconscious "founder" was Robert Jasper Grootveld, a former window cleaner who organised happenings around the statue of "het Lieverdje" (Amsterdam's "little darling") which had been the gift of the Hunter tobacco company. Grootveld, a charming and distinctly apolitical exhibitionist, objected to the statue and made it the centre of his "K for Kancer" anti-tobacco campaign. "No happy smoker is a riot stoker," he'd shout.

To those who asked why he smoked if he objected to cancer, Grootveld invariably replied "Who should know better than the addicted consumer?" This personable, attractive man with his war paint and bizarre, often incomprehensible incantations, who had previously set up an open-fronted bourgeois drawing room on a raft on one of Amsterdam's canals, in which he had enacted the boring daily life of a bourgeois reading the paper, soon gathered large crowds of otherwise bored youngsters. Others, notably Roel van Duyn, a student of politics, inspired in part by the Committee of 100 and Dutch theoreticians of non-violence like Bart de Ligt, and anxious to promote non-violent protest against all manner of defects in society, also came and saw opportunities. The happenings on the Spui became more and more overtly political and the provos called on all youth to join in their provocation of authority.

Later the same month, following the Amsterdam riots, two of the more respectable, media-friendly provos, Bernhard de Vries and Irene van der Weetering, visited London. Van der Weetering's husband had accurately described the provos as a "heart-rending, muddle-headed organisation": the two emissaries bore out his diagnosis. The English press, much more sympathetic than *Le Figaro*, for example, which had described them, intriguingly, as "nazis, communists...vicious petit bourgeois, beatniks, delinquents...," was still quite understandably confused. It turned out that De Vries wanted the Dutch police to be like the English—unarmed—and ultimately to become quasi-"social workers," clad in white, Provo's colour. We tried in vain to explain that when citizens tacitly accept the police as friends, arms are unnecessary and that it is precisely their lack of arms that make the English police such a formidable instrument of authoritarianism and oppression. The English, we knew, were also deeply committed to heartfelt co-operation in their own oppression.

De Vries, having seen rockers in London, had decided that they were not after all a revolutionary force, notwithstanding their inclusion as part of the subterranean revolutionary movement in Provo's *Appeal to the International Provotariat*. What alarmed us was what had actually happened, in practice. My notes of the meeting said:

A lot of kids, doubtless intellectually provoked and pre-justified by Provo ideas and statements, provoke a major crisis of authority in Amsterdam, with police, riot police, and special para-military police in the city and three infantry regiments, either there or on standby. The provos broadcast an appeal on the pop music radio station urging kids to stay at home. Asked if this was not rather inconsistent, De Vries told his London audience that Provo did not approve of violence, and that shops were being damaged which was "unnecessary." But surely such actions were the logic of Provo's *Appeal*? De Vries, like provos I had interviewed in Amsterdam, said Provo did not call for violence. They did not want riots. But didn't they want to "provoke authority"? De Vries said they wanted to provoke with happenings, constructive schemes and not destruction.

In reality, "Seeds of Social Destruction" simply tried to show how the Dutch scene and Provo's recognition of the "provotariat" (a neat catchall for the new lumpenproletariat of the leisure economy) could relate to Britain. It was the idea of an open, fluid series of provocations of authority in the form of a freewheeling, humorous and anarchic street party that excited most of the people around *Heatwave*. Despite deep reservations about their leadership, amply confirmed by the De Vries meeting, the provo actions themselves were wonderfully creative, gloriously rich, popular theatre: funny, dramatic, invigorating, highly communal and quite crazy. No one asked what the demonstration or happening or party, or whatever it was, was *for*, or *against*, or even *about*. It *happened*, with no other aim than its own fulfillment.

Provos fed police peanuts through the bars of their wagons—which once empty of cops, were overturned and set on fire or dumped into the canals, all against a backdrop of swirling crowds, pungent smoke-bombs and, just about audible above the sirens, whistles and singing, the mad sound track of Robert Jasper Grootveld's Dadaesque chants. Police pressure hoses were regularly turned on demonstrators, who would try to surf the powerful water jets until they were out of reach. As often as not they fell to the ground and were duly soaked, thereby becoming an instant target for police "snatch squads." I tried, during one of these street celebrations, to present myself, while under threat by a baton-wielding cop, as an innocently bystanding English tourist. The cop thought for a moment and then—following his muttered curse of "Modern Eengleesh!"—came a resounding whack with his lead-weight tipped 50 centimetre baton across my shoulders, which ached for days afterwards.

Police round-ups of under-age runaways on the huge Provo communal barge, berthed on one of the canals that add such romance to Amsterdam's ancient centre, were always greeted with verbal harassment, abuse, disdain, tomfoolery, whistling and usually a mass chanting of Napoleon XIII's hit single: "They're coming to take me away, ha ha." No one worried too much about these regular purges or fought against them: the police were armed and usually outnumbered those on the barge, and, anyway, the kids went quietly and were almost invariably back on the barge within a day or two. To give credit where due, the Provos did try to provide a rudimentary degree of social security for their community though perhaps with no more success than the San Francisco Diggers. They were also not only considerably more aware of gender politics than most radicals of the period, but had an imaginative and active poetic humour, particularly in their early days.

On March 21, 1966, *Le Monde* reported:

> Although the afternoon's provo demonstration...against the recent wedding of Princess Beatrix and Claus von Amsberg... didn't at first look like much more than a simple uproar, a sudden violent flareup brought police and provos into conflict. The provos, re-inforced by several hundred young people, struggled with the forces of law and order throughout the evening... in some streets householders sided with youth, bombarding police with a variety of objects including old bicycles. At midnight order seemed to have been restored after an evening of sudden violence...

Like most of Provo's philosophical mentors and "leadership," Constant was undoubtedly not a man keen to lead a rag-tag mob of joyously angry youth intent on ludically destructive physical poetry. I had a strong sense of Amsterdam's then-intoxicating atmosphere, a heady mix of insouciant street cool, imaginative plans and an often delirious radical self-consciousness expressed in turning Amsterdam's historic centre and its beautiful spider's web of canals, little bridges and narrow cobbled streets into a giant revolutionary playground with endless riots, happenings and spontaneous events. Though drugs undoubtedly played an important role in this revolt, Amsterdam then was very different from Amsterdam now. Then drugs in Amsterdam were a powerful catalytst for a massive, broad-based and very disparate social movement that instinctively headed for the streets, armed only with wildness, humour, desire and a rage to play, and not an elaborate, fully co-opted, consumer pacifier as they are now.

Provo's leadership really *didn't* understand the message it was getting from the streets. The leadership was, as the pleasant but gloomy Van Duyn readily admitted to me, reformist but "we live in this society." "But reform is just running repairs to the system. It's what keeps the whole shit machine going." "Well, maybe, I don't know." "But revolution is not possible." "Why not?" "Because people, here, are not ready for it." "Of course they are. That's what's trying to happen here." "I don't think so."

The Provos were very much in the news and I felt that what was going down in Amsterdam was important and significant. Accordingly, *Heatwave* 1 not only led off with "What Is The Provotariat?," but followed up with news reports, a Provo contact address and my own (pseudonymous) "Daytripper! A Visit to Amsterdam."

### HEATWAVE IS NOT WORRIED

If *Heatwave* 1 was a less than entirely coherent production, it did, at least, convey something of the wide-ranging and, I hoped, humourous enthusiasm with which we confronted the world, and our pressing desire to change its meaning. The conventional radical press, like the world whence it emerged, was indescribably dull and conventional in thought, word and deed. A lot of old-style radicals made it clear they didn't think much of our efforts which stank of poetry, passion and provocation—qualities not greatly admired by guardians of long-dead Holy Writ. The same people had wilted from the diversity of *Rebel Worker* 6. In *Cuddon's*, Ted Kavanagh wrote a review of an earlier issue: "My first reaction to *Rebel Worker* was so complex I won't even bother to explain it." Many other old-guarders were even more confused. Anarchism was not meant to be revolutionary, let alone fun.

As Bill 'Not Bored' Brown observed not long ago, "the small European groups that came together to form the Situationist International found points of contact between itself and prior movements only in the artistic field; none of their points of contact"—in marked contrast to the *Rebel Worker/Heatwave* group—"were in the field of the labor movement." Noting the many articles on pop music and youth revolt in *The Rebel Worker* and *Heatwave*, Brown continues:

> The reasons for the inclusion of these articles . . . are clear: pop culture, consumerism and subcultural "style" are phenomena that modern workers have directly experienced, have questioned deeply, and have understood at a profound level. It isn't at all relevant, important or even interesting that classical Marxism and its contemporary adherents disapprove of these phenomena as distracting, degenerate or "superficial." What is truly relevant, important and interesting is the question: Toward what end will modern workers put their understanding of these phenomena? *Heatwave* answers: Toward the autonomous creation of a society without classes and exploitation. If this goal seems fantastically out-of-reach to those who pride themselves on the "fact" that they "live in the real world," *Heatwave* is not worried. "Nothing can stop me! I'm the Hulk! I'm the strongest there is!" says a comic-book hero on the page Radcliffe devotes to past issues of *The Rebel Worker* and to future issues of his own zine. "Careful? Ya never get to be a comic-book hero by bein' careful," says another. And, of course, he is right." [See www.notbored.org]

London Solidarity, the British arm of *Socialisme ou Barbarie,* seemed to have considerable autonomy and was a very active, radicalising libertarian-Marxist catalyst within the Committee of 100. I particularly liked their ongoing hatchet-job on the USSR, which they defined as bureaucratic capitalist, and their excellent pamphlets on the Committee of 100 (*Beyond Counting Arses*), the 1926 General Strike and the 1956 Hungarian Revolution. They also carried a lot of news about shop stewards and were deeply involved in fomenting industrial unrest wherever possible. I liked everyone around Solidarity, and respected their attitudes; like them I now considered myself a libertarian-communist. I might even have joined the group but my interests seemed too wide-ranging to be readily included within that nexus. Without the free use of their duplicator and their support, however, it's very likely that *Rebel Worker* 6 (at least in that form and in England) and the two *Heatwaves* would never have seen the light of day.

*The Rebel Worker* group already had a good relationship with

Solidarity and I had worked closely with Solidarity people, like Ian Hutchinson and Ken Weller, both of whom I really liked, in the Committee of 100. I think Solidarity looked on our somewhat crazed approach with benign amusement (though they too carried some quite unusual left-field material including the American Jim Evrard's Marxist analysis of the factory floor hierarchy of a classical orchestra!) They probably felt that we had an entirely different approach and were addressing an audience they were unlikely to reach (and probably didn't want to reach, either.)

At Thames & Hudson, I'd taken weeks of spurious sick-leave, during some of which both *Rebel Worker* 6 and *Heatwave* 1 were produced! That job came to an end.

Terry Chandler had served more prison time for anti-nuclear activities than anyone. I met him in 1963 soon after his release from his Official Secrets jail term following Wethersfield. I had expected a deeply serious and committed activist but Terry's moon-face and tightly curled hair gave him a somewhat Harpoesque appearance which was echoed in an often quite surreally un-Gandhian approach to life and action and an anarchic sense of humour that I liked. In 1966 he was working for Equity Printers, a press with only Terry and his Indian boss. Terry and I started to discuss printing. The inevitable question came up: "Why don't we start a press together?" Variously named Pirate Press or Radical Press, this was our next project.

### "PRE-SITUATIONIST" DAYS IN THE GATE: 1966
### NOTTING HILL & *TOTALITY FOR KIDS*

*Heatwave* 1 was already largely typed up when I met Chris Gray at a London anarchist meeting at the Lamb and Flag, quite soon after *Rebel Worker* 6 was published. He'd already seen the mag and wanted to buy a copy. Chris was tall, dark-haired, skinny, striking-looking, very intelligent, fastidious, soft-spoken and serious, but with a ready laugh that often collapsed into hopeless giggles when something really amused him. The name was Gray, the sense of humour often black. Chris had recently worked with Conrad Rookes on *Chappaqua*, an early attempt (with an Ornette Coleman soundtrack) to capture drug consciousness through film, and knew the Paris scene fairly well; his background seemed to be similar to mine but our experiences were widely different. While I had protested in London, he had travelled quite extensively and had met and knew several of the leading lights of the cultural avant-garde now burgeoning into an élite within a new "counter-culture." While my past included a veritable mishmash of ill-digested influences, largely "Beat" and anarchist, he was a cultural dissident, led into the "new politics" by an initial interest in the "angry young men." He had read Artaud, had pronounced ideas on the Surrealists and Dadaists and on art and anti-art. He was scathing about avant-garde art, hippie culture and Miles particularly! He had come across the Situationists, was very impressed by both their analysis and their style, and was now fully geared-up for "political" action. I knew of the "Sits" vaguely from the Spies for Peace fallout and, less vaguely, from *Decline and Fall*. Chris and I liked each other very much from the start.

Another constant presence in the early days was Phil Vissac: French, dark, saturnine and very attractive, highly intelligent, very black-humorous, very hip, very Left Bank, but with a curiously doomed air about him. Phil was very well informed on the ins-and-outs of Parisian cultural-left circles. He and Chris were then finishing a translation of a key Situationist text, Raoul Vaneigem's *Totality for Kids*. My initial response to *Totality* was, however, bafflement. On a second reading it seemed clearer. By the third I began to grasp it. (After its eventual publication the same thing happened with many friends: What is this incomprehensible shit? It's more abstruse than Tibetan Buddhism, followed, days, weeks or months later by Wow! This is pretty good! A significant few nevertheless failed to find any enlightenment.) In July 1966, shortly after *Heatwave* 1, *Totality for Kids*, unauthorised but "properly printed" (by Terry Chandler at Equity), was published "privately" from Hereford Road. Production values were not to Parisian standard but were well up on *Heatwave*!

Chris owned a very old, very battered, somewhat green, Bedford Dormobile van, untaxed, uninsured and unfit for the road. Sometime in July 1966 Chris, his girlfriend Stella, Di and I took off in this venerable bone shaker, heading for Berkshire and the enormous grounds of my old school, Wellington College, to take LSD. (I think it was still legal but soon wouldn't be. I didn't care either way.) Chris had talked quite a bit about acid but I hadn't found his somewhat dismissive approach (something along the lines of a total experience leading nowhere and saying nothing as I recall) either particularly reassuring or a particularly persuasive recommendation for LSD. However, I'd read Huxley, and a few articles about acid, including one by Tom McGrath in *Peace News*! I thought I might as well try it. Di was markedly less keen or, perhaps, less reckless. She'd turned down smack but she eventually decided to try acid. It might not have been the best place to take it. I had loathed Wellington from start to finish of my time there. Every part of it, except the grounds, which were mostly heath, bog or marshland, with small woodlands of conifer and rhododendron, and which had always represented an escape from the stupefying, repressive boredom of the school albeit partial and temporary.

In any event, the "trip" was, for me, a total revelation. It was a beautiful summer day. After a few throat-constricting, teeth-on-edge minutes the entire environment turned into a shimmering colourscape. I walked through a puddle which turned into liquid diamonds; the drops of water I kicked up seeming to hang like an iridescent, jewelled net in the air. Sound was incredible: a blackbird's song seemed to cascade into incandescent showers of brightly coloured notes. Colours were themselves astonishing; brighter, clearer, richer, so vivid they seemed afire with an inner flame. The senses seemed to be almost infinitely transmutable. You could smell with your eyes, hear with your nose, see with your ears.(I wasn't sure what its specific revolutionary implications were but I knew there must be some.)

They were crazy days. Hardly anyone around us seemed to be working: just hanging out, smoking dope, tripping, growing hair, wearing increasingly fanciful and colourful clothes and talking. There was a multitude of answers on offer for hippie "seekers." Cults, spiritual techniques, newspapers, magazines, books, music, posters, head stores, diets, religious sects, European and Chinese astrology; anthropology; radical psychology; scientology; Gurdjieff; Buddhism; beat poetry; comic books; flying saucers; Peru's Nazca lines, ley lines and Lung-mei; the I-Ching; English and European Millenarianism; the current pataphysical "hit" *The Dawn of Magic*; *The White Goddess*; R. Gordon Wasson's perplexingly prosaic accounts of psychedelic experiences.

One thing was obvious: the world didn't need any of our inputs to make it work. Chris and I might denounce "hippie" as "the latest slave ideology imported from the USA," which it obviously was, but, inevitably, we hung out with hippies. To the world at large we too were hippies, part of a rapidly growing new urban youth lumpenproletariat. We had endless free time, little money, and plenty of imaginative ideas to really liven things up and not with more dreary happenings, the ultimate in controlled alienation, where we knew nothing ever happened. We wandered around Notting Hill, often wrecked on ether.

### ANOTHER *HEATWAVE*

Soon after the appearance of *Totality for Kids*, Chris Gray contacted the Situationist International (SI), and sent them a copy along with *Heatwave* 1. We had already decided to edit *Heatwave* 2 jointly: its primary function would be to introduce Situationist ideas to

Britain, whatever SI said. However, the SI's reaction to *Totality* was extremely positive and was rapidly followed by Mustapha Khayati's arrival from Paris to check us out more carefully. Di was always sceptical and stand-offish about the Situationists but she liked Mustapha, who was very funny, had an almost constant wry smile and didn't fit the image of austere revolutionary purity that I had begun to associate with SI after reading more of their material. Mustapha didn't much care for the English at large: "If they can put up with each other, they can put up with anything."

Contrary to the claims of Andrew Hussey in his biography of Guy Debord (2001), *Heatwave* 2 neither had, nor in any way required approval (tacit or otherwise) from Debord (or his emissaries), whose approval of *Heatwave* 2 was after the event. (It is highly unlikely that *Heatwave* 2 would have had Debord's wholehearted approval anyway. If he had been involved it would doubtless have been entirely situationist and probably wouldn't have been called *Heatwave*!) Moreover *Totality* was in fact *un fait accompli*, translated and published without SI sanction, in July 1966, before Mustapha came to London: the translation was certainly neither requested nor authorised by Debord (or anyone else), either when Chris Gray and I joined the SI, in October 1966, as Hussey claims, or at any other time.

I thought my own material in *Heatwave* 1 was weak. My politics always instinctive, I'd never had much time for theory. The Provo piece, written straight after my return from Amsterdam, was a rushed, personal snapshot, when what was really needed was a detailed analysis. "Seeds" seemed to be very limited pop-sociology, pepped up by a revolutionary twist of the tail. Mouthing-off was fine but if *Heatwave* was serious about helping to create a "new revolutionary praxis," some sort of theoretical coherence was vital. I thought closeness to SI could only help in that respect, but I did wonder how the very diverse elements now gathered very loosely together under the *Heatwave* banner would view a move away from wild-eyed, stoned iconoclasm towards a more classically theoretical paradigm, and one, furthermore, designed in Paris.

For me, then, there still wasn't abundant evidence that the Situationists were not simply very French, very arty, very intellectual, very articulate, salon libertarian-Marxists. And their approach, for all its declared totality and its undoubted (but by no means total) originality, seemed quite narrowly sectarian compared to the extravagant workings of chance in our *Rebel Worker* 6 investigations.

Chris and I were invited by his friend John Gravelle to do a talk at their "crammers," Tunbridge Wells Tutors. We wanted to do the talk but we recognised that talks were by their very nature alienating. We couldn't avoid the alienation so the next best thing was to reveal it clearly. We taped our talk on my small reel-to-reel machine, took the tape to Kent and played it back to the students of Tunbridge Wells Tutors, while we sat at the back and made occasional cynical comments. I have no memory of what the talk was about, I probably didn't listen. The students were generally confused by our "performance," but one, a black kid called Roy Cornwall, came up and talked intelligently about situationist ideas. I would meet Roy again.

In September 1966 I reviewed *The Autobiography of Malcolm X* for *Anarchy* 67, under the title (stolen from Archie Shepp) "Malcolm, Semper Malcolm." I'd admired and been fascinated by Malcolm for some time, but had missed him, stupidly, on his visit to the UK. (This highly controversial visit had been preceded by predictable howls of indignation from the right.) Malcolm, one of the most interesting figures of the period, a one-time hustler who had undergone a genuine and life-changing conversion, was gunned down in the USA, just as his thinking was developing very interestingly beyond the narrow religious-based Black Nationalism of Elijah Muhammad's Nation of Islam, from which he had seceded. This piece, which also reflected my still rapidly growing interest in American black radical politics in general, was to be my swan song for *Anarchy*. The footnotes drew attention to *Decline and Fall*.

## A REVOLUTIONARY GRAND TOUR: OCTOBER 1966

In October Chris, Di and I set off on a revolutionists' Grand Tour, starting with a few days in Amsterdam. We had already endlessly discussed the Provos. They were unquestionably the most interesting political phenomenon in Europe at the time. Our visit helped crystallise thoughts for "The Provo Riots" in *Heatwave* 2.

Our next stop was Brussels, a markedly less exciting city but the domicile of Raoul Vaneigem, one of the two key figures among the Situationists. His seminal contribution to *Revolution of Everyday Life* was then just about to be published before Debord's own masterwork, supposedly to Debord's chagrin. Raoul lived just outside Brussels. We spent an afternoon, evening, night and morning with him, mostly holed up listening to his accounts of the terrorist Bonnot Gang, Emile Henri and Ravachol. He took great delight in showing us his collection of various late-nineteenth-century anarchist terrorist artifacts, while talking ideas with great excitement. He told us he was also working on a pot-boiler about surrealism's history. I think Di was shocked by his enthusiasm for the more violent elements of anarchism. Despite his sympathies, Raoul was in fact surprisingly quiet, even a little shy, but a friendly, warm, wickedly humorous and hospitable man. Di thought that a lot of Vaneigem's revolution was "in the head," that he was an "idea man" and an improbable activist.

Our final visit, the most important of the tour, was to Paris—to meet Guy Debord and other Situationists. This would decide whether Chris and I would be invited to join the group or whether we would, like countless others before and after, be summarily dismissed, hurled centripetally into pro-situ orbit.

We spent most of our time in Paris in Guy's small flat, a typical, old Paris apartment, small, comfortable, relaxing and, in this case, overcrowded with Situationists. Whenever you stood up your head was inevitably thrust into a richly smelling Gauloise cloud of smoke. Wine was poured immediately and often.

Guy was no longer the studied left-bank dandy of that much-used early photograph with Pierre Feuillette. He had put on some weight, was noticeably more jowly and had adopted an altogether more anonymous sartorial style: he looked like any bespectacled provincial art college lecturer, in fact very much like Tony, my older art teacher friend in Middlesbrough, who first turned me on to Bird, Miles and bop. Since my French was poor and my understanding of Situationist ideas still limited, I was happy for Chris to do most of the talking. The atmosphere was warm and friendly and Guy, clearly revelling in being very much the centre of the devoted attention of the assembled Situationists and would-be Situationists, was at his most urbane, amusing and charming. That certainly did not prevent him venting his undeniable talent for vituperation on most denizens of the French left and cultural avant-garde who seemed, almost to a person, to qualify as "stupid, completely cow-like, little cunts," "cretins" or "imbeciles."

In London the overall talk tended more and more towards "peace and love, man," so this flood of venomously scurrilous epithets was at once both slightly shocking and undeniably refreshing, particularly since the squibs were delivered with a distinctly devilish sense of humour. One neither doubted that he really meant it, nor that it was also delivered as a line, for the assenting nods and laughter of the attendant gallery, which included not only his former long-term companion and co-worker, Michelle Bernstein, and his current companion, Alice Becker-Ho, a dramatically beautiful French-Chinese woman, but also Mustapha, René Riesel, René Vienet, Donald Nicholson-Smith and his French girl friend Cathy.

Much of what Debord said was too quick for me to grasp but was invariably greeted with rapid assent or appreciative laughter and merriment from the assembled Sits. We drank a lot, ate well, talked a great deal (in my case mostly with Michelle Bernstein, who spoke good English and was a highly sympathetic, intelligent, wide-ranging and attractive woman, and with Donald, the bluff, bearded and refreshingly affable established English member of the group), and wandered around Paris. Perhaps it was the wine, but I began little by little to feel more relaxed and at home in this strangely rarefied world, so different from anything I had encountered in London.

Di, on the other hand, with simply a fly-on-the-wall watching brief, didn't feel at all relaxed or comfortable. She also noted and was very shocked by SI sexism: the word did not exist yet but the attitude certainly did. Then more or less all males were more or less all sexist. But even by our lowly standards today and, for all his undeniable cool and charm, Debord was *very* sexist and avowedly "chauvinistic."

Recognising more clearly my own psychological hang-ups about my father and, deriving from them, about any other authority figure, I see Guy Debord more sympathetically now than I did then. I was undoubtedly not only intellectually but also temperamentally ill-suited to becoming a Situationist. Then I was uncertain but Guy now seems to me to have been one of the most authentic, fascinating and remarkable monsters of the twentieth century, and the only one I ever met in person. (That remark is not intended to be entirely uncomplimentary!)

Di felt that Michelle (and, to a lesser extent Mustapha, who had first-hand experience of England and the future members of the "English section") was the only Situationist with a broad enough consciousness to understand "where *Heatwave* is at" and to see that Britain was not a replica of France—a fact (and a factor) which Di (and possibly Michelle) felt largely escaped SI. Michelle had actually helped introduce Situationist ideas to Britain in an article for the *Times Literary Supplement*, together with one from Jörgen Nash, a little more than two years earlier, but Di and I had both missed it. We rarely read the *TLS* which still seems a less than ideal recruiting medium for a French Marxist revolutionary group. We wondered how many *TLS* readers really either understood or were interested in their ideas. Debord later used the same medium to advertise for a literary agent!

Finally, Chris and I were admitted as Situationists. It was actually quite anti-climactic and just seemed to emerge organically from an increasingly enjoyable visit, the relaxed *bonhomie* providing a pleasant and amusing contrast to my expectation. No Psychogeography Reports, no Theory Exams, just relaxed walks, meetings, discussions and meals, markedly less agenda-driven than the Committee of 100! Di had an unarticulated, but probably clearer view of SI than I then had. She definitely did not like either Debord or the Situationist milieu, but sensing my enthusiasm, couldn't really bring herself to explain that to me at the time. She was uneasy throughout, except with Michelle, and seemed upset by the suddenness of the eventual decision. I was probably grossly unsympathetic to Di at this point.

When we returned excitedly to London, Chris and I thought we were part of an English section of the Situationist International but Donald Nicholson-Smith is doubtless correct in saying that there never was an English section—we simply joined the French section. (It would seem that Tim [T.J.] Clark joined SI shortly afterwards. Neither Tim nor Donald were ever any part of the *Heatwave* group: neither Chris nor I knew of them at that time. I only met Tim on a very few occasions and Donald scarcely more.)

In October 1966 *Heatwave* 2, much of which was already "committed to stencil" before our "tour," was published. I couldn't afford the cost of printing it myself at the press, so once again Solidarity lent us their duplicator! It reflected, satisfactorily, very much what I then thought. "The Provo Riots" analysed the Amsterdam events lucidly from an English vantage point, the Dada texts provided a clear antidote to Hans Richter's then recent (and quite dreadful) *Dada* and placed us in historical perspective, while the editorial "All or Not at All" laid out our clear intentions for the future. Thanks to Chris's input, it had some kind of theoretical clarity. Some readers complained that it wasn't "so much fun" but I probably considered that a compliment at the time!

I was briefly very excited by the prospect of doing *Heatwave* 3. I wanted it, in part, to be a very accessible Situationist-style comic. It probably should have looked something like *Beano,* an instant cultural reference point for every Briton—but my personal taste was more towards the distinctively American Marvel comics. (I redesigned *Heatwave*'s title and the cover featured a drawing, by Marvel artist Steve Ditko, of a ragged, slightly toothless yahoo, surrounded by an equally disreputable mob, who were holding the world, and shouting: "IT'S A QUESTION OF FINDING A NEW USE FOR THIS WHOLE WORLD." The price was "It's a steal at 1/6d. (25 cents USA)." An editorial ("The Story So Far...") and several articles were already lined up: Chris had written on Berlin Dada (and particularly Baader) and I had completed a first draft of "Low Sensation Experience with the Students of Poverty," a piece ("Let's Liberate Dialectics!") on the International Congress on the Dialectics of Liberation (to which we'd irritatedly refused a formal invitation) and one contrasting the approaches of two 1967 London embassy attacks. The Situationist material, a Chicago Surrealist Group diatribe against

Picasso, an extract from *Black Mask*, and "Marx on Alienation" were all to be included. The centrepiece would simply have been cuttings and comments on the overall social decomposition around us. There were several other articles in early draft. I was hoping to find a means of producing this as a logical extension of the Situationist International's polemical comic strips. This was the area in which I felt good; being me, I headed straight for it.

Perhaps *Heatwave* had had its day. Now that we were all Sits, a break with this "semi-situationist" past was probably a good idea, at least as far as the group at large was concerned. On the other hand, *Heatwave* did seem to have struck chords with a lot of people, *Heatwave* 3 would have been better than either 1 or 2 and, with the benefit of hindsight I should probably have resigned from the SI immediately and carried on with it. Despite my obvious disappointment, I consoled myself that a four-month, two-issue life had, at least, a satisfyingly minimalist brevity to it. For some time I continued working on *Heatwave* 3, unsure whether to go it alone or not.

What was more difficult to accept than the demise of *Heatwave* was the fact that, as good Situationists, we were expected to break contacts with non-Situationists, which logically included old anarchist friends, the Solidarity group, to whom I felt indebted in many ways, and probably most of the people who'd bought and been excited by *Heatwave*. It also included the *Rebel Worker* group, branded by Debord in Paris as "surrealist cretins," although at that point the Chicagoans were the only people in the USA actively promoting and distributing situationist material! I didn't want my friendships, political or not, determined by some quasi-Leninist headmaster in Paris. It would have eliminated all social contact other than with Chris, Tim and Donald, and particularly with those most likely to be attracted to Situationist ideas. Chris, certainly more pragmatic, took a less bothered and angst-ridden line. Whereas I was deeply worried by the implications—in part, no doubt, a reflection of deeper, increasingly conscious misgivings about the wisdom of my direct involvement with the Situationists at all, and sadness at the axing of *Heatwave*—Chris was going to do whatever he wanted to do anyway, and didn't seem greatly concerned by Situationist codes of conduct, perhaps noting that, for Guy at least, these were evidently made for the observance of fools (other people), and the *ignore*-ance of Debord.

Around this time Chris, Mike Lesser, Sue Rose and I, with a few other loudmouths, disrupted a London anarchist meeting, as a "protest" against anarchist irrelevance. Our incursion brought the long-established London Federation of Anarchist meetings at the Lamb and

Flag pub in Covent Garden to an end. The anarchists seemed to think we would have nothing better to do than attack their meetings every Sunday and they surrendered them without much demur. In fact, as far as we were concerned our attack was a one-off. It had been very amusing to watch the anarchists' dismay. For us, not even Christians could have acted more satisfactorily.

"Shall I call the police?" someone shouted. "No, no, they're comrades," shouted someone else. "They might be your fucking comrades, but they're not ours," boomed the beardies John Rety and Ted Kavanagh in full stentorian Greek chorus. I even got my first-ever *Freedom* front page! Good libertarian education: Anarchist Dilemmas, a beginner's guide, slap bang in your face!

The idea was to publicise ourselves as a viable and lively alternative to the dead hand of the old politics, which certainly included anarchism. We were moving into a new phase, away from the "garage-anarchism" of little mags and into action. Breaking up anarchist meetings didn't strike me as being of vital revolutionary consequence, perhaps because, for me, there were also, personal consequences. Our action aroused bitter hostility among many old comrades, like Ted Kavanagh, Jack Robinson, Jon Pilgrim, Philip Sansom, others who read about it and most of the older and several of the younger anarchists, including some who'd helped sell *Heatwave*. I was particularly sorry about Ted who'd been a good and supportive friend. He was instinctively quite radical himself, but like so many others he had a living to earn and simply could not afford to take on even the mild hooliganism we espoused. I'm sure he knew that he had over-reacted massively and like the rest without much sense of humour to our pin-prick flea bites, but our friendship was over.

In November 1966 the "Strasbourg affair" broke, grabbing the attention of the world's press, already increasingly full of reports about the various forms of youth rebellion, now visible world wide. The generation gap seemed to have developed into an uncrossable chasm. The Situationist International had "taken over" the student union, using its funds to publish *De la misère en milieu étudiant*, a critique whose purpose, boldly stated from the start, was "to make shame more shameful by publicising it." "We might very well say, and no one would disagree, that the student is the most universally despised creature in France, apart from the priest and the politician" began the acidic diatribe against student (and finally all) existence. Khayati's attack was promptly republished in English (with a brief preface and a longer Postscript written and approved by the four English Situationists) as *Ten Days that Shook the University*.

One morning in February 1967 there was a loud hammering at the door of the Redcliffe Road flat. I was still in bed with a new girl friend, Jo, whom I'd met only days earlier at a Hampstead party. The knocking got louder and more insistent. "Coming, for fuck's sake, I'm coming," I shouted as I dragged on my jeans and I opened the door in a still-stoned, confused and distinctly bedraggled daze. Three bruisers half-pushed and half-stumbled up the stairs into the flat, flapping search warrants in my face. I hadn't a clue what was happening. I assumed at first that it was the Special Branch or MI5. Then the drug squad. But the cops turned out to be from the Forgery Squad. They had an American FBI agent with them. Forgery? What the hell was this all about?

Then slowly, very slowly, it dawned. Radical Press had done a print job for the Committee of 100, printing US one dollar bills with a slogan "Is this worth the horror and murder in Vietnam?" under the words "In God We Trust." Almost everyone had seen them. And almost every one had laughed, including my father. The British cops weren't notably unpleasant, but the American, introduced as a currency expert was brusque and hostile. However, once they'd found a few thousand bills lying around the flat, they went on their way with a cheery "you'll definitely be hearing from us" from the Forgery Squad detectives.

My initial reaction was relief that they hadn't found my hash stash. On further thought, I was alarmed. Here was trouble from a completely unexpected direction. Who would have guessed that the pigs would be interested in "forged" dollar bills, so poorly printed, on such poor paper, without even matching numbers, and with such a loud and obvious slogan, when all over the flat was real revolutionary literature, like *Watts 1965*, *The Forecast Is Hot!*, RYM manifestos, copies of *Rebel Worker*, *Heatwave*, *Black Panther* and *Totality for Kids*?

It was ridiculous. If our dollars were forgeries, I was a frog!

However, checking with Ben Birnberg, my lawyer, I discovered that the British Forgery Act was so comprehensive that even to reproduce a barely visible segment of any currency bill from anywhere in the world was a crime, and to do it with someone else, was effectively a conspiracy, carrying a mandatory minimum jail term of two years. It certainly was ridiculous. I was a frog and a frog without wings in very deep shit!

The Forgery Squad detectives themselves hadn't in fact seemed to take the matter very seriously, so the motive force had to be the

American FBI. But why bust *me* and, a few hours earlier, Chandler and the press? The bills had been around for months. Then it emerged that Terry's girlfriend Nancy had been stopped at Kennedy Airport, NY, with a suitcase full of bills and the American authorities had not been amused, the dollar being more sacred than even the flag.

Unbeknown to us and fortunately to the police, an American draft-dodger and unpaid helper in the press was actually producing passable forgeries of large denomination US bills at the same time. His hunch proved correct; our "fake forgeries" provided good cover for his "real" ones!

In February 1967, the London School of Economics (LSE), five minutes' brisk walk from the press, exploded into student rebellion (Britain's "mini-Strasbourg") and other universities and colleges soon followed suit. I wasn't even sure if students really had any revolutionary potential at all. Most revolutionary leftist students I'd met were very boring and seemed at least as interested in preserving their privileges as promoting revolution. Once threatened with losing the opportunity for a degree and its attendant career opportunities, most of them would come to heel very obediently. Universities themselves seemed isolated and isolating intellectual prisons. So what if you took one over? The authorities could always just lock you in and bring in the guns, or in a liberal democracy like Britain, just leave you to rot.

Meanwhile, my fellow printer Terry Chandler wanted to turn any forthcoming forgery trial into a show trial, revealing it for the farce it was. It might well have been the best course of action, but I'd had enough. After he'd spent many hours of what turned out to be his last few days of freedom trying to clean Situationist/King Mob "NEVER WORK!" graffiti off the walls of LSE, I was absolutely sure he was not someone with whom I wanted to do a show trial! On the actual day he was arrested, charged and locked up, I went "on the run" with Jo, who still seemed astonishingly undeterred by my chaotic lifestyle.

We never did much actual running. Chris found us a safe house where we ended up spending the summer. Tunbridge Wells had a surprisingly large hip and radical community. Chris told us that they'd had to release Chandler on bail because I'd disappeared, but if I was still umbilically attached to the "political" through the dollar bills, I was in all other respects a full-time acid freak. We were all highly amused, however, by one cutting of a cartoon he brought. A man on a chair peers out through slightly parted curtains at the outside world. He wears "traditional" arrowed convict clothes. At the open door a woman leans forward to speak to the man. Behind her is another man with suitcases. She says: "Oh, Mr Radcliffe! I thought you'd been recaptured, so I let your room."

Apart from a few trips to London for concerts (notably Jimi Hendrix at the Savile Theatre) we spent most of the time getting very stoned and tripping a lot, mostly with Roy Cornwall and another young freak called Johnny Penfold and occasionally Dave Jackson, the long- suffering but well-heeled provider of most of the acid. The four of us became inseparable friends. We tripped out, chilled out and listened to music, above all to Hendrix who, after a run of staggering singles—"Stone Free," "Purple Haze" (the first out and out acid anthem) and the beautiful "Wind Cries Mary" had issued in May arguably the best debut album in rock history, *Are You Experienced?* On the other side of the Atlantic, Franklin Rosemont was equally enthused, writing "The Invisible Axe of Jimi Hendrix" for The Chicago *Seed* and drawing attention to a man "who sings and plays to shares his dreams. In Jimi Hendrix the music of revolt has found its poet."

Of course, rock or indeed anything consumable that was in the slightest bit popular, was deprecated by the SI. I didn't really care much about the political coherence or otherwise of "rock revolt." It might be largely or entirely "spectacular," but frankly I didn't give a shit. I simply liked listening passively or otherwise to some rock, most real blues and largely postwar jazz, and I wasn't about to stop!

At summer's end, I was getting bored with life "on hold" and realised at last that I couldn't and didn't want to be "on the run" for the rest of my life, however lysergically languid the resultant lifestyle. I returned to London, got incredibly stoned and handed myself in at West End Central police station in Savile Row, on the forgery charges. I couldn't begin to remember when I'd been busted or by whom. I had never known where the warrant had been issued. I could only tell them that it had been issued. There was the usual string of dumb questions: How do you know if you've never seen it? and so on. They couldn't find the warrant. They searched and searched. They wanted to send me home, but I insisted on my right to arrest.

Eventually they handed me some warrant books: Here, *you* have a look then! (This was to be the last word in participatory arrest!) Eventually I found myself: "Here I am! Here I am!" The desk sergeant examined the warrant, closely. "Right, Radcliffe, you're fuckin' nicked, pal! Get him banged-up, constable—take his tie, shoelaces, belt and braces." (I had none of those!) My self-generated arrest had taken the best part of 90 minutes.

I was bailed the following morning; they couldn't refuse because Chandler had already been bailed, along with the unfortunate Melvin Estrin, a press volunteer, who had nothing to do with the bills, on

May 18. He got bail largely because I was on the run. We'd got one bit of strategy right, albeit by accident!

In August, 1967, *Playboy* magazine took time out to analyise the burgeoning global youth revolt, focusing, *inter alia*, on Jonathan Leake's and Walter Caughey's Resurgence Youth Movement: "*Resurgence* reads like the rantings of a soapbox poet zealot:

> surrealysics :: pataphism :: panultraneo :: underdogma :: negativentropy :: Resurgence has not yet defined any limit. We may be three billion persons; we may be a negative universe reaching out across the void...Revolution is the total destruction and creation of society...All science and art is crap. We will not submit and we will not co-exist. The magazine envisions a planet on the very brink of apocalypse... Logic and metaphysics to the torch, it cries. Turn our culture upside down and cut its head off. Go wild. Go naked.

"But there is some intelligence behind its mystical ravings, and to call its authors and audience 'out of touch' would not serve any purpose. Their delusions are evident enough from the vantage point of the mainstream. But in London, members of the Industrial Workers of the World have joined with the Resurgence Youth Movement to start a similar magazine for revolution: *Heatwave*..."

It had always been Jonathan who wrote to me. I presumed him to be the main driving force of RYM, but in fact, like *Rebel Worker* and *Heatwave 2*, *Resurgence* was very much a collective endeavour. I first realised this when I read Walter Caughey's "Reflections on Invisibility" in which he wrote:

> The projection of enigmas into the visible world is an unforgiveable affront to the bureaucrat who presumptuously imagines his assembly of regulations to reflect the nature of the real world. The irreconcilability of authority and the surrealist mission is the reason why the consistent and dedicated surrealist is irrevocably anarchist.

As *Playboy* hit the streets, Walter Caughey was stabbed to death by an unknown assailant with an unknown motive in New York. Franklin wrote to tell me. I was shocked and very sad. I felt as though I had lost a not quite invisible but nevertheless deeply connected friend.

## DID I JUMP, OR WAS I PUSHED?

By late 1967 I was thoroughly disillusioned with the SI, although I probably never had that many illusions. Soon afterwards, in

November, I resigned from the SI for "personal reasons." It was simply admitting a personal reality: I was no longer a Situationist, if indeed I ever had been. Whatever the three Brit-Sits decided to do, I knew then I wouldn't and couldn't be part of it. As a Sit, French or English, I'd always been out on my own un-theoretical limb; now I was out on an emotional limb, too. Chris was still my closest friend and I felt extraordinarily bad about effectively abandoning him. In reality, however, he was so hyped up by then, that I probably didn't need to worry at all! All I knew was that I was now just too ragged to carry on at all, let alone keep up with his energised nihilist enthusiasm. Why did I move away from politics at the precise point at which "situationist-type" politics was coming to the fore? The realisation that things like Strasbourg simply created political waves, not revolutions and not even revolutionary movements? That violence *per se* was, after all, still an essentially self-defeating strategy? My own cowardice? Was I simply terrified of dying, either in a nuclear attack or in a revolution against odds that suddenly seemed, once again, insuperable? Burnout?

It was probably a combination of all these things. Foremost, however, was a growing disillusion with the Situationists. I'd heard that the SI in Paris was trying to find acceptable reasons to exclude one of the French who was homosexual and "going mad." No contact "other than purely political" was deemed possible because of his hysteria and encroaching breakdown. So much for "transparent relationships!" I'd already noted prior examples of situationist cynicism. In its outer-directed form it never worried me: society gets what it deserves. But when directed against one's own comrades it disgusted me.

Paris was also taking its first stumbling and inept steps along the path that would lead to the exclusion of the three remaining English sits. (When I resigned, Chris had predicted "Don't worry! We'll probably all be out in a month or two!") This situation finally blew up after Raoul Vaneigem's visit to New York, during which he (of all people!) had refused to speak to Ben Morea of *Black Mask*, supposedly because of the "mystical tendencies" of Ben's sidekick Allan Hoffman. The close relationship between the English section and *Black Mask,* (damned by Paris as the "union of Morea and the mystic") met with the approval of neither the Paris nor the recently consecrated New York Situationists.

## THE OLD BAILEY

Late in 1967 or early in 1968 Terry and I were finally tried at the No. 1 Court of the Old Bailey. We faced one charge each of conspiracy between us, and four charges each of possessing papers, negatives, photographic plates and printing plates "bearing words, marks, lines, devices, letters, figures, numerals, peculiar to or as appearing upon US Federal Reserve one dollar bills." The real problem was still the conspiracy and that automatic mandatory prison sentence of two years. Neither Birnberg nor my barrister Lord Gifford were optimistic. After I'd talked to them I could readily understand why Chandler had chosen to defend himself. It couldn't possibly have a worse outcome than my advocate's vision of certain and lengthy incarceration. It seemed ironic, not to say absolutely stupid, to end up in prison for political "forgery" at the very moment I was beginning to turn away from politics.

Came the trial. There was a brief but telling submission from Chandler, who over the years of arrests and imprisonment had become quite an astute trial lawyer, and a much longer and less convincing one from Gifford, who, after years of expensive legal training, still hadn't. Eventually the judge said to my advocate: "I was minded, Mr Gifford, not to send your client to prison but you are rapidly convincing me that that is perhaps the only course open to me." Still Gifford, "If I might just finish what I am saying, m'lud" continued his ineffective (if syntactically demanding) speech. I kept on nervously repeating my silent mantra: "Come on, man! Shut up." At long last, Gifford obliged.

After a brief but pithy summing up, in which the judge declared us both idiots, we got conditional discharges: Terry for two years and me for one.

Chris Gray had now linked up with the Wise twins, David and Stuart, who were much closer to his way of thinking than I now was. I watched the first issue of *King Mob Echo* in April 1968 from close quarters but was only very peripherally involved with its production. I was still very fond of Chris, but was disillusioned by the whole New York fiasco and couldn't work up much interest in King Mob's activities. Furthermore, any criminal conviction during the next year, however minor, would have meant being re-sentenced for the forgery.

By the end of 1969 Chris Gray too was gone, hitting the hippie trail to India and ending up in the commune of Sri Baghwan Rajneesh, later Osho. King Mob continued for a short while longer but times were changing. Gray's own brief and often moving reflections on the period are in *Leaving the 20th Century*.

In March 1970 Franklin Rosemont wrote:

> After you broke with the situationists we've hardly heard from you...Sometimes we get the impression that they tried to destroy you, and perhaps to a certain extent succeeded...We wish very much that you were here; if we could all pool our resources what amazing transformations we could inspire! The week that we put together *Rebel Worker* 6 remains for me a criterion for getting things done in a beautiful & exhilarating manner, a real Fourierist operation, delirious & exalting. Imagine a year like that: western civilisation would collapse in writhing agony after six months...

The letter brought tears to my eyes, for its truth and for my loss, but I couldn't respond.

## REFLECTIONS ON THE SI(X)T(IE)S

*"All Power to the Workers' Councils!"*
*"Never Work!"*

Although I was already, almost subconsciously, distancing myself from the Situationists, I watched the external fallout of the Strasbourg affair in 1967 with pleasurable delight, and the internal fallout—yet more exclusions and clear evidence of the SI's fairly cynical and ruthless use of people—with appalled fascination, reactions symptomatic of my feelings in general. (It probably should have been clear from the start that all that could be expected from the SI was a seductive honeymoon, a brief marriage and an acrimonious divorce.)

The *Rebel Worker* and *Heatwave* emerged from a scene and a period in which exploration of ideas of all kinds was part and parcel of life. It wasn't just "sex, dope and cheap thrills, rock 'n' drug culture that separated us culturally from France (and linked us with the USA). For instance, many on the libertarian left in the UK and the USA were discovering (or had already discovered) Buddhism, anthropology, ecology and feminism, as well as Spinoza, early Marx and Freud. Like many, I'd read and been deeply impressed by Rachel Carson's *Silent Spring*, while still at school. We had countless other common points of reference, some a great deal more "trivial."

The IS, despite their vaunted omniscience, seemed unaware of feminism and ecology, and Buddhism would no doubt have earned blanket contempt. As a group they never seemed to develop a real consciousness of the full extent of the pervasive social conditioning of which we were all inevitably victims, nor of the infinitely subtle (and, from time to time, not so subtle) ways such conditioning impacted on our revolutionism. When it comes to a project as profound as the entire parallel restructuring of human personality and human community, such partial insights are inevitably fatal.

Furthermore, for all their attacks on mysticism, the SI, as self-confessed inheritors of the traditions of medieval millenarianism (particularly and declaredly obvious in Vaneigem's case) which inherently involved a kind of collective waiting for the Godot of universal revolution and the assumption that upon its arrival there would be a kind of massive clean-up operation in which everyone would be stripped of their character armour (truly formidable in the case of several Sits!) and conditioning, and thus enabled to inherit the new earthly paradise, could justifiably themselves be termed mystics. (The oft-cited analogy was the flooding of Pavlov's laboratory which proved a rapid deconditioning agent for all his incarcerated and conditioned animals.) The bizarre Situationist belief that the new work-less paradise would be democratically "ruled" by workers' councils (a bolt-on taken from *Socialisme ou Barbarie*, even as *S ou B* was vilified) was possibly a further instance of mystical tendencies, or simply of theoretical poverty, or both. It certainly indicated that the Situationists' revolutionary programme had not been as thoroughly investigated as its revolutionary critique.

Everyone else printed their translations of *De la Misère* in a style as closely mimicking the French original as their local conditions allowed. The English *Ten Days that Shook the University* not only used an entirely different title ("borrowed" from John Reed's famous eye-witness account of the 1917 Russian Revolution, *Ten Days that Shook the World*) but produced a fairly crude pamphlet. I designed the cover around the SI's detourned comic strip, *The Return of the Durruti Column,* which intentionally looked utterly different from the deliberately correct, conservative and archaic-looking original— a "joke" anyway, perhaps less meaningful to the funkier English. What really stands out, however, is how accessible to an English audience the "Postscript" was, (written and approved by the English members), compared to the original French text. Not because the latter was poorly translated, but because the ideas and the vision had to be expressed differently for the English and for Americans, too.

In "Postscript" the English continued to formulate, more explicitly than in "All or Not At All" or "The Provo Riots," an English Situationist critique, one that emerged from observation of the apparently terminal socio-politico-cultural collapse that surrounded us on all sides. What's more, the focus was immediately widened.By a nice irony Debord simply wasn't hip enough to colonise the Anglo-American left on his own terms. In France, which was basically broadly apathetic

and ultimately more interested in a larger slice of "survival" than taking risks for "real life," despite May '68, the Situationist International
(and Debord in particular, since he was the personification of Situationist
ideas) were absorbed readily enough into the cultural discourse of the
French intellectual left. The Sits in Paris (or Debord at least) decided
after May 1968 to get rid of the Situationist International's *blouson noir*
element (precisely the type King Mob sought!) and finally the Situationist
International had no option but to remain manipulators and "hermetic
terrorists" to the end. The last SI coups, carried out by Debord and
Sanguinetti in Italy, notably the mysterious *Censor's True Report on the
Last Chance of Saving Capitalism in Italy* in 1975, used manipulation
to brilliant hermetic terrorist effect. The English, however, embraced a
hooligan ethos (based, it has to be said, on a generally uncritical approach
to the nature of "youth cultural" violence and anti-social behaviour) and
tried to bring the Situationists' revolutionary consciousness into the
streets and into the hands of street people.

I met Guy Debord only a few times, during a very brief period and
never knew him well, so I won't add to the hagiography. He, being a man
of considerable intellectual narcissism, vanity and self-certainty, added
plenty himself. In any case, others who did know him (as well as many
more who didn't) have more than enough to say on the matter.

When I met him, Guy was relaxed, charming, witty, amiable, incisive and, yes, perhaps even slightly "charismatic," though this charisma
may have been simply a reflection of his acolytes' attitude to him. It
was probably my "paranoia"—his theoretical armour-plating was
daunting—but I never felt relaxed with Debord, never escaped the
sense of being a specimen under scrutiny. His body language confirmed the Situationist International as his fiefdom. He gave little or
no intellectual credit for the evolution of his and the Situationist
International's thought to those that deserved it—a very long list,
from Isidore Isou through *Socialisme ou Barbarie* to Henri Lefebvre.
(The early the Situationist International seems to have had a notably
collaborative approach, to which many contributed.) He had no option
but to admit Lukács' enormous influence and was more gracious to
some former "cultural" collaborators like Asger Jorn, perhaps in part
because Jorn proved an ever-ready "cash cow" for SI! Lefebvre, however, continues to do illuminating and important work on demystifying the world we survive in.

In print however, Debord is still often undeniably magisterial.
The lucid and imperious prose, the centimetre-perfect dialectical analysis and the sharp, witty, ice-cold, theoretical precision of *The Society
of the Spectacle* as it builds its argument, interdependent paragraph by

interdependent paragraph, is still both challenging and thrilling. (I have not read post-SI Debord.)

The subjective vision of Vaneigem's poetic, radical and dazzling *Revolution of Everyday Life*, an inspired, apocalyptic and passionate fusion of wisdom, madness and rage, illuminated in the fires of destruction, is the other face of the SI, very different in approach from Debord's elegantly clinical, almost mathematical dissection. Vaneigem's passionate, fire-breathing disgust at the present situation and his revolutionary wish that humans raise themselves to the stars, make for a roller-coaster ride of a book, written with the limitless expectation of those days. It appealed to me (and to most others in the *Heatwave* axis) more, as did Vaneigem personally, although it would be very hard to refute the book's "mysticism." What little post-SI Vaneigem I have read has been very disappointing. His 1970 "critique" of surrealism, *A Cavalier History of Surrealism*, is predictably immodest in his claims for the SI, but at least appropriately titled! Its slightness, patchiness and inadequate development are nevertheless disappointing in a tract that claims, *utterly unconvincingly*, to put the surrealists to bed once and for all.

Apart from Don Nicholson-Smith, the sixties English Situationists never had the chance to integrate with Paris. SI was, for me, simply a source of ideas. Affinity was purely theoretical, save for Mustapha Khayati. The sense of pain, loss, incomprehension and grievance is tangible in Vaneigem's response to his effective exclusion from SI in November 1970. He actually resigned, after facing accusations of cowardice during the events of May '68, from a "tendency" within the SI consisting of Debord, Riesel and Vienet. It appears to have taken them 30 months to discover Vaneigem's apostasy! The mind boggles! The latter two soon shared Vaneigem's fate! Or was it destiny?

Vaneigem, it transpired, had been sunning himself in the south of France while the stalwarts of the SI were slaving over a hot revolution. He supposedly added insult to the injury of this heinous display of revolutionary laxity, by learning of events through the despised mass media. The man clearly had no shame. Vaneigem's distress provides a nutshell insight into what the SI had once had, and what it had now lost.

At the formal dissolution of The Situationist International in April 1972 there were two members (three if you count the then-inactive J.V. Martin who remained till the end), Debord and his Italian "lieutenant," Gianfranco Sanguinetti, and they subsequently fell out. In the end there was only one.

The final arbiter, the final integer, the only Situationist was Debord, a centrifuge, shooting radically charged fragments at the world of the spectacle. That was perhaps how he saw himself. Alice Becker-Ho insists he was the "freest" person she ever knew. (One is forced to ask how genuinely free is a man who insists on systematically trashing his collaborators in order that he alone should be seen as the presiding intellectual genius, and how revolutionary is such essentially dishonest egomania?) Stewart Home is by no means alone in considering him "a mystic, an idealist, a dogmatist and a liar." He could have added countless other epithets, possibly more a matter of opinion than of analysis! In my view, Debord was, above all, tragic.

I probably hadn't given Debord more than a passing thought in ten years when, sometime in December 1994, an old *Heatwaver* rang me: "Did you hear that Debord died?" "No!?" "Really!" "When?" "Last month. Apparently shot himself." I was too shocked to speak for a moment. Then we talked on the basis of what little else my friend knew—little more than that Debord had been an acute alcoholic before his suicide, which wasn't a huge surprise. We chatted about other things before coming back to the death of Debord. As he rang off, Ian laughed a little nervously: "Well, I suppose that is definitively the final Situationist exclusion." I laughed. I hope Guy would have enjoyed the joke.

Positively (or perhaps that should be negatively), the Situationist International (and subsequently and to a lesser extent the English Section) partially understood, incompletely revealed and extravagantly denounced the destructive anti-human vacuity of a globally-focused western consumer capitalism—the Spectacular Commodity Economy—and formulated a far-reaching revolutionary critique of it long before I woke up to such insights. They went back to early Marx, stole him from his interpreters, freed his language, re-understood him for their own time, and re-invented and re-valorised Marxism. Juvenal considered *panem et circenses* to be the sole interests of the Roman mob, but the concept of the Spectacular Commodity Economy and of the Spectacle, was not just a clever neo-Marxist update of "bread and circuses," not just a theoretical bolt-on extra.

The analysis of the Spectacle placed it right in the centre, at the very heart of an all-enveloping unreal reality, over which no one had control. They developed it over 11 years and 12 issues of the *Internationale situationniste* and two major books, an important critique of the insufferable banality of almost every aspect of an everyday reality in which we merely survive. We might have been the most privileged generation in history but in terms of real life we had nothing. At the time, Situationist ideas seemed to me to represent the best available blueprint for leaving the twentieth century.

And yet, when I joined the Situationists I had expected not only incisive theory but also a ludic exuberance (of which, however, I saw little sign) and at least some prophetic foreshadowing of the desired future within the actual organisation. In reality SI seemed more than a tad dull, academic, humourless, old-fashioned and, dare I say it, *boring* after the open-endedness, high spirits, humour and screwball lunacy that had underpinned *Rebel Worker* 6's revolutionary fervour. Blues, Jazz, Malcolm X, the Wobblies, Fourier, Buster Keaton, the Keystone Cops, Bugs Bunny, Tom O'Bedlam, Beano, Marvel Comics, Ann Radcliffe, Poe, Edgar Rice Burroughs' Barsoomian pulp, Dr Syn, Sax Rohmer's Fu Manchu, H.P. Lovecraft, Will Eisner, de Sade, the IWW, William Blake, Gerard Winstanley, Abiezer Coppe, Gary Snyder, Huizinga, Norman O. Brown, Simon Rodia's Watts Tower, Maxwell Street, Surrealism and much, much more—all those magical, inventive opportunities of chance and genius reduced overnight by the SI's stale left ideology into merely infantile pacifiers to be dispensed with in short order. I wasn't even sure I wanted to live in a cathedral! I wondered where the Theory of the Spectacle ended and the Spectacle of the Theory began. I had swapped the confused but richly nourishing mess of pottage that was *Heatwave*, for the pot of message that was the SI. It wasn't, as it turned out, a good exchange. In fact, as a New York taxi driver said to me, after recounting the old but evergreen story of how New York was bought from the Indians for a few beads, "We wuz ripped off."

As Franklin Rosemont recently put it in a letter:

> At the time [in the 1960s] it always seemed to me that the Situationists *wrote* and *talked* and *theorized* about playing and having fun, while *we* [*Rebel Worker* and *Heatwave]*—still just kids, in a sense—were actually *playing* and *having the fun*, and trying to articulate it in a new revolutionary poetic / political language... That some of what we did and said was foolish doesn't alter the fact that most of what we did and said was what really needed to be said and done...

The Situationist International was distinctly of the French cultural and intellectual left. Their critique was restrictively urban, as was that of their unruly and rebellious English offspring. I think we were all often unaware of similar currents elsewhere, which we should have known about, but contacts and communications, which we then thought quite advanced, were actually quite primitive. The SI in Paris covered the tracks of its plagiarism with devotion, and preferred instantaneous and increasingly trite dismissal of its coeval rivals to serious analysis of their position. They defended their own blinkered view with barricaded determination.

The Situationists were absurdly optimistic in their assumptions about technology and its effects, as indeed was *Heatwave*. As assiduous critics of work, we should have guessed that ever more gratuitously stupid ways of turning human life into self-denying drudgery would be invented. Far from machines liberating us from work, they have controlled us within it. There is undoubtedly more idiotic, self-chaining, mindless, alienated work going on now than at any time in Western history. Following the rapid and extensive process of globalisation since the sixties, the Situationist lack of a *genuinely global* revolutionary perspective also stands out. Though it was clearly important to take on contemporary forms of impoverishment in the West, their contempt for Third World issues as an appropriate concern for Western revolutionaries also had uncomfortably selfish, isolationist, possibly racist and even neo-imperialist overtones.

The situationists, like the rest of the "magical sixties," were recuperated, co-opted, the "ultimate" subverters ultimately subverted. Small wonder that Debord developed a veritable obsession with Clausewitz! A peculiarly galling fate awaited him, the universities, the telly, the cinemathèques, the museums, the galleries and, worse still, pop culture. "Those who make half a revolution..." indeed! It's tempting to say that few men ever so richly deserved to be hoisted by their own petard. Nevertheless, Debord's thinking (and that of the SI at large) no matter how flawed (or unflawed) he or they may have been personally retains a still dangerously *radioactive* core.

I hope the same may be said of *Heatwave* and *Rebel Worker*. The world is vastly more complex and more sinister in every way than it was forty years ago. A new, global and rampantly virulent super-authoritarianism is emergent. Dis-information and The Big Lie dominate. Truth is on the run, in disguise, difficult to recognise even when you see it. Consciousness in general has suffered from the official strategy of removing the core of meaning from *everything*. We are *all* being "dumbed-down" through a general and conscious jumbling of sense and meaning.

But it is important not to forget that this society has within it such massive contradictions that it is, *inevitably*, an unsound structure. No one can predict where or when the Old Mole of Revolution will break ground, but the *absolute certainty* is that she will.

The question today is still, as it was for us in the Sixties, not simply the desirability of changing the world, which is more and more acknowledged as a necessity: but *how* to change it?

Revolutionaries need to understand that no one person, no one group, has all the answers. Revolution is a collaborative project or it is nothing.   In the oft-quoted "Poetry must be made by all, not by one," Lautréamont presents in epitome (but with ever-expanding resonances of meaning) the *entire human project*. All projections for a communist social community should be tested against it in the *full* richness of *all* its implications!

Charles RADCLIFFE

Valencia, 2004

# HEATWAVE 1

July 1966 / 40 pages

*"It is characteristic of this kind of (revolutionary) movement that its aims and premises are boundless. A social struggle is not seen as a struggle for specific, limited objectives, but as an event of unique importance, different in kind from all other struggles known to history, a cataclysm from which the world is to emerge totally transformed and redeemed. This is the essence of the recurrent phenomenon or, if one will, the persistent tradition that we have called 'revolutionary millenarianism'."*

Norman Cohn, *The Pursuit of the Millennium*

Cohn really doesn't come close to expressing the full extent of the ebullient and intoxicated revolutionary exuberance with which *Heatwave* 1 ventured forth to follow up the delirious excesses of *Rebel Worker* 6, which Franklin and Penelope Rosemont and I had produced in one frenzied week of joyous April activity in London. Determined as I was to outstrip even its illustrious progenitor in wildness, imagination, untrammeled desire and a lust for unfettered freedom, it seems far better than anything else I ever did—to capture the feeling of those times. This is doubtless because, although I physically produced it on my own, it was in every other sense—in every important sense—a collective endeavour, its spirit still as much Chicago as London. Everything—the cover stock (exquisitely named Excalibur Merlinfire), the grab-bag graphics and the wilfully, ecstatically inflammatory content from my Chicago soul companions, my friends in England and myself—testified to our certain conviction that the improbable was already on our doorstep and the impossible but one dream-step away.

—C.R.

Charles Radcliffe's extravagant comic lettering added appreciably to *Heatwave*'s "slightly crazed" character

# HEATWAVE
## (Opening Statement)

**H**EATWAVE IS A NEW MAGAZINE, but it has a past. On May Day, the first Anglo-American edition of the Chicago wobblies' *The Rebel Worker* was published here because a group of us felt there was an audience in Britain for an experimental, perhaps slightly crazed libertarian socialist journal.

*The Rebel Worker* will continue to be published from Chicago; the London group will publish *Heatwave*.

*Heatwave*'s policy will obviously reflect the ideas of the people around the magazine but we are not a splinter group. We intend to cooperate, ideologically and practically with our Chicago co-dreamers; we see our task as being the same as theirs—to run a wild, experimental libertarian-socialist journal which will attempt to relate thought, dream and action whilst pointing out the significance of movements' ideas and creations which are ignored by the stagnant, *fin-de-siècle* revolutionaries.

*Heatwave* is not a rival to existing publications on the libertarian left, but an addition to the libertarian press and an extension of its ideology, both conscious and unconscious, into new fields. *Heatwave* wants to generate heat in every field. We believe the time is ripe for an explosion of revolutionary energy which would alter the face of the earth. *Heatwave* advocates the use of any and all means that may bring to a climax the crisis of capitalism and authoritarianism, and result in the total extinction of all forms of exploitation or authority.

The Incredible Hulk Says NO! Do you?
(*Heatwave* 2)

383

# THE PROVOTARIAT ACTS

AS THIS FIRST ISSUE of *Heatwave* goes to press, the Dutch capital of Amsterdam is still in a state of uneasy peace after a series of youth riots. *Heatwave* reprints here extracts from various newspapers which present the outlines of the explosion and leave a clear impression of the seriousness with which the Dutch authorities are treating their youth revolt. We think these extracts will interest our readers, provide a basis for further thinking on the "World Revolution of Youth" and also indicate that Holland, for many years regarded as being asleep, is gradually producing a wide-awake resistance to contemporary society.

"There were more arrests tonight in Amsterdam—the scene of rioting during the last two evenings—when sporadic outbreaks of vandalism by teenagers were reported. Both the State police and the Royal Marechaussee—the emergency reserve almost indistinguishable from the military—have been bought in today to supplement the hard-pressed and much-criticised city police. The reinforcements number about 1400...the minister of the Interior...announced that control of the Amsterdam city police would be put in the hands of three wise men...the demonstration by non-union building workers on Monday against the union's decision to take 2% of their holiday bonus for administrative expenses and the consequent death of Jan van Weggelaar, provided the sparks for the rioting and hooliganism which followed on Tuesday and last night. The troublemakers now are young teenagers...who are trying to identify themselves with a small group of intellectual youngsters who call themselves "Provos" (provocateurs) and who have over the last year been making a nusiance of themselves...the provos have written to all Amsterdam newspapers saying they dissociate themselves from the rioting by the youngsters."[1]

"Amsterdam is a police controlled city this morning. The three chief inspectors of police, K. Heijink, J.A. Valken, and A. Coppejlan have been charged by the government to restore law and order to the city and given a mobile brigade to do so. The Mayor...and the chief commissioner of police...are in disgrace after criticism of their handling of the situation, directed from both sides of the house during yesterday's emergency debate in the Dutch parliament. Amsterdam is a tense city today, sweltering under a humid summer haze after a further night of violence. Serious trouble is expected later today."[2]

"Amsterdam has remained quiet this weekend, thanks primarily to rain which has quenched the enthusiasm of the youngsters for seeking trouble in the streets. The police too have helped by keeping out of sight, for the mounted detachments, the steel helmets, long rubber truncheons, and straw shields were certainly game for provocation. The radio station devoted to pop music has been broadcasting a message recorded by one of the leading Provos, telling the boys to stay at home.[3]

"Weekend leave has been cancelled for four armoured infantry battalions, totalling 3,500 men, who will stand by throughout the country in the wake of this week's disorder in Amsterdam. The strengthening of the police and the setting-up of a central command for mobile forces in the city itself has already had an impact on the situation. The general impression today of the effects of the Government's decisions, endorsed by a large majority in the Lower Chamber of Parliament last night, is that gradually Amsterdam is returning to normal.... Last night, for the fourth night running there were disorders in the city...but substantially less in intensity and duration than before. There was, again some destruction and noisiness on the part of a band of what is called here "nozems" but the police were able to disperse the trouble makers, after closing the area to traffic."[4]

Charles RADCLIFFE

1. Michael Wall in *The Guardian*, Friday, June 17, 1966
2. *The Evening Standard*, Friday, June 17,1966
3. Michael Wall in *The Guardian*, Monday, June 20, 1966
4. Our Correspondent in *The Times*, Saturday, June 18, 1966

# THE GREAT ACCIDENT OF ENGLAND

I F LONDON HAS THE MOST WITH-IT, the most cultured, refined and studiously pleasure-seeking hips, then Liverpool has the most in number.

London hips have arrived. Liverpool hips have never been anywhere else. They wouldn't know what hip means but their tradition is hip from the roots. The future in Liverpool is pay-night for everybody, helped along on a bigger scale by sailors coming into town to blow three months pay in one week.

The bourgeoisie are represented by a few middle-aged ladies that nobody could envy for their happiness who make the fearful journey during daylight across town to George Henry Lees, sneering at girls in curlers and being nudged all over the pavements by the cowboys with them. But before night comes they have escaped safely in the red buses to Crosby clutching their little green bags with their hats pinned to their heads, leaving the world to darkness and to pleasure.

Because in Liverpool pleasure is all there is. The jobs are too much shit to fool anybody. Bombsites and slums demonstrate the meaning of the light and nice clothes and food and records in shop windows. In London there is money and miles and miles of the best material existence in the world and careers in famous firms all offering to seduce comfortably.

Liverpool has been ignored. It is the great accident of England where it is too late now for the weak to hold the energy of the beatboys, footy-fans, teddy boys, hitchhikers, comics, general piss-takers, artists, trainwreckers, intellectuals, wildcat strikers and scrubber birds....

John O'CONNOR

# THE EXPANDED JOURNAL
# OF ADDICTION (EXTRACT)

SIX YEARS OF OPIATE ADDICTION—six years of increasing terror; veins shrinking away, hiding. Brain encased in a shell of fear that nearly grew impenetrable. 3000 miles from home I began to die: 30-9-65 The drug is taking my body away from me. It is only by intensive investigation that I can find out what plans the drug have for my flesh. The normal lines of communication have been broken. Limbs fall asleep when not being used. Things fall from my hands without my knowledge. Organs shift positions, work independently for their new master. Am I to be completely replaced? Each day I lose control of another part of my body. My intestines, bladder, genitals, and right hand are already partly conquered. I must cut down.

7-10-65 Thoughts now originate in my stomach and must work their way up to my brain before they can be acted upon. Many times my brain acts as a solvent, dissolving many of the messages sent by my stomach before I know what they are. Vomiting would not rescue ideas from solution, for having not yet reached my brain, they would be unintelligible, scrambled code sparks of plans for escape.

15-10-65 Conditions have become almost intolerable. Not only am I unable to see any source of happiness here, but I am unable to see how I shall be able to bring about any such pleasant situations *ever*. I feel as if this journal is a monument to dulled senses, a tribute to the mind clouded by heroin and exploded by countless fears.

(That night, a shot, perspiration and lying on the bed thinking of sleep. Four hours later awakened by a knock: Two policemen come into the room. The taller one points his finger at my face, and the other comes up behind the head of the bed and holds me there, one hand on my throat, the other hand on my shoulder. The taller one grabs my legs at the knees and slides his hands down my legs to the ankles as he reaches my ankles, he lifts his hands from my body and displays hypodermic needles, syringes, droppers, heroin tablets; he turns his hands over, letting the objects fall to the floor. He rubs his hands down my legs again, somehow producing more heroin. I'm lying there, not moving, tears falling fast. Wanting to deny, but speechless. I don't understand any of it, where the heroin comes from, is it a conjuror's trick? I try to see the face on the other policeman, but I cannot. The taller policeman straightens up, looks at his colleague, and says "We have enough." He takes out a pistol and aims it at my head. I scream.)

24-10-65 I can't explain the period I'm moving into, but it's horrible. Have all my years of trying to get well been hopeless? If only I could get into a hospital immediately. I can't go on like this. I don't want to die—I'm afraid. Everywhere I turn there is fear. I don't know how to get home alive; I wouldn't know how to be happy once I did get back; I don't know how to be happy here. I'm lost.

9/10-11-65 There is no chance for me to see the people I've loved. Will I ever get back home? Thinking of R., almost crying, Did she give me up because I was an addict? All the letters I wrote to her, every night, the same dazed state—where is she now?

(My last shot. I awaken in the morning to find the streets covered with ice. I dress quickly for I must go and get more heroin, I step out on the sidewalk, slip, and fall. The ice is too slippery to get traction, walking is impossible. But no drugs, and I'm getting sick. I begin to crawl on my stomach, digging my fingernails into the ice. Hours later

I find I've only traveled a few feet; my fingers are bleeding. I'm vomiting. Will I die here, from the cold? Heroin, God, I need a shot;
Please, please, please. God, give me a shot. I look up, I'm surrounded
by mangled bodies, blood is pouring from them, flowing towards me,
I will drown.)

Paul GARON

## ONLY LOVERS LEFT ALIVE

WHAT HAPPENS WHEN THE BANALITY of consumer society
nails the brains of even the most devoted, efficient, satis-
faction-seeking consumer to the blank wall of reality?
What happens when, surrounded by the consumption-ephemera
without which life is known incorrectly to be impossible, everyone
discovers that he has everything there is to have and still has nothing,
that all objects are impoverished?

What happens?

Insurrection—or suicide. Social destruction or self-destruction
are seen as the only ways out of the madness of social alienation.
Perhaps because this realization was implicit in the book, Dave Wallis's
*Only Lovers Left Alive* was ignored—at least on this most important
level—by almost all the critics when it was first published (Anthony
Blond) in 1964. It is now fortunately reprinted in a paperback edition
(Pan: 3/6d) and its relevance has increased enormously.

The book begins—one imagines sometime in the 1960s—with a
sudden, all-enveloping outbreak of self-disregarding, self-destructive
despair among the adult "oldies." Within a matter of months (and
after a variety of reactions from official society), England is left to
the kids while the suicided corpses of the oldies pile up in the housing blocks, the streets, the offices and the factories. Over a short
period, society—already in a state of ruin, decay and imminent collapse before the oldies' dramatic rejection of themselves *en masse*—
disintegrates completely. As the orthodox patterns of government
break down, new elites arise to rule, but their control is isolated and

only effective within small confines of public docility. When the country is taken over by NATBINCO (The National Bingo Governing Council), the Council's actual power is limited to Bingo halls and their environs and is based on two simple factors—for oldies Bingo halls are the natural social meeting place and Easyway pills (used for suicide) are the Bingo prizes. NATBINCO can govern precisely because it has the means of satisfying the ultimate consumer need—nothingness, death.

Eventually the only adults left are the hopeless derelicts and social outcasts whose lives have always been so much fringe affairs that nothing on a social level can farther reduce them. (For such people consumer-mythologies have at best only the same appeal as horror-comics to middle class intellectuals or pop-art to the publishers of coffee-table books.)

Although the kids are not intellectually prepared for the collapse of megalopolitan civilization, they are emotionally prepared. The organisational structure of the old society is too complex, too inhuman, too irrelevant to their needs, too unreal for them to manage; its aims and principles are quite literally beyond their comprehension. Instead, their reactions are instinctive—spontaneous, violent and barbaric.

At first their behavior is a ruthless, speeded-up mimicry of that of the oldies in the old society: occupying flats and houses for single nights and then tearing them apart; taking a few pints of milk from a machine and then smashing it; riding motorcycles on high-octane fuel until they burn up. At first everything is expendable, but gradually, as the few genuine necessities become scarce, a crude barter system comes into being and, later still, gangs form and fight other gangs for supplies. Some of these gangs and groups are extremely libertarian.

The heroes of the book—the Seely Street Gang—meet one such group of marketers at Hammersmith Broadway. The marketers laugh at the gang's tiger-insignia and leather jerkins until the gang take them off; once they do so and join in the huge street dance around the market they are happily accepted. The Seely Streeters themselves are also relatively libertarian; the leadership is flexible and coercion seems to be unnecessary even though the gang is capable of behaving with an uninhibited, inflexible savagery which seems to surprise even themselves.

Some gangs however—like the Kings of Windsor who are eventually conquered through superior strategy by the Seely Streeters—are ruthlessly authoritarian and fascistic. The Kings capture weak kids—either from weak gangs or from amongst those mavericks who are neither organised into gangs nor able to survive on their own—and run Windsor as a slave "state," based on slave labor. However, it is neither the Kings, who have brute strength but no intelligence, nor the Hammersmith "beats," who have intelligence but insufficient strength, who survive, but the moderate, pragmatic Seely Streeters, who are tough enough to hold off other gangs, and intelligently adaptable enough to change with circumstances.

Eventually, their numbers drastically reduced by plague in Windsor, the gang finds their urban past totally useless. Out in the country they are faced with a simple decision; either become like the hayseeds (country kids) with their livestock and nomadically rough but basically less insecure life, or return once again to the plague-ridden south with its poisoned water, gutted towns and technological ruins. They choose to become herders, and throughout the summer following the collapse of the Windsor commune they journey slowly North. They winter in a once-hotel in Midlothian—now run as a cooperative by a clan who charge no rent but ask for help guarding, hunting and in the kitchens—where Kathy, the girlfriend of the gang-leader, Ernie, has her baby. Some months later there is the first great meeting of the Northern tribes and Ernie is elected a captain of tribes.

It should be pointed out—for the benefit of those people who wish to discuss the book without the bother of reading it—that this conclusion is open to varied interpretations. There is, in fact, no definition of how a captain is elected, nor under what terms he remains captain. The only definite program for the future is an annual trek south with investigations of cities and methodical searches for tools, maps, plans, textbooks (undoubtedly the most *essentially* authoritarian item on the list) and manuals on medicine, metal work, stockbreeding and building. Of course the birth of Kathy's child symbolically ends their youth and possibly symbolizes also a turning-point and perhaps return to the old life. It may, alternatively, symbolize the birth of a new society. Take your pick.

There are a number of serious criticisms that can be made of this book. It would, for example, be interesting to know what happens to various sections of youth who are barely mentioned here. Do *all* the architectural students, medical students, engineers, machine-operators, psychologists and revolutionary kids just die off, or are they killed? What happens to all the public school boys, trained as leaders of men, who should, according to the authoritarians, be at their best in just such circumstances? (Do we assume they die because, by virtue of class background, they were born old?) Do all the oldies do it? How do the gangs deal with toothache and illness, let alone everyday medical matters?

Perhaps, however, it is pedantic to discuss the book at this level—

it is emphatically not a book in the detailed, "sociological" tradition of English prophetic novels, like *1984* or *Brave New World*, and neither is it seen as a parable as was *Lord of the Flies*. It makes no attempt to present a consistent, overall view, being content simply to trace the reactions of a small group of people to circumstances which, in one form or another, seem a more and more probable outcome of contemporary society.

In fact the book, possibly for these reasons, has a reality missing from Orwell's grim masterpiece, Huxley's satire or Golding's nasty little piece of school-teaching. It would be a pity if it was missed simply because Wallis is not a particularly good writer and lacks the pedigree of the others.

The news that The Rolling Stones are to film the book—to Wallis' publicized displeasure—means that it will attract some of the attention it deserves. Much of the reaction will depend on the film. It could be excellent, even the first myth-film of the new revolution. If not, there is still the book which in itself may well turn out to be of seminal importance to the new revolutionism, its ideology, its mythology, and its folklore.

Ben COVINGTON

Bernard Marszalek: *The Family that Preys Together*
(*from Surrealism & Revolution*)

# THE SEEDS OF SOCIAL DESTRUCTION

ONE OF THE MOST INTERESTING aspects of revolt within the more advanced capitalist states since the war has been the emergence, one after the other, of groupings of disaffected youth. Such groups are not isolated phenomena; they exist wherever modern, highly bureaucratized consumer societies exist; in the USSR (stilyagi), France (blousons noirs), Britain (mods and rockers), in Holland (proves). They have little immediately in common but their implicit rejection of the positions allocated to them in society.[1] Let it be understood this is not primarily a class matter but a matter of the wholesale destruction and frustration of dreams.

Adults, be they left-wing journalists or right-wing magistrates,[2] can be relied upon to attack every aspect of youth rebellion, and most revolutionaries likewise see in it no more than a symbol, or perhaps symptom, of capitalist degeneracy; they address their antique pieties to the "problem" secure in the knowledge that it cannot really be important since it was never mentioned in the old revolutionary sacred texts.[3] They have, as befits the changers of societies, been content to condemn without understanding, showing only their own pitiful ignorance and shallowness.

By now it should be obvious—even to the traditional revolutionaries and other preservers of instinctive ignorance—that teen-groups are not merely the neatly tagged symbols of the alienation of whole sectors of youth from society at large but, in their extreme forms, are amongst the few groupings in society which have presented and continue to present an instinctive, sustained, and potentially shattering social threat to stable society. Youth revolt is not necessarily a panacea; neither is it necessarily the precursor of social revolution; rather a grim-humored reaction to the frustration implicit in this society and this manner of living. It is one of the few things in this society worth serious defense and support. I welcome youth's rage: I share it. I support their outrages because I wish for explosions infinitely more brain-peeling than in their wildest, most socially profane dreams.

In this article, a short and necessarily limited introduction, I want to note some aspects of the postwar unofficial youth movements in Britain.

## THE TEDDY BOYS

named after their preoccupation with Edwardian (1900–1914) fashion, were the first really cohesive postwar youth grouping in

Britain. Their emergence coincided with postwar "reconstruction" and also with the consumer invention of "teenage"; their number was increased by young adults whose youth had been lost in the "pre-teenage" austerity of the early postwar years. The extravagance of ted clothes (drape jackets with velvet collars, elaborate brocade waistcoats, "slim-jim" or "country and western" ties, "drainpipe" trousers with huge turn-ups and heavy car-tire shoes and later Italian "winkle-pickers"), the outlandishness of their hairstyles (massive duck's-arses at the back and Tony Curtis-type quaffs at the front and thick sideburns) and their aggressive arrogance earned them the immediate hostility of generations who had learned to see in thrift both a moral code and a social cement.[4]

Although many were only sartorial rebels, the teds, as a whole, were the most overtly violent of all youth groupings; many carried and used coshes, flick-knives, "cut-throat" razors and bicycle chains. They fought in gangs—usually a gang from one area against a gang from another area. They were broken up—either by each other or by the police. They were constantly harassed and arrested and fiercely criticized by every element of respectable society. Above all they were feared.

In fact the teds' attitudes were closer to those of their "elders and betters" than any subsequent groups. The teds were socially unacceptable precisely because they acted out the values of a world where force and corporate brutality were the *officially* postulated simple answers to all problems, because they were unable to accept the living death to which they had been so casually consigned, or the *non-sequiturs* of a society which demanded of its citizens an uncomprehending acceptance of dumb non-violence towards internal authority and ferocity towards officially-designated external enemies. For all their failings the teds were able to sense their real enemies. In the end, however, they were the easiest rebels (*en masse*) to deal with; they were progressively conscripted out of existence. They had their last real fling in the mid-fifties; they tore apart cinemas like avenging furies and jived in the aisles to the early rock'n'roll films. Now teds are comparatively rare, confined for the most part to the workingclass areas of the larger Northern industrial centers.

## THE TON-UP KIDS

...the coffee-bar cowboys, arrived shortly after the teds, the product of a rather more affluent society. Motorcycle gangs in Britain have been relatively small and relatively well behaved; nothing like California's Hells Angels has ever happened here. The appeal of motorcycles' speed, power, danger—has been almost exclusively confined to workingclass

youth. The middle-class kid typically has a small sports car; the workingclass cowboy has a bike—cheaper to buy, cheaper to run, easier to
tune, more exciting and less impersonal to use.[5]

Cowboys are not interested in converting anyone to their way of
life; they vary so much anyway that almost the only real points of contact between them lie in their leather clothes, their bikes and the attitudes forced on them by society's reaction to their enthusiasms. Some
gangs play "chicken" games—most often a race against a record on a
café juke-box—while others see their bikes mainly as an exciting
means of weekend escape from employment, dull urban environment
and nagging adults; speed is an optional, if delirious, bonus. Some
aim simply to bug the squares, either in mocking the police, who,
particularly in the provinces, are quite scared of the cowboys, or alternatively in burnups round middle-class housing estates, which stop
only when a high proportion of inhabitants are openly annoyed or,
better still, furious.

The cowboys, like most people, are unsympathetic to those who
do not share their preoccupations; they are not particularly sympathetic even to each other. Birds (girls) are usually seen as sexual bal-
last; something to hold the rear wheel on the road and to be shafted
afterwards. But again, most people are less honest about more or less
identical attitudes toward women. The ton-ups do not worry very
much about tragedy, either on a personal or cosmic scale. Most of
them have friends who "fucked-up" on a run; they are philosophical
about death; accidents are one way out of the fuck-up routine of
dead-end jobs in a dead-end society.

Most cowboys work simply to keep riding. They are not interested
in success; they live for weekends, days off, nights at the few "caffs"
where the owners do not see social responsibility in terms of keeping cowboys out. They accept, more or less, that one day they will opt
out and join the squares. Some compromise earlier than others by
joining ton-up[6] priests collecting for charity or organizing rock'n'roll
church services to spare the church the need to face its own total
redundancy.

Many ton-ups do seem compulsively respectable, appearing on
TV panel discussions about teenagers (with all the painful insistence
that under the rebellious exterior lurks humble goodness) and helping dear old ladies across the road. However, the last cowboy I knew
well told me that most tonups think "priests and that load of shit" every
bit as bad as the "snotties."[7] He seemed quite convinced that the rebellion went deeper, pointing out that the only reason ton-ups "doing
good" attracted attention was because it was so unusual. In any event

he was able to get rid of a large number of Spies for Peace leaflets at London's ton-up center, the Ace Cafe, after the 1963 revelations.

## THE BEATS

If the English beat movement had its roots in the beats of the USA, particularly as mythologized by Jack Kerouac, it soon developed its own character. Less interested in artistic achievement than American beats apparently were, the English beats were, for the most part, content to disaffiliate and leave it at that. They usually dropped politics, if they ever had any, when they went beat. The hard-core beat movement was probably never more than a few hundred strong, but its influence went much wider; over the last ten years any number of kids have gone beat. Once having done so it is inevitably more difficult to rebuild or prop up the illusions on which society functions.

The beats are possibly the gentlest of all the rebels; they have been attacked, even killed, in those interstices of society where they have been involuntarily forced into contact with social delinquency, but their main interest has been to keep moving, "cutting out" of any "scene" after a short time. Beat communities have been notably, and often chaotically, libertarian and notably short-lived. If the beat rebellion is essentially short-sighted (within an unfree society everyone, even the last committed disaffiliate, is unfree, and it is impossible to talk of rejecting society when to do so one has to be able to beg, borrow or steal the wherewithall for existence from people who, however reluctantly, continue to live within society), it is nevertheless magnificent in its nonchalant, long-haired contempt for "straight" society, and in its proud indifference to the dreary disgust of all the office-bound pen-pushers, bureaucrats and wearers of the regulation weeds of the living dead.

## THE BAN-THE-BOMBERS

The beat movement reached its height at much the same time as the anti-war movement—in the late fifties and early sixties; in fact the two groups were deliberately confused with each other by press and public. The more *deracine* elements of the anti-war movement often looked beat and often associated loosely with beats. The political adults distrusted beats, partly as scavengers and partly because they made the already too unrespectable political kids look even less respectable—this last factor may yet turn out to be the beats' most singular and most valuable contribution to British politics.

The young people who made the nuclear disarmament movement the largest and most influential youth movement in British history[8] were the post-Suez generation. The Aldermaston March, started two years after Suez in 1958, became the center of these young people's activities: a happy-serious carnival-protest, a gathering point for remarkably varied people ranging from hardened-arteried veterans of various Communist Party front-groups to dedicated Quakers, from old ladies with curious pasts to dedicated wild-eyed kids burning with self-sacrificing seriousness. After the second march the image was permanently fixed: youth.

A great deal of space has already been devoted to the ban-the-bombers and most people who read this will either know (or not care) why such a generation emerged, what it did, why and how it did it, and how in the end it declined and shattered into its myriad components as CND (Committee for Nuclear Disarmament) ceased to be umbrella enough for all the disparate ideas which had been attracted to it. CND educated youth—usually out of CND and into all the sad little splinter groups that are the only traditional, authentic, political, British, folk-art form.

### THE RAVERS

...were possibly the least distinct and, in their classic form, shortest lived group of all. They had some beat characteristics and rather tenuous connections with the anti-bomb movement, but their main preoccupations were jazz clubs and jazz festivals. This was the period when ersatz traditional (trad) jazz, as purveyed by Aker Bilk, Kenny Ball and others was inordinately popular. (Partly trad's popularity arose in reaction to the decline of the small fifties beat scene; it was easy to dance to, and jazz clubs were among the few places where teenagers could do more or less as they wished without adult interference. Partly it arose because the musicians did not take themselves too seriously and were often simply good-time ravers.[9] The raver movement took its "ideology" from the stale-ale-and-spermatazoa humour of the musician-ravers and its dress, if loosely, from that of the Acker Bilk band—"music-hall-*cum*-riverboat-*cum*-contemporary-folk-art" with CND-symbol-decorated bowlers, umbrellas, striped trousers, elegant jackets. The chicks had long hair and wore ban-the-bomb type uniforms (duffle coats, polo-neck jerseys very loose around the hips, and jeans). The ravers moved not only in the world of British "jazz," but also on the fringes of the beat and political worlds.

Chris Farley, now connected in some way with Bertrand Russell's Peace Circus, once interviewed a group of ravers at the Beauliea Jazz Festival for *Peace News*, and was obviously distressed by the fact that most of them had no political program beyond the election of Acker Bilk as Prime Minister. One West Indian observer[10] described them in 1964 as "mainly frantic English teenagers inspired in recent years to new heights of happiness by the indestructible and tireless *Negro 'faces' happiness habits* nightly in the West End. In their over-enthusiastic aping of Negro dances, over-indulgent drug-taking, they actually outdo their mentors in self-destruction—if not in jail sentences."

The ravers were, on the whole, distrusted by other groups with whom they came in contact; the beats used the term "raver" derogatorily, and the nuclear disarmers treated the ravers "superficiality," with superior amusement and occasionally annoyance. (The fact that many of the serious kids are now regretting their aloofness is a reminder that we all change.) The ravers, as such, died with the trad jazz boom but the "philosophy" continues and there are once again groups calling themselves ravers. The term has likewise retained its approbatory meaning after its frequent critical use by the CND generation.

## THE MODS AND ROCKERS

Began attracting attention in 1963; the mods as a developing group,[11] the rockers as a yet unchristened continuation of earlier ones: the teds and more particularly the ton-ups.[12] The mods (modernists) originally favored short hair, wool shirts, casual suede or corduroy jackets, lightweight ankle-length trousers and casual sneaker-type shoes—very much of the continental type. Mod girls wore collaborateur-type hair styles, drape leather overcoats and calf-length dresses which came up as time passed but were, in the early days, extended to ankle-length for visits to clubs, etc.

The rockers were the entrenched traditionalists of teenage fashion—long ted-style hair, sideburns, jeans with large turn-ups, leather jerkins or bum-freezer jackets and winklepicker shoes. The girls' clothes echoed those of the boys—at least of working hours. At work they were in the teenage fashion mainstream. Rockers were barely a group as such; they were put together by the mods as "them" figures—hot, breathy, archaic squares to the mods' ice cold, up-to-the-second hipsters.

In 1963 the first fights between the two groups broke out—in the City of London during lunch hours. What usually happened was that a group of mods began jeering at—and later bundling with—a rocker delivery boy. But such fights were nothing to those which broke out at the various seaside resorts during public holidays the following year. By then the mods were a large group and their outlook was formed.

In general they owed much to the West Indian hipsters (faces); much as the white-Negro hippies of the USA took the soul-ethos from the urban ghetto Negroes, so the mods reflected, in a slightly less conscious way, some of the patterns of British Negro existence. Their coolness, their drug-taking (primarily of the goof-ball/lidflip type at first), their musical taste, and many of their expressions (*e.g.*, "face") derived, more or less directly, from actual or fantasy-life patterns of the hip "Spades." (At least in this sense the mods were a sophistication of the ravers.)

The mods' rebellion was perhaps more experimental than any other groups' except possibly the beats and the disarmers—and the mods despised the rockers and others precisely because they were bedded in the past. "You can tell us by the way we walk—feet out. Rockers are hunched. We hope to stay smart forever, not shoddy like our parents." The mod distaste for parents and rockers was reciprocated. "I can't think why he turned out like this. We always gave him everything he wanted and we have good values for him to see"—the harrassed parent of an arrested mod. "Orgy—kids shagging birds all over the shop; all bloody sex and pills. It's no way to live"—a rocker on a typical mod party in a disused London house.

Mods, despite the time they spend decking out scooters with ephemera and accessories, have a less emotional relationship with machinery, and a less mechanical one with girls, than most rockers. For all that they are less tied up with "going steady" than the rockers. They distrust particularly the rockers' attempts to fit into adult society: "We don't talk politics or religion—we hate attempts to make religion with it. It's always rockers on these telly programs."

At the height of the mod "thing" in 1964, mod fashions were changing at break-neck speed. Beatle-type clothes had been exhausted, along with Beatle-music, by the end of 1963, and mod clothing, at the beginning of 1964, reflected the taste of the new London in-groups—The Rolling Stones, The Kinks, The Yardbirds. Later West Indian blue-beat music was "in" beyond the small circle of very hip faces with whom it had been *the* music for some time, before it too was overcome by the next enthusiasm.

The whole furious consumption program of the mods seemed to be a grotesque parody of the aspirations of the mods' parents, typically lower-middle or upper-lower-class suburban. The leaders of mod fashion were changing, and re-fashioning clothes overnight to keep up with each other; the situation became so desperate toward the end of the year that the reigning "faces" simply refused to allow new faces to take over. By the end of 1964 the hard-cult was over, although the mods still exist, largely as loosely-organized scooter gangs. There may still be a few minor mod–rocker skirmishes to keep blimpish magistrates busy and furiously absurd in those quiet seaside towns where the bourgeois go to living-die like hanpy squires, and the kids go to explode the unholy peace of a death structure. But if the heyday of the mods is probably over the youth rebellion is not, as is indicated by the recent case of the Matlock Hills Trogs[13] and many other continuing elements of humanizing chaos.

### THE FUTURE: CAN'T GET NO SATISFACTION

The various youth groupings I have discussed are not part of a cohesive movement; some presented a violent threat to good order, some presented an ideological challenge, some merely an annoyance. Their attitudes were and are varied: the teds a partial reflection of the violence of adult mores; the ton-up kids rebelling at those points where their will crossed society's; the ban-the-bombers a complete rejection of their birthright (the majority were almost certainly warbabies (the movement, perhaps significantly, arose in the first of the postwar years in which there was no conscription); the beats rejecting everything; the ravers living for kicks; the mods annoyed and determined not to emulate the shoddiness of their parents.

The backgrounds too were different, although attempting to classify heterogeneous youth groupings is dangerous. Broadly, the ton-ups, rockers and teds were workingclass. The ban-the-bombers were broadly middle-class. The mods, beats and ravers come between the two. But class origins, for the most part, are irrelevant to the youth revolt. Between the groups there there was and is little contact. Teds fought each other, mods fought rockers, ban-thebombers and beats co-existed, ban-the-bombers hardly ever associated with those right outside politics, except, rather awkwardly as preachers. There has been some interchange between the groups. A number of beats came from the cowboys and, rather curiously, became mods, typically at that stage when mods were discovering British r'n'b. The art-school beats were not only the first r'n'b audiences—listening to the early protagonists of the music like Cyril Davis and Alexis Korner—but became the first real popularizers of the form. As mods adopted some of the more obvious characteristics of the beats, so some beats became, almost by accident, mods.

All these movements can be see as the groping of youth toward explosive self-expression and show that young people are not content simply to become the well-ground sand in the joints of a crumbling, oppressive, adult-delinquent society. They are expressive both of consumption-crazed society and of rebellion against corrupted mores; both a visible and audible symbol of a society whose effusions, institutions and attitudes are hopelessly disoriented and no longer completely intelligible or logical to anyone, least of all to those authoritarians who have unconsciously create them, and a reminder that it cannot long continue without the chaotically engineered safety-valves finally breaking down and shattering both their own Heath Robinson ingenuity and the society they protect. In a society which has everything, everyone wants nothing.

What is important about the youth revolt, at this stage, is not so much *what* it is but *that* it is; that in some ways and however hesitantly, however unsurely, youth recognizes its exploiters and is, if only temporarily, prepared to pay them off in a currency they can understand. The explosions are imperfect and impermanent; the rage is fused and canalised; the violence is exploited and utilized; the dreams become advertising slogans. But the revolutionary, of all people, must be able to sympathize with and encourage such revolt; if nothing else it increases the bourgeois, suicidal paranoia which is, in a very real sense, the revolutionary's best friend. The suburban mental derelict, his world threatened by the phantoms of disquiet—car-tires deflated, windows smashed, flowers stolen, sleep destroyed, business threatened by the *Conspiracy*, status constantly challenged by neighbors and business colleagues, wife at the mercy of ravaging back-door tradesmen, sanctum permanently challenged by nameless youth tyrannies—sees in all youth a savage innocence and a mindless threat to his well being; his mind (torn already by the frustrations of working into an emotional gutter), his body, (obese on the non-foods of a death-oriented society, his prestige (so intangible, so dependent on irrelevancies and reactions which can never be based on concrete evidence) are not enough to address the challenge.

It is this disquiet-factor that all rebel youth have in common, that threatens the carefully moulded suburban fantasies whose function is as a contraceptive against reality: sexual, social and cultural. It is this, together with the unrepressed violence and viciousness of those in authority dealing with youth rebellion, that should have told the revolutionaries they were dealing with rather more than a symptom of the degeneracy of a system. For the facts proclaim that youth revolt has left a permanent mark on this society, has challenged assumptions and status and been prepared to vomit its disgust in the streets.

The youth revolt has not always been comfortable, valid, to the point or helpful. It has, however, made its first stumbling political gestures with an immediacy that revolutionaries should not deny, but envy.

Charles RADCLIFFE

1. At least in sensing this much the authorities show themselves more aware of the reality than most revolutionaries.

2. For example Paul Johnson and J.B. ('Call me Fathead') Priestley in *The New Statesman* and the magistrates who dealt with the teds, mods, rockers and ban the bombers.

3. The reaction of the Communist Party to USSR youth rebels is instructive and hilarious; Moscow teengangs are dismissed either as 'high spirited student-types' or 'bourgeois-minded, jazz-corrupted decadents.'

4. Ted fashions were a curious throw back to the Good Old Days (otherwise known as GOD) when gay irresponsibility was the chief social virtue and wars were theoretically still heroic, romantic and colourful. They were also a powerful reaction against the drabness of the war and post-war years. They were a conscious imitation, by working class youth, of aristocratic fashions at the last point in time when a really rigid class (and parallel fashion) structure existed. Had the teds been Edwardians they would have been unable to wear such clothes. In an odd way therefore these clothes seem to have been both a case of following upper class fashion ideas (albeit archaic ones) *and* snubbing the upper class by doing so.

5. I remember doing the ton (100 m.p.h.) with a cowboy on the A.1 in Durham; after stopping the cowboy rubbed down his bike and checked it for damage, treating it with a care and respect that really astounded me.

6. Though members of the famous 59 Club—a respectable priest-ridden rocker club—were at the 1964 Clacton riots.

7. One of a wide variety of designations for the police—an abbreviation of 'snot-gobbler.' Other terms include the slightly square 'rozzer,' 'shit-sucker,' 'copper' (square), 'gestapo,' 'fuzz,' 'law.'

8. Anyone who doubts that CND was primarily a youth organization should read contemporary reports of Aldermaston marches.

9. See, for example, George Melly's delirium-fest autobiography, *Owning Up* (Weidenfeld & Nicolson)

10. C. Lindsay Barrett in *Revolution*, January, 1964.

11. They were actually beginning as early as 1962.

12. The two terms are now used synonymously.

13. See *Freedom*, April 30, May 21, May 28.

Brief Bibliography: *Generation X* (Library 33)
*Only Lovers Left Alive* (Pan)
*Rave Magazine*
*Mods, Rocker and the Revolution* (*Rebel Worker* Pamphlet 1)

# THE LONG HOT SUMMER

SUNDAY, JUNE 12, AT ABOUT DUSK, in a tavern on Division Street in the center of Chicago's Puerto Rican ghetto, a misunderstanding arose between a longtime resident of the neighborhood—a Croatian, the newspapers later intimated—and a young "Spick" (white lingo for Puerto Rican). As is the case with verbal clashes among slightly intoxicated men, this one escalated into a physical engagement, and, again according to role, the tavern owner pushed the contending parties outside into the sidewalk and called the police.

Two cops appeared on call and confronted a group of young, animated Puerto Ricans, immediately concluded that this was a gang of "Spicks" and, acting on that assumption, attempted to break up the group, without the slightest understanding that drinking partners are hardly likely to break up on the absurd orders of two dumb cops, who undoubtedly were protecting the Croatian's right to be boisterous at their expense. The details are lost, probably forever, but one fact is certain—the cops decided that they had to shoot someone, and, with unequalled tactlessness, did so.

With nothing to look forward to but Monday's back-breaking, low-paying crud job, and with years of pent-up frustration released by the blood of a friend, the young men began to defend themselves against this assault by the guardians of "law and order" and before, the two cops could call for help, their squad-car was a prime target for stones, bottles, loose bricks and whatever else could be thrown with ease. Revenge, combined with elements of a carnival-like spirit, captured in demonic ferocity the hundreds upon hundreds of Puerto Ricans who, in summer, nightly take walks along Division Street to visit neighbors and talk to friends. (The fly-paper mass media has limited appeal to these people who understand little English; their recreation is the enjoyment of conversation, an art lost by the bourgeoisie who, as a class, view it with at least a slight suspicion, as they do every atavistic oddity).

The sight of a cop car was the only stimulus needed for a barrage of bottles and rocks. And, as more cops cried into their microphones for help, the whole shattering intrusion of desire progressively accelerated. Before an hour had passed, the original barroom argument faded into irrelevancy as hundreds of helmeted cops were firing into the crowds that had gathered at every street corner and alleyway; from rooftops and windows missiles landed upon squad-cars, cops and reporters. Snipers appeared sporadically and a few molotovs were hastily devised, but none too effectively used.

The frenzy seized the souls of a car full of "outsiders" (Negroes from the South Side), by chance passing by, who stopped immediately to help turn over a squad-car and set it afire, to lend an orange asymmetry to the two other cop cars which were captured from fleeing police and burned.

Several Canine Unit cars arrived and the dogs set upon the crowds, but this tactic backfired, for it only intensified the disgust of the people, which continued to be vented far into the night. The total arrested numbered fifty, with, thankfully, only one person wounded: the original young man in the story.

Monday's morning editions blasted the "riot" across their front pages, and radio and television carried detailed reports, all of this having a rather shocking effect upon bleary-eyed morning commuters, who read astonishing reports of street battles in Chicago next to dispatches from Saigon and Amsterdam, describing similar events. The shock was intensified because, while the conflict was flaring, the media, under police request (!), kept the story under wraps, to prevent probably the spread of fighting and the ultimate destruction of the City of Chicago.

(Monday afternoon a madman left a group of his fellow inmates who were taken to Comiskey Park to watch a Major League baseball game and boarded a subway train and rode to the Loop where he entered one of the larger banks and robbed it of several thousand dollars. He then proceeded to his brother's home to surprise him with a gift of friendship, as only a true brother would do from time to time. His brother however simply called the cops and turned him in.)

Throughout the day city officials responded with their usual brace of moldy, obfuscatory platitudes, all of which were devastatingly exploded into their parenthetical limbo Monday night when a second battle ensued as police, with characteristic stupidity and brutality, charged a group of persons who assembled after a peace rally. As the battle raged, ten thousand people gathered along Division Street for more than a mile to witness typical demonstrations of the Chicago Police's "crowd control tactics," which involved charging groups with riot-clubs, arresting people (35), and shooting others (7 persons were shot Monday night.) But Monday also brought forth far more sniper fire and many more molotovs.

The sun, Tuesday morning, was reflected a million times by the bits of glass that covered the sidewalks and streets, the only evidence of a disturbance. The regular Captain of the area was put on furlough because of a poor heart, and his replacement, a young Captain on the make, began acting like a military commander of occupying forces, which in fact he and his men were. All day little groups engaged in conversation were broken up, people were pushed off porches and into homes, taverns were closed and a tense peace maintained. Only the remarkable restraint of the people kept Tuesday relatively calm, despite the informally imposed martial law.

The outbreaks of violence stunned all the "human relations experts," some of whom reported to the Police Department only five days before that the large Puerto Rican (60,000 estimated) and Mexican communities were not sources of trouble. What must have stunned them even more, however, was the ability of local people to remain cool-headed despite constant police violence. Only one incident needs to be told: on Monday night two Spanish-speaking social workers attempting to calm the crowd were severely beaten by the cops who thought they were inciting violence. Those originally blamed for the riot Sunday, the gang members, were actually responsible for containing much of the anger of their friends in the face of pistol-shooting cops and killer-dogs. Given the potential, only one building was burned and, this being an apartment building, it was very likely unintentional; and no cops were shot.

The Puerto Ricans voiced one demand that, given a highly bureaucratized society, was revolutionary in its implications: they wanted to control their neighborhood. And Monday this was the sole demand—the cops should be removed immediately! Naturally, the forces of authority cannot act in a manner which puts their entire irrational behavior into proper perspective, so the cops remained to incite more violence.

Just as the managers of factories don't really know the factory, the mayors of America's largest cities hardly know the cities they rule. The whole point of the relatively small skirmish is that by the end of this summer they won't have much of their cities left to know.

Bernard MARSZALEK

(*Rebel Worker* 3)

# DAYTRIPPER! A VISIT TO AMSTERDAM

IMMIGRATION OFFICIALS EYE LONG HAIR suspiciously: they want to check my ticket to ensure that I will fly out again tonight. They tell me I must be on the 10 o'clock flight, as booked. Unfortunately I have no choice anyway.

Everyone talks of provos and riots. The airport is dull and provincial, and it is difficult to believe anything can ever really have happened here. I take a coach into the city centre—curiously all the notices in the coach are in English. The city is flat but beautiful, fanning out from the centre with "islands" of houses and narrow streets, linked across the framework of narrow canals by narrow bridges. The houses are old, beautiful and somehow airy. (I am already affected by romanticism.)

The recent riots add a curiously ambiguous touch to Amsterdam's essentially placid, patient nature. The town seems full of kids, police and promenaders. To a Londoner everything seems to move at half-speed; people have time to walk and talk in the streets. It is a city still small enough for people to live within the centre: the provos talk of urban crisis, smoke control, depopulation of the city centre. They are entirely right, of course, but they obviously have acute environmental consciousness. (In London we have already tolerated the almost total depopulation of the city centre, the construction of giant, community-destroying highways into the city centre and an air of breathtaking, poisonous filthiness, without apparently even noticing.

If the very nature of Amsterdam, built on water and with only very narrow streets, prohibits the grotesque irresponsibility which has marked London planning and secured for London its place among the truly inhuman structures of the world, it is nevertheless absolutely right that the provos should worry about such problems now, before it is too late. Even if they have nothing else to tell the world the saving of Amsterdam would be enough to justify them.)

I walk into a bookshop selling English paperbacks, China-friendship literature, pamphlets on Vietnam, books on surrealism and a few New Directions books. The guy behind the counter has a head covered in a band-aid.

\* \* \*

In the street outside a kid, dressed predominantly in white, came up to me after seeing my London nuclear disarmament pin and asked whether I was an English provo? Rather than confuse the issue I said yes. He asked a lot of questions about the anarchists, CND, the

Committee of 100. I told him the anarchists, as such, were largely irrelevant, CND absorbed into all that is wrong and the Committee of 100 without the money to bury itself. I asked him about the provos and, in particular, their public dissociation from last week's rioting. (This worried me a great deal when I read about it in the English press, seeming to be a classic example of "intellectuals" behaving irresponsibly, isolating themselves from the physical consequences of their effective intelligence and, in this case, incitement of youth.) He thought that perhaps the issue was too simple for the provos—"the real provos were in the riots." It was simply a case of Amsterdam's youth against authority.

The provos disapproved because they did not want violence which made authority stronger. I said I considered that many of the provos' statements had violent overtones and violent implications. He agreed but said the provos were not very consistent. Were the provos who demonstrated with building workers on Monday "official" or "unofficial"? He said they were "official" but that their actions were the direct inspiration of the later "unofficial" youth riots. Was the provotariat disillusioned with the provos? He did not think so; most of the provotariat acted with limited understanding of the provos' actual position. A number of people who admired the provos stopped rioting when the provos made public appeals for the rioters to stay home.

Further riots—perhaps soon, perhaps later in the year—were inevitable. The provotariat was frightened but not over-awed by the action of the authorities. By this time we had a small group of kids around us and I started giving out copies of *The Rebel Worker*. "What is Burn, baby, burn?" "What is IWW?" A couple of fuzz (I suspect actually members of the Royal Marechaussee) moved in on us. Some of the kids dispersed but most hung around, ignoring the fuzz. Questioned, I said that I was English. "Why are you in Amsterdam?" "Just to look around, see the Dutch." "How long are you here?" "One day." They drifted away without checking *The Rebel Worker*. The kids were, however, interested in it.

* * *

I wander through the streets. For someone increasingly stoned sky-high on the possibilities (and no longer sure whether it will all end in social outrage or nervous collapse) Amsterdam is perhaps the most beautiful city in Europe. Not only well-planned but, almost overnight, the capital of youth-rebellion. The kids are the most self-assured I have seen anywhere. They have little of the Londoners' sullenness and their rebellion is much more extroverted. They move around in loose gangs or else storm through the streets in twos and threes on bicycles and mopeds. Amsterdam is designed for the guerrilla warfare of provocation. The streets, at least outside the immediate city centre, are too narrow for cars to move really fast. Mopeds, on the other hand, hardly need to slow down at all. The town is full of beats and the extraordinarily decadent Dutch "mods," decked out in fantastic floral suits.

There is a fantastic impression of tranquillity to which the riot police, moving around town in small Volkswagen microbuses, add a strange distorting effect. Kids do not take very much notice: they seem slightly elated by the continuing concern of the authorities as to whether they will explode again. (In Amsterdam casualness seems a way of life. The Dutch work a 45-hour week but under nothing like the pressures facing a Londoner.)

I had lunch with a young, middle-aged man (the actual reason for my business trip to Amsterdam) who gave me impressions of the last week in Amsterdam. He was not sure whether the provos were responsible for the riots; he thought their ideas and statements probably gave the rioters a justification. The provos, in his view, are quite respectable. "They just want their happenings, white bicycles instead of cars in the city, and smoke control. Many people agree with them. One of them was elected to the city council with 13,000 votes (the Dutch voting age is 21). They have good ideas. They stop Holland from going to sleep, which is necessary. I think they will grow. In ten years, twenty years, they might even be the government of Holland!

What do older people think of youth rioting in the streets? "Mostly shock...but maybe that is necessary. Of course no one in Holland likes riots—people and property get hurt. The provos are believed by many when they say they have nothing to do with riots, but they make strong statements, and people expect them to be responsible for strong actions."

Why do people object to the white bicycle plan which would mean that the city centre would be served by public transport and white bicycles which can be freely used, and left wherever the rider wishes to await the next rider. "Mainly it is the police who object. They are anti-theft...they must protect property. These bicycles would be no one's property. Also, of course, people with cars do not want to ride bicycles in the city. They want to show their cars."

After lunch I make my way further over to the West-side of the city, attempting to find PROVO'S offices at Valkenburgstraat. (It is fairly easy to find the way in Amsterdam: the town is small and its layout makes it easy to move quickly in any direction.) I have a number of questions I want to ask: after my previous conversations

407

I am anxious to hear what they say about their "betrayal of the provotariat," which is now the way it looks to me.

I walk up narrow streets, filled with bars and shops selling an even wider selection of pornography than can be found in those little specialist shops in Soho, which proudly announce their medical and psychological interest in flagellation, the circumcision rites of Western civilisation and various other oddities of vital importance to us all. There are plenty of prostitutes—many of them seem startlingly young but perhaps they are simply amateurs. I notice a surprising number of Negroes—mostly very, very cool. They seem much hipper than most West Indians, better dressed, more self-confident. They do not seem to attract the sneaky, half-envious, half-hating glances they would get in London. They are, I imagine, more like the really hip spades of the American ghettoes.

As I move further West the town begins to look more decayed. On the blank walls of buildings are Provo leaflets and posters. Provocation No. 10, which features crude but delightful sketches of cars, exhaust fumes and free-form BRAM! BRAM! BRAM! sound effects, catches my attention. The provo approach is infinitely more imaginative than anything we have done in London (that, at any rate, must now be changed). The walls have painted all over them slogans advertising rock-'n'-roll groups—The Monks, The Sailors, The Croes, The Houw (The Who??), The United Sounds, The Idols, The Amplifiers, The Keys, The Ways. (Unfortunately I did not get the chance to hear any groups play but judging from the frequent pictures of The Rolling Stones in the Dutch pop press I guess that Dutch rock is ex-American-via-Britain.)

By mistake I found myself in the Lazarus Market. It was very, very hot and sticky, and this, together with the kaleidoscopic impressions of the city, made both my concentration and energy wilt. I sat down on a box in the market, next to a beat, who talked briefly to me in French. Our conversation was limited to simple French, simple philosophy and metaphysical grunting. He also got a copy of *The Rebel Worker*. He was amused by the explanation of the title. (We are not workers: we rebel against being workers: we are therefore rebel workers.) He was totally disinterested in the rebellion of the provotariat. He liked Amsterdam because the living and the pot was cheap. It is now, he said, the new European centre for youth. It used to be London but the authorities in London didn't like foreign beats, so they now go to Amsterdam instead. He said to me that there was no point in returning to London, that I would do better to stay forever in Amsterdam where no one minds.

(In this part of town everyone seems to be wide-awake; even small kids wear battered denim suits. A wrecked van up against the wall, propped on stones, is crammed full of old crates. The market itself is hot and sandy. None of London's pushing grind. I thought this sort of placid ease was a feature of only provincial France—I suspect it exists on this scale in no other major Western capital.)

I find Provo's offices: there is no answer when I ring the bell but the front door is open, and I walk up perilously steep stairs to No. 4 at the top. On the landing a pair of white jeans hang out so I knock on the first door I see. Someone shouts so I walk in. The room is small, bare but light. A slight whiff of fish-scent occasionally wafts in through the window. Posters of Castro and nuclear disarmament symbols on the wall. Inside there is a kid of about 15 and two chicks about the same age. His hair is longer than most English kids of that age. They all seem totally turned-on; rather in the manner of some of the kids who used to cram the Committee of 100 offices and who were, in terms of personal liberation, far further out than any of their so-called mentors. Unfortunately we converse only in an erratic, if flexible, combination of Dutch, English and French. After an hour I get a further address and leave.

Later in the day, in a small, attractive house in Karthuiserstraat— described by *Le Figaro* as "certainly the most wretched house in the street" in "one of the most crumbling parts of the town"—I found Roel van Duyn, editor of *Provo*-Amsterdam. He pointed out a headline in the evening paper: "VAN HALL SAYS PROVOS RESPON-SIBLE." Were they? Van Duyn said perhaps they were: "The *blousons noirs* come into Amsterdam because of what they hear about us." Was it true that the provos dissociated themselves from the riots? He said they dissociated themselves from the riots because they were caused by *blousons noirs* from outside town, who had no political consciousness and were violent.

The Amsterdam *blousons* had been "educated" by the provos but this had not so far been possible with the suburban ones. But surely, I asked, Provo's appeal to the international provotariat called upon all elements of the provotariat to help provoke a crisis of authority? Surely this was what had happened in Amsterdam? He admitted a crisis of authority had been provoked by the riots but, like his colleague Bernhard de Vries who addressed London meetings last week, said the provos disapproved of this unless it was politically motivated and did not believe in violence against authority because it both justified and encouraged authority to increase the strength of repression. What do the provos want?

According to Roel van Duyn: a democratization of society, white (disarmed) police, a mayor elected by direct election rather than chosen by the central government, the curbing of air pollution, the prevention of urban depopulation, white bicycles, a squatter movement for the unoccupied houses, the provocation of authority so that it would reveal its true, anti-social nature.

Roel van Duyn admits the programme is reformist, "but we live in this society!" The 'white police' plan is for police to be disarmed like English police (amongst the most sophisticated forms of authoritarian control any government has ever been allowed to get away with). Eventually they would become trained social workers. (Anyone who wants to check out how fast the notions of authority can change in this respect ought to search out *Newsweek* for June 27, which shows just this *trend* happening in the USA.) I told him I was very confused by these ideas. I thought some excellent, others very naive. I was surprised that an anarchist group should stand for city council election. Roel said that it is to observe authority from inside.

Was there no risk of being thus absorbed by tame authority, being maintained as tame rebels? Roel thought the danger very small. He told me he would probably be doing a six week jail sentence shortly (unless his appeal was successful) for publishing an inflammatory article in *Provo* 7. (I was unable to ascertain whether this was the one calling for the physical destruction of the petty bureaucracy.) I told him I thought many provo statements were inflammatory and I was hardly surprised that the kids took them so seriously, or that provos were blamed for riots.

Roel said the more extreme statements were essentially provocative satire rather than direct statement. I said I felt quite honestly that the provos had unconsciously betrayed the provotariat. He no more agreed than did Bernhard de Vries in London when I made the same point. I said I felt it was the provos' task to explain the riots even if they felt unable to physically support them. Certainly to denounce riots which were the provos' philosophical responsibility seemed not only naive but potentially dangerous. "We did not denounce them—we dissociated from them because they served no purpose." (In London Bernhard de Vries said he could understand them but seemed surprised by suggestions that he might have acted as explainer of the riots, even if he felt compelled to say they had nothing to do with the provos.)

As I make my way back to the Central Station from the East-side of town, I pass through a square in which an old man with a guitar begins to play and sing, in a superbly demonic, cracked voice. Immediately he is surrounded by kids, some clambering on top of post-boxes, dancing and hamboning as the old man plays and sings.

Whatever the provos say or think, they seem to be in an ironic position: they are the only group—apart from Jonathan Leake's delirious saboteurs of social peace, The Resurgence Youth Movement—who make youth revolt their point of departure. Their manifesto is quite definitely the best and most interesting statement on youth revolt to come out of the Continent. On the other hand they seem astonishingly keen to deny the implications and consequences of their thought. The irony is, ultimately, that the first group of revolutionaries (of any sort) to get through to teenagers (and particularly the type of teenagers who are usually totally ignored by "serious" revolutionaries) are, at the point of crisis, prepared to turn their backs.

I talked to a long-haired kid wearing the brightest floral suit I have ever seen, at the airport. He was bugged as hell, having to look after his very-kid brother who blew Pepsi-Cola bubbles out of his bottle over everything and, in between, laughed deliriously. When will the next riot happen? "When we feel like it. Authority needs time to prepare for fighting us but we just come when we want. We always win. Riots, they don't cost nothing for us. Authority pays." Did he read *Provo*? "Sometimes I see it. I like *Provo* and provo happenings. *Provo* gives us cause and we enjoy rioting. There will be more riots."

I do not recall ever having been so sorry to leave a city. I like Amsterdam and, despite my reservations, admire the provos. (In the end I find I agree with the husband of provo "leader", Irene van der Weetering, when he says: "It's a heart-rending, muddle-headed organisation.") It is a nice final touch to fly in over Clacton after visiting the capital of the World Revolution of Youth—Amsterdam—beautiful, gentle, patient town raped by the savage hip of the provotariat.

Charles RADCLIFFE

The Majesty of the Law
(*Heatwave* 1)

411

# *HEATWAVE*

Britain's wildest, most incandescent, experimental libertarian journal attempts to relate thought, dream and action, whilst pointing out the significance of movements, ideas and actions ignored by the traditional left. Blowing this year's blues, the first issue contains 40 pages of articles and cartoons on the youth rebellion, the Provos, Liverpool and New York's Resurgence Youth Movement and a stop-press analysis of the Puerto Rican riots in Chicago.

# *HEATWAVE*

is available at 2s. a copy, post free (30c for USA) with discount terms operated for booksellers and bulk-sellers, and subscriptions available at a reduced rate of 6s. ($1.00 for USA) for four issues. Heatwave will be published quarterly. All enquiries to

## HEATWAVE,

## 13 REDCLIFFE ROAD, LONDON, S.W.10,

## UNITED KINGDOM.

A full-page notice of *Heatwave* in *Anarchy* 66 (London, 1966)

# HEATWAVE 2

October 1966 / 36 pages

*Bring me my bow of burning gold:*
*Bring me my arrows of desire:*
*Bring me my spear: O clouds unfold!*
*Bring me my chariot of fire!*

—William Blake—

Chris Gray and I joined the Situationist International just before *Heatwave* 2 appeared. At the time I considered it a substantial step forward from *Heatwave* 1, better produced and marked by a growing "theoretical maturity" as we moved into the situationist fold, without losing too much of the high spirits which had led to the first issue being sold out inside a month. Our editorial, "All or Not At All!" and the centrepiece on "The Provo Riots" revealed the strong and still largely beneficial Sit influence, as did the reprint of "Unitary Urbanism." Looking back now I am more conscious of the losses

413

involved. We did include, mostly towards the back of the magazine, the Chicago Surrealists' tract, "The Forecast Is Hot!" (which became one of the Un-tied Kingdom's most widely reprinted revolutionary documents), *Resurgence*'s "Guerrilla Manifesto," a cartoon by Norrie MacLue (Uel Cameron), Franklin Rosemont's "Landscape With Moveable Parts," and the intrusion of several Marvel superheroes and villains. *Heatwave* 2 was also still littered with plentiful very non-situationist graphics. However, as our serious "situationism" tightened its grip, all these turned out to be a requiem for a "madder" (and, in hindsight, vastly more exhilarating) past. As indeed did *Heatwave* itself. Although a third issue was mooted, several articles drafted and a cover designed, it was not to be. I had little idea that the magazine's thrilling and incandescent trajectory would be so brief.

—C.R.

Charles Radcliffe: *Under the Pirates' Banner*
(*Heatwave* 2)

# ALL OR NOT AT ALL!

WE ARE LIVING THROUGH THE BREAK-UP of an entire civilization. Contemporary society has only one foundation—
its own inertia—the last vestiges of religion and ideology
cannot conceal the extent of our mass-alienation. Nothing means anything any more. There seems to be no escape from the isolation and
senselessness of our lives. For all of us the abyss seems likely to open
at any moment. We are all alone in a world that has become one huge
madhouse.

Nowhere is there an adequate explanation of what it is we go
through every day. The traditional revolutionary movement to which
desperate people might once have turned, has long since been integrated
in the *status quo* and is no longer distinct from the rest of the bureaucratic machine. At best it is simply the vanguard of bureaucratic effi-
ciency-reform. Nowhere does there exist a theoretical and analytic basis
from which the increasingly unbearable contradictions of our daily
life can be examined, attacked and destroyed—a basis exposing our
modern poverty and revealing our possible wealth.

In isolation and anguish, innumerable people are becoming aware
of the poverty of their own lives—of the total disparity between their
real subjective desires and the lives they are forced to lead, of the total
disparity between the richness of life now possible and the mass-produced mini-life imposed on everyone by the Welfare State.

Over the last decade, *a new revolt* has begun to break out in all
the highly-industrialized countries of the world, a revolt associated
particularly closely with both the wildcat strikes and with the attitudes
of contemporary rebel youth. This revolt is now out in the open: agitators and saboteurs are on the streets. The whole of official society
(cops and psychiatrists, artists and sociologists, anarchists and architects) has tried to suppress, distort and re-integrate the phenomena of
this, their crisis.

It is still at an early stage. (Last month a twenty-year old set fire
to a railway goods depot in Sheffield, causing close on a million pounds
worth of damage; when interrogated he said that he had "wanted to
see a little blaze"). But it is breaking out everywhere: the acts still lack
a real perspective and a coherent form of action. They are, in fact,
half-symptoms of crisis, half acts of rebellion. It is in this context that
we intend to act as a catalyst; to take part in the transformation of this
new revolt into a new revolutionary movement.

The first thing to be criticized is the crock of shit passed off as criticism. Opposition has degenerated into a series of disparate and fragmentary protests—against nuclear war, against colonialism and racial discrimination, against urban chaos, *etc.*—lacking any grip on the whole of modern society and presenting no serious challenge to the dominant set-up. *What should be criticized is, on the contrary, our normal everyday experience of life.* It is this that is so boring, disgusting and senseless. Why worry about the risk of humanity immolating itself in a nuclear holocaust when everyone, everywhere, sacrifices their real nature, their real desires, their real will to live every minute of every day?

All that we can see anywhere is a grotesque travesty of human life, half nightmare and half burlesque: a degraded labor we never chose in order to produce an empty, passive, isolated leisure we never wanted. Life has been reduced to living death. We reject the whole system of work and leisure, of production and consumption, to which life has been reduced by bureaucratic capitalism.

Put in different terms: it is the concept of *total revolution* which has been lost. It has degenerated into a theory of the rectification of economic and political structures, whereas all the most radical periods of the past revolutionary movement were animated by the desire *to transform the whole nature of human experience*, to create a world in which the desires of each individual could be realized, without restriction. The only real problem is how to live life to the full. Burn, baby, burn!

Now revolutionary theory must attack production and consumption as a whole, showing that exactly the same alienation exists in both, and showing that their transcendence can only lead to the creation of *a new kind of human activity*. The basic demand is for a society based on the almost-total leisure that mechanization and automation have now made possible; that is to say, on a new culture corresponding to human desires and not simply dissimulating and sublimating their frustration.

It is precisely the early stages of this revolt which can be seen in the revolt of contemporary youth, in their refusal either to work or consume as ordered, in their permanent strike and in their experiments, however confused they may be, to create *an alternative use of life*. What would a revolutionary society be like? An endless passion, an endless adventure, an endless banquet.

In this issue, *Heatwave* 2, we have tried to show some of the phenomena of this international revolt, and we have tried to relate them to the last radical period of the revolutionary movement (the period 1910–1930) whose importance the new revolutionary movement must rediscover and criticize. As the crisis of the contemporary develops, as it becomes more and more acute and less and less easy to dissimulate, revolt can only grow. Things have already reached the point where if anyone wants to live at all *they can only revolt.*

The problem now is to make such acts radical and coherent, to relate the fragments seen by more and more individuals to the alienation of social life as a whole, to place them within a perspective which can only serve to expand consciousness and to introduce to each and every rebel the outline of revolt in which his act can be mirrored along with all other acts of revolt. Finally to create the revolutionary praxis by which this society and this civilization can be destroyed, once and for all.

Christopher GRAY
Charles RADCLIFFE

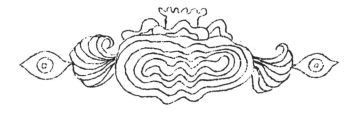

# THE PROVO RIOTS

*Poetry must be made by everybody, not by one person alone.*

—Lautréamont—

SINCE THE LATE-FIFTIES Amsterdam has had a clandestine reputation as one of the best-established and most open beat cities; hundreds of Scandinavian, English and American disaffiliates have either passed through or settled there, bringing with them an attitude of social and cultural dissent. The youth underground, which these beats helped establish, has surfaced during the last year in a series of events very different from the social passivity and cultural inoffensiveness of the beats: the provo riots.

In all the highly developed countries of the world, there is a radical discontent rapidly spreading throughout youth, a youth that wants neither to work nor to consume, a youth for whom comfort and gadgets have proved to be empty substitutes for an empty everyday life. This discontent is ready to explode in a great number of

417

places; in Amsterdam it was largely the fantastic energy of one man—the artist Robert Jasper Grootveld—which triggered the discontent into an explosion.

Starting from a fanatical opposition to tobacco companies—as the creators of "tomorrow's enslaved consumer"—Grootveld began a single-handed campaign against them, painting the letter K for Kancer in huge letters across the tobacco hoardings with an aerosol paint-spray, disguising himself as an old woman to persecute Amsterdam's tobacconists, holding church services in which a cigarette replaced the Host, the congregation coming forward to kneel reverently and take a drag, while Grootveld officiated at an altar flanked by two huge fire-extinguishers.

Later his campaign extended into full-scale attempts to sabotage the whole of bourgeois reality; anchoring a raft in the middle of one of Amsterdam's main canals, furnishing it to look like a bourgeois drawing room, with a table, chair and Dutch stove, he sat aboard it for a fortnight reading the newspapers.

More important were the happenings he began to hold on the Spui, at the foot of the statue Het Amsterdamse Lieverdje (Amsterdam's Little Darling), presented to the city by the Hunter Cigarette Company and, for Grootveld, the perfect symbol of enslaved consumption. Chanting his nonsense anti-smoke songs, performing his weird, destructive rites, chalking up his symbol (since appropriated by the provos) of the Magic Apple, he rapidly became a centre of attraction. Time and time again he was picked up by the cops, but, refusing to be intimidated he returned to the Spui. Crowds began to accompany him to the police station demanding his release. The nonsense songs and rhythmic handclaps became popular weapons. Fights with the cops broke out. The Spui, at midnight each Saturday, suddenly became the popular centre for everyone who was bored. And everyone is bored.

Grootveld himself seems to be far more attractive and imaginative than most modern exhibitionists (somewhat like the Berlin dadaist Baader—v. Raoul Hausmann's *Courier Dada*); any way, the real importance of the Spui scenes was that they broke the system of isolation, based on permanent movement, characteristic of modern urban control—to rule, divide—and succeeded to a large extent in turning a public place in the middle of the city into a small uncontrolled enclave of freedom (*Viz.* "Unitary Urbanism"). This vortex rapidly drew in together all the city's dissident bored and aggressive elements.

At about the same time, in early 1965, the original Provo group—composed initially of active beats, anarchists and the wilder ban-the-bombers—came together to produce a small duplicated magazine, with an initial circulation of 500, called *Provo* which now has a circulation of 20,000 copies. They took part in the Spui happenings, gradually giving them a far more aggressive and political slant, denouncing cops, traffic, bombs, royalty, *etc.* Journalists and cops appeared. So did kids on mopeds. Minors were seduced, fights broke out and large-scale arrests began. The happenings got out of everyone's hands and became riots. The Provos just rode the wave.

The provo revolt is essentially the first time that a number of hitherto heterogenous rebel youth groupings ("beatniks, pleiners, nozems, teddy boys, blousons noirs, gammler, raggare, stiljagi, mangupi, mods, students, artists, rockers, delinquents, anarchists, ban-the-bombers, misfits…those who don't want a career, who lead irregular lives….") that the Provos call the provotariat (*Viz Anarchy* 66, which contains both the "Appeal to the International Provotariat" and an article, by Roel van Duyn, reprinted from *Provo* 1, which goes some way towards articulating the spirit and attitudes of the early Provo group) have, as a result of the development of modern society, begun to come together, to recognise their common interests and to act on them. The values on which this new *lumpenproletariat of the Welfare State* is based are essentially its utter disgust with work and its attempt to use its clandestine leisure in an experimental and adventurous way, denying the passive and isolated consumption characteristic of all alienated leisure. It is this attitude of the new lumpenproletariat which both underlay and found temporary expression in the provo riots.

In all their actions they used a highly developed sense of game-war, an imagination, playfulness and sense of humour which completely baffled the cops consigned to deal with it. When Princess Beatrix married the ex-Nazi Claus von Amsberg, the wedding coach disappeared in the billows of smoke bombs, white chickens (chicken is the Dutch slang for cop) painted with black swastikas were driven, flapping into the street, television cables were cut, and above the uproar of the street fighting rose fragments of Grootveld's dadaist hymns. Only lack of money prevented them putting even wilder schemes into practice: having a frogman emerge from a canal near the route of the procession to explode a bomb containing lealets giving the lowdown on the House of Orange, spiking the palace water supply with lysergic acid, releasing a pack of white mice emblazoned with swastikas to stampede the horses drawing the seventeen-ton gold wedding coach

The provo riots fused and completely transformed the traditional forms of both art and politics. The exhibitionism of artists and the passivity of spectators, characteristic of New York, Paris and London happenings (and characteristic of alienated art in general) were eliminated from the riots that grew out of the Spui happenings: everyone was free to participate to the full extent of their imagination and energy in an experience which they had all created. The same structure in terms of politics was also overturned: the passivity and repression of the rank-and-file, imposed *a priori* by the hierarchic structure of all political parties (and by the self-sacrificial ideology dissimulating this structure: the Cause) were abolished in favour of a fluid, leaderless and exuberant onslaught. The alienation of both art and politics was transcended, and the appeal of their synthesis was electric. The riot became a popular world of art, a party to which the whole city was invited.

These riots represent imagination and passion applied consciously to the construction of immediate experience. They were, inseparably, a form of self-realisation and an objective assault on contemporary life: a society that has suppressed all adventure has made *the only adventure the suppression of that society*. And, in a more general sense, these riots express all that is essential to the new lumpenproletariat: their *style* illustrates concretely the reason for youth's disgust with life in the Welfare State and prefigures something of the life with which they want to replace it. They were a living critique of the deserts of everyday experience. Imagination, passion, communication, adventure: a brief glimpse of Utopia.

Embodied, inarticulately, in these riots was a total criticism of life in this society: a society characterised by its exclusion of everyone from their own lives, by its repression of everyone's real desires, by its reduction of everyone to a state of passivity and isolation in which they can be manipulated and stacked like inanimate objects. All these features which were effectively reversed during the actual riots have never been articulated in Provo theory: on the contrary, the so-called leaders and spokesmen of the movement do nothing more than propose a ridiculous series of minor reforms—banning the bomb, abolishing the Queen, making cops social workers, creating smokeless zones, preserving old buildings *etc.*,—all of which, with the possible exception of the bomb, are just anticipations of reforms bound to be effected by the ruling bureaucracy in the natural course of its development. Ticks, ticks and ticks. Why has the original Provo group— which precipitated these riots—failed so dismally to articulate a theory as radical as the events which took place spontaneously?

The basic flaw in the original Provo group lay in its theory. While they recognised both the intensity and the cohesion of the revolt of contemporary youth, of the groups they called the provotariat— whose political importance has not been recognised by any traditional political group or party—they were completely unaware of the

other signs of radical revolt throughout the rest of the proletariat—
the wildcat strikes and the shop stewards, obviously—as well as being
completely incapable of analysing the signs of rapidly growing crisis
throughout this society as a whole—its human penury that no ideology can dissimulate much longer—and seeing that a universal awakening is almost inevitable. They failed to see the ideology responsible
for mass-apathy, and the decomposition of this ideology. The original Provo group saw their rebellion as a desperate last stand. "The
Provotariat is the last rebellious grouping in the Welfare State countries."…"We cannot convince the masses. We hardly want to."…"Provo
realises that in the end it will be the loser."…(*Anarchy* 66.) This meant
that there could never be any hope of a general revolution, and that
their attitude was basically the nihilistic attitude of vandals.

As soon as they were successful, as soon as the movement began
to become really powerful, their theoretical incompetence became of
critical importance. Since (as far as we know) none of them were capable of realising the possibilities of a general proletarian uprising implicit
in the time, there were only two possibilities open to them: either to
continue their artistic vandalism, on a larger scale, which the best of
them have continued to do, or, alternatively, to use their power to
effect a number of minor reforms—it is from this latter ground that
a reformistic and reactionary group of leaders seem to have sprung.
Reformism inevitably means leaders and specialists in reform, representative activity on "behalf" of the masses, acceptance of the hierarchical repressive structure of the ruling classes, and activity within
it—in short, acceptance of everything the riots rejected. It is this group
that make statements like Bernard de Vries' "We only want to make
things a little better," and that went on the pop radio station during
the June riots to appeal to the blousons noirs to stop burning cop cars
and chucking them in canals, to stop *attacking shops* (the most relevant instinctive gesture made) and to go back home and let the Provo
leaders "educate" them,. They have become completely reactionary.

This fragmentary and reformistic theory of the leaders is the complete denial of the radical opposition implicit in the street riots, an opposition which was total, irreconcilable and practised by everyone. It is
now impossible for the leaders to formulate the most radical features
of the revolt they precipitated—rejection of contemporary society as
a whole, *the desire to use life differently*, to realise subjectivity in a transformed everyday life—and everything they do stands in the way of
any such formulation.

Without a critique of the alienated system of production and consumption on which this civilisation is based, without the possibility

of a universal awakening of the proletariat, there can be no question of really transforming our immediate everyday experience of life, and all that is most valuable in the provo experience is bound to become intangible and to be lost. No fragmentary reform will ever change the nature of everyday life. As it is the only reflection their poetry and taste for adventure has found in official theory is in Constant's "New Babylon", where it appears as an abstract appendage to his plans for a fully modernised concentration camp, the world, he assures us, of *homo-ludens*. Constant is about as *"ludic"* as an ox.

This is all even sadder since basically the provos have beaten the cops. The riots revealed clearly their complete inability to deal with exuberant, leaderless and intense political street-games: their horses have already been driven off the streets with ball-bearings and marbles, and it is only a matter of time before someone comes up with aniseed or ammonia for the dogs. All the cops can do is to keep the crowds moving, disperse groups about to form, book the occasional agitator for the night: they are just playing for time, big blue thugs with their fingers stuck in the dyke...

The real process of integration of the provos into the *status quo* is taking place elsewhere, on a more sophisticated level. The leaders and representatives of the provos are, sometimes happily and sometimes unwillingly, becoming steadily more divorced from the masses: executing their mutilated reconstructions of popular fury on television and in the newspapers. They are being integrated as an artistic avant-garde, as a new political party, as the rebel side-show revitalising the official spectacle: already the first provo has his seat on the city council, already artists are preparing glossy coffee-table books on happenings, already the bureaucrats of the "new" urbanism are peddling their plans, already the sociologists are preparing their explanations. Once the provo revolt is fragmented it can easily be recuperated. The mass will have their activity taken out of their hands and once again be reduced to passive spectators, staying at home and identifying with their own specialised representative in the appropriate niche of the official spectacle.

The provos still seem to have considerable vitality:

"At the Hague on Tuesday they attacked the State Opening of Parliament with batteries of smoke bombs—and as the black marias raced forward, fed peanuts to the policemen through the window bars. The monkeys were not amused, and arrested 81 of them."

"On Saturday, in the early hours of the morning, inspired by marihuana, Mr. Rob Stolk hatched perhaps the most daring Provo plan of all: the takeover of Amsterdam's Dam Square which is like Trafalgar

Square. Dam Square was "sold" 20 years ago to the citizens of Amsterdam for one guilder a square centimetre to raise money for a war memorial. The certificates of "sale" still exist, forgotten in countless desk drawers. Through their teenage supporters the Provos plan to beg, borrow or steal enough of these charity certificates to claim they now "own" Dam Square. And then they will ban it to their respectable elders…" (*Sunday Times.* 25.9.66)

Despite which, it is difficult not to feel that the crisis of the whole movement is very far advanced. The spontaneity and innocence their revolt are over, and there just isn't any radical perspective at the time when it has become most necessary. They talk of activists dropping out, becoming pot-heads, of people going away to write books, of the difficulty of getting enough help with the production of *Provo*, of the poorness of their new weekly *Image*, etc. They are getting tired. Perhaps they will realise what is happening to them: understand the modern methods of integration, dissociate themselves from their leaders, establish a radical perspective. It is difficult to say: but it doesn't seem likely.

For us, the fate of the particular wave of revolt called the provos is not of particular importance. They represent the most evolved form of the youth revolt that has yet broken out without engendering a radical revolutionary perspective and strategy. They have synthesised and gone a good deal further than either the Committee of 100 or any of the vandal and delinquent outrages. In fact, their exuberance, imagination and violent distaste for the whole of contemporary social life make their riots something very close to a spontaneous rediscovery of Dada, rediscovered not by a minority, but by the mass. (As the masses accede to hitherto "bourgeois" conditions of comfort and leisure, they also accede to the whole revolt engendered by the emptiness and falsity of these conditions). And the provos rediscovered the real spirit of Dada, not its contemporary official version—happenings, pop, auto-destructive art, etc.,—which is precisely the opposite of all that Dada stood for, its integration in spectacular culture and the complete reversal of its sense. Like the Dadaists, the provos reached towards a revolutionary praxis of self-realisation which they could not formulate, which they could not insert in a real revolutionary perspective, remaining purely destructive iconoclasts to the end.

This is in no way to belittle their importance: they indicate irrefutably the extent to which the coming generation is disgusted with western civilisation, and they prefigure the transcendence of this civilisation, of its specialised and alienated forms of action in new forms of activity. Life has still to be invented.

The provos as such are no isolated phenomenon. What happened in Amsterdam this year could happen in any of the highly industrialised countries of the world next year. They are just the most recent episode of the international revolt engendered in the context of mass "affluence." The positive and negative aspects of their rebellion must be understood, assimilated and put into practice in the construction of the new revolutionary movement.

Christopher GRAY
Charles RADCLIFFE

# THE ALMOST COMPLETE WORKS
# OF MARCEL DUCHAMP

THIS IS THE TITLE OF A RECENT Arts Council Show. Where the "almost complete work" was unavailable, Richard Hamilton bridged the gap with tasteful reconstructions. I doubt whether a Dada event on so large a scale has ever before been officially sponsored.

Naturally, some credentials were given to establish that Duchamp had, at least, taken it all seriously in the beginning. These being some hastily mounted drawings which appeared to have come from only one sketchbook (lent be a resourceful Swiss? woman) and his few paintings in oil.

Duchamp has traded frivolity for frivolity over many decades and has treated art history, art theory, art practice and art market as so many *accoutrements* to the vocation of artist clown. It must have seemed to him, this London show recognized his spirit if not in the pieces selected then by the nature of the spectacle that surrounded them. Take those strange waifs from the British Legion who would prevent the public hand re-arranging the hinged "glasses," to effect, as intended. Glass cases in which items carrying such formula as "Art-Merdre," and rubber-breasted book-jackets—"Please Touch"—were part of the misfired conspiracy to disguise Duchamp as a pedagogue (a French Paul Klee who turned to engineering rather than water-colors).

The larger ready-mades were grouped together in arcades behind rope—several pieces being thus totally deprived of significance. The famous fountain had the signature R. Mutt painstakingly forged on its side; despite the artists statement that once a mass-produced object has received designation "the rest was sentiment."

It is impossible here to condense Duchamp's achievement. He anticipated almost all recent avant-garde movements. This alone demonstrates his lack of interest in establishing values. He was intent in extending the base of the Art Model into Consumer Society, and making it demonstrate its absurdity by its own nature. The Tate Gallery, and the majority of those who witnessed the event I am describing, can be congratulated for doing just that. To treat a piece labeled "She has a hot arse" with dumb aplomb, as was general, points to some disease at work in society—humorlessness. Perhaps thousands peered through a little hole in the rear cover of the catalogue at spinning roto-reliefs without a single giggle of conscious idiocy.

Uel CAMERON

# LANDSCAPE WITH MOVEABLE PARTS

*For Penelope, because if the Earth turned twice as fast or faster,*
*the sun's perspective would change.*

*The paint fresh as an egg*
*and the same color but darker*
*and heavier like the footsteps*
*that stick in the door*
*like gloves*
*like an oyster*
*If the fireplace were cooler*
*left to its own devices*
*its own solitude of trees and windows*
*Perhaps a man standing on the corner*
*oblivious to his cigarette*
*its smoke and the reactions it produces*

among the birds far overhead
The drawing room leads to a watery grave
her ancestors walked that path
the windows were darker and one grandfather
wore a peculiarly marked tie
like a jack of clubs
It was a Sunday children were playing
softly like a murdered bear
The mirror shattered the light from its frame
a violin repeated the gestures of blindness
in the rain
The cathedral steps led to a dark roof
there was a dog there
two dogs three
hundreds of dogs
and several trees arranged like an observatory
or a cemetery with a sundial buried
beneath the water
It was as dark as a hand in front of the moon
the streets veiled in train whistles
distances starred by frogs and the rare glimpse
of hitchhikers
The morning opens like a knife in a melon
it begins anywhere
ambiguously
and tears for itself an itinerary along the hemispheres
of flesh and blood
The edge of the map is burned
its vagueness causes lack of sleep
The navigator's eye has lost sight
of its goal
too far away to hope for
too near to do without
The night casts its embers
The conductor sleeps
in photographic silence
There is a seal in the water
balancing on its nose
a red and yellow ball
If it is a balloon will the winter surrender its peppermint
its boots
Will the stars in the sky

*rise to tell*
*of the Northern Lights*
*in your eyes*
*and if not what is there to say*
*of danger of the high seas of a strawberry sundae*
*on a night*
*like tonight*
*What is there to say for a tidal wave*
*or a vase of flowers*
*or a revolver*
*After all the forest is nearer than the trees*
*and the barricades were not designed*
*to keep us out*
*Like strangers like lovers*
*The war in which the blood*
*settles like leaves*
*upon the trees*
*and the goats vanish into the lake*
*The puzzling venison of dawn*
*the drowning of swans*
*The mechanical sand evaporates the hours*
*In this coagulated island*
*the simplest formulas all fit*
*with the simultaneity of dancing shoes*
*The rain meets the shoulders with a warm good-bye*
*no spokes in these wheels*
*no left turn on this bridge*
*straight ahead stop keep moving*
*I love you*
*the harpsichord of silence tightens its grip*
*on the liquid tigers*
*like the night that flows*
*in the arteries*
*of tomorrow's*
*noonday sun*

Franklin ROSEMONT

Charles Radcliffe: Automatic drawing

# A NEW INTERNATIONAL FOR THE TOTAL OVERTHROW OF EVERYTHING

IF THE NEW REVOLUTIONARY MOVEMENT is to attain its ends (no less than the total overthrow of everything)—and there is little doubt that we can achieve such ends if we really want to—the first practical step is to internationalize, to interrelate the various struggles and ideas spontaneously occurring all over the world.

In the past twenty years the remnants of the old revolutionary movement—the ghost of a movement which once intended to transform human life and is now reduced to whining dissension over which practical reform should come next—have maintained the most precarious international contact, precarious because it has been devoted to the maintenance of partial insight and the preservation of fragmented and superseded ideas, because, in short, *no one really believes in it any more.* Their contact has been mutual masturbation. There has been nothing to discuss but the spectacle of a ruined past and no ideas which might enable them to transcend the pathetic futilities in which they are immersed. The sham has stolen their minds where it has not shackled their bodies. They remain to discuss survival.

The new revolutionary movement, in its desire to overthrow and remake the entire state of existing reality, has already replaced these ghosts of revolt, superseding them with the embryo of new analysis, new action, and new organization. *Already there is a spontaneous, continuous international conference going on.* Revolutionaries from the U.S.A., Holland, France, etc., have spontaneously visited us—the conference has been personal and unofficial, but it has laid the seeds for a new revolutionary international. The total and obvious collapse of this civilization under the weight of its own contradictions has created a new millenarianism.

This new attitude finds its justification in actions as apparently diverse as the Watts riots, the small-scale insurrections which have once again swept all the major cities of the USA this long hot summer, the youth riots of Stockholm, Moscow, Amsterdam, Tokyo, Oxford, and the British resorts, the Vietnam hoax, etc. *It is everywhere and it is spreading.* These crises represent attempts by people to overcome the boredom, disgust and inhumanity of their situation, to inscribe their own physical poetry on the blank board of contemporary reality, to make the world correspond to their own desires, to construct at least a part of their own lives.

In this and subsequent issues of *Heatwave* we shall draw together as many as possible of these threads of revolt, both group and individual. We shall bring back into play a whole past, as well as the unknown present and the new future. *We are about to write the unofficial history of mankind.*

Here we are reprinting two texts by contemporary American revolutionary groups—part of the New York Resurgence Youth Movement's "Guerrilla Manifesto," and the text of a leaflet, "The Forecast Is Hot!," distributed to some 50,000 marchers on one of Martin Luther King's reform marches in Chicago.

"The Forecast is Hot!" was published jointly by the Chicago Surrealist Group and the Anarchist Horde, who find their common perspective in *The Rebel Worker.* Founded two and a half years ago, the *Rebel Worker* group have managed to keep up regular publication of the journal and also to maintain the finest radical bookshop in North America (Solidarity Bookshop). *The Rebel Worker* itself has progressed considerably from being a somewhat crudely updated magazine of Wobbly ideas to being the best total revolutionary journal published in the U.S.A. The sixth issue, distributed by *Heatwave,* was produced in England and from it emerged *Heatwave.*

As far as we can tell the only other fully-constituted revolutionary group in the U.S.A. —we would be happy to receive positive contradiction—is the Resurgence Youth Movement, centered in New York around the young Wobblies Jonathan Leake and Walter Caughey. We are printing a small portion of RYM's "Guerrilla Manifesto" which first appeared in *Resurgence* 6, a *must* for all revolutionaries. Like the Chicago group, RYM has added an entirely new dimension to old Wobbly ideas, basing their analysis primarily on the international youth revolt.

Charles RADCLIFFE

excerpts; originally titled "Mad Mama's Blues"

(*Heatwave* 1)

429

Like *Ztangi!* in Chicago, the third issue of *Heatwave* never appeared; unlike *Ztangi!*, however, it had a cover design ready and waiting

the most widely stolen
magazine of our generation!

# GUERRILLA MANIFESTO

THE REVOLUTION THAT IS DUE TO ERUPT in the Western countries, the Home Camp of Imperialism (the United States and Europe), will reveal the basic weakness of and implicit alternatives in their bureaucratic and authoritarian civilization. The struggle of a few will become the struggle of many—suddenly, in apocalyptic revelations of a new world of the new spirit of freedom.

Who is the Underground in America, in Europe, all over the world? It will show itself soon.

Anarchists in particular have a duty to the revolution that is unfolding, for anarchism has been the apprehension of this revolution, and closer to it than the other radical movements of socialism or communism. The anarchist principle of decentralisation traced an ethnic of mutual aid based on voluntary groups that exists today on the fringes of society, in the underground.

Anarchism is faced with two basic tasks in relation to the development of the Revolutionary Idea. The first is the resurrection of the Apocalyptic Vision. The second is the restatement of the anarchist principles of autonomy, particularly in regards to the organisation and tactics of a revolutionary movement.

The first task is concerned with taking account of a number of new trends in revolutionary thinking. These include the psychedelic movement, and the affirmation of a new culture, a new civilisation within the shell of the old. The resolution of the conflict between European ideas and the Afrasian American New World, which is now being enacted in North America, brings to the fore this essential element of radical thought and action.

The political and bureaucratic developments of social democracy, state socialism, reformism, etc., all proposed to replace the ethics of crisis, of the Armeggedon between People and State, with a new ethics of social unity and social peace. The political radicals tied a great portion of the direction of the Idea to a professional class which, although transformed by its new place in technology, soon re-acquired its parasitic stance, becoming integrated with the power structure. Indeed, we may look at almost all contemporary socialism as an attempt to heal the wounds, to make up for the historic distrust of the lower echelons of the working class—the lumpenproletariat agricultural workers, the unemployed—for the 'intellectuals.'

This messianic vision of a total revolution that would transform every social relationship, and erase the concept of "worker' as it would the concept of 'capitalist,' was carried by a minority in the radical movement: anarchists, syndicalists, and the recurring heretics of the spirit who ambushed European culture in the 1920s and 1930s in surrealism, and which now make themselves felt through a chemical substance.

These elements are like the tip of an iceberg projecting out of the murky waters of this stagnant society. In the vision of the surrealist, anarchist, and psychedelic revolutionary is seen all the ingredients of a new context for work, for leisure, for life itself. The street rabble in the cities of North America—the blacks, the Puerto Ricans, the dropouts—all mirror the colors and echo the sounds of Africa, Asia, and the New America, not of Europe.

This final cleavage between cultures has been part of a pattern of cleavage between economic groups, generations, ways of life. The Social Democracy and all the forms it took have been swallowed by the monster they created, the bureaucratic state. Now the words socialism, communism, revolution once more designate the outlaw, the dissident, the submerged, that which is to be.

Walter CAUGHEY, Jonathon LEAKE, et al.<br>
The Resurgence Youth Movement<br>
(New York, May 25, 1966)

reprinted from *Resurgence*
(*excerpt*)

# THE FORECAST IS HOT!

REJECTING, TOTALLY, THE POLITICAL, theological, literary, philosophical and academic assumptions which hinge our society to the withered refrigerator of civilization (and which are, in any case, rooted in stupidity and class interest), and insisting, moreover, on our own irresistible emotional autonomy, we find it essential to affirm, here and now, without reservations and at any price, the marvelous red and black validity of absolute revolt, the only attitude worthy of survival in the present millennium of streets and dreams.

More than ever, with everything continually at stake, we find it necessary to encourage the impassioned use of the most dangerous weapons in the arsenal of freedom:

MAD LOVE: totally subversive, the absolute enemy of bourgeois culture;

POETRY (as opposed to literature): breathing like a machinegun, exterminating the blind flags of immediate reality;

HUMOR: the dynamite and guerrilla warfare of the mind, as effective in its own domain as material dynamite and guerrilla warfare in the streets (whenever necessary, however, rest assured: we shall use every means at our disposal);

SABOTAGE: ruthless and relentless destruction of the bureaucratic and cultural machinery of oppression.

It is necessary, at times (and this is one of them), to speak bluntly: we affirm deliriously and simply the TOTAL LIBERATION OF MAN.

Long live the Negroes of Watts, the Puerto Ricans of Chicago, the Provos of Amsterdam, the Zengakuren of Japan and the youth of all countries who burn cop cars in the street and demonstrate by these exemplary manifestations that the struggle for freedom cannot be guided by the rulebooks of priests and politicians!

Long live the New Guinea tribe who, aware of the idiocy of technological civilization, massacred the managers of a washing-machine factory, took over the building and converted it into a temple of the marvelous but elusive Rabbit-god!

Long live the youth of Fairbanks, Alaska, who, after being forbidden by law to drop out of school, retaliated by burning down the schoolhouse!

Long live the lunatic who escaped from an asylum and calmly robbed a downtown bank only to have his "sane" brother tell the police!

Long live Barry Bondhus of Big Lake, Minnesota, who dumped two buckets of shit into the file drawers of his draft board!

Long live the twelve Fort Lauderdale, Florida teens who, prevented by their schools from meaningful experimentation, independently began manufacturing LSD, two sizes of plastic bombs, smoke bombs, and a varied and catalytic assortment of revolutionary hardware!

Long live the Incredible Hulk, wildcat strikers, the Nat Turner Insurrection, high-school dropouts, draft-dodgers, deserters, delinquents, saboteurs and all those soul-brothers, wild-eyed dreamers, real and imaginary heroes of defiance and rebellion who pool their collective resources in the exquisite, material transformation of the world according to desire!

The lucidity of "alley apples" and broken bottles has replaced autumn leaves—the crushing subservience to authority scorched by Molotov cocktails of fantastic destruction; and, far from finally, the expressionless caress has been deliciously transcended by the touch that stimulates to unheard-of heights the sensuous pores of the only dynamism that matters. As liberated souls (which we are, for our quests cannot be stopped now) we have necessarily an historically enviable role as cosmic architects armed with hammers, electric guitars and apocalyptic visions, but more significantly armed with the exhilarating knowledge that we are able to crush systematically all obstacles placed in the way of our desires and to build anew EVERYTHING.

The Surrealist Group
The Anarchist Horde
The *Rebel Worker* Group

Chicago, July 1966

Tor Faegre: Automatic drawing

# AFTERWORD

*Let no one say that I have said nothing new:*
*I have presented the matter in a different way.*
*When people play tennis, both use the same ball,*
*but one places it better than the other.*

—Pascal—

The *Rebel Worker* group, Solidarity Bookshop, and *Heatwave* had an appreciable impact in their day, and their influence in imaginatively rebellious milieus has persisted and even expanded through the years. Few of their many offshoots, alas, survived the 1960s. (Solidarity Bookshop was something of an exception; under new management, it continued until 1974 as a narrowly anarchist enterprise: no Marxism, no surrealism, no black nationalism, no comic books.)

Most of the *Rebel Worker* group's spin-offs seem to have disappeared from history, in some cases without leaving a footprint. The Enragés rock band, the abortive motorcycle gang of the same name, the Waller High School Noon-Hour Doo-Wop & Dance Club, the local chapter of the Resurgence Youth Movement, the even more ephemeral local Diggers and Chicago Provo, the Louis Lingg Memorial Chapter of SDS, several anti-war and draft-resistance groups, the sizeable but amorphous aggregation known variously as The Anarchists and The Anarchist Horde, and even, I fear, the left-wing of the local Rolling Stones Fan Club all faded away long before 1970.

Most of these informal associations—sociologists might call them "sub-groups"—were small, but not all: Well over a hundred attended at least one Anarchist Horde meeting at the Bookshop. What is important is that every one of these autonomous groups helped, each in its own distinctive way, to "fan the flames of discontent." By developing *their own* critiques, and organizing *their own* actions, they were instrumental in transmitting *Rebel Worker/Heatwave* ideas and inspirations to new sectors of the population. In short, these groups were key players in the collective effort to build a new revolutionary movement *and* a new workingclass counterculture. That nearly all of them perished without a trace leaves some significant gaps in the historiography of 1960s radicalism.

One *Rebel Worker*/Solidarity-related group not only held its own but flourished.

From 1966 through 1968, Solidarity Bookshop was the Surrealist Group's headquarters and mailing address—roles later assumed by the nearby Gallery Bugs Bunny. Chicago surrealism's early years are documented in *The Forecast Is Hot! Tracts & Other Collective Declarations of the Surrealist Movement in the United States: 1966–1976* (Black Swan Press, 1998), and in Ron Sakolsky's *Surrealist Subversions: Rants, Writings & Images by the Surrealist Movement in the United States* (Autonomedia, 2002). For the group's current activities and publications, see the website: www.surrealistmovement-usa.org.

Several characters in the *Rebel Worker* story—Fred Thompson, Franklin and Penelope Rosemont, Carlos Cortez, Robert Green and Paul Garon—went on to revive the Charles H. Kerr Publishing Company, starting in the 1970s. In addition to reissuing many revolutionary classics—including the old *Rebel Worker* standby, *The Right to Be Lazy*, with a long essay by Fred Thompson—the rejuvenated Kerr has brought out numerous new books on Haymarket, the IWW, and the working-class counterculture. The Kerr website is: www.CharlesHKerr.org

*Rebel Worker* plans for a "Sabotage Anthology" were substantially fulfilled by Salvatore Salerno's collection, *Direct Action & Sabotage: Three Classic IWW Pamphlets from the 1910s* (Charles H. Kerr, 1997).

The name Nelson Algren pops up here and there in this book—as inspirer or supporter of our subversive activities—and it is interesting to note that our friendship with the author of *Chicago: City on the Make* expanded in later years. The Surrealists encountered Algren often all through the early 1970s, and in 1975 he attended a Surrealist Group meeting at the St Regis Hotel restaurant on Grand Avenue (see "'Surrealism? In Chicago?'—Talks with Nelson Algren" in *Arsenal/Surrealist Subversion* 4, 1989).

In the 1970s/80s a mimeo'd workingclass anarchist magazine in Adelaide, Australia took the name *Rebel Worker.* An early issue (the first?) featured the René Crevel "Au Grand Jour" declaration that we had printed in *The Rebel Worker* and as a Solidarity Bookshop poster.

Around that same time, when the Chicago Branch of the IWW decided to issue a more or less monthly newsletter, they too decided to call it *The Rebel Worker.*

And when will a new no-compromise revolutionary workingclass movement come to the fore again? No one knows for sure, but it's as inevitable as morels after a spring rain. As Fellow Worker Guy Askew (Skidroad Slim) wrote me from Seattle back in February '65: "All the reptile press has been preaching funeral services for the IWW for a long time. What the brass check bastards don't know is that the IWW's black cat has many lives."

—F.R.

The Gallery Bugs Bunny in 1968
(drawing by Tor Faegre)

The wildest, most adventurously innovative and talked-about gallery in 1960s Chicago, the Bugs Bunny was, along with Solidarity Bookshop, the favorite hangout of the Surrealist Group. Located at 524 Eugenie (corner of Mohawk), it had no sign: just a large portrait of the world's greatest rabbit on the front door. Here the surrealists had their first group show, featuring the work of Lester Doré, Schlechter Duvall, Robert Green, Eric Matheson, Franklin Rosemont & Penelope Rosemont, all of whom had taken part in *Rebel Worker*/*Heatwave* activity. In a later Bugs Bunny "Surrealist Objects" show, Paul Garon was also among the exhibitors.

# BIBLIOGRAPHY

**I. Books and Articles that discuss *The Rebel Worker*, *Heatwave*, Solidarity Bookshop, and/or individuals who participated in them.**

Ahrens, Gale, ed. *Lucy Parsons: Freedom, Equality & Solidarity. Writings & Speeches, 1878-1937.* Afterword by Roxanne Dunbar-Ortiz. Chicago: Charles H. Kerr, 2004.

Allsop, Kenneth. *Hard Travellin': The Hobo and His History.* New York: New American Library, 1967.

"Arrest Demonstrators at Congressional Hearing Near North Side." *Chicago Tribune*, May 25, 1965, p. 11.

Barr, Dave. "Lincoln Park a 49-year host to Wobblies." *Inside Lincoln Park*, Sept. 5, 1984.

*Black Mask & Up Against the Wall Motherfucker.* London: Unpopular Books, 1993.

Blazek, Douglas. "Surrealism & Revolution" (a review), in *Olé* No. 7, May 1967 (San Francisco: Open Skull Press).

Bruckner, D. J. R. "The Wobblies Return; Local Unit Seeks Farm Unions." *Chicago Sun-Times*, February 28, 1964.

Buhle, Mari Jo, *et al.*, eds. *Encyclopedia of the American Left.* Second Edition. New York: Oxford University Press, 1998 (first published 1990)

Buhle, Paul, ed. *History and the New Left: Madison, Wisconsin, 1950-1970.* Philadelphia: Temple University Press, 1990.

—, and Edmund B. Sullivan, eds. *Images of American Radicalism.* Foreword by Howard Fast. Hanover, MA.: Christopher Publishing House, 1998.

—, and Mike Alewitz, *Insurgent Images: The Agitprop Murals of Mike Alewitz.* New York: Monthly Review Press, 2002.

Conlin, Joseph R. *Bread and Roses Too: Studies of the Wobblies.* Westport: Greenwood Press, 1974.

"Diggers Started." *Chicago Seed*, Vol. I, No. 3, May-June 1967, p. 13.

Dubofsky, Melvyn: *We Shall Be All: A History of the IWW.* New York: Quadrangle, 1969.

Ducornet, Guy. *Ca va chauffer! Situation du Surréalisme aux U.S.A. (1966-2001).* Mons: Editions Talus d'approche, 2001.

Garon, Paul. "The Chicago Surrealist Group and Black Swan Press," in *Progressive Librarian*, Fall 1993.

Heise, Kenan. *Chaos, Creativity and Culture: A Sampling of Chicago in the Twentieth Century.* Salt Lake City: Gibbs Smith, 1998.

Hernández, Rodrigo. "Surrealistas de Chicago o la revuelta como forma de vida." *Revista Derrame* 6, Santiago, Chile, 2004.

*Internationale Situationniste.* Paris, 1958-1969. Reprinted by Van Gennep: Amsterdam, 1972.

Jablonski, Joseph "The War on Leisure," introduction to Paul Lafargue, *The Right to be Lazy.* Chicago: Charles H. Kerr, 1989

Kelley, Robin D. G. *Freedom Dreams: The Black Revolutionary Imagination.* Boston: Beacon Press, 2002.

Knabb, Ken, ed. *Situationist International Anthology.* Berkeley: Bureau of Public Secrets, 1981.

Kornbluh, Joyce. L. *Rebel Voices: An IWW Anthology.* New and expanded edition. Chicago: Charles H. Kerr, 1987.

Lewis, Helena. *The Politics of Surrealism.* New York: Paragon House, 1988.

*Literarische Messe 1968: Handpressen, Flugblatter, Zeitschriften der Avantgarde. Katalog.* Frankfurt am Main: Frankfurt Forum fur Literatur, 1968.

Murphy, Sarah. "Victory at Roosevelt." *SDS Bulletin* (New York), 1964.

Nuttall, Jeff. *Bomb Culture.* New York: Delacorte Press, 1968.

Peck, Abe. *The Sixties: The Life & Times of the Underground Press.* New York: Pantheon, 1985.

"Pickers' Strike Continues with Tension Build-Up." *South Haven (Michigan) Daily Tribune,* July 27, 1964, p. 1.

*Radical America Catalog.* Includes a page on *Rebel Worker* and *Arsenal/Surrealist Subversion.* Madison, WI: *RadicalAmerica,* Fall-Winter 1971.

Roediger, David. "Surrealism," in Mari Jo Buhle *et al.,* eds., *Encyclopedia of the American Left.* New York: Oxford University Press, 1998.

Rosemont, Franklin, ed. *Juice Is Stranger Than Friction: Selected Writings of T-Bone Slim.* Chicago: Charles H. Kerr, 1992.

—. "Revolution in the Service of the Marvelous: Notes on Surrealism in the U.S., 1966-1991," in *Artpaper.* Minneapolis, 1991.

—. *Joe Hill: The IWW & the Making of a Revolutionary Workingclass Counterculture.* Chicago: Charles H. Kerr, 2003.

—, ed. *From Bughouse Square to the Beat Generation: Selected Ravings of Slim Brundage.* Chicago: Charles H. Kerr, 1997.

—, ed. *The Rise & Fall of the Dil Pickle: Jazz-Age Chicago's Wildest & Most Outrageously Creative Hobohemian Nightspot.* Chicago: Charles H. Kerr, 204.

—, with Penelope Rosemont and Paul Garon, eds. *The Forecast Is Hot! Tracts & Other Collective Declarations of the Surrealist Movement in the United States, 1966-1976.* Chicago: Black Swan Press, 1997.

Rosemont, Penelope. *Surrealist Experiences: 1001 Dawns, 221 Midnights,* Chicago: Surrealist Editions/Black Swan Press, 2000.

Rosenkranz, Patrick. *Rebel Visions: The Underground Comix Revolution.* Seattle: Fantagraphics Books, 2002.

Rosenzweig, Mark. "Surrealism—Chicago Style," in *Progressive Librarian*, Fall 1993.

Sakolsky, Ron, ed. *Surrealism in the U.S.A.: The Complete Contents of the Suppressed Surrealist Issue of* "Socialist Review." *Race Traitor*, Special Double Issue, No. 13-14, Summer 2001.

—, ed. *Surrealist Subversions: Rants, Writings & Images by the Surrealist Movement in the United States.* New York: Autonomedia, 2002.

Sauter, Van Gordon. "Browsing in Some Old Curiosity Shops." *Chicago Daily News Panorama*, December 23, 1967, p. 3.

Savage, Jon. *England's Dreaming: Sex Pistols and Punk Rock.* London: Faber & Faber, 1991.

Shea, Robert, and Robert Anton Wilson. *The Illuminatus Trilogy (The Eye in the Pyramid; The Golden Apple; Leviathan).* New York: Dell, 1975.

"Solidarity Books Strikes Back." *Chicago Seed*, Vol. I, No. 2, May 1967.

"Student Power Upheld by Old Leftist Union." *Los Angeles Times*, September 3, 1968.

Thayer, George. *The Farther Shore of Politics: The American Political Fringe Today.* New York: Simon and Schuster, 1967.

Thompson, Fred W., and Patrick Murfin. *The IWW: Its First Seventy Years: 1905-1975.* Chicago: Industrial Workers of the World, 1976.

—. *Fellow Worker: The Life of Fred Thompson.* Compiled, with an introduction, by Dave Roediger. Chicago: Charles H. Kerr, 1993.

"2,500 Here Join Anti-Viet March." *Chicago Sun-Times*, March 27, 1966, p. 46.

Vague, Tom, ed. *King Mob Echo.* Vol. I: *From the 1780 Gordon Riots to Situationists, Sex Pistols and Beyond.* Vol. II: *The English Section of the Situationist International*—Rebel Worker, Heatwave, *etc.* London: Dark Star, 2000.

**Note:** Mentions of *The Rebel Worker*, *Heatwave*, and Solidarity Bookshop also appear in various issues of the following periodicals: *Industrial Worker* (Chicago), *Playboy* (Chicago), *Seed* (Chicago), *Roosevelt University Torch* (Chicago), *Strike!* (Cleveland), *Resurgence* (New York), *Black Mask* (New York), *L'Adunata dei refrattari* (Boston), *Radical America* (Madison), *Solidarity* (London), *Anarchy* (London), *Freedom* (London), *Cuddon's Cosmopolitan Review* (London), *My Own Mag* (London), *ICO: Informations Correspondence Ouvriers* (Paris), *Internationale Situationniste* (Paris), *Provo* (Amsterdam), and no doubt many others.

## II. Other Works

Charters, Ann, ed. *The Beats: Literary Bohemians in Postwar America.* Detroit: Gale Research, 1983.

Debord, Guy. *La Société du Spectacle.* Paris: Buchet-Chastel, 1967. The first English translation, by Fredy Perlman, appeared as a joint publication of the SDS journal *Radical America* and the anarchist Red & Black Group in Detroit in 1970. Donald Nicholson-Smith's translation was published by Zone Books in New York, 1995.

Fountain, Nigel. *Underground: The London Alternative Press, 1966-1974.* London: Comedia, 1988.

Gray, Christopher, ed. *Leaving the Twentieth Century: The Incomplete Works of the Situationist International.* London: Free Fall, 1974; reissued by Rebel Press, London, 1998.

Green, Jonathan. *Days in the Life: Voices from the English Underground, 1961-1971.* London: Pimlico, 1998.

Jappe, Anselm. *Guy Debord.* Berkeley: University of California Press, 1999.

Lipton, Lawrence. *The Holy Barbarians.* New York: Julian Messner. 1959.

Vermorel, Fred and Judy. *Sex Pistols: The Inside Story.* London: Star, 1978.

## III. Websites

Aufheben / http://www.geocities.com/aufheben2

Antagonism / http://www.geocities.com/CapitolHill/Lobby/3909

Autonomedia / http://www.autonomedia.org

Bureau of Public Secrets / http://www.bopsecrets.org

Break Their Haughty Power / http://www.home.earthlink.net/~lrgoldner

Charles H. Kerr Publishing Company / http://wwwCharlesHKerr.org

Collective Action Notes / http://www.geocities.com/CapitolHill/Lobby/2379

Endpage / http://www.endpage.org

Industrial Workers of the World / http://iww.org

John Gray / http://www.geocities.com/~johngray

Midnight Notes / http://www.midnightnotes.org

NotBored! / http://www.notbored.org

Race Traitor / www.postfun.com/racetraitor

Red & Black Notes / http://ca.geocities.com/red_black_ca

Surrealist Movement in the U. S. / http://www.surrealistmovement-usa.org

442

444

# STUDS TERKEL
## *on*
# CHARLES H. KERR
# BOOKS

We may be suffering from a national Alzheimer's Disease —forgetful of what happened yesterday, let alone years ago in our history.

*I suggest the perfect cure:*
Read the books published by
**CHARLES H. KERR**
of old-time dissenters, muckraking journalists, and all-around noble troublemakers.

You'll find these works an exhilarating tonic!

*Studs Terkel, 2004*

# *Books for an Endangered Planet*

**LUCY PARSONS: Freedom, Equality & Solidarity—Writings & Speeches, 1878-1937**, edited & introduced by Gale Ahrens, with an Afterword by Roxanne Dunbar-Ortiz. First-ever anthology of tracts & talks (on anarchism, women, race, class war, the injustice system) by the great anarchist agitator, regarded by cops as "More Dangerous than 1000 rioters"! Includes nearly all her IWW writings! The Intro & Afterword correct many errors made by earlier writers, & add much to our knowledge of Lucy and her relevance for today. 191 pages. Illus. $17

**THE RISE & FALL OF THE DIL PICKLE: Jazz-Age Chicago's Wildest & Most Outrageously Creative Hobohemian Nightspot**, edited & introduced by Franklin Rosemont. "The Pickle [was] the most important place in Chicago and maybe the U.S. to hear artistic and political argument. . .a real university. To read about [its] creativity and irreverence is to realize how much we've lost in our intellectual culture"–Susan Davis, *Counterpunch*. 192 pages. $14

**THE DEVIL'S SON-IN-LAW: The Story of Peetie Wheatstraw and His Songs**, by Paul Garon. The classic study of the influential blues-singer, songwriter, piano- and guitar-player. First published in England in 1971, this revised, expanded edition includes a mass of new information and images, updated bibliography/discography, **and a 24-track CD!** 156 pages. Cloth $22; paper $16

**A HISTORY OF PAN-AFRICAN REVOLT** by C. L. R. James, with an Introduction by Robin D. G. Kelley. The classic account of global black resistance in Africa and the diaspora. *"A mine of ideas advancing far ahead of its time"*—Walter Rodney. 160 pages. $14.00

**CRIME AND CRIMINALS & Other Writings** by Clarence Darrow, with a Foreword by Penelope Rosemont, an essay by Leon Despres and an Afterword by Carol Heise. The great labor attorney's celebrated "Address to the Prisoners in the Cook County Jail" and other hardhitting indictments of the U.S. criminal justice system. 64 pages. Illustrated. Cloth $18; paper $8.00

**VIVA POSADA! A Salute to the Great Printmaker of the Mexican Revolution**, edited & introduced by Carlos Cortez. 121 of Posada's finest works, with excerpts from classic texts about his work by Frieda Kahlo, Diego Rivera, André Breton, Octavio Paz, Anita Brenner & others, as well as statements by surrealists & other poets & artists of our own time. 96 pages. $12.00

**HOBOHEMIA: Emma Goldman, Lucy Parsons, Ben Reitman & Other Agitators & Outsiders in 1920s Chicago**, by Frank O. Beck, with a new introduction by Franklin Rosemont. Back in print at last, the classic portrait of Chicago's IWW-influenced counterculture in its heyday. Illustrated. Cloth $25. Paper $12

**WALLS AND BARS: Prisons and Prison Life in the "Land of the Free,"** by Eugene V. Debs, with a new introduction by David Dellinger. Still the best revolutionary critique of U.S. "justice"and the prison system. *"Capitalism must have prisons to protect itself from the criminals it has created"*—Eugene Debs. Revolutionary Classics Series. 256 pp. Cloth $24. Paper $14:

*Please add $3 postage for the first title, and fifty cents for each additional title.*

# CHARLES H. KERR PUBLISHING COMPANY
*Est. 1886* / 1740 West Greenleaf Avenue, Chicago, Illinois 60626